ISBN 960-7401-65-4

© ATHENS 2004 City of Athens
Foundation of the Hellenic World
Poulopoulou St. 38, Athens 118 51,
Tel : (+30) 210 34 22 292 Fax : (+30) 210 34 22 272
http://www.fhw.gr/ E-mail : info@fhw.gr

The reproduction or reissue of this whole or in part, is strictly forbidden, as is translation, adaptation or exploitation in any form, spoken or otherwise, in accordance with the provisions of law 2121/1993 and the International Agreement of Bern-Paris which was legalised by the law 100/1995. Reproduction of the typesetting of the page layout, the cover and in general any of the aesthetic elements of the book through photocopying, electronic or any other method is also forbidden, in accordance with article 51 of law 2121/1993.

From Antiquity until Today - History, Archaeology, Architecture, Museums

STROLLING THROUGH ATHENS

CITY OF ATHENS

Dear Friends,

The Olympic Games offer an excellent opportunity to promote our country and our city. For over a month, Greece and Athens will be the focal point of global interest. However, even if one puts the Games aside, Athens needs a contemporary, easy-to-use and pleasant guide for its visitors, both Greeks and foreigners. Reliable guides inspire, generate ideas, increase visitors' enjoyment, open up new possibilities about what there is to see and encourage a longer stay – a benefit both to the visitor and the city's economy.

The City of Athens has undertaken a new publishing initiative, which, using the proven expertise of the Foundation of the Hellenic World, provides visitors with an opportunity to learn about the culture and history of our glorious city in the form the guidebook, Strolling Through Athens, from Antiquity until Today – History, Archaeology, Architecture, Museums.

What makes this new guide really remarkable is not only the exceptional quality of its research but also the fact that it covers such a wide range of subjects, examining them from an interdisciplinary viewpoint.

History, architecture, City-Planning and museums, issues that are apparently, at least in part, unrelated, assume new dimensions through the pages of this Guide and reveal a different picture of our city. There is a multitude of historical information available to the reader regarding people, events, public and private buildings, archaeological sites and museums, which enable him or her to experience, and even create, an extraordinary image of "our" Athens.

The texts, based on the highest levels of research, are accompanied by an unprecedented wealth of visual material, such as maps, original pictures of monuments, architectural drawings and much more. The skills and structured approach of those who drew up the guide are also evident from its user-friendly character, making it easy for readers to deal with and assimilate its material.

I would like to express my warmest congratulations to all who contributed to the City of Athens' new publishing venture. I am certain that the reader will appreciate the professionalism, consistency and enthusiasm that has gone into this new guide to Athens – our city.

Dora Bakoyiannis
Mayor of Athens

Dear Reader,

The guide you are holding suggests certain walks for you to explore, each one pointing out places that would be ideal to visit even if you haven't got much time at your disposal. If you are walking around the city and happen to see a monument, you can go straight to the index and find the reference that will give you all the useful information you need. The museums, the monuments of the archaeological sites of the Acropolis, the Ancient Agora and Kerameikos form separate units in the index. Each walk is accompanied by a corresponding map with all the stopping off points, and each one, route and map, is in a different colour.

Have a pleasant tour!

MAP KEY

Insertion	Important Insertion
Museum	Cemetery
Modern Times	Modern Buildings
Middle Ages	Church
Antiquity	Archaeological Sites
Metro Station	

CONTENT

INTRODUCTION IN THE HISTORY OF ATHENS	11
ENVIRONMENT	12
MYTHOLOGY	15
HISTORY	18
ARCHITECTURE AND SCULPTURE	50

WALK 1
Walking on the hills of the Acropolis — *61*

WALK 2
Admiring the Parthenon — *87*

WALK 3
Small but interesting museums — *131*

WALK 4
View over Athens – View over Greece — *151*

WALK 5
The panorama of Byzantine Athens — *177*

WALK 6
The garden of Athens — *201*

WALK 7
The Plaka: Walking in Athens' old city — *221*

WALK 8
The heart of ancient Athens — *251*

WALK 9
The Town Hall of Athens and the municipal marketplace — *285*

WALK 10
An unusual walk — *313*

WALK 11
The National Archaeological Museum — *337*

WALK 12
The centre of the centre and its charms — *355*

IN THE PERIPHERY OF ATHENS
Archaeological sites — *385*

GLOSSARY	408
BIBLIOGRAPHY	412
INDEX	418

INTRODUCTION IN THE HISTORY OF ATHENS

THE NATURAL ENVIRONMENT OF ATHENS

INFORMATION ABOUT ATHENS' NATURAL ENVIRONMENT

The basin in which Athens lies constitutes the central and largest plain of Attica, stretching over an area of 383 square kilometres. It is surrounded and demarcated by the following mountains: Hymettus (1026m) to the east, Penteli (1109m) and Parnes (Parnitha) (1413m) to the north and Aigaleo (468m) to the west. In the south it is lapped by the Saronic Sea. A series of hills divides it lengthwise from the north-east to the south-west: Tourkovounia Hill (338m), which is dominated nowadays by telecommunication and television antennae; Lycabettus Hill (277m, crowned by the small white Church of St George; Strefis Hill (163m), almost entirely covered by the urban development; Ardettus Hill (133m) above the Panathenaic Stadium; the hill of the Acropolis (156m) crowned by the Parthenon; and Areios Pagos (115m).
Philopappos Hill or the hill of the Muses (147m), Pnyx Hill (109m) and the hill of the Nymphs or hill of the Observatory (104m) provide a green oasis south of the Acropolis and lead up to the hill of Agoraios Kolonos (68m) with the Hephaisteion. Further to the south, the hill of Sicily (78m) is today partly quarried. To the north-west of the city, in the Kolonos district, are the hills of Skouzes (67m) and Ippios Kolonos (55m).
Athens' climate is characterized by generally light annual rainfall, and the composition of the soil and the small size of the river basin formed by the surrounding mountains have

not allowed the creation of big rivers. Two streams flow through the basin, the Kifissos and Ilissos. The Kifissos flows from Parnes and empties into Faliron Bay. Its most important tributaries are Kefalari and Podoniftis. Today it is mostly covered up by Kifissos Avenue. The Ilissos has its sources on Hymettus and also empties into Faliro Bay. Formerly it debouched into the

Kifissos through another smaller river, the Eridanos, which flowed from Lycabettus. Part of the River Eridanos can be seen at Kerameikos.

Attica in general and the area of Athens in particular have no significant mineral wealth. The Laurion silver mines once contributed to the prosperity of Classical Athens and operated anew for a short period of time during

the late 19th century. Penteli gave the purest and finest-grained white marble of Greece. Today it is no longer quarried. Hymettus produced a darker (blue-grey) marble, and a grey marble was extracted from the Eleusis region, mainly used in architecture. In addition, various kinds of limestone and poros stone were quarried from the hills of the city and the surrounding areas. For the needs of the renowned ancient Attic pottery local clay was used, derived from the metamorphic argilliferous sandstone of the Athenian schist, a characteristically thick geological layer.

The existence of Athenian schist led at times to the simplistic belief that Athens was resistant to earthquakes. However, recent studies have shown that strong earthquakes had occurred during ancient times (1641, 1805, 1874 BC, etc.), and earthquakes in recent times have testified to the existence of focuses at the south foot of Penteli and at the south-west slope of Parnes. The latter was the cause of the severe earthquake of 1999. Athens has a Mediterranean climate. It is characterized by low annual rainfall, most of which occurs during the winter, by hot summers with drought and heat waves, by mild winters with ample sunlight and by short springs and autumns. Strong north and north-west winds are frequent, mostly in the winter. The sea has a temperizing effect on the cold of the winter and the heat of the summer. However, urban pollution and the scarcity of vegetation are factors that diversify the microclimate from area to area. The pollution caused by human activity (cars, heating and, to a smaller extent, industry), combined with the morphology of the basin and the mountains that surround it, contributes to the accumulation of pollution and very often to the creation of smog that looms over the capital. Nevertheless, on days when it has rained or when a mild wind is blowing, the clarity of the atmosphere and of the Athenian sky is surprising.

Vegetation has been confined, due to the dense urban layout, to very few parks, where one can see a large variety of bushes and trees, and to pine-clad groves that cover

THE NATURAL ENVIRONMENT OF ATHENS

some of the Athenian hills. Apart from pines, palms, acacias, mulberries, sour orange trees, eucalyptus and, more seldom, olive trees, plane trees and various kinds of poplar are the commonest trees that cast their shade on certain squares or create avenues on a few roads. What is left of the olive grove that covered the entire basin before urban development is located in an area at the borders between the Municipalities of Aigaleo and Rentis, a part of a wider district bearing the name Elaionas (meaning "olive grove"). The parks and groves of the city shelter several types of birds. In addition, the Hellenic Ornithological Society has set up a bird-watching centre in the National Garden. Sparrows, swallows,

blackbirds and wild pigeons are often seen, but only the latter – which frequent most of the city's squares – are totally accustomed to the boisterous city life and the pollution.

The Mythology Of Athens

The numerous myths regarding the gods, founders, heroes, kings and the name of Athens have survived in the ancient texts of the Classical and Hellenistic periods, but can be traced back to yet more ancient traditions.
Two gods, Poseidon, master of the sea, and Athena vied for dominance over Attica. The former drove his trident into the rock of the Acropolis and salty water

gushed from a spring, the "Erechtheis Sea". Next to it, Athena planted the first olive tree. The two gods almost fought. Zeus separated them by hurling his thunderbolt. The issue was put to the judgement of King Cecrops, who in turn put the matter to vote among the twelve gods. Zeus abstained, and as the goddesses supported Athena and the gods voted for Poseidon, Athena led by one vote and thus gained control of the city, which was named after her. The myth regarding the autochthony of the Athenians, meaning the claim that they were not immigrants but had always lived there, is founded on King Erichthonios, who was born out of the Attic soil. Tradition has it that Hephaestus tried to rape Athena. The goddess managed to escape, but Hephaestus ejaculated on her thigh. Athena wiped herself with a lock of hair and disgustedly threw it on the ground near Athens, thus inseminating Gaia. The child that was born, Erichthonios, was half human and half snake. Athena took upon herself to bring up the child. She hid him in a covered basket, which she entrusted to Aglauros, Cecrops' daughter. Cecrops had been married to Agraulos, who gave him three daughters, Aglauros, Erse and Pandrosos. Erse, Pandrosos and their mother were curious to see what was inside the Athena's basket and lifted the cover. The sight shocked them so much that they jumped off the Acropolis.
According to the tradition accepted by most Greeks, Xouthos, son of Hellen and brother of Aiolos and Doros, married the daughter of King Erechtheus, Kreousa, and had two children, Ion and Achaios. Therefore, the four Greek tribes, the Aeolians, the Dorians, the Ionians and the Achaeans all originated from Hellen. However, the Athenians maintained a second version, according to which Ion was the fruit of the illicit love between Apollo and Kreousa, whereas Doros and Achaios were sons of Xouthos.

Cecrops was succeeded by his son Pandion, who was later exiled by the claimants of the throne at Megara. There, he had four sons, Aegeus, Pallas, Nisos and Lykos. After his

THE MYTHOLOGY OF ATHENS

death, his sons took hold of Athens and shared power. Aegeus got the city of Athens, Nisos Megara, Pallas the Mesogaia (midland) Attica and Lykos secured for himself Euboea. Aegeus was unable to have a successor; and as he returned from the oracle of Delphi where he had gone to seek advice, he passed by Corinth. There, Medea made him swear that he would shelter her in his house – should this be necessary – and in return she would help him with her sorcery to have a son. After that, Aegeus went to Troezena and with Medea's magic he won Aethra, daughter of the local king. However, that same night she lay with Poseidon as well. The child that was born, fathered by the god of the sea, was Theseus. When Theseus became an adult, Aethra led him to the rock where Aegeus had hidden his sword and sandals. Theseus removed the rock and took them without any difficulty. He then decided to go to Athens by land. As he travelled he encountered brigands, whom he defeated, inflicting on them punishments that corresponded to their crimes: Periphetes at Epidaurus, Sines Pityokamptes (he who bent the trees) at the Isthmus, Skiron at Megara, Kerkyon at Eleusis and Prokroustes at Korydallos. Before arriving at Athens, the hero was purified at the sanctuary of Zeus Meilichios near Kifissos. Meanwhile, Medea had taken refuge in the city and had married Aegeus. She

convinced her husband that Theseus intended to kill him, so they decided to poison him during a feast that they had organized in his honour. Aegeus recognized Theseus when the latter drew his sword to slice the meat. Then Theseus defeated Pallas and his sons, who were suspicious of his presence at Athens, and sacrificed, in honour of Athena, the bull that Herakles had brought from Crete. The beast had caused much damage to the region of Marathon and had even killed Androgeus, son of Minos, King of Crete. In retaliation, Minos had demanded that the Athenians send seven young men and seven virgins every nine years to be fed to the Minotaur, the monster of the Labyrinth. Theseus took part in the expedition, after having agreed with Minos that, should he defeat the monster, the heavy toll on the Athenians would cease. Upon his arrival in Crete, he proved to Minos that he was the son of Poseidon by drawing up from the bottom of the sea a ring that belonged to the king and by offering to his daughter, Ariadne, the crown that Thetis or Amphitrite had given him. This scene was represented in the 5th century BC by the famous painter Micon in the sanctuary of Theseus. Ariadne fell in love with Theseus and gave him the magical thread that had been entrusted to her by Daedalus, creator of the Labyrinth. This thread would allow him to find his way out of the Labyrinth. That same night the plan was completed, Theseus killed the Minotaur, freed the young men and embarked to Athens taking Ariadne with him. They stopped off at Naxos, where Theseus abandoned Ariadne. Whether because of remorse for abandoning her or joy for his return, Theseus forgot to change the black sails of his ship with white, which would signal the success of his expedition. Aegeus, who watched

THE MYTHOLOGY OF ATHENS

from Cape Sounio, saw the black signal and fell into the sea, which thenceforth took the name Aegean Sea.
According to legend, Theseus is accredited with the synoecism of Attica. Until then, Attica consisted of 12 rival communities, which did not recognize the king of Athens. Theseus convinced everyone to give

up and founded an assembly and a tribunal at representatives of Athens. The 16th day of the month Hekatombaion was dedicated to the celebration of Athena and of the synoecism; and from his time onwards the Athenian games were called the Panathenaic games.
Theseus participated in the expedition against the Amazons in Asia Minor, where he met Antiope, who fell in love with him at first sight and followed him. The Amazons invaded Athens in order to avenge her betrayal, and after a mortal battle around the Acropolis, the Amazons were beaten and chased off, but Antiope was murdered. According to another version, it was Theseus himself who killed her, because she opposed to his marriage to Phaedra.
Theseus was a friend of the Lapith Peirithous. During the latter's wedding, the drunken Centaurs tried to abduct the wives of the Lapithae. Theseus saved the bride, Hippodameia. Theseus and Peirithous had both been suitors of Helen of Sparta, whom Theseus had abducted when she was twelve years old, hiding her in Dekeleia. But the hero Akademos pointed the hiding place to her brothers, the Dioskouroi. Akademos was the eponymous hero of the deme (district) of Akademeia. Out of respect for his action, during the Peloponnesian War, the Spartans avoided ransacking the grounds of Akademeia. Together with the audacious Peirithous, Theseus descended into Hades to seek Persephone. Plouton kept them held on the chairs of Lethe (oblivion) for four years. When Herakles descended to take Cerberus, he freed Theseus but not Peirithous. After that, Theseus dedicated a temple to Herakles the Deliverer and granted him most of the altars that had been dedicated to him.
After his return from Hades, Theseus decided to go to Crete, but a storm brought his ship to Skyros. Lykomedes, king of the island, received him with honours; but walking together, threw him down a precipice and then said that the hero was drunk and fell by accident. Around the mid-5th century BC, in an attempt to demonstrate the heroic Athenian past, Cimon brought the relics of Theseus from Skyros and dedicated a sanctuary to him near the gymnasium.

THE HISTORY OF ATHENS

PREHISTORIC TIMES

The history of Athens begins many centuries before the cultural wonder of the Classical period. Archaeological evidence testifies to the existence of organized life and significant accomplishments as early as Prehistoric times. However, due to intense building activity through centuries at the locations where traces of the first settlements have been found, namely the Acropolis, the Agora and the Olympieion, most of the evidence that would give a clear picture of the prehistory of Athens has been lost forever. The reconstruction of the earliest phases of Athens is based on results of excavations that have brought to light mostly tombs and portable finds. Athens was first settled during the final Neolithic period (4500–4000 BC), around the Acropolis. From the scant finds it seems that the Neolithic inhabitants of Athens were in contact with the coasts of the Saronic Gulf, with Aegina, and Kea, where important settlements have been discovered. During the Bronze Age (3200–1100 BC), settlement continued uninterruptedly around the Acropolis but new sites also bear witness to the spread of inhabitants over a wider area. During the early Bronze Age, the Acropolis was settled, around the Erechtheion and on the hill of the Olympieion. The Kerameikos area began to be used for the burial of the dead, and at the Agora there were early traces of a road leading westwards. Cultural evidence bears witness to contacts with the Cyclades, which thrived during this period, and with the important coastal settlements of Attica, such as Agios Kosmas. During the middle Bronze Age there was considerable expansion and organization of the settlements on the Acropolis, on its south and north slopes, at the Agora, on the hill of the Muses and at the Olympieion. What is impressive is the large quantity and variety of findings, demonstrating the constant communication with Central Greece, the Peloponnese and the Cyclades. During the late Bronze Age or Mycenaean period, the inhabitants of Athens were quite late in adopting the organization and practices of the

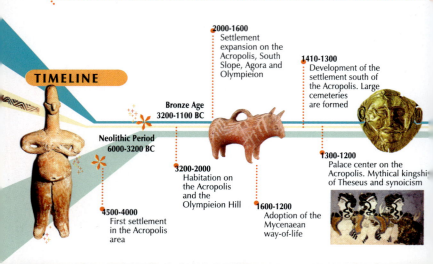

TIMELINE

Neolithic Period 6000-3200 BC

4500-4000 First settlement in the Acropolis area

Bronze Age 3200-1100 BC

3200-2000 Habitation on the Acropolis and the Olympieion Hill

2000-1600 Settlement expansion on the Acropolis, South Slope, Agora and Olympieion

1600-1200 Adoption of the Mycenaean way-of-life

1410-1300 Development of the settlement south of the Acropolis. Large cemeteries are formed

1300-1200 Palace center on the Acropolis. Mythical kingship of Theseus and synoicism

Mycenaeans, but eventually, from 1500 BC onwards, they assumed a Mycenaean character. A new settlement with a cemetery made its appearance at Ilissos. The greatest settlement development, especially south of the Acropolis, occurred between 1410 and 1300 BC. The creation of large cemeteries in the Agora, on the hill of the Nymphs and on the Areios Pagos, where the richest burials were found, affords evidence of the prosperity and growth of the population. The existence of different places of burial suggests perhaps that the inhabitants were organized into independent groups, "kata komas", a fact that concurs with the ancient sources and the name of the city, Athinai, in the plural. The early 13th century BC marks the beginning of the most important stage of development. The biggest differentiation is noticed in administrative organization, seeing that by then it was clear that the Acropolis was the palatial, administrative, military and cultural centre. The few relics of the Mycenaean palace were located on the site where the Erechtheion and the first temple of Athena would later be built. Later the inhabitants fortified the hill perimetrically with a cyclopean wall and created entrances. The coordination and planning of works on the site planning suggest that a powerful authority was in existence. The Athenians interpreted the Mycenaean hegemony as the rule of Theseus, to whom was attributed the synoecism of Athens. In the early 12th century, the prosperity of the final Mycenaean phase came to an end, as was the case in the entire Mycenaean world. The population grew sparser and dispersed, but the city was never deserted.

ATHENS DURING HISTORICAL TIMES

At some point during the early historical period the whole of Attica was united and made up a political entity centred in Athens. All the inhabitants of Attica were called Athenians and Attica became synonymous with Athens.

Cylon and Draco

The 7th century BC was a century of major political activity in municipal terms: the "polis" had achieved its social and

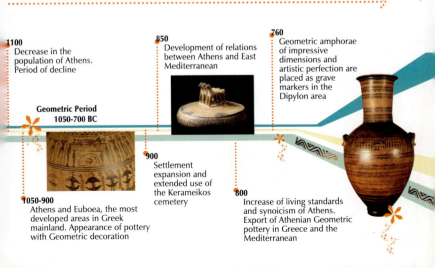

1100
Decrease in the population of Athens. Period of decline

Geometric Period 1050-700 BC

1050-900
Athens and Euboea, the most developed areas in Greek mainland. Appearance of pottery with Geometric decoration

850
Development of relations between Athens and East Mediterranean

900
Settlement expansion and extended use of the Kerameikos cemetery

760
Geometric amphorae of impressive dimensions and artistic perfection are placed as grave markers in the Dipylon area

800
Increase of living standards and synoicism of Athens. Export of Athenian Geometric pottery in Greece and the Mediterranean

THE HISTORY OF ATHENS

administrative shape in the previous century. Originally, there was conflict among the powerful aristocratic families of the cities, some of whom attempted or even managed to monopolize power, in certain cases favouring the lower strata, especially artisans and merchants, and established tyrannies.

In Athens, in about 635 BC, Cylon, instigated by his father-in-law, Theagenes, the tyrant of Megara, established a tyranny by seizing the Acropolis with his supporters. The Athenians besieged them and finally gained control of the sacred rock. Some of them managed to escape, but most, including Cylon, took shelter at the altar of Athena Polias and left it only when they were guaranteed a regular trial. But the Athenians broke their promise and killed them, thus staining the city with the so-called Curse (Agos) of Cylon. Later, Epimenides the diviner was summoned to cleanse the city of the unholy deed.

A few years later, around 624 BC, the Athenians assigned Draco to make laws and write them down publicly, with a view to abolishing the exclusive right of the aristocratic families to interpret and apply unwritten laws arbitrarily. Draco's laws, which most probably concerned only cases of murder, have made their mark in history because of their harshness.

Solon

Solon was a true ruler during those unsettled times (638–559 BC). In 595–594 he persuaded the Athenians to reconquer Salamis, which had been in Megarean hands since the time of the Curse of Cylon. Having succeeded in this, he was elected archon in 594–3 and appointed "diallaktes", meaning arbitrator on social issues. As part of his jurisdiction, he publicly enacted and inscribed laws that pertained to constitutional, family and civil law. The most important part of his legislation was the "seisachtheia", measures dealing with the prescription of peasant debts so that the peasants would not have to be subjugated to aristocratic landlords, and the redistribution of

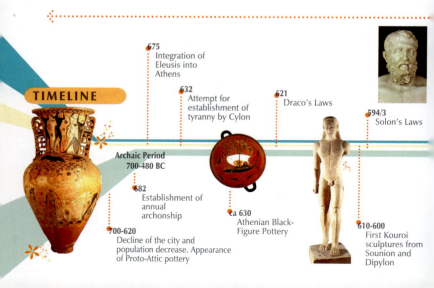

TIMELINE

- **675** Integration of Eleusis into Athens
- **632** Attempt for establishment of tyranny by Cylon
- **621** Draco's Laws
- **594/3** Solon's Laws
- **Archaic Period 700-480 BC**
- **682** Establishment of annual archonship
- **ca 630** Athenian Black-Figure Pottery
- **700-620** Decline of the city and population decrease. Appearance of Proto-Attic pottery
- **610-600** First Kouroi sculptures from Sounion and Dipylon

land. An important step towards democracy was the institution of the collective exercise of power to include the lower strata, through the assembly of the citizens (Ecclesia tou Demou) and the people's court (Heliaia). In order to make this measure work, Solon associated the holding of high offices with property rather than with descent and founded the Council of the 400.

Peisistratos' tyranny
It seems that the legislation of Solon, which aimed to secure stability, did not have lasting results, because in about 560 BC Peisistratos managed to establish a tyranny using a mercenary army and taking advantage of his good external connections. However, he paid attention to satisfying the demands of the people, such as the effective redistribution of land, but also to safeguarding the privileges of the aristocrats, harming only those who threatened his power. Peisistratos and his successors organized in grand fashion the cult of traditional aristocratic deities: under Peisistratos the Younger the Olympieion was built on the banks of the Ilissos in honour of Zeus and a temple in honour of Athena was built on the Acropolis. The festival of the Panathenaea was reorganized under Peisistratos, bringing all Athenians together. In addition, he introduced the worship of Dionysus, who became particularly popular and was associated with the flourishing of drama. After the death of Peisistratos, power devolved upon his sons, Hipparchos and Hippias. Hipparchos was murdered in 514 BC, most probably for reasons of personal revenge, by Harmodios and Aristogeiton: Hippias was overthrown in 510 BC by the Spartans.

Cleisthenes
Following the overthrow of the Peisistratid tyranny, Cleisthenes the Alcmaeonid returned to Athens. Annihilating his political rivals, he succeeded in enforcing a series of administrative changes that paved the way for a more representative constitutional system. The core of his reforms,

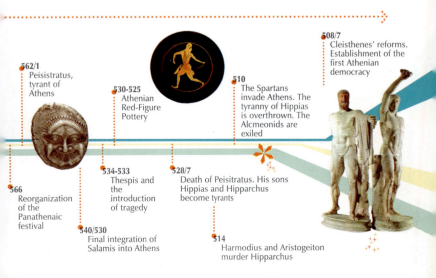

562/1 Peisistratus, tyrant of Athens

530-525 Athenian Red-Figure Pottery

510 The Spartans invade Athens. The tyranny of Hippias is overthrown. The Alcmeonids are exiled

508/7 Cleisthenes' reforms. Establishment of the first Athenian democracy

566 Reorganization of the Panathenaic festival

534-533 Thespis and the introduction of tragedy

540/530 Final integration of Salamis into Athens

528/7 Death of Peisitratus. His sons Hippias and Hipparchus become tyrants

514 Harmodius and Aristogeiton murder Hipparchus

THE HISTORY OF ATHENS

instituted in 507 BC, was the restriction of aristocratic power in political issues, as well as in issues of religion and cult. To this intent he replaced the system of the former four tribes with a new system consisting of ten new tribes, each with their own heroes and cults. In this way, he weakened the aristocratic families and the dependence of citizens on them. At the same time, Cleisthenes increased the number of the representatives from 400 to 500, so that each tribe elected 50 persons each year. The Council prepared the resolutions and the Assembly, which by then convened at regular intervals, passed them or voted against them. The combined attack by the Spartans, Boeotians and Chalcideans against Athens was firmly rebuffed. On the occasion of the Athenian victory over the Chalcideans and the seizure of the latter's property, Cleisthenes inaugurated the institution of the "cleruchies", distributing Chalcidean land to 4,000 Athenians.

The Persian Wars (490–479 BC)
The new administrative reforms brought about by Cleisthenes had a strong influence on the composition of the army, which was soon to be put to the test. In 500–499 BC the Ionian cities, originally under Lydian and then under Persian suzerainty, revolted against the Persian King Darius and the extremely heavy taxation that he had tried to impose. In 494 BC Darius finally managed to crush the Ionian revolt, preparing the ground for the conquest of the Greek mainland. Between 490 and 479 BC the Greeks waged war with the Persians. At the battle of Marathon (490 BC), the Athenians, led by Miltiades, spearheaded the victory against the Persians. However, what determined not only the outcome of the Persian Wars but especially the political developments inside Athens, was the naval battle of Salamis (480 BC). In this battle, the Athenians, headed by Themistocles, succeeded in sinking the Persian fleet, after the army had destroyed the unfortified city.
Themistocles, having averted the

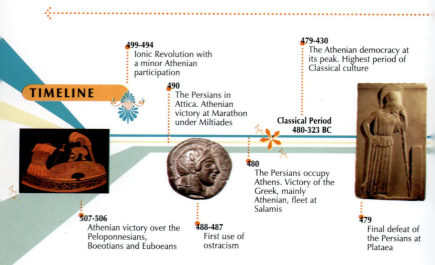

TIMELINE

499-494 Ionic Revolution with a minor Athenian participation

490 The Persians in Attica. Athenian victory at Marathon under Miltiades

479-430 The Athenian democracy at its peak. Highest period of Classical culture

Classical Period 480-323 BC

480 The Persians occupy Athens. Victory of the Greek, mainly Athenian, fleet at Salamis

507-506 Athenian victory over the Peloponnesians, Boeotians and Euboeans

488-487 First use of ostracism

479 Final defeat of the Persians at Plataea

ANTIQUITY

Persian danger, advised the Athenians to wall the city; so Athens was fortified with the Themistoclean Wall.
The Persian danger led to the creation of the First Athenian League in 478. Originally, its members included the majority of the cities of the Aegean islands and of the coasts of Asia Minor. At the same time, the reinforcement of the fleet resulted in the increase of landless free Athenians, given the fact that only free citizens worked in the ships. This, combined with the political changes brought about by Themistocles and Ephialtes (462 BC), spread and consolidated the institution of democracy.

The Fifty-Year Period

Nevertheless, these reforms would not remain in force if Athens had not gained increased power among the Greek cities after the end of the Persian Wars. The Athenian League became an instrument for Athens' rule. Its seat was transferred from Delos to the Acropolis. Instead of contributing ships, many cities started giving money, which Athens used to complete its building programme, but also to improve defence (construction of the Long Walls, which linked Athens to Piraeus and Phaliron) and the fleet. The "architect" of all the plans of this period was Pericles. This period was characterized by a marked growth in literature and the arts – this was the period of Aeschylus, Sophocles, Aristophanes, Herodotus, Thucydides, Socrates, Pheidias and many more. It was also a period of economic growth for all categories of citizens. Lastly, in 449 BC, Athens achieved a monopoly over the circulation of its silver coins to the cities of the League and in that same year it negotiated on its own the 30-year Peace of Callias with the Persian king.

The Peloponnesian War (431–404 BC)

Pericles' successful building and defence programme made the leader popular. As a result, he was elected general (strategos) uninterruptedly between 444–443 and 429 BC, with the sole

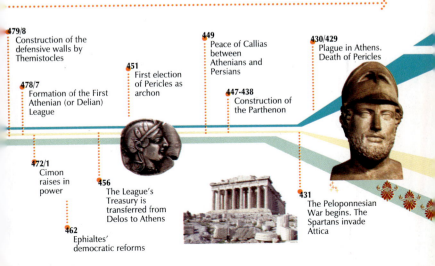

479/8 Construction of the defensive walls by Themistocles

478/7 Formation of the First Athenian (or Delian) League

472/1 Cimon raises in power

462 Ephialtes' democratic reforms

451 First election of Pericles as archon

456 The League's Treasury is transferred from Delos to Athens

449 Peace of Callias between Athenians and Persians

447-438 Construction of the Parthenon

430/429 Plague in Athens. Death of Pericles

431 The Peloponnesian War begins. The Spartans invade Attica

exception of the year 430 BC. The Peloponnesian War had already broken out by 431 BC. During its first phase, Athens was hit by pestilence, some form of epidemic disease. One of the victims of this epidemic was Pericles himself, who died in 429 BC. This war was the culmination of the increasing enmity between Athens and Sparta, which had begun in 462 BC with the sending away of the Athenian auxiliary military corps from Sparta during the Helot uprising. The main reason for the conflict among the Greek cities was the perpetuation of Athenian hegemony despite the Peace of Callias that had averted the Persian danger. In 446 BC Megara and Boeotia defected from the League and in the same year Athens and Sparta concluded a peace that ensured that the former would abandon its designs on central Greece and the Peloponnese. But Athens started behaving all the more domineeringly towards its allies, behaviour that culminated in the subjugation of Samos (439 BC) after its failed uprising. What sparked off the war was commercial conflict between Athens and Corinth, due to the westward expansion of Athenian trade.

After the death of Pericles, new leaders emerged for Athens, which was at war by that time. Among the most eminent was Nikias, who belonged to the moderate party. Thanks to the reconciliation he effected between rival parties, mostly Athens and Sparta, the first phase of the Peloponnesian War ended in 421 BC with a treaty that was named after him. However, he was confronted with the war supporters, in particular with Cleon, a demagogue and wholehearted democrat, and with Alcibiades. Despite his objections, he played a leading part in the Sicilian expedition (415–413 BC) with disastrous consequences for the city. Consequent on the defeat, the 30 tyrants took hold of Athens: they were invested with extended jurisdictions, whereby all democratic freedoms were abolished and democratic citizens were proscribed. This oligarchic regime in Athens was short-lived;

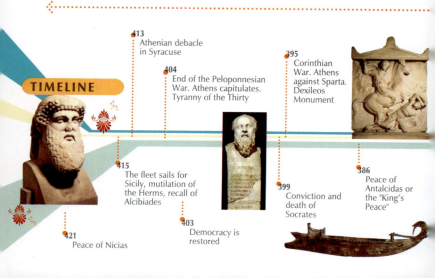

TIMELINE

- **413** Athenian debacle in Syracuse
- **404** End of the Peloponnesian War. Athens capitulates. Tyranny of the Thirty
- **395** Corinthian War. Athens against Sparta. Dexileos Monument
- **415** The fleet sails for Sicily, mutilation of the Herms, recall of Alcibiades
- **421** Peace of Nicias
- **403** Democracy is restored
- **399** Conviction and death of Socrates
- **386** Peace of Antalcidas or the "King's Peace"

it was overthrown by the allied exiles, mostly seamen, democrats headed by Thrasyboulos, and in 403 BC the regime regained a moderate democratic character. A few years later, the Spartan autocracy led several cities, including Athens, to ally against it. In the war that ensued, known as Corinthian, Athens won important victories, especially at sea, near the coasts of Asia Minor. These victories alarmed Persia, which rushed into concluding the Peace of Antalcides or the King's Peace in 386 BC. This treaty, which favoured Athens, enabled her to regroup and to found the Second Athenian League. But, once again, Athens proved autocratic in governing the League. The displeasure of its allies led to the War of the Allies (357–355 BC), paving the way for king Philip of Macedon to invade the Greek mainland and the Peloponnese.

Lycurgus (336–324 BC)
After the battle of Chaeronea, the orator Lycurgus ruled Athens from 336 until 324 BC. His primary concern was to increase income and economic reserves, allowing Athens to create an effective army and fleet and contributing to the creation of splendid buildings, such as the Panathenaic Stadium, the portico at the sanctuary of Asclepius and the temple of Apollo Patroos in the Agora. In addition, Lycurgus is accredited with the reconstruction of the Theatre of Dionysos and the completion of the works at the Pnyx, at Eleusis and at the Amphiareion of Oropos. The city had not seen such building activity since the time of Pericles.

The beginning of Macedonian rule
The already tense situation between Athens and Macedon came to a head in 323 BC, when Alexander died. Athens played a leading part in the creation of an anti-Macedonian alliance with the Aetolians, the Thessalians, the Phoceans, the Lokrians and certain Peloponnesian states. The alliance was decisively defeated by the Macedonian general Antipater in 322, in Krannon, Thessaly. Athens capitulated with extremely onerous

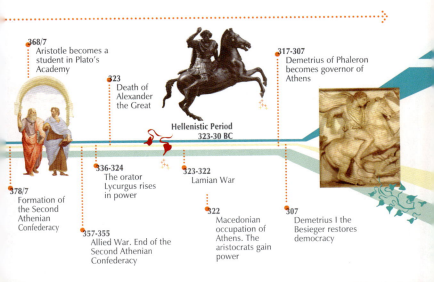

368/7 Aristotle becomes a student in Plato's Academy

323 Death of Alexander the Great

Hellenistic Period 323-30 BC

317-307 Demetrius of Phaleron becomes governor of Athens

378/7 Formation of the Second Athenian Confederacy

336-324 The orator Lycurgus rises in power

357-355 Allied War. End of the Second Athenian Confederacy

323-322 Lamian War

322 Macedonian occupation of Athens. The aristocrats gain power

307 Demetrius I the Besieger restores democracy

THE HISTORY OF ATHENS

terms: a Macedonian garrison stationed at the port of Mounychia, the democracy abolished, those responsible for the war sentenced to death, and Oropos and Samos detached from the city. The leadership of the city fell to the senior general Phokion, who was put to death in 318 BC, when the democracy was restored. In 317 BC Athens was obliged to ally with Cassander of Macedon and power was held for ten years by a pupil of Aristotle, Demetrius Phalireus, an eminent scholar and lawgiver.

Demetrius the Besieger (307–287 BC)

In 307 BC, Demetrius, the son of King Antigonus, sailed with a large fleet to Piraeus and abolished the regime of Demetrius Phalireus. The city was declared free and the democracy restored. Demetrius assisted Athens financially and by sending grain. He also ceded Imbros, Lemnos and Oropos to Athens.

Cassander did not accept the loss of Athens and between 307 and 304 BC he tried – without success – to retake it. The Athenians took part in the battle of Ipsos (301 BC) on the side of the defeated Antigonus and Demetrius. Lachares became tyrant of Athens, but soon Piraeus passed to the hands of his opponents and, in 295 BC Demetrius successfully besieged Athens. In 287 BC Demetrius, by now king of Macedon, was defeated and forced to abandon his kingdom. He thus finally failed to keep Athens, but Piraeus remained in Macedonian hands.

From the Macedonians to neutrality (287–200 BC)

In 268 BC Athens, in alliance with the Ptolemies of Egypt and King Ares of Sparta, declared war against Antigonus Gonatas, King of Macedon, son of Demetrius the Besieger. The city was besieged and forced to capitulate in 262 BC. It remained under Macedonian influence until 229 BC. After the death of Demetrius II, son of Antigonus Gonatas, the Macedonian garrison withdrew and returned Piraeus, Salamis and the forts of Mounychia and of Rhamnous to the Athenians. The

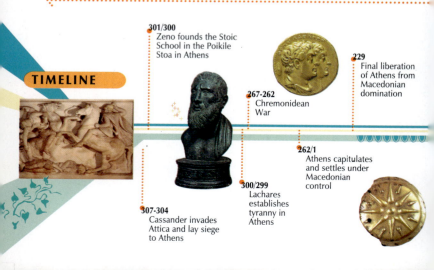

TIMELINE

301/300 Zeno founds the Stoic School in the Poikile Stoa in Athens

267-262 Chremonidean War

229 Final liberation of Athens from Macedonian domination

262/1 Athens capitulates and settles under Macedonian control

300/299 Lachares establishes tyranny in Athens

307-304 Cassander invades Attica and lay siege to Athens

ANTIQUITY

city leaders pursued a policy of strict neutrality with regard to the conflicts that prevailed during the last quarter of the 3rd century on the Greek mainland, remaining however under the protection of the Ptolemies.

On the side of Rome (200–88 BC)
This situation was reversed in 200 BC, when the city declared war against Philip V of Macedon, who had already gone to war with Rhodes and with Attalos of Pergamon. The Athenians, unable to wage war by themselves, solicited the help of Rome. The city was besieged by the Macedonians, to be saved only thanks to Roman intervention. In 197 BC, the defeat of Philip at Cynoscephalae led to peace. Athens adhered to Rome conclusively and assisted it in 192 BC, against Antiochus III of Syria, and in 171–167 against Perseus of Macedon. In return, Athens won Lemnos and Delos, which over the following years became a link between Asia and Italy, contributing considerably to the new affluence of the city. During that period, building activity started afresh and added lustre to the city, thanks to donations from the rulers of Pergamon and other Asian kings.

Mithridates and Sulla
Allegiance to the Roman alliance was set aside in 88 BC, when Athens sided with Mithridates VI Eupator, king of Pontus. The Athenians collaborated with Archelaos, the general of Mithridates, and subjugated the larger part of Greece, while the king freed most of the cities of Asia Minor and of the islands from the Romans. In 87 BC Sulla, at the head of five legions, spearheaded the Mithridatic War on behalf of the Romans. He besieged Athens and Piraeus for many months: when the city eventually fell, there was a terrible massacre that Sulla in the end stopped himself. A little later he seized Piraeus and set fire to the famous "skeuotheke" (arsenal) of Philon and the dockyards.
Athens' audacity in confronting Rome cost her dearly. She lost Delos and Salamis and was decimated by the war, the siege

146 Athens is a free state and an ally of Rome

88-86 Athens supports Mithridates, king of Pontus, against the Romans

86 Siege and sack of Athens by Sulla

58 Athens is subject to Rome

42 Mark Anthony arrives to Athens and transforms the city into his most important, after Alexandria, seat

30 After his victory at Actium, Augustus visits Athens

THE HISTORY OF ATHENS

and the ensuing massacre. Numerous works of art and precious metal offerings fell into the hands of the besiegers and were taken to Rome. Many city monuments were destroyed or seriously damaged. The city survived thanks to its name and prestige in the Roman world.

Roman rule in Athens
Nevertheless, the city was quick to recover after these disasters. During the 1st century BC Greek culture began to appeal to the Romans. As a result, many Romans settled in Athens and the emperors embellished it with remarkable new buildings. Julius Caesar inaugurated the new Athenian Agora, known as the Roman Agora, completed after the termination of the civil wars. Under Augustus, the aspect of the ancient Athenian Agora changed, with the Odeon of Agrippa and the transfer of temples from the Attic countryside to the Athenian Agora, such as that of Ares from Acharnai. The government of Tiberius and Claudius was oppressive, but in the Emperor Nero, despite his disreputable historical image, Greece found a real benefactor: as a new Flamininus, he declared again the independence of Greek cities, followed by large tax alleviations. During this period, specifically in AD 50, Paul the Apostle preached Christianity in Athens, a fact that had little importance then but assumed gigantic proportions in the course of the time. The reign of the Flavians was marked by opposition between the men of letters and the Roman administration, since the former began to criticize the excess of power of the later. Several intellectuals were persecuted, some Athenians among them.

During the Antonine period Athens enjoyed a time of rebirth, beginning with Trajan (98–117) and continuing with that great benefactor of the city, Hadrian (117–137) and his successors. Hadrian, fond of Greek philosophy and of the city itself, visited Athens three times (124–125, 128–129, 131–132). At his command, the residential area of the city expanded eastwards,

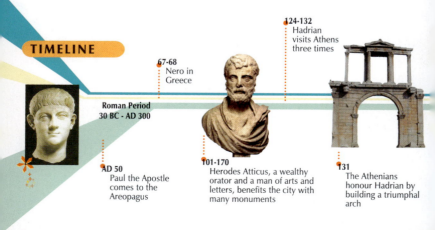

TIMELINE

Roman Period 30 BC - AD 300

AD 50 — Paul the Apostle comes to the Areopagus

67-68 — Nero in Greece

101-170 — Herodes Atticus, a wealthy orator and a man of arts and letters, benefits the city with many monuments

124-132 — Hadrian visits Athens three times

131 — The Athenians honour Hadrian by building a triumphal arch beyond Ilissos, while public buildings of great importance were built or completed under imperial benefaction (the aqueduct and the nymphaeum, the library, the Olympieion and the temple of the Panhellenic Zeus, the Pantheon, the temple of Hera, a new gymnasium and a new Pompeion). This was not all, though: it was clear that Hadrian intended to give back to Athens its intellectual grandeur. The construction of the temple of Panhellenic Zeus was accompanied by the foundation of the Panhellenion, a federation of all the Greek cities headed by Athens, and by the institution of the Panhellenic games that were held every five years in the honour of the emperor. In addition, Hadrian saw to the protection of the lower social classes against the avarice of food merchants, forbidding unlimited exports of oil. The city, in order to honour the emperor, dedicated an arch to him near the Olympieion that bears his name.

This beneficent policy towards Athens continued under Antoninus Pius (138–161), a period during which Herodes Atticus offered the city more splendid buildings, such as the Stadium and the Odeon, as well as under Marcus Aurelius (161–180), the emperor-philosopher.

Around mid-century the traveller Pausanias wrote the "Hellados Periegisis" (a description of Greece), a significant part of which was dedicated to Athens and its monuments, thus preserving for future generations a picture of the city in the heyday of the Roman period.

About a century later, this picture of the city was to change for good. The invasions of barbarian tribes in the Balkans and in Greece had an effect on Athens as well. Under Valerianus (253–260) there was a last effort to fortify the city against the imminent invasions, but the wall, constructed hastily, did not prevent the Herulians from seizing the city and destroying a large part of its public and private buildings.

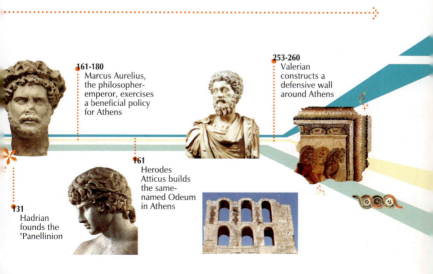

161-180 Marcus Aurelius, the philosopher-emperor, exercises a beneficial policy for Athens

253-260 Valerian constructs a defensive wall around Athens

161 Herodes Atticus builds the same-named Odeum in Athens

131 Hadrian founds the "Panellinion"

THE HISTORY OF ATHENS

ATHENS DURING THE MIDDLE AGES (267-1456)

The year 267 is a significant one to the history of Athens. It was when the Herulians, a Germanic tribe from the north coast of the Black Sea, invaded the city and razed it to the ground almost in its entirety. As a result, the physiognomy of the city, as this had been formed during the Roman period, with the expansion of the residential tissue and the splendid public buildings, changed completely. A small area, around the Roman Agora, would thenceforward constitute the main residential area, which was enclosed by a wall in about 280, known as the Late Roman wall, and which would be the main part of the city for several centuries.

However, efforts were made towards the restoration of at least some of the public buildings under the aegis of the emperor Diocletian, who assigned the reconstruction to a special official, the "corrector" of the province of Achaia (Corrector Provinciae Achaeae), since Athens came under the administrative jurisdiction of that province. The first building to regain its former appearance was Hadrian's Library, probably because it was the place where the tax archives were kept. Albeit confined, 4th century Athens was intellectually radiant. Its schools continued to operate and gathered students from all over the world, especially those who wanted to study philosophy and rhetoric. Important philosophers and orators, such as Libanius and Himerius, Longinus and Porphyry, taught in the city's schools, whereas some of the students of the 4th century were the future emperor Julian, Basil the Great and Gregory of Nazianzos. The blow dealt to the city by the Visigoths and their leader Alaric in 395-396 was not enough to impede its dynamic course as an intellectual centre. However, the historian, and later bishop of Cyrene, Synesios, who visited the city, was not very positive in his descriptions. The late 4th century saw an extensive building activity, which led to the expansion of the city beyond the Late Roman wall. This was the period during which were reconstructed the Theatre of Dionysos, as a meeting place, the Tholos and the Metroon (at the Ancient Agora). Two new constructions were the Gymnasium of the Ancient Agora, a

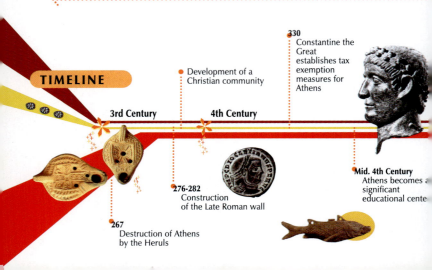

TIMELINE

3rd Century

267 Destruction of Athens by the Heruls

276-282 Construction of the Late Roman wall

4th Century

Development of a Christian community

330 Constantine the Great establishes tax exemption measures for Athens

Mid. 4th Century Athens becomes a significant educational centre complex that included teaching halls, a library, a training site and baths, and a building dedicated by the eparch Aetius to the emperors Arcadius and Honorius. Many private schools of philosophy were built near the Areios Pagos and on the south slope of the Acropolis. The repairs at Hadrian's Library were made thanks to Herculius, eparch of Illyricum, who had shown a great interest in the city.

The 5th century was a period of thriving for the Neo-Platonic Academy. During that period it was headed by outstanding philosophers, such as Plutarch, Syrianus and Proclus (412-485), the most renowned, who was put in charge of the Academy in 437. The commentarial work by Proclus covers a very wide range of works by ancient philosophers. His most important works include the commentaries on the Platonic dialogue "Timaeus" and on the first book of the "Elements" by Euclid, as well as an overview of the astronomical theories set out until that time. Recent excavations have brought to light the location of his residence, at the south slope of the Acropolis. Proclus had lived most of his life at Athens, with the exception of a short period of time, in about 450, during which he left the city on the grounds of religious conflicts, and had been one of the most active citizens, seeing that he participated in the common affairs of the city until his death (485). Under his guidance, the school acquired great prestige and his works, despite the subsequent religious conflicts, have survived to a large extent.

Throughout the 5th century, the city maintained a pagan way of life, following the Greco-Roman tradition. Institutions of the Classical period were still in force, such as the eponymous archon, as well as rituals, such as the procession of the Panathenaea. Certain renowned families seem to have played a significant role in it. One of the archons of that time was sponsor of the Panathenaic procession: the archon patrician and senator Theagenes, eminent member of the imperial court, who was married to Asclepigeneia, grand-daughter of the Neo-Platonic Plutarch. Another well-known name was that of the teacher of the Academy, Leontios, father of Athenais. Athenais is better known under the name Eudocia, which she took when she was baptized a Christian and became the wife of the emperor

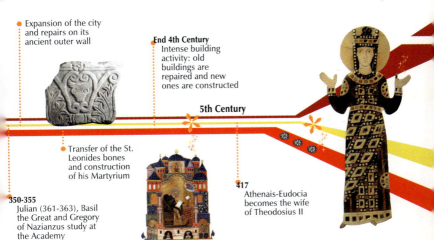

- Expansion of the city and repairs on its ancient outer wall

End 4th Century
Intense building activity: old buildings are repaired and new ones are constructed

5th Century

- Transfer of the St. Leonides bones and construction of his Martyrium

350-355
Julian (361-363), Basil the Great and Gregory of Nazianzus study at the Academy

417
Athenais-Eudocia becomes the wife of Theodosius II

THE HISTORY OF ATHENS

Theodosius II (408-450). Although she had received a classical education and was intellectually broad-minded, she did nothing to prevent Theodosius from effecting persecutions, to a limited extent, against all pagans and from carrying off from the city works of art in order to enhance the beauty of Constantinople, the capital of the empire. However, she maintained relations with her native city, as reveals the palace that she had built near the Acropolis.

Throughout the late antiquity, paganism and Christianity seem to have co-existed rather peacefully. As early as from the time of Dionysius the Areopagite there was a small Christian community in Athens that made its presence more felt from the 4th century onwards. Its existence is evidenced by clay lamps bearing Christian symbols and tomb slabs found at the excavations in the Agora. Perhaps the oldest Christian church in the city was founded in the 5th century at the centre of Hadrian's Library. It was a central plan church known as Tetraconch, which later, in the 7th century, would be replaced by the basilica of the "Great" Virgin Mary (Megali Panagia). At the same time a large three-aisled basilica was built on the banks of Ilissos river, next to the martyrium that housed the relics of martyr Leonides. It seems that the followers of Christianity multiplied dynamically after the measures taken by Theodosius, in 437, and the community received members of a particular economic and social prosperity. By the end of the 5th century they had almost prevailed over the pagans. This is clear judging from the appropriation of the sanctuary of Asclepius, following the death of Proclus, which until then was the main sanctuary of the Academy, but also from the temporary exile of Marinos, the new head of the school.

The conclusive defeat of the pagans was brought about by the decree of Justinian in 529, which imposed the shutting down of the Neo-Platonic school. The last teachers, its head Damascius and Simplicius, Priscianus, Eulamius, Hermeias, Diogenes and Isidorus of Gaza, abandoned the city and sought refuge in the court of the Persian king Chosroes. The predominance of the Christians is also reflected in the conversion of the ancient sanctuaries into Christian churches. In the mid-6th century the

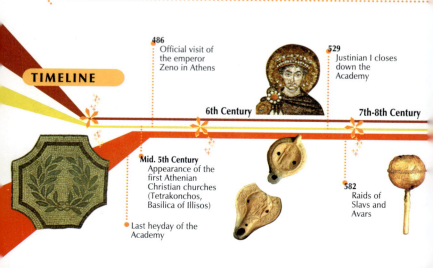

TIMELINE

486 Official visit of the emperor Zeno in Athens

529 Justinian I closes down the Academy

6th Century   7th-8th Century

Mid. 5th Century Appearance of the first Athenian Christian churches (Tetrakonchos, Basilica of Illisos)

582 Raids of Slavs and Avars

• Last heyday of the Academy

temple of Athena Parthenos in the Parthenon was converted into the church of the Virgin Mary of Athens (Panagia Athiniotissa). In the early 7th century the Erechtheion changed into a three-aisled basilica, the temple of Hephaestus at the Agora was dedicated to Saint George and later the sanctuary of Artemis Agrotera on the banks of Ilissos became a church dedicated to the Virgin Mary. At the same time, a number of churches were built on or very close to ancient monuments, such as the three-aisled basilica built on the site of the sanctuary of Asclepius, which was dedicated to St Anargyroi, and the basilica at the Theatre of Dionysos. An interesting remark is that the ancient sanctuaries were dedicated to saints of the Christian religion to whom are attributed similar qualities. The sanctuary of Asclepius became the church of St Anargyroi (healing saints) and the fountain was transformed into holy water, the temple of the ancient doctor Toxaris was converted into the church of Saint John, the healer of fever etc. This habit, which continued throughout the following period, was indicative of the religious syncretism that was prevalent. The caves of the Acropolis were also transformed into Christian churches (for example that of Pan became the chapel of St Athanasios, that of Clepsydra became the chapel of Holy Apostles (St Apostoloi at Marmara) etc.

During these two last centuries of the late antiquity, Athens seems to experience a fruitful prosperity, judging from the numerous pottery workshops that have been discovered at the excavations but also judging from the new fortification of the city by Justinian at the border of the former Themistoclean Wall, a fact that reveals the expansion of the settlement.

In the late 6th century, however, in 582, Slavs and Avars attacked the city causing complete devastation. This invasion marks the transition to a new era, for which very little information is available. Of course, this new period was the conclusion of a series of changes – administrative, economic and social – throughout the empire, which signified the end of the cities as they were known since antiquity, namely as autonomous centres.

MIDDLE BYZANTINE PERIOD

During the first years of the Middle Byzantine period, after the schools of

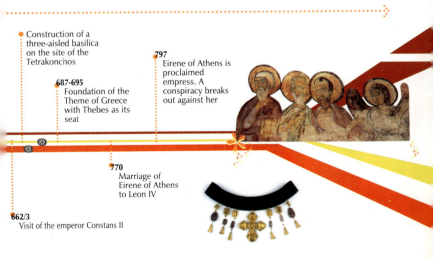

- Construction of a three-aisled basilica on the site of the Tetrakonchos

687-695 Foundation of the Theme of Greece with Thebes as its seat

797 Eirene of Athens is proclaimed empress. A conspiracy breaks out against her

770 Marriage of Eirene of Athens to Leon IV

662/3 Visit of the emperor Constans II

THE HISTORY OF ATHENS

Athens had ceased to operate and Christianity had predominated completely, Athens became a provincial city, cut out from the centre of power, with limited strategic significance. Evidence concerning the life of the city during that time is scant. For example, it is known that the emperor Constans II had spent the winter of 662/663 in the city, on his way to Sicily. Also, the bishopric of the city became a metropolis, in about mid-9th century, a fact that reveals certain potency. With regard to its administration, as from the 7th century the city came under the Theme of Greece seated at Thebes, whereas the local power was exercised by the archon of Athens (athenarchos). Apparently, the economy of the city was mostly based on agriculture. However, the fact that two Athenian women ascended the throne of the Eastern Roman Empire testifies to the existence of aristocratic families. One of these Athenians was the empress Eirene of Athens, wife of Leo IV the Khazar and mother of Constantine VI. She was the first woman to ascend the imperial throne (797-802). The other was her niece Theophano, wife of the emperor Stavrakios (811).

From the 9th century the city probably became the seat of the Theme, as reveals the tomb – situated on the Acropolis – of Leo, the strategos (general) of Greece, who died in 848. In any case, the development of the city is established by the reissue of the folles, which were bronze coins for everyday transactions, and by the extensive building activity, as evinced by the archaeological research. A great number of churches have survived especially from the 11th-12th century, which have given shape to the so-called Athenian type: these were small-sized cross-in-square churches with an exquisite eight-sided dome, fine cloisonné masonry and brickwork decoration with denticulated bands and kufic motifs. The use of such motifs of Arabic influence reveals possible relations with Arabs, and perhaps even the existence of an Arabic community in Athens. Another characteristic was the extensive use of marble members from ancient monuments. Typical churches of that period are the Holy Apostles of Solakis, the Kapnikarea, the Holy Incorporeal (St Asomatoi) at Thisseio etc. Many of these were founded by members of the Athenian aristocracy,

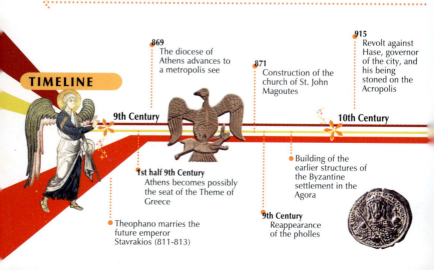

TIMELINE

9th Century

869 The diocese of Athens advances to a metropolis see

871 Construction of the church of St. John Magoutes

1st half 9th Century Athens becomes possibly the seat of the Theme of Greece

Theophano marries the future emperor Stavrakios (811-813)

10th Century

915 Revolt against Hase, governor of the city, and his being stoned on the Acropolis

Building of the earlier structures of the Byzantine settlement in the Agora

9th Century Reappearance of the pholles

THE MIDDLE AGES

which had acquired at that time affluence in a city that grew demographically as well, as attested by the archaeological remnants that bear on the development of its districts. The main urban tissue covered the area around the Agora and the Acropolis, at the border of the ancient wall. An important district was the Tzykanisterion, named after the place where the game tzykanion was played, which resembled today's polo. Another district was that of the konchyliarioi, namely the purple dyers, that of the elafos, near St Marina etc.

Economy was based on agriculture and industry, namely pottery, oil-industry, tannage, the production of soap and purple. Trade was also a growing sector and, what is more, in the 11th century the Venetians obtained the right to conduct free trade in the city. On the politics front, there were not any significant events, with the exception of two that bore on the central power. One was the result of the heavy taxation that at times gave rise to severe tensions. Such an incident occurred in 915, when the Athenians rose in rebellion and stoned at the Parthenon the administrator Chasse, because they held him responsible for the State policy. The other event was the visit of the emperor Basil II, in 1018, to church of Virgin Mary of Athens (Panagia Athiniotissa) in the Parthenon, where he prayed for victory against the Bulgars. Panagia Athiniotissa had become an important shrine, as attest the visits by eminent people of the Church, as for example Holy Loukas, Nikon etc.

Until 1203, Athens had not been greatly affected by the general instability of the Eastern Mediterranean and continued to act as the peripheral centre of the Eastern Roman Empire, facing certain occasional difficulties, such as the Norman and Arab invasions, in 1147 and in the second half of the 12th century respectively. Descriptions of the city, such as that of the Arab geographer Al-Idrisi, in the 12th century, present it as a greatly peopled city surrounded by a rich country. Its past as a cultural centre started to be reminisced about by the eminent scholars who appeared in Constantinople from the 11th century. Influenced by that past, Michael Choniates, who had profound knowledge of the classical literature,

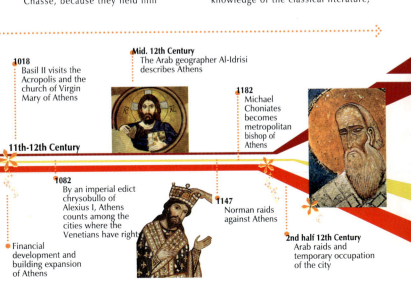

1018 Basil II visits the Acropolis and the church of Virgin Mary of Athens

11th-12th Century

Financial development and building expansion of Athens

1082 By an imperial edict chrysobullo of Alexius I, Athens counts among the cities where the Venetians have rights

Mid. 12th Century The Arab geographer Al-Idrisi describes Athens

1147 Norman raids against Athens

1182 Michael Choniates becomes metropolitan bishop of Athens

2nd half 12th Century Arab raids and temporary occupation of the city

THE HISTORY OF ATHENS

came to the city in 1182 in the capacity of metropolitan. He was disappointed by the poverty and the illiteracy with which he was confronted. His term of office as metropolitan coincided with very difficult times for the city. In 1203, Leo Sgouros, ruler of Nauplion, attacked the city. The ruinous attack was withstood by the inhabitants with the help of Choniates. Ultimately the city was seized in 1204 by the Frankish crusaders led by Boniface of Monferrat, as part of the Fourth Crusade. This event introduced a new phase in the history of the city.

FRANKISH OCCUPATION

Boniface ceded Athens and Megara to Othon de la Roche of Burgundy, who had already Thebes in his possession. Otto (Dominus Athenarum, Sire d' Athenes), organized his territory in imitation of the western medieval model. His nephew and successor Guy I received from king Louis IX the title of the duke and the territory of Athens and Boeotia were officially named duchy. Right from the beginning a Latin bishop was seated in the city and was recognized by the Orthodox priests after the self-exile of Choniates to Kea and Euboea.

The seat of the new political and ecclesiastical administration was the Acropolis, which was strengthened by fortifications and took the form of a medieval castle (Castel de Setines). A high tower, later known as the Frankish fort, was built south of the Propylaia, which survived until 1875. However, the residential area was confined within the Late Roman wall. In the first half of the 13th century a fortification enclosure, the Rizokastro, was built in order to reinforce the castle. On the Acropolis, the Propylaia were converted into the residence of the duke, the Erechtheion into the house of the bishop and the church of Panagia Athiniotissa became a church of the catholic creed.

Under the de la Roche Athens knew a peaceful period: the Venetians and Genoese who had settled permanently in the city contributed to the growth of trade and industry, especially the silk industry whose centre was Thebes. Under Guy I, on the other hand, coins were issued in the mint of Glarenza. This was the only coin minted in the duchy. The artistic production of the Athenian workshops of that time, which had incorporated the western influences, was noteworthy as well.

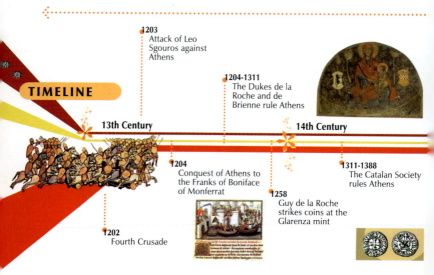

TIMELINE

13th Century

- **1202** Fourth Crusade
- **1203** Attack of Leo Sgouros against Athens
- **1204** Conquest of Athens to the Franks of Boniface of Monferrat
- **1204-1311** The Dukes de la Roche and de Brienne rule Athens

14th Century

- **1258** Guy de la Roche strikes coins at the Glarenza mint
- **1311-1388** The Catalan Society rules Athens

THE MIDDLE AGES

The rule of the Burgundian dukes came to an end with the seizure of the city by the knights of the Catalan Company after 1311. The Catalans offered the rule first to the kingdom of Sicily and then to the kingdom of Aragon. The kings of Aragon accepted the offer and designated a vicar in the city. Thebes became the seat of the duchy, whereas the Catalan became the official language and the law of Barcelona was introduced. The natives had no rights of property and the only profession that they could exercise was that of the notary.

The Catalan rule, which has been considered a sombre page in the history of the city, came to an end with the seizure of the Acropolis by the Florentine Nerio Acciaiuoli. The Acciaiuoli maintained the rule, discontinued by a short period of Venetian rule (1395-1403), until the conclusive surrender of the city to the Ottomans (1458). Prior to this, in 1397, the Ottomans had invaded the city under Bayezid, but the invasion had been unsuccessful.

The Acciaiuoli made Athens the capital of the duchy again and engaged in infrastructure and embellishment works. They had the port of Piraeus (Porto Leone) repaired, they constructed roads and restored churches. The Propylaia became a resplendent palace and the church of the Virgin Mary on the Acropolis (Santa Maria de Setines) was renovated. Trade and production were improved. Greek was designated the official language and the Orthodox metropolis was reinstated. Under those circumstances certain native families, the most eminent of which was the Chalkokondylis family, managed to distinguish themselves and acquire wealth. At the same time, the prosperity was associated with the settlement of the Arvanites (Albanian-speaking population) in the wider region of Attica and Boeotia. The interest shown by the Florentines was evidently associated with the movement of humanism, which had started to develop in the Italian cities and was based on the rediscovery of the ancient literature, the cradle of which was deemed to be Athens. As a result of this interest, certain Western travellers, such as Cyriacus of Ancona (1436 and 1444), embarked upon tentative visits to the city in order to get in touch with its glorious past. The Ottoman conquest, in 1456, which was concluded with the fall of the Acropolis in 1458, interrupted this tide and introduced the city into a new phase of its history.

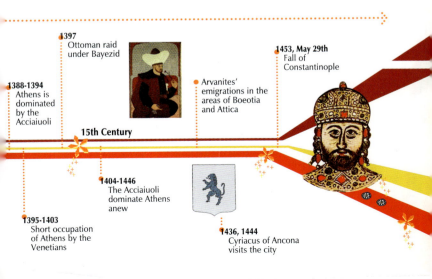

- **1388-1394** Athens is dominated by the Acciaiuoli
- **1397** Ottoman raid under Bayezid
- Arvanites' emigrations in the areas of Boeotia and Attica
- **1453, May 29th** Fall of Constantinople
- **15th Century**
- **1395-1403** Short occupation of Athens by the Venetians
- **1404-1446** The Acciaiuoli dominate Athens anew
- **1436, 1444** Cyriacus of Ancona visits the city

THE HISTORY OF ATHENS

ATHENS IN THE MODERN TIMES

15th-17th CENTURY

Athens was taken by the Ottoman army in 1456, and in 1458, with the surrender of the Acropolis, the occupation was sealed. In that year Sultan Mehmed II Fatih (the Conqueror) came to Athens on his way back from his campaign in the Peloponnese, when he visited the sites of the "city of the wise men", as Athens used to be called by the Ottomans. The sultan gave the metropolitan of Athens most of the dioceses that were under his jurisdiction during the Byzantine era. Catholic churches were also given to the Orthodox Church, except for those that were turned into mosques, such as the Parthenon.

Athens was an administrative centre (kaza). The highest ranks of the city's executives were the voyvoda (governor) and the kadi (judge). Under Ottoman rule non-Muslim citizens were free to practise their religion; however, they were burdened by heavier taxation than Muslims and were prevented from holding public office. From the 17th century the Orthodox community of Athens was led by a group of elders (dimogerontes) elected by community members who acted as mediators between Christians and the Ottoman authorities.

The peace that followed allowed the city to flourish economically. The population of Athens increased, reaching 15,000 during the 16th century, making Athens one of the largest cities of the Ottoman Empire in the Balkans. The majority of the population were Orthodox Christians. The increase of the population and the ever-growing need for water supplies led the Ottomans to construct an aqueduct, to repair older fountains and build new ones.

According to information provided by travellers, during the 17th century the streets of Athens were narrow and slated and the houses were small and built of stone. The city was divided into eight areas (platomata) covering what is today the area of the Plaka, Monastiraki and a small part of Thisseio and Psirris.

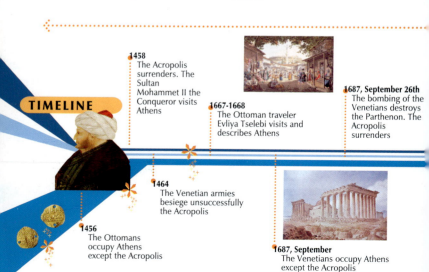

TIMELINE

1458 The Acropolis surrenders. The Sultan Mohammet II the Conqueror visits Athens

1667-1668 The Ottoman traveler Evliya Tselebi visits and describes Athens

1687, September 26th The bombing of the Venetians destroys the Parthenon. The Acropolis surrenders

1464 The Venetian armies besiege unsuccessfully the Acropolis

1456 The Ottomans occupy Athens except the Acropolis

1687, September The Venetians occupy Athens except the Acropolis

MODERN TIMES

In 1687 the Venetians, who had just taken over the Peloponnese, took over Athens as well. From their stronghold on Philopappos Hill, they besieged and bombarded the Acropolis, where the Ottomans had taken refuge, and destroyed the Parthenon. The Ottomans surrendered the Acropolis and left Athens. However, the Venetian army in its turn left Athens in 1688. Much of the Christian population abandoned the city then in fear of acts of revenge on behalf of the Ottomans, since numerous leaders of the Christian community had encouraged the Venetians to take over the city. By the end of the 17th century, however, most of the population had returned to Athens.

THE UNSETTLED 18th CENTURY

The 18th century is considered to be a period when the local, communal authorities, Muslims and non-Muslims, flourished. In Athens as in other places this meant intense conflict over the control of the community; the conflicts involved both Christian religious leaders and the local Ottoman authorities. In around 1710 a man of Christian Orthodox faith, Dimitrios Palaiologos, was appointed voyvoda for the first time. He was later assassinated by Muslims, although powerful members of the Christian community were probably also involved in the killing.

In 1754 Athenian Christians and Muslims rose up in protest against the arbitrariness of the voyvoda Sari Musellem. The uprising was suppressed by troops from Chalkis, and in 1758 Mustafa Ali Tzistarakis became the new voyvoda; later he built the mosque that carries his name.

Conditions for the Christian population of Athens worsened during the Russian-Ottoman War of 1768–74 and especially with the campaigns of the Russian Admiral Orlov in the Aegean, in which a large number of Christians took part. During these operations Salamis was taken over by armed Christians, which led to a deterioration of Christian–Muslim relationships in Athens, since Muslims considered the Christians

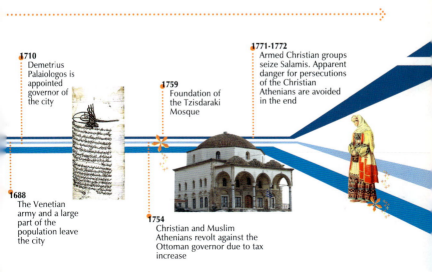

1688
The Venetian army and a large part of the population leave the city

1710
Demetrius Palaiologos is appointed governor of the city

1754
Christian and Muslim Athenians revolt against the Ottoman governor due to tax increase

1759
Foundation of the Tzisdaraki Mosque

1771-1772
Armed Christian groups seize Salamis. Apparent danger for persecutions of the Christian Athenians are avoided in the end

THE HISTORY OF ATHENS

as potential allies of the Russians. The years 1775–95 were marked by the presence of the city's voyvoda Hadji Ali Haseki. To begin with he maintained good relationships with the metropolitan and the elders of the community; however eventually a large part of the Christian community turned against him. Later the metropolitan also opposed him, and with the support of the majority of the Christians protested in Constantinople against his heavy taxation. Haseki was replaced for a short time but managed to regain his position in 1788, and to hold on to it until 1791. His violent policies meant that this was an unsettled period for many Athenians, some of whom had to abandon the city. Haseki was beheaded in 1795 by order of the Great Vizier, and many Athenians returned home. However, the city's population had been dramatically reduced because of these conflicts and outbreaks of plague in 1789 and 1792.
Soon after those events Lord Elgin, Ambassador of Great Britain in Constantinople obtained permission from the sultan to remove materials from archaeological monuments in Athens and take them to England. Thus, the monuments of the Acropolis were deprived of much of their sculpted decoration, which today can be seen in the British Museum in London.

THE GREEK WAR OF INDEPENDENCE

Just before the Greek War of Independence of 1821 the population of Athens was around 11,000, Greek- and Albanian-speaking Christians and Turkish-, Greek- and Albanian-speaking Muslims, the majority being Christian. Haseki had built a defensive wall around the city to protect the inhabitants against the raids of armed "Arvanites" (Albanian-speaking population) from rural Attica. The walls followed the line of more ancient defences, and started from the theatre of Herodes Atticus, reached Hadrian's Gate and continued along what is today Amalias Avenue, Sintagma Square, Stadiou Street, Psirris, Thisseio and the southern side of the

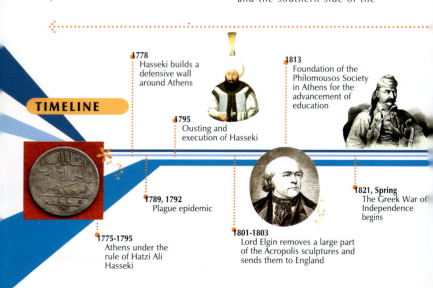

TIMELINE

- **1778** Hasseki builds a defensive wall around Athens
- **1795** Ousting and execution of Hasseki
- **1813** Foundation of the Philomousos Society in Athens for the advancement of education
- **1789, 1792** Plague epidemic
- **1775-1795** Athens under the rule of Hatzi Ali Hasseki
- **1801-1803** Lord Elgin removes a large part of the Acropolis sculptures and sends them to England
- **1821, Spring** The Greek War of Independence begins

MODERN TIMES

Acropolis, covering some 1,100,000 square metres in total. Athenian houses at this time were stone-built with wooden roofs covered with tiles. The city's administrative and financial centre was the area around Monastiraki, where the markets were also held. The largest market was behind Pandrossou Street, at the end of what is today Aiolou Street.

The military campaigns of Greek War of Independence destroyed much of the city. In April 1821 the revolutionary army took over the city and besieged the Acropolis, where the Ottomans had taken refuge. In June 1822 the Ottomans surrendered, but in August 1826 the situation was reversed: after their military successes in the Peloponnese, the Ottomans took over Athens and the Greeks took refuge on the Acropolis, which remained under siege until May 1827, when the Greeks surrendered and left Athens, only to return to Athens after the declaration of the independence in 1830; however, the Ottomans remained on the Acropolis. Finally, in March 1833, the Acropolis was returned to Greece and the Ottomans left Athens for good.

1834-1922

The first capital of Greece was Nauplion in the Peloponnese. Very soon, however, Athens became the capital. The choice of Athens had several symbolic and practical advantages. The city had been the focus of ancient Greek civilization, which dominated the ideology of the newly founded Greek State. Furthermore, since Athens had been largely destroyed during the campaigns of the Greek War of Independence, it could develop into a new city, unburdened by the Ottoman past.

Town planning studies were initiated to enable Athens to cope as the new capital. The first study by the architects Stamatis Kleanthis and Eduard Schaubert aimed to promote the ancient heritage and the new public buildings of the kingdom. The fact that Otto, son of Ludwig of Bavaria, an admirer of ancient Greek civilization, had been selected as the first king of

1822
The Acropolis falls to the Greeks

1835
First municipal elections in Athens

1830
Foundation of the Modern Greek state

1833, March
The Acropolis is handed over to the Greeks

1827, May
The Ottomans occupy the Acropolis

1833, January
The first king, Otto, arrives in Greece

1834, December
Athens is proclaimed capital of the Greek state

THE HISTORY OF ATHENS

Greece emphasized the identity of the capital as the symbol of a glorious past and as the administrative centre of an organized modern state. Kleanthis and Schaubert envisaged the creation of a city that would be equal to the other European capitals and suggested the remodelling of the urban environment with plenty of wide, open spaces and gardens, wide streets and boulevards. Their plan included the demolition of the old Ottoman city and the suggestion to transfer the centre of Athens to the area between Omonoia and Sintagma Squares. As the plan entailed radical change in the use of land and widespread compulsory purchase, it came into conflict with many powerful individuals and brought serious objections. The Bavarian architect Leo von Klenze was therefore invited to Athens to draw up new plans. Klenze's scheme was based on the earlier one, particularly regarding the site for the new city centre. The main difference was that he suggested that Athens should have a quainter character, without wide roads and open spaces. Furthermore, the network of the Ottoman roads and centre would remain intact. The plan was approved in September 1834, but in fact it was never implemented. The city's population changed both quantitatively and qualitatively: from 6,000 people in 1832 it reached 41,000 people in 1870. Athens was attracting people from other urban centres in Greece and the Ottoman Empire, and Greeks of the diaspora who came to work in the public services, as well as immigrants coming to work as labourers and small-scale merchants and manufacturers. The city was expanding without any specific planning and there was only a spontaneous separation of the different social classes in different areas. The lower classes settled in the southern and south-western areas, in the old Ottoman part of the city, in Thisseio, Psyrris and later in Metaxourgio and Gazi. People from the middle and upper classes settled in today's city centre and around Vassilissis Sofias Avenue.

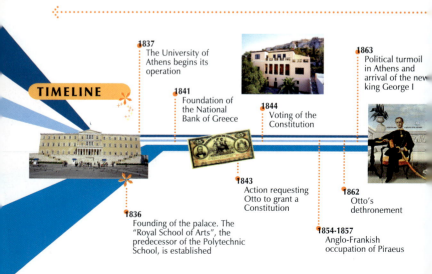

TIMELINE

1836 Founding of the palace. The "Royal School of Arts", the predecessor of the Polytechnic School, is established

1837 The University of Athens begins its operation

1841 Foundation of the National Bank of Greece

1843 Action requesting Otto to grant a Constitution

1844 Voting of the Constitution

1854-1857 Anglo-Frankish occupation of Piraeus

1862 Otto's dethronement

1863 Political turmoil in Athens and arrival of the new king George I

MODERN TIMES

As the country's capital Athens was closely related to events that shaped the history of the newly founded Greek State, starting with the uprising of 1843, when the people gathered in Sintagma Square and demanded a constitution from King Otto. Athens suffered in the years 1854–57, when the port of Piraeus was besieged by British and French forces to prevent Greece from participating in the Crimean War on the side of Russia. The situation deteriorated with an outbreak of cholera in Athens at that time.

In the following years there was increasing discontent with Otto's interference in political affairs in Greece, which resulted in a widespread movement against him that continued until 1862, when he finally left Greece. In the period before his successor to the throne, King George I, arrived in 1863, different parties vied for political control, resulting in the violence outburst of June 1863, known as "Iouniana", when many people lost their lives. These conflicts ended with the appointment of a temporary government, which remained in power until the arrival of King George.

In the following decades, until the end of the 19th century, succeeding governments tried to modernize and strengthen the country's economy. This was the time when the first vital infrastructure was put in place (Athens–Piraeus railway, the gas factory, Evangelismos Hospital) and numerous public buildings were constructed. It was also in this period that increasing waves of urban migrants made the population of Athens soar to 123,000 by 1896. The city expanded to the south and south-west (Metaxourgio, Gazi) and to the north and north-west (Neapoli, Exarcheia, Kolonaki). The first industrial developments took place at this time, although they didn't alter the city's character: Athens remained a city of merchants and manufacturers with a large number of public servants. The port of Piraeus on the other hand developed rapidly into an industrial zone.

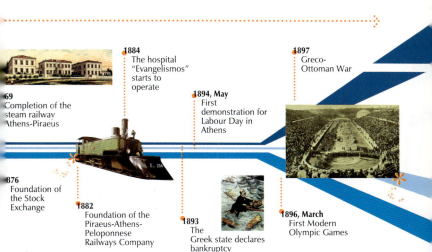

1869 Completion of the steam railway Athens-Piraeus

1876 Foundation of the Stock Exchange

1882 Foundation of the Piraeus-Athens-Peloponnese Railways Company

1884 The hospital "Evangelismos" starts to operate

1893 The Greek state declares bankruptcy

1894, May First demonstration for Labour Day in Athens

1896, March First Modern Olympic Games

1897 Greco-Ottoman War

THE HISTORY OF ATHENS

Athens was not only the capital of the Greek State but also a national focus for Greeks all over the world. This was combined with Greece's irredentist aspirations in those parts of the Ottoman Empire with Greek-speaking communities. Athens' institutional framework, particularly the education system, and its European aura attracted not only the Christian Orthodox population of the Ottoman Empire, but also the Greeks of the diaspora. Wealthy diaspora Greeks made significant financial contributions to the creation of an industrial infrastructure and to numerous educational and cultural organizations.

The beginning of the 20th century in Athens was marked by a series of conflicts; the first ("Evangeliaka"), in November 1901, concerned the translation of the Bible into Demotic Greek. The second ("Oresteiaka"), in 1903, concerned the translation of Aeschylus's Oresteia. Both conflicts reflected the ideological schism between the supporters of katharevousa (purist Greek), an official version of the Greek language that resembled ancient Greek, and those who supported the use of the Demotic; furthermore the conflicts reflected a larger pool of social unrest in Athens.

The disappointment caused by serious economic difficulties, the defeat in the war of 1897 and a general distrust of the political establishment resulted in the Goudi movement of 1908; its aims were to reorganize the army, improve the country's military capability and state institutions and functions. The movement was a landmark in the modernization process in Greece; it brought Eleftherios Venizelos to Athens and the development of new national and international policies aiming at social, political and economic modernization and the expansion of the state.

In the same period, the first years of the 20th century, additional vital infrastructure was completed in Athens as the supply of electricity throughout the city gradually increased, the public transport system developed, roads were opened up, municipal

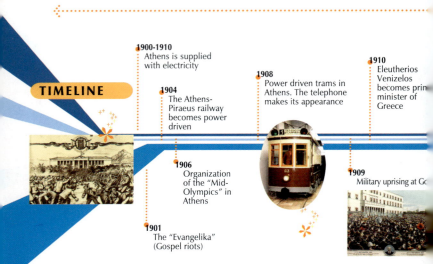

TIMELINE

1900-1910
Athens is supplied with electricity

1904
The Athens-Piraeus railway becomes power driven

1901
The "Evangelika" (Gospel riots)

1906
Organization of the "Mid-Olympics" in Athens

1908
Power driven trams in Athens. The telephone makes its appearance

1909
Military uprising at Go

1910
Eleutherios Venizelos becomes prin minister of Greece

administrative services provided by the municipality of Athens (founded in 1835) were reshaped and municipal abattoirs constructed to improve public hygiene. Much of this endeavour was achieved through the mayors Spiros Merkouris and Emmanouil Benakis.

In the years that followed Athens lived in an atmosphere of national pride thanks to victory in the Balkan Wars. However, disagreements between Venizelos and King Constantine I about Greece's stance in World War I resulted in the so-called National Schism ("ethnikos dichasmos"). Conflict between Venizelos' supporters and opponents resulted in two governments operating at the same time, one in Athens and one in Thessaloniki led by Venizelos. The schism came to a peak in November 1916. Immediately after World War I Greece became involved in the Asia Minor campaign. Nation-wide exhaustion from continuous military involvements quickly took its toll in political affairs in Athens. Venizelos was defeated in the 1920 election. The Asia Minor disaster of 1922 and the wave of refugees that followed led in autumn 1922 to the trial and execution of the politicians and officers who were held responsible.

1922 - 1949

The arrival of refugees from Asia Minor and the Balkans caused the population of Athens to increase dramatically, to 460,000 in 1928, while in the entire conurbation including Athens and Piraeus it reached 800,000. The most important problem facing the already exhausted country was the rehabilitation of refugees, most of whom were housed in quickly built shacks on the outskirts of the city. Government initiatives and international assistance led to a unique (in Greece) housing programme that was put in place in areas inhabited by refugees, such as Nea Ionia, Kallithea, Neos Kosmos, Nea Smirni, Nikaia and Kaissariani. On several occasions political innovation was matched with advanced architectural ideas,

1913, March
Murder of king George in Thessaloniki. Constantine I raises to the throne

1922, August - September
Withdrawal of the Greek military forces from Asia Minor

1922, September
Plastiras' coup

12, October
Beginning of the 1st Balkan War

1913, June
Beginning of the 2nd Balkan War

1919-1922
Greek expedition to Asia Minor

1916
National Division

1922, November
Trial and execution of those thought of as the ringleaders for the defeat in Asia Minor

THE HISTORY OF ATHENS

in accordance with European modernism.

The refugees invigorated the city's economy. The availability of inexpensive labour promoted industrial development, which flourished in the mid-war period. However, social inequality increased at the same rate. Many refugees settlements, particularly in shanty town areas, were marked by poverty and marginalization.

As across Europe at the time, the political situation was also unsettled. Athens and indeed the whole country was divided by the conflict between the supporters and opponents of Venizelos, the leader of the Liberal Party, which initiated the country's development and modernization between the second and fourth decades of the 20th century. Those who opposed Venizelos were generally in favour of the monarchy, which had been abolished between 1924 and 1935. Although the majority of native Athenians opposed Venizelos, most of the refugees supported him, since his governments had taken measures for their relief.

An increasing population in Athens had resulted in the introduction of "horizontal ownership" and through that in the construction of multistoreyed blocks of apartments (polykatoikies). This development marked the urban image of Greece and Athens in particular, especially in the years after the war.

The labour movement had already began to develop in the early 20th century but the influence of the left increased significantly in the capital during the 1930s as a result of the city's industrial development and the ever-growing working class, as well as the international economic crisis of 1929. In the same period the feminist movement also grew stronger, particularly in the capital. At that time the so-called 30s generation, a group of writers and artists who found expression mostly through urban novels had a strong presence in Greek literature, suggesting new ways of aesthetic expression and new

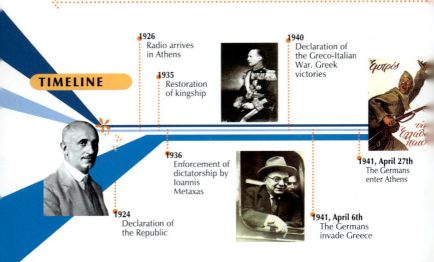

TIMELINE

1924 Declaration of the Republic

1926 Radio arrives in Athens

1935 Restoration of kingship

1936 Enforcement of dictatorship by Ioannis Metaxas

1940 Declaration of the Greco-Italian War. Greek victories

1941, April 6th The Germans invade Greece

1941, April 27th The Germans enter Athens

MODERN TIMES

ideological positions.
This unsettled and tense political, ideological and social atmosphere in mid-war Greece was terminated with the reestablishment of the monarchy in 1935 and the dictatorship of Ioannis Metaxas one year later. A few years on, Greece became involved in World War II.
Greek victories against the Italians (1940–41) were followed by German invasion of Greece (April 1941). During the difficult years of the occupation (1941–44) Athens suffered a lot. The economy was destroyed and the occupying forces had control over food supplies, so the winter of 1941–42 became a nightmare for the people of Athens. Food supplies were sparse and the little available was sold on the black market at extremely high prices. The majority of the population was starving and a large number of children and elderly people lost their lives. The sight of dead people piled up in horse carts left terrible memories and a constant sense of insecurity, which has been overcome only with the social well being of recent decades.
Athenians did not tolerate the Nazi occupation without resistance. From very early on, as in other parts of Greece, resistance groups were formed in Athens and took decisive action against the Germans. The central resistance group was EAM/ELAS which, despite its communist leadership, attracted people from the entire political spectrum between centre and left. The political differences between EAM/ELAS and another of the main resistance groups in Greece, the right-wing EDES, began in the years of the German occupation. In December 1944, a few months after the liberation from Germany, EAM/ELAS confronted the British army and pro-government forces in Athens. The polarization led to the civil war of 1946–49 that ended with the final defeat of the communists. The civil war affected Greek society deeply and scarred political developments after the war for many decades.

1941-42, winter
Famine in Athens

1943, February
The funeral of the poet Kostis Palamas develops into a widespread demonstration against the Nazis

1943, March
Large-scale strike against the mobilization of the Greeks by the Nazis

1944, December
Battles between ELAS and British troops in Athens

1946-49
Civil War

1944, October 12th
Liberation of Athens

1941, May
Manolis Glezos and Apostolos Santas bring down the swastika. First act of resistance against the conquerors

THE HISTORY OF ATHENS

THE POST-WAR YEARS UNTIL TODAY

Greece's economy, although destroyed by the German occupation and civil war, began to grow again in the 1950s thanks to the assistance of foreign countries, mainly the US, and to the so-called "Greek economic miracle". Instrumental in this was the building of a public infrastructure, particularly while Konstantinos Karamanlis was Prime Minister, and, mainly, the growth in the construction and building sectors of the economy. The sharp increase in the construction of new buildings was fuelled by a huge wave of immigrants into Athens at a time when large numbers were emigrating abroad, to Australia and the Federal Republic of Germany. Masses of people from the country arrived in Athens so that the city's population increased from 1,124,000 people in 1940 to 2,540,000 in 1971 and 3,016,000 in 1981. Large numbers of these new residents settled in areas outside the city centre. In 1940 42% of the population still lived within the boundaries of the Municipality of Athens. By 1971 this percentage had been reduced to 34% and was further reduced in following years. In 1940 the population of Athens was 15% of the population of Greece as a whole, while by 1971 it had doubled to 30% of the entire population.

Unfortunately, the settlement of immigrants and the expansion of the city took place without any form of government planning, which resulted in uncontrolled and unauthorized building activity. Particularly important in the construction process was the so-called "antiparochi" system: many old detached houses were demolished and gave way to apartment blocks through an agreement between the former house owners, the builders and the purchasers of prospective apartments. The owner offered his building plot in exchange for some apartments in the new block and the purchasers gave the builders the capital necessary for construction.

At the same time Athens

TIMELINE

1952 Greece accedes to NATO

1957 The railway Piraeus-Kifissia is completed

1960-70 The internal migration towards the capital reaches its peak

1965 Demonstrations in Athens during the political crisis of "Iouliana"

1967, April 21th Establishment of military dictatorship in Greece

1973, November Students' revolt against the dictatorship in Athens

MODERN TIMES

developed at an extremely fast pace, sometimes faster than the city's infrastructure could cope with. An example of this is the transport problem. Even in the 1960s the roads in Athens did not guarantee a regular flow of traffic – and this in a period when very few Athenians owned a motorcar. The military dictatorship of 1967–74, another indirect result of the civil war, interrupted the political and cultural progress of Athens during the 1960s, when music and theatre flourished in Athens, with artists of international fame such as Mikis Theodorakis, Manos Hadjidakis and Karolos Kuhn.

A year after the student uprising at the Technical University of Athens, the dictatorship came to an end, the monarchy was abolished and Greece came into a new era during which the marks of civil war were erased, the country's political life stabilized and democracy became self-evident. Athens benefited most from these developments as the country's capital. Today, following the end of the unregulated expansion between 1950 and 1970 and at the beginning of the 21st century, Athens is trying to be successful as the metropolis of a wider area. Athens' new immigrants come not from the Greek countryside, but from the Balkans, Eastern Europe and Third World countries. The position of Athens in international affairs was also affected by Greece's joining the European Union in 1981 and the Economic and Monetary Union in 2001. Athens is today a vibrant, multicultural city of some 3,200,000 people who have numerous problems, but also optimism for the future. The small Athens of 1896 took leave of the 19th century by hosting the first modern Olympic Games; Athens of 2004 welcomes the 21st century by hosting the global festival of the 28th Olympics.

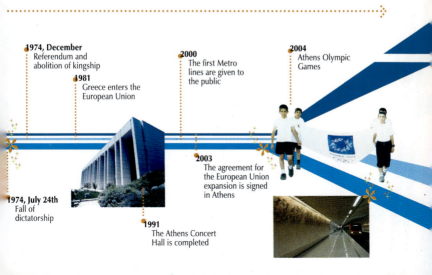

1974, December
Referendum and abolition of kingship

1981
Greece enters the European Union

2000
The first Metro lines are given to the public

2004
Athens Olympic Games

1974, July 24th
Fall of dictatorship

1991
The Athens Concert Hall is completed

2003
The agreement for the European Union expansion is signed in Athens

ARCHITECTURE AND SCULPTURE

ANTIQUITY

Architectural terms

ARCHITECTURAL ORDERS

DORIC CAPITAL   IONIC CAPITAL   CORINTHIAN CAPITAL   PERGAMENE CAPITAL

IONIC KYMATION   LESBIAN KYMATION   ASTRAGAL   LION-HEAD WATERSPOUT

TYPES OF ANCIENT GREEK TEMPLES

DISTYLE IN ANTIS   AMPHI ANTIS DISTYLE   AMPHIPROSTYLE

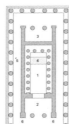

1. Cella
2. Pronaos
3. Opisthodomos
4. Cult Statue
5. Pteron
6. Anta
7. Interaxial Distance
8. Intercolumniation

PERIPTERAL
ATHENS, HEPHAISTEION

DIPTERAL
ATHENS, OLYMPIEION

ARCHITECTURE AND SCULPTURE

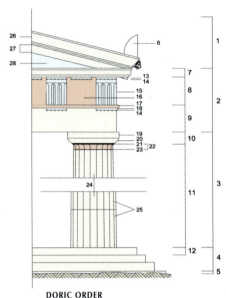

DORIC ORDER

1. Pediment
2. Entablature
3. Column
4. Crepis
5. Euthynteria
6. Acroterion
7. Horizontal Cornice
8. Frieze
9. Architrave
10. Capital
11. Shaft
12. Stylobate
13. Mutule
14. Guttae
15. Triglyph
16. Metope
17. Taenia
18. Regula
19. Abacus
20. Echinus
21. Annulets
22. Hypotrachelion (Neck)
23. Necking Rings
24. Flutes
25. Drums
26. Sima
27. Raking cornice
28. Tympanum

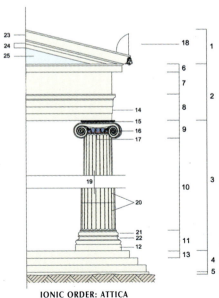

IONIC ORDER: ATTICA

1. Pediment
2. Entablature
3. Column
4. Crepis
5. Euthynteria
6. Horizontal Cornice
7. Frieze
8. Architrave
9. Capital
10. Shaft
11. Base
12. Plinth
13. Stylobate
14. Fascia
15. Abacus
16. Volute
17. Echinus
18. Acroterion
19. Flutes with Fillet
20. Drums
21. Spira / Torus
22. Scotia, Trochilus
23. Sima
24. Raking Cornice
25. Tympanum

ARCHITECTURE AND SCULPTURE

The Theatre of Dionysos

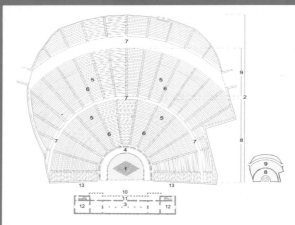

1. Orchestra 2. Cavea 3. Skene 4. Prohedria 5. Kerkides
6. Stairways 7. Diazoma 8. Lower Cavea 9. Upper Cavea
10. Proskenion 11. Logeion 12. Paraskenia 13. Parodoi

The Odeon of Herodes Atticus

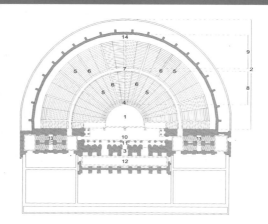

1. Orchestra 2. Cavea 3. Skene 4. Prohedria 5. Kerkides
6. Stairways 7. Diazoma 8. Lower Cavea 9. Upper Cavea
10. Proskenion 11. Logeion 12. Vestibule 13. Staircase
14. Stoa

ARCHITECTURE AND SCULPTURE

Sculpture

Severe Style:
The term applied to the sculptures of the second quarter of the 5th century (480–450 BC), in which the weight of the body is supported by an extended member, the other member being loose. The structure of the body is natural, following the position of the skeleton, and reveals exact anatomical knowledge on the part of the sculptor. The faces show an inner sense of concentration, while the facial expressions reflect the ethos, character and psychological state of the subjects.

Kore:
An Archaic statue of a young female, dressed.

Kouros:
An Archaic statue of a young male, dressed or naked.

Votive Relief:
A rectangular marble plaque with relief decoration, dedicated to a deity usually depicted as receiving offerings from the votaries.

Ornate style:
The term applied to the sculpture of the last 20 years of the 5th century BC, that reveal a special interest for the structure of the bodies, the dress and the ornate rendering of the folds. The figures are airy and tend to turn around a central axis. Gradually, the female body reveals itself with nobility and elegance.

Funerary relief:
A rectangular marble plaque with relief decoration, set on a grave. It depicts the dead person in a typical lifetime activity, among his loved ones. The person's name is inscribed on the upper or lower part of the stela.

ARCHITECTURE AND SCULPTURE

MIDDLE AGES

Ground plan types of Byzantine churches

EARLY CHRISTIAN THREE-AISLED BASILICA

(Ilissos Basilica)

MIDDLE BYZANTINE CROSS-IN-SQUARE CHURCH TYPES

DOMED OCTAGON

(Sotira of Lykodemos)

COMPLEX FOUR COLUMNED

(Kapnikarea)

SEMI-COMPLEX FOUR COLUMNED

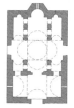

(Gorgoepekoos)

CENTRAL PLAN TETRACONCH

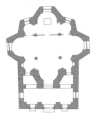

(Holy Apostles Solaki)

FOUR-COLUMNED

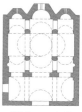

(St Assomatoi) Thisseio

TWO-COLUMNED

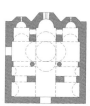

(St John the Theologian)

ARCHITECTURE AND SCULPTURE

POST-BYZANTINE BARREL-VAULTED CHURCH TYPES

THREE-AISLED WITH SQUINCHES

AISLELESS WITH SQUINCHES

SIMPLE AISLELESS

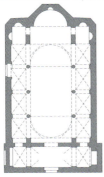

(St Dionysius the Areopagite)

(St Anargyroi Kolokinthi)

(Agia Dinami)

ARCHITECTURAL ELEMENTS OF BYZANTINE CHURCHES

Dome of Athenian Type

Masonry with ceramic kuific decoration

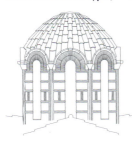

Elevation

Section

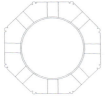

(St Assomatoi) Thisseio

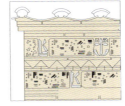

ARCHITECTURE AND SCULPTURE

Modern Times

Otto's style

This style can describe buildings representing folk architecture during Otto's era. Those buildings were harmoniously adapted to the neoclassical style and formed a bridge between that style and more traditional forms. As far as their ground plans are concerned, they have a simple arrangement of space (yard, open-air space, enclosed space) in a closed, functional formation. The construction and decoration of the façades is simple and the houses are usually two-storeyed. The general forms are strict and the cornices are slightly protruding.

Example of Otto's style building

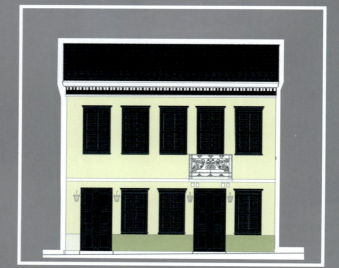

ARCHITECTURE AND SCULPTURE

Classicist form

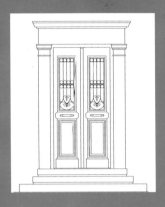

The term refers mainly to the arbitrary use of the neoclassical style, which resulted in the alteration of its character in Athens. These variations of the neoclassical style often managed to adapt to the demands of the period in an immediate and flexible manner.

Example of classicist building

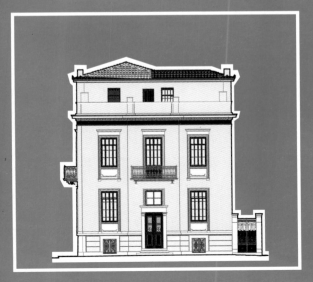

ARCHITECTURE AND SCULPTURE

Neoclassical style

An artistic movement across Europe with monumental character and symbolic references to the historic archetypes from the Classic era. Those elements had already matured in the German tradition and were represented in Greece by European architects (Ernst Ziller, Theophilus and Christian Hansen, Leo von Klenze) and their Greek counterparts who had studied in Europe (Stamatis Kleanthis, Lissandros Kaftantzoglou).

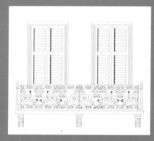

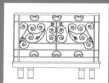

Example of neoclassical building

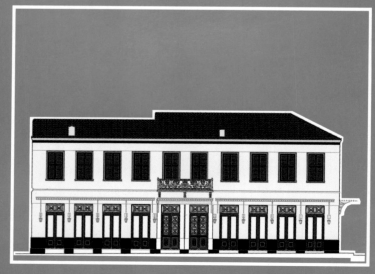

ARCHITECTURE AND SCULPTURE

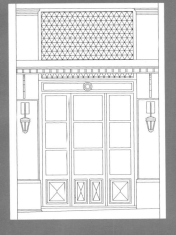

Example of neoclassical building

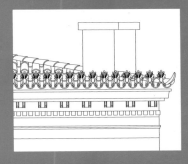

WALK 1

1. St Assomatoi
2. Centre for the Study of Traditional Pottery
3. The Jewish Synagogue
4. The Kerameikos
5. The Themistoclean Wall
6. The Sacred Gate
7. The Dipylon and the Fountain-House
8. The Pompeion
9. Funerary Periboloi and Monuments
10. Tumuli (Tombs)
11. The Kerameikos Museum
12. St Athanasios Kourkouris
13. The Cultural Centre "Melina Merkouri"
14. Apostolou Pavlou Street
15. Thisseio Square
16. Antiquities of the St Marina-Thisseio Area
17. St Marina in Thisseio
18. The Observatory
19. The Pnyx
20. The Areios Pagos
21. St Demetrius Loubardiaris
22. The Philopappos Monument
23. The Atelier of Spiros Vassiliou

ARCHAEOLOGICAL SITE OF THE KERAMEIKOS

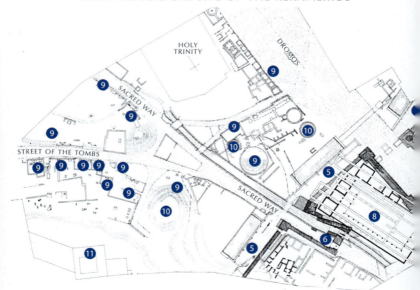

1 WALKING ON THE HILLS OF THE ACROPOLIS

Three hills with political importance: Areios Pagos (the hill of justice), Pnyx (the hill of Democracy) with the little Church of Loubardiaris decorated by Pikionis, and the hill of the Muses, which the Athenians chose to honour their benefactor, Philopappos. A fourth hill is dominated by the Observatory, where one can walk among the trees and have an interesting view day and night.

St Assomatoi

The small Byzantine church of St Assomatoi is situated next to the Thisseio metro station on Ermou Street, in the centre of Thisseio Square.

The church dates back to the second half of the 11th century. During the 1960s it underwent repairs that restored the building almost to its original state by eliminating the various additions that had been made in the course of the years. Today the church is in a particularly good condition.

With its characteristic four-columned, domed, cross-in-square form, the church of St Assomatoi is typical of Athenian Byzantine churches of this period. The exterior is of sculpted stone surrounded by bricks (cloisonné masonry). Typical characteristics of the period are the large stones on the lower parts of the side walls in a cross-shaped arrangement, as well as the brick dentils on the sides of the building.

There are also two ceramic plates with kufic decorations mounted on the western wall. They probably formed part of a larger frieze, similar to the one of the church of St Theodoroi in Klafthmonos Square. These decorative elements (kufic) imitate the old Arabic writing in which the Koran was first written in the city of Kufa in present-day Iraq. Above the northern entrance of the church there is a horseshoe-shaped arch inspired by Islamic architecture. Islamic influences can actually be traced in various Byzantine artefacts, such as textiles, sculptures and small ornaments, and these influences stem from the trend to imitate oriental decorative elements. With regards to Athens in particular,

St Assomatoi, Thisseio

these influences are also related to the documented presence of a small Arab community in the city towards the end of the 10th century, mostly merchants and manufacturers.

THE JEWISH SYNAGOGUE

Old Synagogue

The Jewish Synagogue on 5 Melidoni Street, opposite the Museum of Traditional Pottery is called "Beth-Shalom" which means "House of Peace" in Hebrew. The Jewish community of Athens decided to acquire this plot of land and build a new Synagogue as the older one on 8

Synagogue Beth-Shalom

Melidoni Street, founded in the early 20th century, was not sufficient to cover the needs of the community that expanded with the arrival of Jewish refugees from Asia Minor.

The neoclassical building is made of marble from Penteli and was completed soon before World War II, when in Greece, as in other parts of Europe most Jews were brutally exterminated by the Nazis. The Synagogue's interior decoration was completed in 1975. Today mostly the recent Synagogue is in use and the older one only operates on big celebrations, attended mainly by the older members of the Jewish community who are sentimentally attached to that building.

CENTRE FOR THE STUDY OF TRADITIONAL POTTERY - GEORGIOS PSAROPOULOS FAMILY FOUNDATION

The Centre for the Study of Traditional

Banded stamnos

Pottery, also known as the Museum of Traditional Pottery, is situated on 4-6 Melidoni Street in Kerameikos. The museum owes much to the inspirational work of Betty Psaropoulou, who over many years acquired a large collection of traditional ceramics and researched the various types, methods of production and materials. She founded the centre in 1987; in her property on Ipitou Street in the Plaka. Teams of younger

researchers continued her work in different locations, gathering additional material and publishing a number of books on the subject.

mounts temporary exhibitions, educational activities, events and research programmes.●▪

View of the area of periodic exhibitions

In 2000 the museum was transferred to its present location, a neoclassical building with a central yard paved with slabs, which was provided by the Greek Ministry of Culture.
Visitors to the museum can explore the different stages of pottery-making in a specially set up atelier, with explanatory audio-visual displays; they also admire some of the collection's 4,500 ceramics. Those items not on display are kept in the centre's original building. The museum

KERAMEIKOS

The archaeological site of the largest and most important necropolis of Athens, Kerameikos, is situated north-west of the ancient Agora on Ermou Street, near the junction with Peiraios Street. The area is bordered by Peiraios, Ermou, Melidoni and Salaminas Streets and by the church of Holy Trinity (Agia Triada). The River Eridanos, which in former times rose from Lycabettus Hill, flows through the site in a south-east–north-west direction. The main entrance to Kerameikos is on Ermou Street while the museum that displays archaeological finds from the excavations is within the site itself. Other discoveries include, to the east, the ruins of Athens' defensive wall with the two main gates of the city – the Sacred Gate and the Dipylon – and public buildings inside the walls, such as the Pompeion and the Fountain-House. To the west, the extended ancient cemetery shows impressive private funerary monuments along with

Workshop of pottery production in ceramic wheel

tombs of men killed at war and buried at public expense. According to the traveller Pausanias (2nd century AD), Kerameikos was named after the potters' patron Keramos, son of Dionysos and Ariadne, who was the eponymous hero of the deme of potters (Kerameis). This indicates the early existence of a potters' settlement along the banks of the Eridanos. The excavation site constitutes only a part of the ancient deme. Finds suggest that Kerameikos extended from the north-west slopes of the Acropolis to the grove of the hero Akademos, a distance of about 1.5 kilometres. The historian Thucydides (5th century BC) mentions that before the construction of the wall in 478 BC the entire Kerameikos area was outside the ancient city walls. Thus, when the new defensive wall was erected by Themistocles, the deme was divided into an urban area and a suburb, the "inner"

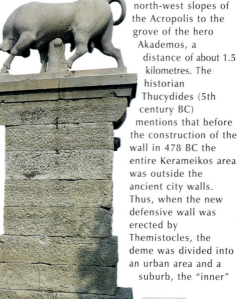

Kerameikos, marble bull

 ### BURIAL CUSTOMS IN CLASSICAL ATHENS

In Classical Athens custom dictated that citizens were to be buried in Attica; refusal to comply with the custom was considered a heinous and punishable action. Cemeteries were usually situated outside the city walls, and the deceased were either buried or incinerated. Funerals consisted of three stages: the "prothesis", or the laying out of the dead for three days at home so that family and friends could mourn; the "ekphora", or the taking of the deceased to the cemetery, escorted by a silent procession, and then the burial; and the "perideipnon", the funerary banquet at the house of the deceased, in which relatives participated. The burial was accompanied by libations (the ritual pouring of liquids on to the ground), as attested by large amounts of pottery found close to tombs. Sometimes more expensive votive offerings were placed in tombs. People of high rank and wealth expressed their status through the erection of funerary monuments, which was regulated by special laws. Following the funeral, first degree relatives had to perform rituals every year, on specific dates, in honour of the deceased.

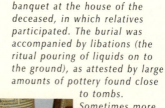

The exposition of the corpse of the dead

and "outer" Kerameikos. Kerameikos functioned as a burial place from the 12th century BC, primarily for the inhabitants of the surrounding settlements. Since the beginning of the 6th century BC, Athenians – and people from other Greek cities – ceased to bury their dead inside the city limits. Hence their choice of Kerameikos as their chief cemetery, which remained in use until 86 BC when Sulla besieged and destroyed the city. Afterwards the area was deserted and gradually was covered by in-filling (c. 10.60m deep) from the Eridanos. The Greek Archaeological Society began excavating the site in 1871, but from 1913 the German Archaeological Institute has been in charge of ongoing work in Kerameikos.

Thucydides. After its destruction by the Persians, Themistocles managed to enclose anew the city with walls within a year (479 BC). The haste was due to the eventuality that the Spartans would issue an order preventing Greek cities from fortifying themselves after the Persian Wars. The walls were reinforced with towers while fifteen gates enabled the access to the other demes of Attica and the Piraeus port. The height of the walls varied from 6 to 10 m. and their width from 2.5 to 4.5 m. A few years later, Cimon completed the walls of the Piraeus and the Long Walls that connected the city to its harbour, thus securing sea access. At that time the Phaleric wall was constructed protecting the entire Phaleron bay. In the 4th century BC, the "Diateichisma" was built which connected the Hill of the Nymphs to that of the Muses. The main gates of the city were the "Thriasian Gates" (later Dipylon) and the Sacred Gate, the ruins of which have been preserved inside the Kerameikos cemetery. Following the defensive wall southwestwards, before the point where the Long Walls and the Diateichisma started, the Piraeus Gate and the Demian Gate were built. Ruins from this part of the walls have been revealed in the corner of Erisichthonos Street and Irakleidon Street in the Thisseio area. Along the Diateichisma –a great part of which is still visible today– the Melite Gate and a second one south of the Pnyx had been constructed. Along the part of the enclosure between the south side of the Long Walls and the Olympieion four

THE THEMISTOCLEAN WALL

The defensive wall around the center of Athens had a total length of ca. 6.5 km or 43 stadia, according to

Part of the Themistoclean Wall in the area of the Kerameikos

gates existed: the West Phaleric (or South Gate), the East Phaleric or Halade Gate, the Itonian Gate and the Diomeian Gate. In the remaining section of the walls there were the Aigeus or Hippades Gate, the Diochares Gate, the Northeast Gate, the Acharnian Gate (visible today in front of the new building of the National Bank of Greece) and the Eriai Gate.

The visible part of the wall that crosses the Kerameikos is one of the longest and best preserved sections. When it was constructed, it divided Kerameikos in a part that was inside the city and a suburb. The Themistoclean wall protected Athens during the 5th century BC and at the first years of the Peloponnesian War. Restoration works at the enclosure took place during the period of Nikias's Peace in 421-416 BC while after the Athenians' defeat at the Peloponnesian War in 404 BC the walls were demolished. More restoration and repair works took place in 394 BC under Conon, in 338 BC after the battle of Chaeronea, during the period 307-304 BC under Demetrius I the Besieger, in 229/8 BC and in the 1st century BC after the destructions caused by the Romans under Sulla. The Themistoclean wall, as an outer enclosure, remained in use as it was formed during the reign of the emperor Valerianus (253-265 AD). A part of it was incorporated in the Late Roman wall built at the end of the 3rd century AD after the invasion of the Herulians. Although the "Royal wall", as the ancient enclosure was called in the Byzantine period, was reinforced during the emperor Justinian's reign (527-566 AD), it gradually lost its defense worth because the inhabitants of the city could no longer maintain and defend it.

THE SACRED GATE

The nearest gate of the walls to the entrance to the archaeological site of Kerameikos is the Sacred Gate. One of the most important in ancient Athens, it was named after the Sacred Way which started at that point and led to Eleusis. This was the

Sacred Gate

Way followed by the procession of the Great Mysteries.
The Gate has an oblong ground-plan. This is due to the courtyard formed by the construction of a second gate ca. 18 m. further inside the defensive enclosure. The Gate had been reinforced by high walls and square corner towers. It had a double doorway opening that led to two divided passages. One of them covered the Eridanos river which flowed through the Gate and the other covered the Sacred Way. In order to protect the Way from a possible flooding of the river, a wall was built along its banks.
The first building phase of the Gate is dated to 478 BC under Themistocles. Significant and quite expensive repairs took place at the structure in 394 BC under Conon, during the reconstruction of the walls. The written sources refer to hasty repairs at the Gate after the battle of Chaeronea in 338 BC. The extensive restorations, however, that came to light are probably related to the building activities of Demetrius I the Besieger in 307-304 BC. Works at the Gate, especially at its towers, were done in the beginning of the 3rd century BC and in the 1st century BC. The defensive enclosure underwent renovations during the period 253-260 AD, under the emperor Valerianus, and in the 6th century AD under Justinian. At that time the riverbed was covered, as this is testified by the marble arch visible today in the site.

THE DIPYLON AND THE FOUNTAIN-HOUSE

Around 40 metres north of the Sacred Gate lies the most important gate of Athens. Its size (almost 1,800 square metres) places it among the largest gates in the ancient world. The earliest building phase is dated to the time of Themistocles, in 478 BC. The gate was constructed at the end of a courtyard (13.5 x 7m) which was open to the west and protected by strong walls and large corner towers. Part of the south-western tower has survived.
Until the end of the 4th century BC the gate was known as the Thriasian Gate because the "Dromos", the wide road that crossed it, led, via the suburb

View of the Dipylon and the Fountain

of Akademos (the Akademeia) to the deme of Thria near Eleusis. Inside the walls the Panathenaic procession, in honour of the patron-goddess Athena, started from this gate and continued through the ancient Agora to the Acropolis. In around 307/306 BC the old gate was destroyed, possibly because of an earthquake and flood. Demetrius I the Besieger built a new gate, the Dipylon: the name probably refers to the two entrances that stand side-by-side facing the city. To the rear of the remains of the central, dividing wall is a circular altar on a square base. According to inscriptions, it was dedicated to Zeus Herkeios, Hermes and the local hero Akamas. Presumably, this gate collapsed after the destruction of Athens by the Herulians in 267 AD.

At the corner formed by the east wall of the Dipylon and its east tower lie the ruins of a fountain, contemporary with the gate, which supplied the city and travellers with water. The cistern of the Fountain-House with a three-column Ionic stoa on its façade formed the letter Γ.

POMPEION

In the area between the south of the Dipylon and the Sacred Gate lie the ruins of buildings that belong to different historical periods.

The earlier ruins are of the Pompeion, a rectangular structure built at the beginning of the 4th century BC, with an interior courtyard with various rooms around it. As the name suggests, the Pompeion was where Athenians prepared for important processions. Heavy equipment, such as carriages and whatever was needed for the Panathenaic festival was kept here. In addition, the building functioned as a gymnasium, and in cases of emergency, as the city's granary.

The entrance to the building was through a propylon at the east corner. The Pompeion court had a peristyle of six columns on the narrow sides and thirteen on the long ones. It is actually said that this place was favoured by the Cynic philosopher Diogenes. The visitor can also see the orthostates on the east and part of the south wall of the

View of the Pompeion

WALKING ON THE HILLS OF THE ACROPOLIS

Lysippus. Outside of the west and north side of the court are the ruins of square dining-rooms, one of which still has the remains of a mosaic floor.
The building was destroyed in 86 BC, during the seizure and sack of Athens by Sulla. Much later, in the time of Antoninus Pius (2nd century AD), a two-storied building was constructed on the same site. This was probably used as a storage area and was razed to the ground during the raid of the Herulians in 267 AD. Between the end of the 4th century and the beginning of the 5th century, two stoas were built on the west side of the ruins, which were connected by a monumental arched gate.

courtyard, made of marble from Mount Hymettus. The Pompeion was decorated with painted portraits of comic writers as well as with a statue of the philosopher Socrates by the famous sculptor

THE KERAMEIKOS CEMETERY

FUNERARY PERIBOLOI AND MONUMENTS

The Kerameikos cemetery extended outside the Dipylon and the Sacred Gate, along and between the Sacred Way and the Dromos. The entire area was full of funerary periboloi (percincts), tumuli (tombs) and monuments. The Sacred Way, the

---

DEMOSION SEMA

In the course of the same winter (431/430 BC) the Athenians, following the custom of their fathers, celebrated at public expense the funeral rites of the first who had fallen in this war. The ceremony is as follows. The bones of the departed lie for two days in a tent erected for that purpose, and each one brings to his own dead any offering he desires. On the day of the funeral coffins of cypress wood are borne on wagons, one for each tribe, and the bones of each are in the coffin of his tribe. One empty bier, covered with a pall, is carried in the procession for the missing whose bodies could not be found for burial. Any one who wishes, whether citizen or stranger, may take part in the funeral procession, and the women who are related to the deceased are present at the burial and make lamentation. The coffins are laid in the public sepulchre, which is situated in the most beautiful suburb of the city; there they always bury those fallen in war, except indeed those who fell at Marathon; for their valour the Athenians judged to be prominent and they buried them on the spot where they fell. But when the remains have been laid away in the earth, a man chosen by the state, who is regarded as best endowed with wisdom and is foremost in public esteem, delivers over them an appropriate eulogy. After this the people depart. In this manner they bury; and throughout the war, whenever occasion arose, they observed this. (Thucydides, History of the Peloponnesian War 2.34, trans. C. Foster Smith)

earlier of the two, with the adjoining streets, was reserved for the graves of Athenian citizens, metics and other Greeks.

Walking along the Sacred Way towards Eleusis, keeping Eridanos on the right, one comes across the first monuments. To the left, at the point where the Street of Tombs starts, in front of the tomb called "South Hill", stand the 5th-century BC stelai of the Ambassadors. One names the consul (proxenos) Pythagoras from Selybria in the Black Sea. The other two are for two ambassadors from Corcyra (Corfu), Thersandros and Simylos.

At the Tritopatreion (the shrine of the ancestors), a small street, called South Way, starts from the Street of Tombs. At the corner are five periboloi forming the corner terrace (4th century BC). Next to it is the peribolos of two sisters, Demetria and Pamphile, including the inscribed relief monument of the late 4th-century BC, on which the two women are depicted inside a temple-shaped structure. The loutrophoros of Hegetor also survives inside the peribolos. Of the same period is the next – and up to this point the last of the South Way – peribolos of Philoxenos from Messene. The small loutrophoros

Funerary stela of Hegeso

The Dexileos Monument. On the base.
'Dexileos, son of Lysanias from Thorikos, born when Teisandros was archon, died when Euboulides was archon in Corinth, one of five horsemen.'

The Monument of Dionysios of Kollytos. On the epistyle (1) and on the base (2).
1. 'There is no need for any strenuous search to find praise for virtuous men, there is always a reason for praising words. As it was your lot Dionysios, when you settled yourself in the chambers of Ananke-Persephone, she who accepts all.'

2.
'The earth covers your body, Dionysios, but the soul of the common treasurer is immortal. You left your friends, your mother, your sisters grieving by your departure, grieving at the immortal thought of your love. Two countries, the natural and that by the law, loved you for your wisdom.'

The Monument of Ampharete. On the epistyle.
'The beloved child of my daughter, here, I hold, which I held on my knees when we, alive, were looking at the sunlight. Now, I hold it dead, me myself dead.'

of Parthenios and the relief of the anonymous seated woman belong to this peribolos.

The Street of Tombs is marked by impressive funerary complexes of the 4th century BC. Among them, the following periboloi stand out: a) that of the Thorikians, with the large equestrian monument of young Dexileos, son of Lysanias from the deme of Thorikos, killed in 394/393 BC in a battle against the Corinthians, b) that of the brothers Agathon and Sosikrates from Herakleia of Pontus, with the tall palmetted stele of Agathon and the grave relief of his wife, c) that of Dionysios from the deme of Kollytos, with the imposing marble bull on a high pedestal, d) that of Lysimachides of Acharnai, with the marble Molossian dog on the façade wall, e) that of Koroibos from the deme of Melite, with the high palmetted stele of Koroibos, the stele of his grandson Kleidemos with a loutrophoros scene and the grave relief of Hegeso, daughter of Proxenos, one of the most beautiful examples of Attic art of the end of the 5th century BC, and f) that of the Potamians, with Bion's column and the stele with the relief decoration of three figures.

In the area between the Street of Tombs and the Sacred Way in the direction of the church of Holy Trinity (Agia Triada), stands, on a pedestal, the 4th-century BC marble loutrophoros of Olympichos. Ascending the Sacred Way towards Athens, one comes across many other graves of the 4th century BC. The peribolos of Aristomache contains a marble lekythos with a relief scene depicting her bidding farewell to her husband Kephisodotos (a dexiosis scene), etc.

In addition, in the same area one finds grave structures from Classical, Hellenistic and Roman times. Near the Tritopatreion, above the Eridanos, is the small bridge leading to the Lateral Way and to the area between the Sacred Way and the Dromos. Numerous funerary periboloi and monuments from the 4th century BC to Roman times can be found here (e.g. the peribolos of Kleomedes).

The city's public cemetery was situated along the Dromos. This was where the Athenians and their allies, killed in war, were buried in honour. Their ashes were placed in a communal tomb, the Demosion Sema.

On the left of the Dromos towards the Akademia, close to the Lateral Way, lies the Tomb of the Lacaedemonians killed in 403 BC, during the battle against the Athenian democrats. This is an episode described in detail by the historian Xenophon, who gives information on their burial outside the Gates of Kerameikos.

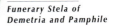

Funerary Stela of Demetria and Pamphile

TUMULI (TOMBS)

In the Sacred Way near the Sacred Gate a good number of tombs can be seen. The first is on the right at the north bank of the Eridanos and contains burials dated between the 7th and 4th centuries BC. Due to the continual succession of burials it is assumed that this is the burial site of an aristocratic Athenian family. Beside it is another tomb, which covered three marble sarcophagi of 450–425 BC. In between these two, others were made in the years following 394 BC. Among these is one with the plain palmetted stele of Myrte and her mother Pythogeneia. Close to the Sacred Gate, one more tomb can be seen, the so-called "South Hill". It was made between 550 and 525 BC and contained two burials. The next tomb lies right behind the sacred peribolos of the Tritopatreion at the point where the Sacred Way meets the Street of Tombs. It is a little earlier in date that the previous one and covered funerary periboloi, tombs and funerary structures of the 8th to 6th centuries BC. During the 6th and 5th century BC, other shaft graves were placed there in circular arrangement. In the area between the Street of Tombs and the Sacred Way lies the tomb with the funerary relief of the young girl Eukoline. It belongs to the period after the battle of Chaeronea (338 BC), at the time

Attic burial amphora

when digging took place to widen the defensive ditches. The earth was used to cover the area between the two streets to a depth of up to 3 metres. In this landfilled layer, new burials took place, among which that of the young Eukoline. Her name is inscribed on the monument, together with those of her parents and possibly her grandmother, while Eukoline herself is depicted with her dog. One more tomb has been located on the left of the Dromos coming out of the Dipylon Gate: it can be dated to the 6th century BC, and covered a shaft grave.

Funerary stela of Dexileos

WALKING ON THE HILLS OF THE ACROPOLIS

Stela of Ampharete

THE KERAMEIKOS MUSEUM

The Kerameikos Museum was built in 1937 to the designs of H. Johannes and with funding from Gustav Oberlaender. In the 1960s it was expanded, thanks to the financial support of the Boeringer brothers. Today, the museum is under reconstruction and is scheduled to reopen to the public shortly. The museum houses findings from excavations in Kerameikos, mostly objects directly connected to the cemetery and the burial customs of ancient Athens, such as funerary urns, grave offerings and as funerary monuments: these latter, like the inscribed reliefs, the stelai and the loutrophoroi, dominate the displays, while exact cast replicas can be seen in situ. Excellent examples of pottery can also be seen at the museum, such as an early Geometric urn amphora (860–840 BC), the Amasis Lekythos, with a scene of the god Dionysus and two satyrs (mid-6th century BC), the hydria by the painter Meidias with a multifigured scene, and others.

Another piece prominently displayed is the mid-6th century BC marble stele with a man carrying a stick and a sword, as well as its contemporary marble sphinx that functioned as the crown of a funerary stele. Particularly remarkable among the funerary marble reliefs are those of Ampharete in a scene with her grandchild (430/420 BC), and of Eukoline (380/370 BC), as well as the stelai of Eupheros (420 BC) and of Dexileos (394/393 BC). The first grave relief of the above was inscribed, and in the epigram of the epistyle, Ampharete mourns her own death and the death of her daughter's child, which occurred at the same time. On the relief of Eukoline, daughter of Antiphanes, the young woman stares sadly at some object she holds in her hand (which has not survived). The relief is accompanied by an epigram, which laments the fate of the unfortunate girl. The relief stele of Eupheros was found on top of the grave with the rich offerings of the young man, as if it too was buried, its colours almost intact. The background of the relief decoration was deep blue, the ribbon at his feet red and the hair bears traces of yellow. It was set up next to the modest pedimental stele of Lissos, the brother of Eupheros. The large equestrian monument of Dexileos,

WALK 1

son of Lysanias from the deme of Thorikos, was found when his father's family grave was discovered. The relief, standing on an inscribed base, depicts the young man as horseman and victor. However, according to the inscription, the young warrior Dexileos was killed at the age of 20 during a battle against the Corinthians in 394/393 BC. His monument looks towards the Dromos and the public cemetery of Athens because Dexileos was buried in the Demosion Sema while the bones of his brother Lysias and his sister Melitte were placed in his cenotaph. Dexileos's name is written on a marble stele near the Demosion Sema with the names of the rest of his dead comrades.
Looking to the future, it is anticipated that there will be a new exhibition of the most significant articles of the museum, to include striking sculptures (kouros, sphinx) found in recent excavations undertaken in Kerameikos by the German Archaeological Institute.

St Athanassios Kourkouris

The small post-Byzantine Church of St (Agios) Athanassios Kourkouris is situated on the pedestrian Eptachalkou Street in Thisseio and is named after its donor, Kourkouris.
As was common practice in those days, the church was built on the site of an ancient monument, in this case dedicated to the Attic hero Chalkodon.
The original building was a vaulted basilica with weight-bearing arches on its longer sides. Today this original structure forms the sanctuary of a church of later build, while on the northern side there used to be a smaller chapel, also vaulted.
On the eastern side of the small church stands the church of St Athanassios Athonitis, built in 1756 with a veneer that imitates regular brickwork. Its belfry and marble propylon are truly impressive.

Cultural Centre "Melina Merkouri"

See Route 10b

Apostolou Pavlou Street

Apostolou Pavlou Street is an extension of Dionissiou Areopagitou Street. It stretches from the foot of Philopappos Hill to Assomaton Square and Thisseio metro station. It was recently turned into a pedestrian zone, as part of the project to unify the archaeological sites of Athens; since then it has become a favourite location for walks.
People walking along the street from the Acropolis can see the

Saint Athanassios Kourkouris

WALK 1

Apostolou Pavlou Street

Pnyx Hill on the left side of the road and further down the Hill of the Muses, at the foot of which is the Thisseio district, with many neoclassical houses. During the summer there is an open-air cinema on Apostolou Pavlou Street. On the right side of the road, inside the archaeological site, one can see part of the ancient city of Athens at the foot of Areios Pagos Hill, while further down from Thisseio Square is Thisseio Park, stretching between Apostolou Pavlou Street and the Agora. ▪▪

THISSEIO SQUARE

Thisseio Square is on the pedestrianised Apostolou Pavlou Street, the extension of Dionissiou Areopagitou Street. On the one side of the square there are several low neoclassical buildings, typical of the area, while the rest of the square is full of open-air cafés, where one can have a cup of coffee on sunny days. Opposite the square is the garden of Thisseio dating back to 1862; it was the first public garden of Athens as the then Royal (the present National) Garden was still closed to the public. ▪▪

ANTIQUITIES OF THE ST MARINA – THISSEIO AREA

Looking up from Apostolou Pavlou Street towards the church of St Marina (Agia Marina) one can see a long and rocky slope. The gray limestone, which prevails on this slope, bears multiple carvings, often quite deep. These carvings formed the foundations of houses dating from the Classical period; the steps, benches and pediments of these houses are visible from the courtyard of

Thisseio Square

the church. At the bottom of the slope the recent work for the unification of the archaeological sites of Athens revealed the existence of a Classical sanctuary,

St Marina

dedicated to Zeus, probably with the attribute "Exopsios". At the junction of Nileos and Irakleidon Streets a small temple was accidentally discovered in 1958, dedicated by Themistocles to Artemis Aristoboule after the Persian Wars. In Roman times a statue of the Athenian general and politician was placed on the same spot. It was also in this area that the executors used to put the clothes and nooses of the hanged men in display. The remains of the temple are not visible nowadays.
To the northwest, not very far from this spot, just at the junction of Irakleidon and Erisichthonos streets one can see the remains of yet another bit of the Themistoclean wall. ••

St Marina In Thisseio

The impressive church of St Marina (Agia Marina) in Thisseio is situated on the Hill of the Nymphs, near the Observatory. The church's foundations were laid in 1922, based on the architectural drawings of Achilleas Georgiadis on the site of an older, 19th-century church. In its present form the church follows an inscribed cruciform plan with a dome in the middle and four smaller domes on the corners. The interior was decorated by mural paintings during the 1930s, mostly by the painters A. Graikos and A. Kandris. This was also when the wooden screen was crafted, designed by the

Chapel of St Marina

architect Georgios Nomikos. The mural paintings form a rare example of religious painting in Greece, influenced by the Jugendstil of Central Europe.
South-east of the church is a small Byzantine church carved into the cliff, next to which the new church was built. This small church was also dedicated to St Marina; it must have been built between the 11th and 12th centuries. Thirteenth-, 17th- and 19th-century wall paintings were found inside; most of them were removed and placed on the northern part of the new church. On the smaller church's side walls there are still several 17th-century mural paintings.
The location of the church had been associated with religious practices related to childbirth and child health. Expectant

mothers and those with sick babies would come here to pray for safe labour or the cure of their children. Pregnant women actually used to crawl over a steep cliff in order to make their wish for a safe labour come true. On 17 July a celebration for St Marina is held in this area. •=

Observatory

The National Observatory of Athens is situated in Thisseio, a little further up from the church of St. Marina on the Hill of the Nymphs. The building, which can be seen from a great distance, houses the first Observatory ever built in Greece and the Balkans.

The neoclassical building was built in 1842 by the Danish architect Theophilus Hansen. Its construction was funded by the baron Georgios Sinas, a leading figure in Austrian business and finance and ambassador of Greece in Vienna. It is a cross-shaped building pointing to the four cardinal points. Until 1884 it operated with funding from the Sinas family and since then it has been funded by the Greek State. Today the operations of the Observatory have been expanded and the foundation consists of four institutes: the Institute of Astronomy and Astrophysics, the Institute of Geodynamics, the Institute for Environmental Research and Sustainable Development, and the Institute for Space Applications and Remote Sensing. •=

The Pnyx

The hill of the Pnyx is situated to the west of the Acropolis, between the hill of the Nymphs and the hill of the Muses. It can be reached by following the paved street off Apostolou Pavlou, past the church of St Demetrius Loubardiaris and then turning right at the first earthen track.

In Classical Athens Pnyx was the gathering place of the Citizens' Assembly ("Ecclesia tou Demou"). The minimum number of participants necessary

The Athens' Observatory

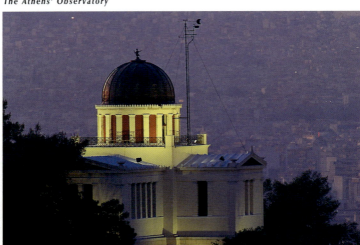

for voting on a certain issue was 6,000; these had to be Athenian citizens and over 20 years of age. From the mid-5th century onwards it was the Citizens' Assembly that took all important decisions regarding the city. From the 4th century members were remunerated for their services, so that farmers and artisans could serve too. After the Macedonian conquest the institution was not abolished, but meetings were limited to 40 a year.
In the Classical period the assembly met in the open air and members sat either on the ground or on portable seats on the slightly hollowed-out slope, which accommodated about 10,500 people. Under the thirty tyrants (404/3 BC) the area probably underwent transformation (the phase known as Pnyx II). What we see today is the third phase, dating from c. 330 BC (Pnyx III). It consists of a semicircular wall, which must have supported an amphitheatrical construction, and a tribune carved into a protruding rock. By 88 BC the Pnyx had already been abandoned and the assembly gathered at the theatre of Dionysos. Around 100 BC, to the east of the tribune an open-air sanctuary was built, dedicated to Zeus Hypsistos. Excavations have revealed several votive objects of clay, such as tablets on which depictions of human limbs were carved; these tablets were situated in carved cavities on the rock. Just above the tribune is a large rectangular carving on the ground, which is thought to mark the area where the altar of Zeus Agoraeos stood before it was transported to the Agora. Just opposite the hollowed-out space are the marks of two oblong foundations, probably destined for porticoes.

The Pnyx

AREIOS PAGOS

The hill of Ares (Roman Mars) or of Arae (or Erinyes), better known as Areios Pagos, is situated to the north-

The Areios Pagos

west of the Acropolis. It is a limestone hill 115m high, with steep sides and a rocky summit accessible only by somewhat slippery steps cut out of the rock. In the Archaic era, a formative period for Athenian civic institutions, Areios Pagos was chosen as a meeting point of the aristocratic council. After the reforms of Kleisthenes, this political body, which by then had been named after its venue, upheld a purely judicial role and judged only murder cases. On the feet of the hill on its northern side there is a small cave which was dedicated to the Erinyes, the goddesses who tormented the murderers. Hence the etymological explanation, which connects the place with Arae, or curses. On the top of the hill is a stone block, which has been identified either as the altar of Areia Athena or as one of the two tribunes of the open-air court, the Hybris,

ST DIONYSIUS AREOPAGITE

Excavation on a plateau on the north-eastern side of Areios Pagos uncovered the remains of a post-Byzantine three-aisled basilica. This was identified as the documented church of St Dionysius Areopagite: Saint Dionysius was a disciple of Saint Paul, patron saint and first bishop of Athens. It is believed that it was on the site of the church that Saint Paul made his speech about the "unknown God" to the Athenians gathered in Areios Pagos. In this area the remains of a 6th-7th century church, active until the 11th century, have also been discovered. The post-Byzantine church of St Dionysius was built in the mid-16th century and was the cathedral until the first half of the 17th century, when it was destroyed, probably by an earthquake; the bishop's mansion used to be close by, to the west. The architectural form of the church is particularly interesting: it is a three-aisled barrel-vaulted basilica, with the central aisle raised higher than the others, and internally there are blind arches, several of which have small windows. This architectural form became the prototype for many churches in Athens during the Ottoman rule, particularly in the 17th century, due to the cathedral status of the church. Examples include the church of Pantanassa in Monastiraki, St Anargyroi (the Metochion of the Holy Sepulcre) and Panagia Romvi. It is a mixed architectural type based on a basilican plan, with a number of original solutions for the roofing of the rectangular space with a barrel-vault and conches at the ends. This new architectural form was based on St Sophia in Constantinople, and since the 15th century it had been widely used for Ottoman buildings, such as the Hadji Ali Hamam in Athens, which probably inspired the city's barrel-vaulted churches.

where the accused stood, or the Anaedia, from which the accuser spoke.
Areios Pagos is also known as the site where St Paul taught when he visited Athens in AD 54. His preaching brought at least one proselyte to the new faith, St Dionysius Areopagite. Today, on the northern side of Areios Pagos one can see a small, almost ruined church, dedicated to this Athenian saint.

ST DEMETRIUS LOUBARDIARIS

At the foot of the wooded hill of the Nymphs, near the hill of Pnyka and the monument of Filopappou, opposite the Acropolis, there is a little chapel dedicated to Agios (Saint) Dimitrios, known as

St Demetrius Loubardiaris

'Loubardiaris'. It is a one-aisled arched basilica dating from the Ottoman period. In the interior, the surfaces of the walls have blind arches on the long sides. This solution saves both material and room without consequences for the building's statical stability, while the chapel externally acquires a vivid appearance and motion. The outside walls are decorated with geometrical shapes from clay and marble. The decoration is part of the restoration works of 1955, carried out by the known architect Dimitrios Pikionis. Restoration works revealed wall paintings dating from 1735.

THE HILL OF THE MUSES – THE PHILOPAPPOS MONUMENT

If you follow the paved street (designed by Dinitrios Pikionis) that goes past St Demetrius Loubardiaris, you come to the top of the Hill of the Muses,

THE NICKNAME «LOUBARDIARIS»

According to travellers' accounts, around the mid-17th century, on the name day of Agios Dimitrios (26 October) a cannon ('loumbarda') blew up resulting in the explosion of the powder stored in the Propylaia. The Propylaia was inevitably destroyed. The little chapel, which celebrated its name day, has been called 'Loubardiaris' ever since.
Some other travellers' accounts provide a more folklore version: Jusuf Aga, an Ottoman officer, wanted to pull Agios Dimitrios down. He used three cannons, which he would fire the following day. But lightning struck the powder magazine that night, thus annihilating the officer, his cannons and his family! Thanks to this miracle Agios Dimitrios has been attributed the nickname 'Loubardiaris' (gunner) ever since.

WALK 1

84

south-west of the Acropolis. Athenians chose this summit in AD 114-116 for the site of a funerary monument to Gaius Julius Antiochus Philopappos, grandson of the last king of the Syrian kingdom of Commagene, and prominent citizen and benefactor of Athens, whom they wanted to honour. The monument is 9.80 metres high and 9.30 metres long and is made of Pentelic marble. The sculptural decoration on the façade, facing the Acropolis, depicts Philopappos on a quadriga (tehtrippon) heading for Rome; this alludes to the consulship accorded to Philo-pappos in AD 109. On the upper part, within niches, are statues of Philopappos (centre), flanked by Antiochus and Seleucus Nicator. Inscriptions on the front of the monument offer information about the deceased and his career. The monument contained the sarcophagus of Philopappos.

It was from this hill that the soldiers of Fr. Morosini bombarded the Acropolis in September 1687 in order to destroy the Ottomans, who used the site as a fortress. The Philopappos Hill is today one of the favourite walking areas in Athens; it is one of the few green spaces of the capital and it offers an excellent view of the Acropolis and the sea. On "Kathari Deftera" ("Clean Monday", the first day of the Lent), Athenians celebrate here, as on the nearby Hill of the Nymphs, in the open air with music, eating, drinking and flying kites.

DIMITRIOS PIKIONIS

Dimitrios Pikionis, the pioneering architect, painter, writer and thinker, was internationally established with his masterpiece: the arrangements in the area around the Acropolis and the Philopappos hill (1951-1957). Pikionis combined the principles of modern architecture with the morphology of folk tradition as well as the archaeological findings and ancient materials with the features of the scenery and the geophysical environment, thus realising in the best way his aesthetic theories about modern Greek architecture. In his vision modern Greek architecture escaped the imitation of western standards and elevated Greek historical continuity from Antiquity to date.

WALK 1

Sp. Vassileiou: "The microcosm of Webster Street"

ATELIE OF SPIROS VASSILEIOU

The great artist Spiros Vassileiou lived and worked in a house on Webster Street, near the Acropolis. His family decided to open the house to the public in 2004, converting it into a museum, thus creating the "Atelier of Spiros Vassileiou". The purpose of the museum is to familiarize visitors with the painter's life and work. The museum houses Vassileiou's archive; several paintings of the artist are on display. Spiros Vassileiou was born in Galaxidi in 1902 and died in Athens in 1985. He studied art at the School of Fine Arts in Athens and in other European cities, settling in Athens in 1932. His early work includes theatrical sets and the pictorial decoration of St Dionysius Areopagite in Kolonaki. His themes are inspired by everyday life in Greece. He was especially inspired by the small neighbourhoods of Athens and the life of their simple people, which he often depicted in a surreal manner. He used the Acropolis as a background in his paintings – he saw it every day from his house on Webster Street – and composed urban landscapes with a unique atmosphere, attention to detail and colourful personalities. In his work one can discern a subtle irony towards Athens' modernisation and the loss of the city's old character together with its neoclassical and traditional houses – in effect, the passing of an entire era.

Sp. Vassileiou: "Incident in Dionissiou Areopagitou Street"

WALK 2

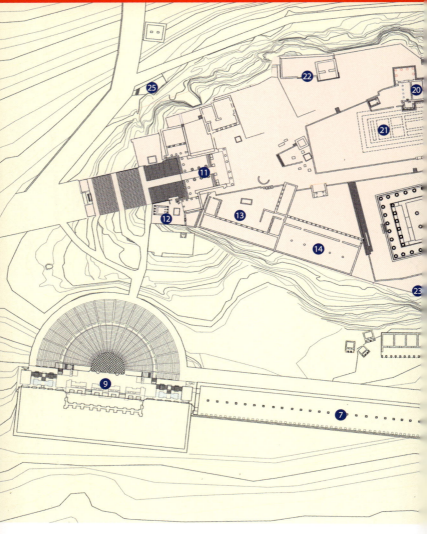

1. Dionissiou Areopagitou Street
2. The Sanctuary of Dionysos
3. The Theatre of Dionysos
4. The Choregic Monument of Thrasy
5. The Odeon of Pericles
6. The Asclepieion
7. The Stoa of Eumenes
8. The Choregic Monument of Nikias
9. The Odeon of Herodes Atticus
10. The Acropolis

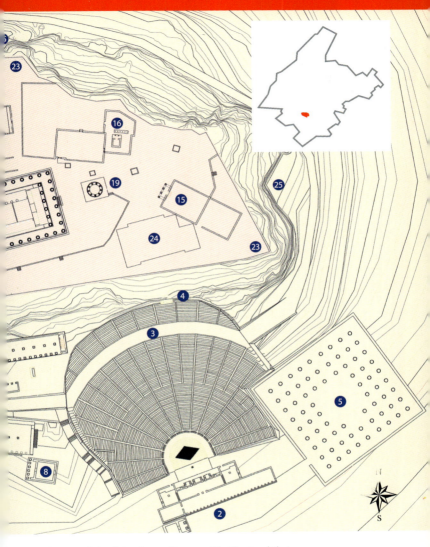

11 The Propylaia of the Acropolis
12 The Temple of Athena Nike
13 The Sanctuary of Artemis Brauronia
14 The Chalkotheke
15 The Sanctuary of Pandion
16 The Sanctuary of Zeus Polieus
17 The Parthenon
18 The Altar of Athena Polias
19 The Temple of Rome and Augustus
20 The Erechtheion
21 The Ancient Temple of Athena
22 The Arrhephorion
23 The Acropolis Walls
24 The Acropolis Museum
25 Monuments on the North Slope of the Acropolis

2 ADMIRING THE PARTHENON

As one walks along Dionissiou Aeropagitou Street one admires the synthesis of eras, a feature of a city lived in throughout the centuries. Modern blocks of flats, neoclassical residencies and the landmark of Athens, the hill of the Acropolis, with the Parthenon and the Odeon of Herodes Atticus. Classical finesse, Roman magnificence, post-independence and modern periods are harmoniously combined in an entity which proves that Athens was and is a city very much alive.

DIONISSIOU AREOPAGITOU STREET

Walking along Dionissiou Areopagitou Street is a good way to experience a few of the many faces of Athens. The street begins from Amalias Avenue, opposite Hadrian's Gate, and continues all the way to the foot of Philopappos Hill, with a densely populated area on one side and the Acropolis on the other. For years vehicles were allowed to pass through the street, but recently it was pedestrianised, making it a street favoured by Athenians and tourists alike. On summer evenings the otherwise quiet street comes alive with the various shows and concerts that take place in the Herodeion Theatre (Odeon of Herodes Atticus) during the Athens Festival. Furthermore, open-air sculpture exhibitions are often organized here. Walking along Dionissiou Areopagitou Street one becomes aware of the different eras, all present at once in a city that has been inhabited for centuries: one can see modern apartment blocks, neoclassical houses and the city's landmark, the cliff of the Acropolis with the Parthenon at the top and the Herodeion Theatre at the foot. Classical elegance, Roman grandeur, the post-revolutionary era and the modern years all work in harmony to prove that Athens was, and still is, a living city.

THE SOUTHERN SLOPE OF THE ACROPOLIS

Scattered in the area of the southern slope of the Acropolis are archaeological monuments

---

THE HOUSE OF PROKLOS

On Dionissiou Areopagitou Street, between the Odeon of Herodes Atticus and the sanctuary of Asclepios, one can see on the street's pavement the outline of a big house, dominated by a room with an apse and conches at the perimeter. According to the specialists, this was the house of the philosopher Proklos. Proklos was born in Constantinople in AD 412 and arrived in Athens in around 429. Being a worshipper of Athena, he chose to stay on the southern feet of the Acropolis, near the Asclepieion. In around 450 he took over Plato's Academy, which he ran until his death in 485.

Altar of Dionysos

of great importance for the history of ancient Athens. In Antiquity the area was accessible from the Tripods' street, and it was connected to the main site of the Acropolis through the Peripatos, exactly as it does today. Nowadays it consists a unified archaeological site, the entrance to which is situated on the east side of Dionissiou Areopagitou Street. ••

SANCTUARY OF DIONYSOS

The first monument that the visitor meets is the sanctuary of Dionysos, which occupies the eastern part of the southern slope. Its precinct is not surviving entirely. Its walls are built of conglomerate stone from the shores of Piraeus, whereas its foundations are built of large conglomerate rocks. The propylon of the entrance, which is not extant today, was situated at the eastern part of the precinct, where the Tripods' street ended. It is possible that a secondary entrance existed on the western side of the precinct. Scattered within the precinct area are situated the bases of altars and votive objects, whereas cylindrical altars of the Hellenistic and Roman periods, decorated with garlands and theatrical masks of Satyrs are preserved.

A Doric portico measuring 63 by 9.5 meters marks the northern part of the precinct. It consists of a Doric colonnade on the side towards the sanctuary, and its northern wall supported the scene of the theatre of Dionysos. It dates in the 4th century B.C. In front of the western end of the portico is preserved the foundation of the Archaic temple, where the wooden idol ("xoanon") of Dionysos was kept; this idol had been transported from the Boeotian city of Eleutherae at the time of Peisistratos (546-528 B.C.). The temple was small (13.5 by 8 meters) distyle in antis, made of local poros stone of the Acropolis. Two statues were discovered recently, torsos of a satyr and a warrior, which are considered to be part of the sculpted decoration of the temple, dating from the beginning of the 5th century B.C. The new temple, the foundations of which are visible just a few meters to the south, did not replace the Archaic one. The two temples co-existed at least until the 2nd century when the traveller Pausanias visited them. This temple was larger (22 by 10.5 meters), Doric in style, with a pronaos, and it contained the golden and ivory statue of Dionysos, possibly made by Alcamenes, the renowned student of Pheidias. Scholars are not unanimous on its dating: it is either dated at the end of the 5th century or in the middle of the 4th century. ••

New temple of Dionysos

The Theatre Of Dionysos

To the north of the sanctuary and higher by three meters, is situated the theatre of Dionysos, the most ancient and important theatre of the Greek world, where the masterpieces of Aeschylus, Sophocles, Euripides and Aristophanes were performed. Today its state of preservation is not that good.

From the early, mid-5th century phase of the theatre remains only a part of the wall which supported the oval orchestra and some stone benches from the lower row of the cavea, which was Π-shaped. The rest of the rows of the benches were wooden at that time. The theatre acquired its present form at about 340-330 B.C., during the governing period of the Athenian orator Lykourgos. During the same period copper statues of the tragic poets were erected. The cavea was decorated with marble benches and a sewage drain was constructed all around the henceforth circular orchestra and the scene and off stage were created. The cavea is divided in three parts by two diazomas. The second diazoma coincided with the Peripatos, the peripheral road of the Acropolis. The first part of the cavea, the only one preserved in a good

Marble throne from the theater of Dionysos

condition, had 32 rows of seats, divided radially by steps in 13 wedges. The second part of the cavea had also 32 rows of seats, but divided in 26 wedges. The theatre had a capacity of about 17,000 spectators. From the 2nd century B.C. onwards, the first row of seats was gradually replaced by tall marble thrones for the Athenian priests. These thrones are preserved in excellent condition and on them survive inscriptions. The central throne was the one reserved for the priest of Dionysos.

The scene building was wooden in the Classical period. In the Hellenistic period however it acquired a second floor. The scene building and the off stage were made of marble. During the 1st century the scene building was expanded thus reducing the space of the orchestra which ceased to be circular and became petal-shaped; the scene building consisted now of three floors and was decorated with sculpted reliefs. In this period dates an extant marble architrave with a votive inscription dedicated to Dionysos and the emperor Nero. The orchestra, which consisted until then of just padded earth, became paved. In the 3rd century it was covered

Theater of Dionysos

by the marble floor revetment with the rhomboid decoration, which is still extant today. During the same period, when Phaedros was archon of the city, a tribune was made, the so called "bema of Phaedros", and was decorated with relief depictions inspired by the Dionysiac myth and with colossal figures of kneeling Satyrs. In the

THE BIRTH OF THEATRE

Drama was born from Dionysiac rituals, and specifically from the dithyramb, a song accompanied by a flute and dancing or mime. Drama maintained the religious character of the dithyramb, since it was always presented during celebrations in honour of Dionysos. In satyrical drama, after all, the dancers represented satyrs, the companions of the god.

According to tradition, around the mid-6th century BC, under the tyranny of Peisistratos in Athens, the poet Thespis, from the Deme of Icarios (the modern suburb "Dionisos") added a new feature to the traditional dithyramb sung by the chorus: he introduced verses in a different rhythm and without melody, with which the actor answered the words of the chorus. Thus, Thespis is considered to be the father of tragedy and of theatre in general. At the same time Peisistratos inaugurated the Great Dionysia (Dionysia in the City), a major religious celebration in honour of Dionysus, which took place at the end of March (in the Attic month Elaphebolion) and lasted initially five and later six days. Three (later four) of these days were dedicated to theatrical performance, which took place in the theatre of Dionysos on the southern slope of the Acropolis.

Theatrical mask

Performances were also given during the other major Dionysiac celebration, the Lenaia. Three poets participated in the final conquest, each with three tragedies and a satyrical drama. The appearance and development of dramatic poetry is a product of democratic Athens per se. Tragic themes were drawn from mythology, and yet in elaborating them the poet expressed his contemporary Athenians' problems and anxieties, which reflected the organization of the city's social and political life. Comedy, on the other hand, took its inspiration from everyday life and social reality: human superstition and defects, up-to-date political or social events formed the "mythical" core of comedy. Drama theatre reached its peak in the 5th century BC, with the three tragic poets Aeschylus, Sophocles, Euripides and the comedian Aristophanes. At the end of the 4th century BC Menander (342–291 BC) significantly modified comedy and introduced "new comedy", with themes taken from contemporary everyday life.

Statue of Sophocles

3rd or 4th century a row of marble tiles formed a balustrade between the orchestra and the cavea, thus transforming the orchestra into an arena for gladiatorial games. The first excavations started under the direction of the Archaeological Society in 1841. They were continued with particular vehemence from 1882 until 1895 by the German Archaeological Institute, whereas some archaeological research did take place during the 1960s and 1980s by the Greek Archaeological Service. For the immediate future a wide restoration programme has been planned, which is going to change completely the present appearance of the site.

Restoration of the Odeon of Pericles

THE CHOREGIC MONUMENT OF THRASYLLOS

Above the cavea of the theatre, attached to the mouth of a cave, was erected in 319 B.C. the choregic monument of Thrasyllos. The façade of the monument had three pillars supporting an architrave, where the dedicatory inscription, the frieze and the cornice stood. On a base of three grades on the top of the monument was erected a tripod. In 295 B.C. Thrasycles, son of Thrasyllos, erected two more tripods. During the Roman period the tripods were replaced by statues. The central one, depicting Dionysos on a throne, was taken away by lord Elgin and is situated today in the British Museum. After the end of Antiquity the monument was transformed into a church dedicated to Panagia Spiliotissa ("Virgin Mary of the Cave"). It was maintained in perfect condition until 1827, when it was ruined during the siege of the Acropolis. Above the monument of Thrasyllos, on the rock, are situated two columns with Corinthian capitals, which supported Roman tripods.

The Monument of Thrasyllos

THE ODEON OF PERICLES

The Odeon was situated to the east of the cavea of the theatre. Today its condition is deplorable and only few ruins are visible in the archaeological site. Its construction was completed in 443 B.C. under the supervision of Pericles. Pausanias relates that its shape was an imitation of the tent of the Persian king Xerxes. The building was rectangular, measuring 62.40 by 68.60 meters, with benches in the interior and with a wooden roof supported by nine rows of columns. It hosted concerts, musical contests, but it was also used as a court of justice. It was completely ruined in 86 B.C. by Sulla and was rebuilt in 61 B.C., probably on the same pattern, but completely out of marble, funded by the Cappadocian King Ariobarzanes II. It was probably ruined in 267, during the Herulian invasion, whereas in the medieval period the Byzantine castle, Rizokastron, passed from that spot. ●■

THE ASCLEPIEION

The path which passes over the cavea of the theatre to the west leads to the sanctuary of Asclepios, which is situated between the Peripatos and the hill of the Acropolis. The worship of Asclepios was introduced into Athens in 419 B.C. by some Telemachos from Epidaurus. The choice of the site was to some extent due to the spring which existed in a cavity of the nearby rock, as running water was necessary for the performance of the rituals. From the Peripatos one approached the sanctuary through a propylon built in the 1st century B.C., situated slightly to the left of nowadays entrance. The sanctuary took its monumental form mainly in the 4th century B.C. Only the foundation survives today from the little Doric prostyle tetrastyle temple, once measuring 10.40 by 6 meters. The site is nowadays used for the deposition of architectural parts and its restoration is imminent.

To the east of the Asclepieion there was an altar measuring 6 by 3.50 meters, whereas to the north, just on the bottom of the rock, there was a two-storey Doric portico measuring 49.75 by 9.75, consisting of seventeen columns, with a second, Ionic colonnade in the interior. This was the space of the "encoemeterion", where the sick people slept waiting for the god to reveal to them in their dreams their cure, just as Aristophanes describes in his comedy "Ploutos" (Wealth). To the western side of the portico there was a square pit dedicated to the worship of chthonic deities. To the west there was one more portico, dating from the end of the 5th century. It had an Ionic colonnade with 12 columns on the façade and four square rooms at the back, measuring 6 by 6 and provided with couches for the visitors. This building served either as an additional "encoemeterion" or as a guest-room, or as a tabernacle, i.e. restaurant for the pious visitors. During the Roman period a second portico was added to the south of the sanctuary, with eight columns at the front. The sanctuary was destroyed in AD 267, but it was rebuilt in the 4th century, obviously by the emperor Julian. In the 6th century it was transformed into a three-naved Basilica dedicated to St (Agioi) Anargyroi. Nowadays this church is ruined to a great extent. In the cave of the spring, which was transformed into a baptistery, is situated today the chapel of Zoodochos Pege ("Holy Fountain of Life"). To the west of the Asclepieion there is one more spring, which in the Archaic period had been transformed into a fountain of a rectangular shape with a well almost 3 meters deep, dedicated to Pan and the Nymphs.

Asclepios

Sanctuary of Asclepios

Two Medieval cisterns are also visible as well as the substructures of two temples, dedicated to Isis and Themis, dating from the time of Hadrian.

THE STOA OF EUMENES

Between the theatre of Dionysos and the Herodeion was built the portico donated to Athens by the Pergamene king Eumenes II (197-159 B.C.). This portico constitutes one of the masterpieces of Pergamene architecture and is in many ways similar to the Stoa of Attalos in the Agora, to the extent that it is now considered designed by the same architect. It served for protecting the visitors of the theatre from the sun. Its length was 163 meters and width 17.65 meters. On the ground floor façade there were 64 Doric columns and in the center there was another Ionic colonnade of 32 columns. On the upper storey there was a colonnade of Ionic double columns on the façade and an interior colonnade with columns bearing Pergamene capitals. Today the ground level of the portico has been restored and

Part of the Stoa of Eumenes

some of the double columns and the Pergamene capitals of the upper storey are still extant.
At the two ends of the building there were external staircases leading to the upper storey, whereas later on there was added another staircase at the western part, leading to the Odeon of Herodes Atticus. From the east side of the portico access to the theatre was possible through the Peripatos from the upper storey and through the parodos of the theatre from the ground floor. At the back of the portico one can still see the buttresses connected to each other with semicircular arches and supporting the dam of the Peripatos. Only on this part there was used the local limestone and

grey Hymettus marble. The cornice and the columns of the building were made of Pergamene marble. Over the bows of the portico was built the Ottoman fortification, called Serpentze, which was demolished by the Archaeological Service in 1877.

THE CHOREGIC MONUMENT OF NIKIAS

Close to the southeastern end of the portico of Eumenes there are the foundations of one of the largest choregic monuments of Athens, in the shape of a hexastyle prostyle Doric temple, built in 320/319 B.C. by Nikias. During the 3rd century the upper structure of the monument was incorporated almost intact to the Beulé gate of the Acropolis.

The Beulé Gate

WALK 2

ODEON OF HERODES ATTICUS

Walking along the Dionissiou Aeropagitou pedestrian zone towards the Acropolis, after having passed the theatre of Dionysus and the Stoa of Eumenes, one reaches the Odeon of Herodes Atticus on the southern slope of the Acropolis. Today the Odeon, known mostly as Herodeion, functions as an open-air theatre, where during the summer Athens Festival artistic events such as concerts of classical and contemporary music, dance and theatre performances and operas take place.

The Athenian tycoon Herodes Atticus offered the Odeon to the city of Athens after the death of his wife Regilla in AD 160. It was dedicated to her memory and it hosted musical and mimic contests.

The construction of the Odeon started shortly before AD 160 and was completed before 173, when Pausanias visited it on his travels. At the time of its construction, the older Odeon of Agrippa in the Ancient Agora had ceased to function as a stage for musical performances and hosted only lectures by philosophers and sophists. The Herodeion functioned as an odeon for about a century, until it was burned down, probably during the Herulian invasion of AD 267, along with most of the monuments on the southern slope of the Acropolis. It was never used as an odeon after.

During the Ottoman period the building was incorporated into the defensive wall, the Serpentze, that surrounded the slopes of the hill and served as a refuge for the city's inhabitants during hostile attacks. The interior of the Odeon was transformed into a workshop for silk manufacture. Occasional burials, the existence of a church and the use of building material from the Odeon for other uses led travellers and visitors between the 15th and 17th centuries to call it Aristotle's School, the Academy of Aristotle and Miltiades and even to identify it erroneously with the theatre of Dionysos.

In 1764 the British doctor Richard Chandler identified the Odeon as that built by Herodes Atticus, its interior covered with 12 metres of earth. The excavations carried out by the Ephorate of Antiquities between 1848 and 1858 restored it to its original form, and after restoration and conservation it resumed its former use.

Architecturally the Herodeion is like an ancient theatre and consists of three parts: the three-storied scene 35.5 meters long and 28 meters high, the semicircular orchestra (9.5 metres) and the semicircular cavea (38 meters), on which the stone seats are supported on the natural slope of the rock. The scene façade consists of three arched gates flanked by pairs of niches. On the first floor there are

HERODES ATTICUS

Herodes Atticus (AD 101/3–AD 177) was a politician, philosopher, sophist and one of the biggest benefactors of Athens. His projects include the Odeon of Athens, the conservation of the Stadiums at Athens and Olympia, the construction of the fountain of Regilla at Olympia and the restoration of the Odeon in Corinth.

seven larger arched openings, the middle of which protrudes because of its size. The two upper floors were probably originally the same. In the niches were statues of the Roman Emperor, Herodes Atticus and his family, as well as other sculptures. The proscenium consisted of podiums with columns and antes supporting architraves. After the proscenium follows the raised, oblong logeion, on which the actors and musicians played. Behind the stage was an oblong space, whose mosaic floor was decorated with geometrical and floral decoration; this is now covered with a modern marble pavement, to the south of the Odeon. Mosaics decorated also the spaces in front of the staircases that led to the middle passageway of the cavea and are situated next to the dressing rooms, i.e. the adjacent rooms to the logeion, which one entered through the gates at the narrow sides of the proscenium. Five wedges with 20 rows of seats each were formed at the lower part of the cavea, by means of the middle passageway. The first row of seats of the lower zone was called "Proedria" (presidency) and was designated for the supreme political and religious authorities of the city. A portico on the upper path crowned the Odeon. An important feature of the Herodeion was that it was roofed with cedar wood. Although scholars are not sure whether the roof covered the entire building or only the logeion, or whether it was a combination of a wooden roof and a velarium (tent), the use of cedar wood was an impressive element for visitors in ancient times. According to Philostratus, cedar wood was so precious that it was used for making statues. He also mentions that the Herodeion stood out not only for its roof, but also for its sculpted decoration.

The walls of the Herodeion must have been equally impressive. The interior walls are built in the opus cementitium technique and the exterior ones with poros stone blocks, their internal façades covered with marble tiles.

The unique character of the Herodeion lies, according to ancient writers, in the following architectural features: 1) Pausanias mentions that the Herodeion surpasses all other odea in Athens both in magnitude and in appearance. Its dimensions were indeed larger than those of other similar odea of that time in Greece. 2) The Herodeion combines features of Greek and Roman architectural models. The cavea, instead of having an artificially built foundation, on the Roman model, lies on natural rock – the Greek model.

The immediate topographical relationship between the Herodeion and the theatre of Dionysos and the Stoa of Eumenes, with which it was organically linked on the eastern side (from the upper storey of the Stoa the middle passageway of the Odeon was accessible), reveal in an obvious manner that Herodes aspiration was to present himself as the perpetuator of the cultural tradition of Greek paideia and at the same time to be included among the benefactors of Hellenistic times.

ADMIRING THE PARTHENON

THE ACROPOLIS

The sacred hill of the Acropolis forms one of the most recognizable archaeological sites worldwide, and probably the most important landmark of ancient Greek civilization. It also constitutes the symbol of the city of Athens.

The hill reaches 156 meters of height (above sea level) whereas in relation to the surrounding area it is 70 meters high. Its maximum length is 270 meters and its maximum width 156 meters. Its flat top has a total surface of 30,000 square meters and a polygonal form, due to human interventions, particularly during the Archaic and Classical periods (6th-5th centuries B.C.), when several supporting walls were built and the northern and eastern slopes –higher and more abrupt initially - were leveled. The earliest traces of human presence on the hill of the Acropolis date from the Neolithic period. Important development took place in the Mycenaean period, particularly in the 13th and 12th centuries B.C. The hill of the Acropolis was the centre of administrative authority of the Mycenaean kings and the most important religious centre of the city. At the same period, or a little later, the rock was fortified with a cyclopean wall, the so-called Pelargikon, which was attributed to the Pelasgoi, the pre-Hellenic inhabitants of Attica, according to the mythological tradition. In historical times, the Acropolis was for the Athenians the holy site of the goddess Athena, who protected the city. This belief is reflected particularly in the myths concerning the foundation of the city of Athens, when Athena won her contest against Poseidon and gave the city her name.

The peak of the early sanctuary, which was situated at the spot where today stands the Erechtheion, is attested by hundreds of votive objects dedicated by pious Athenian men and women: bronze tripods and animal figurines initially, marble statues and reliefs later, bronze statues and figurines of athletes who won at the Panathenaic Games, precious vessels and

Euripides, "Medea", summer 2002

objects or pottery with impressive depictions. The most impressive of these votive objects, as the Korai, statues of girls originating from aristocratic families of Athens and possibly dedicated themselves to the goddess, and the wonderful horsemen, are on display today in the Museum of the Acropolis, together with the statues of the temples and the other buildings of the Archaic period. The sacred hill of the Acropolis in the Archaic period was a magnificent place where Athens projected itself, creating a "city of images" as has been justly said.

The conquest and destruction of the Acropolis by the Persians in 480 B.C. left behind a jumble of ruins and destroyed works of art, which the Athenians respectfully buried, saving them thus for the archaeologists. The Acropolis of the Classical period was built from fresh and was designed as a complex of religious buildings through the political will of Pericles and the inspiration of Pheidias. Despite its magnificence, the building project of Pericles was not the main focal point of the 5th century Acropolis. The eye of the Athenians was beheld by the colossal statue of Athena Promachos, a work by Pheidias, which stood in the space between the Propylaia and the Parthenon. It is said that the tip of the helmet and that of her spear were visible from cape Sounion. Next to this statue stood also a chariot with four horses (quadriga), which commemorated the victory of the Athenians against the Chalcideans. The three most important points of the hill were the holy olive tree of Athena, the fountain Erechtheis, from which salted water sprang,

A view of the sacred rock of the Acropolis

and the traces of Poseidon's trident on the rock.

The most important cult object was not the golden and ivory statue of Athena in the Parthenon, as someone might have thought, but the ancient coarse wooden statue ("xoanon") of the goddess, which was kept in the Erechtheion. During the second half of the 5th century B.C. on the Acropolis was kept the treasury of the Athenian League, a large part of which was used for the building programme of the city. The "legend" of the Acropolis, particularly of the Propylaia –which were considered a more innovative and

ADMIRING THE PARTHENON

important building than Parthenon- was created by the Athenians themselves in the 4th century B.C., in commemoration of the glory of Athens during the Persian Wars, and was maintained throughout Antiquity. Indeed, the Roman generals, who fought the Athenians in several battles during the 1st century B.C., out of respect for the city's past and the grandiose monuments of the Acropolis, withheld their destructive frenzy and did not harm the city to the extent that they did with other insubordinate cities. During the Roman period, a few buildings were added to the 5th century complex and those were placed always in less prominent positions, so that they left the view unimpeded for the masterpieces of the Periclean period, which attracted visitors from all places of the Greek world.

The picture changed with the coming of the first Christian emperors, the abolition of the old cult and the transformation of the temples into Christian churches, a practice which in fact contributed to the survival and good maintenance of some among them. At the time of the Frankish rule the Acropolis was the administrative center of the Dukes of Athens, whereas around the end of the 14th century the Catalans were besieged in its walls for two years. During the Ottoman period it was

A votive sculpture in the form of an owl

the strongest fortress of the city, which had a destructive effect during the siege of the city by the Venetian Morosini (1687). The last dramatic episodes took place at the beginning of the 19th century: Lord Elgin plundered the marbles, the Greeks used the Acropolis as a fort and the Turks recovered it in 1826-1827.

THE FIGURES OF ATHENA

During the 6th and the beginning of the 5th century BC the figure of Athena Hygieia was important, whereas after the introduction of the cult of Asclepios, in the 420s BC, this type began to wane. Simultaneously, the cult of Athena Ergane became particularly widespread, as she was offering protection to the artisans. The most important iconographic types of the goddess was Athena Pallas (or the Palladion), a depiction of the goddess standing and holding in one hand the lance and the other the aegis, following the model of the ancient wooden statue kept in the Erechtheion, the Athena Promachos, in the same posture as the Palladion, but fiercer, with one protruding leg, and finally Athena Parthenos with the elaborate helmet, in the form which was established by the golden and ivory statue of Pheidias. Unique is the iconographic type of Athena Lemnia by Pheidias, which was dedicated by the Athenians who colonized the island of Lemnos at about 450 BC.

Bronze statuette of Athena Promachos

WALK 2

THE MONUMENT OF AGRIPPA

In front of the northern aisle of the Propylaia stands a tall rectangular podium, known as the monument of Agrippa. Traces on its top attest that a copper quadriga stood on it. Its total height is over 13 meters and it is made of Pentelic and Hymettus' marble. An inscription on its western side mentions that it was dedicated by the people of Athens to Marcus Agrippa (63-12 B.C.), son in law of the Roman emperor Augustus and important benefactor of Athens. However, its similarities from the point of view of typology and construction with other podiums of the Hellenistic period led scholars to attribute its original fabrication to Eumenes II, king of Pergamon (197-158 B.C.), whereas it is possible that for a short while it bore the statues of Marc Anthony and Cleopatra.

Following the Greek War of Independence and the foundation of the Greek state, an extensive archaeological research took place. The Greek classicists and the Bavarian archaeologists chose to divest the hill of every monument, which altered its pure classical character. Thus Medieval and Ottoman buildings were demolished, among them the Frankish tower, the Ottoman mosque and the houses, as the fortress known as Serpentze. In the 20th century the Acropolis underwent two important periods of restoration. The first phase (until the outbreak of World War II) was marked by the personality of the engineer Nikolaos Balanos and his unfortunate choice to use iron junctions, which caused the marbles severe damage, probably graver than the pollution that followed. The second, more scientific phase started around the middle of the 1970s and is still going on. It was paired by a grandiose effort to scientifically register the role of conservation in our days. This effort forms a point of reference for the whole scientific community worldwide. Nowadays the Acropolis is comprised in the World Watch List for Monuments of the UNESCO.

THE PROPYLAIA OF THE ACROPOLIS

The first building one meets going up the hill of the Acropolis is the Propylaia. The modern path, covered with stone slabs, coincides in general with the ancient route, except for the final part, which has been covered with protective wooden stairs and flooring. The Propylaia, forming the official entrance to the sanctuary on the western side of the Acropolis, were built in the period between 437 and 432 BC, after the completion of the Parthenon. They formed an indispensable part of the Pericles' building programme for the sacred hill in the 5th century BC. Their monumental character prepared the visitor for the magnificence of the buildings that followed. An extremely large sum for those times (2012 talents, i.e. about 52 tons of silver) was spent on construction, as attested by surviving

ADMIRING THE PARTHENON

building accounts.
The Propylaia were built of Pentelic marble and dark-coloured Eleusinian limestone over the foundations of an older propylon and of Archaic buildings, ruined by the Persians. The originality of their design was due to the architect Mnesicles. They were 48m wide and formed a complex with three spaces, a central building and two wings, one to the north, the other to the south.
The central building was rectangular, measuring 18 by 25 metres. It had six Doric columns on each of the narrow sides, which supported a Doric entablature and gables. The interval between the middle columns was larger and allowed visitors and sacrificial animals to pass through during the Panathenaea. Inside, a wall from which five doors opened, divided the central building into two parts, eastern and western.
The two wings of the Propylaia were formed to the north and to the south of the central building. The northern one had a portico with three Doric columns and a square room in the background. This room, known as the Pinakotheke, i.e. the Painting Gallery, was decorated with paintings by famous painters of the time. Couches were placed here, which is why it has been identified as a room for ritual banquets or for waiting and relaxing. Matching the northern wing, a portico of three columns was constructed on the southern side, without a back room, however. This wing was open from the west and allowed access to the temple of Athena Nike. The initial design of the Propylaia allowed space for the construction of additional rooms and buildings on the eastern side of the building. The outbreak of the Peloponnesian War, however, prevented the completion of this plan. After Antiquity, the monumental entrance to the Acropolis underwent alteration and transformation. In the 13th century, during the period of Frankish rule, the Propylaia acquired a defensive character and a tower was raised on their southern wing. In the 19th century alien accretions were removed, while conservation work began, which lasted throughout the 20th century.

THE TEMPLE OF ATHENA NIKE

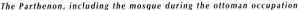

To the southwest of the Propylaia, on the

The Parthenon, including the mosque during the ottoman occupation

rampart which protected the main entrance to the Acropolis, is built the temple of Athena or Apteros Nike. It is an Ionic, amphiprostyle, tetrastyle temple, built entirely of marble. An elegant and graceful building, it was probably designed by Kallikrates. Its construction began around 426 BC and was accomplished around 421 BC. The frieze, which ran all around the building, depicted on the east side the banquet of gods, and historical and mythical battles of the Athenians on the other three sides. Parts of this frieze are displayed today in the British Museum. Battle scenes formed also the themes of the gables, Gigantomachy on one side and Amazonomachy on the other. The central acroterion depicted probably Bellerephontes with the Chimaera, whereas the corner acroteria were formed by figures of Victories. The tower on which this small temple was erected was revetted with limestone slabs and crowned with a marble parapet with depictions of Victories which led oxen to be sacrificed in honour of goddess Athena.
The temple was maintained until 1687, when the Ottomans demolished it completely and used the material for the fortification of the Propylaia during the siege by Morosini. The architectural members of the building were maintained intact, however, and allowed its reconstruction, which was attempted for the first time in 1842, whereas the building was restored again in 1936 and 1941.
In 2001 the temple was demolished to be placed in its proper position and to be cleaned of the concrete additions of the former phases of restoration, which are now going to be replaced by marble elements; it is hoped that after this phase of restoration the entire building will have better proportions. This phase is expected to be completed in 2004.

Temple of Nike Apteros

Nike with sandal

THE SANCTUARY OF ARTEMIS BRAURONIA

The ruins of the north and west wall of the sanctuary of Artemis Brauronia still survive today on the south-western corner of the Acropolis, east of the temple of Athena Nike (or Apteros Nike) and west of the Chalkotheke. The structure, dated probably to the decade 430–420 BC, was a stoa (portico) with two wings on either side. Today one can still see the steps carved into the bedrock, which led

Kore with "polos" hat

to the sanctuary from the north side. Inside one of the wings the "xoanon" was kept – presumably a wooden seated figure of the goddess – along with another statue, a work by the famous sculptor Praxiteles.

SANCTUARY OF ZEUS POLIEUS

To the north-east of the Parthenon, at the highest point of the Acropolis, lie the foundations of the sanctuary of Zeus Polieus, which included a small, north-facing temple. This complex was part of the rebuilding programme dated to the third quarter of the 5th century BC, in the area north-east of the Parthenon. Sacrifices were offered here during the festival of Dipolieia or Diipolia or Bouphonia in honour of Zeus Polieus. The celebrations took place in the end of June (the Athenian month Skirophorion) as a thanksgiving for the successful harvest. It was also here that Pausanias must have seen two sculptures of Zeus: one from the Archaic period, the other by the sculptor Leochares, dating to about 330 BC.

CHALKOTHEKE

To the west of the Parthenon and almost attached to the east side of the sanctuary of Artemis Brauronia lie traces of limestone foundations and walls carved into the rock. These belong to a large oblong room with three entrances to the north and six internal columns. According to inscriptions, the building can be identified as the Chalkotheke, constructed in the mid-5th century BC to house offerings in bronze given to goddess Athena. At the beginning of the 4th century BC a stoa with nineteen columns was added to the northern façade: today its north-east section can be made out by the carved steps of the Parthenon. Important restoration of the building took place during the Roman period.

SANCTUARY OF PANDION

At the south-eastern end of the Acropolis, where the Acropolis Museum stands today, are the remains of a sanctuary. According to most scholars this area was dedicated to the mythical King Pandion (son of either Erichthonios or Cecrops). The structure has been dated to Pericles' time, c. 440 BC. It consisted of a big open space with a propylon. Behind the sanctuary was a smaller area that probably functioned as the workshop of the sculptors who worked on the Acropolis building project.

Bronze strap depicting Athena

The Parthenon

The Parthenon, the ruins of which still dominate the center of the Acropolis, is without doubt the building most strongly connected to the city of Athens. However, its architectural structure, its technical perfection and the harmony of its decoration have elevated the Parthenon to the status of the symbol of ancient Greek civilization and of the universality of its principles. It is definitely the monument with the heaviest ideologically and aesthetically symbolic load for Western civilization. The Parthenon's importance does not belie only on its unequalled architectural and artistic conception and creation but also on the sociopolitical and ideological conditions under which it was erected.

THE BUILDING

It constitutes the core of Pericles's building programme and its construction began in 447 BC. It was inaugurated at the Panathenaia in 438 BC, though -according to the work accounts preserved on inscriptions- its decorative sculptures were completed in 432 BC. It stands in place of an older Parthenon whose construction started right after the battle of Marathon (490 BC), but it was destroyed by the Persians in 480 BC before its completion. The first phase of this earlier temple, usually referred to as the "Pre-Parthenon", has been placed by certain researchers even to the end of the 7th century or the beginning of the 6th century BC while by others to a more recent phase dated to Cimon's time (470-460). It is certain though, that the temple preceded the Periclean Parthenon, was in Doric order too but of slightly smaller dimensions and had a pteron of 6x16 columns.

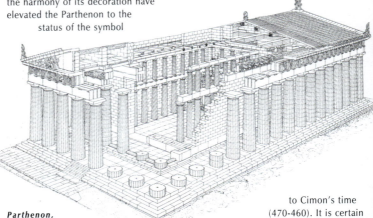

Parthenon, axonometric drawing

The Parthenon –there have been many opinions regarding its name– was dedicated to Athena Parthenos. The first reference to the temple with this name dates to the 4th century BC and was given by the orator Demosthenes. Contrary to the usual practice, the Parthenon was not built to house some old cult statue. Rather, it had the function of a splendid public Treasury where the votives to the goddess, the city's treasuries and the Treasury of the Athenian League were kept.
The architects of the Parthenon were Iktinos and Kallikrates, though, according to all indications and information given by Plutarch, it was Pheidias who had the overall supervision of the works.
The Parthenon was entirely made, from the crepis to the tilling and the

acroteria, of Pentelic marble. The only exception was the limestone foundations and the roof which was made of cypress-wood.

On the stylobates level the Parthenon was 69,51 m. long and 30,86 m. wide. Its total height to the top of the pediment was 13,72 m. It belongs to the type of the Doric peripteral temple with 8x17 columns and an inner line of six columns along the two narrow sides. According to the latest research, in around the middle of the north pteron there was a small temple with a single room – an incorporation of an older cult- and a round altar. Due to the fact that the main temple was 100 Attic stadia long it was initially called "Hekatompedos". It was divided by a lateral wall –not preserved today- into two unequal areas did not communicate with one another and had entrances to the east and west respectively. The roof of the smaller west section, the opisthodomos, was supported by four Ionic columns. The cella was surrounded by a two-storied, Π-shaped, Doric colonnade (5x10 columns), which surrounded and brought out the gold-and-ivory statue of Athena Parthenos. Two large windows opened up in the east façade for the better lighting of the place while in its north section a staircase was incorporated in the thickness of the wall.

OPTICAL REFINEMENTS

Since earlier on, a series of metrical divergences had been already applied to the Doric temples. These were called "refinements" and their purpose was the optical and aesthetic perfection of the result. In the Parthenon these refinements reached their peak. The Doric columns narrow down towards the top in order to create the illusion of greater height. However, their profile is not a straight line rather, it is an occasionally visible or very slight curve, called entasis (swelling), which adds to the column a sense of flexibility, lightness and intense vigour. In the Parthenon, this imperceptible entasis is at its most at the one third in the height of the columns without, however, the diameter exceeding that of the base. Also, it is known that when an object is lighted from the back appears to be more slender than in reality. In order to correct this optical illusion in the Parthenon, the corner columns are somewhat thicker. Nevertheless, the most significant innovation is the replacement of the straight lines with curves. It has, already since the 19th century, been observed, that the crepidoma and the stylobates are not straight lines but slight curves. The same applies to the straight lines of the entablature. In order, though, to avoid the sense of disintegration of the whole outwards, the vertical lines (axes) of both the columns and the walls are in reality very slightly leaning to the center of the structure. This happens in a way that, if they were to be extended they would create a huge pyramid. This constructive prevention emphasizes the height and the unity of the building, defines it explicitly and renders it "self-existent" in space.

THE DECORATIVE SCULPTURES

The entire iconographic programme of the Parthenon deals with the myths of the goddess Athena, the prevalence of the Greeks against the barbarians, the power and the glory of the city. The combination of the Doric metopes along the full perimeter of the epistyle with the Ionic frieze

Gathering of the Gods, detail from the Frieze

along the perimeter of the temple's walls is completely unusual. The triglyphs were painted blue as in the background of the frieze while the background of the metopes was white. The metopes and the frieze must have been placed before 438 BC whereas the pedimental sculptures were added until 432 BC.

THE METOPES

Of the initial 92 metopes only 54 have been preserved. Most of them are in the British Museum whereas a fair number of them are awfully mutilated. The differences in their style led some of the researchers to suggest that certain friezes belong to an earlier phase of the Parthenon. However, these differences are more possibly due to the dissimilar artistic education and skill of their creators. On the west side –the first the visitor sees– Amazonomachy scenes are depicted. On the north side, scenes from the fall of Troy are shown while on the south and east sides, episodes from the Centauromachy and Gigantomachy have been chosen respectively. All these mythical conflicts are thought to symbolise the fights of the Greeks against the Persians or more generally against the barbarians, and perhaps even the battle "of good against evil" as a whole.

THE FRIEZE

Of the initially 160 m. long frieze, around 30 m. have been lost. The representations on half of them, however, are known to us through the drawings of the travellers. The more prevailing opinions agree that these are representations of the Great Panathenaic procession that have a distinctly symbolic character. Two divided groups of figures start from the southwest corner of the temple to meet at the center of the east side. On the west frieze, riders are depicted preparing for the procession. These are followed by parallel scenes along the long sides: galloping horsemen, chariots, thallus-bearers (old men holding branches), musicians, hydria-bearers (young men with water vessels) and animals for sacrifice. In addition, on the north side skaphephoroi (men with troughs) are portrayed and on the south pinakophoroi (men with plates). On the east frieze, groups of men and women appear together with the twelve gods who seat in two groups framing the central scene of the offering of the peplos to Athena

THE PEDIMENTS

On the pediments, the myths related to Athena are presented in compositions carved in the round. On the east pediment –of which the figures on the ends are better preserved- the birth of

Hydria-carrier, detail from the Frieze

ADMIRING THE PARTHENON

THE CHRYSELEPHANTINE STATUE OF ATHENA

Pheidias, began in ca. 446 BC and was completed in 438 BC for the inauguration of the temple. It was the biggest, until that time, composite statue of the ancient world (11.7 m. high) and its appearance is known to us through small-scale copies and other representations. From a technical point-of-view it was an unprecedented achievement. On a wooden frame, pieces of ivory for the bare body parts and sheets of gold –which could have, very easily, been detached and weighed- for the garments and the weapons had been attached. For the maintenance of the ivory's humidity, a large cistern, few centimeters high, full of water was made in front of the statue. The goddess stood on a high pedestal of dark Eleusinian marble that had relief decoration with scenes from Pandora's myth of birth. She was represented standing with a long Doric peplos that formed an overfold girt by a belt at the waist. She wore sandals decorated

The Varvakeion Athena

with Gigantomachy scenes. On her outstretched right hand stood a Nike form (1.8 m. high) while with her left she held her shield and her spear. The goddess carried an aegis on her breast while her helmet was decorated with Pegasus figures and a Sphinx. Behind the shield coiled the sacred snake of the Acropolis, the "oikouros ophis". The shield bore a gorgoneion in the center and Amazonomachy scenes all around. The story goes that Pheidias gave his own physical characteristics and those of Pericles to two figures on the shield. This, in combination with the management of huge amounts of gold for the making of the statue, led to a big political scandal that resulted in Pheidias's self-exile. In truth, 40 to 50 talents of gold –more than a tone of precious metal- was used for Athena's statue.

At the time when Lachares was archon (295 BC), the gold sheets were detached from the statue to finance the war expenses of the Athenians. Very soon, though, they were replaced. According to certain researchers, the statue was entirely rebuilt in the 2nd century BC. It remained, however, in place in the 2nd century AD when Pausanias saw it. It was possibly transferred to Constantinople in the 5th century AD where its traces were lost.

PHEIDIAS

Pheidias lived in the 5th century BC and according to the ancient sources he was the greatest artist of his age. He worked mostly in Athens and Olympia. He is known primarily as a sculptor but he worked as an architect, a painter and a goldsmith as well. Being a truly great and creative mind he became Pericles's artistic advisor. He was a teacher of notable influence. Agorakritos and Alkamenes are included among his distinguished students. He managed to comprise a very skillful team of artists to work on the Parthenon sculptures. He was able to inspire and lead them in such a way as to be impossible today for us to tell his own work from his students'. His most significant works were the chryselephantine Athena Parthenos and the bronze Athena Promachos on the Acropolis, Zeus in Olympia, Athena and Aphrodite Ourania in Elis (all three chryselephantine) and other marble sculptures such as Athena Lemnia and a wounded Amazon made for the city of Ephesos.

Athena was depicted. The goddess with her father, Zeus, stood in the middle framed by Hephaestus and Hera. Other Olympian gods were watching the scene. At the angles, the course of the chariots of Helius (Sun-god) and Selene (Moon-goddess) defined Athena's time of birth, the dawn.

the city, like Cecrops. Although both compositions cannot be accurately restored, both emanate the dynamism and harmony of Classical art.

Restoration of the East pediment of the Parthenon

Athena and Poseidon dominated the west pediment, standing one against the other during their conflict for the possession of Athens. Perhaps, in between them rose the sacred olive-tree or Zeus's thunder in an attempt to divide them. Behind each one there was a chariot as well as certain mythical heroes and kings of

Restoration of a part of the entablature

ADMIRING THE PARTHENON

THE ACROTERIA

On the four corners of the temple and level to the sima were four lion's heads. The acroteria formed intricate plant compositions. Lately, it has been argued that the corner acroteria were winged female figures.

THE HISTORY OF THE MONUMENT

The information on Parthenon's fate during Antiquity are few and not always credible. The first among the ascertained interventions on the building occurred in 334 BC. Alexander the Great dedicated part of the spoils of his victory at Granicus and more precisely, he offered the shields. The holes from the nails used to secure them on the eastern epistyle are visible even today. A fire –dated by some to the 2nd century BC- caused serious damage and possibly destroyed even Pheidias's statue. The supporters of this theory think that the statue

The frankish tower in the northern side of the Partehnon, Engraving, 1835

a Christian church. At that time, an apse was added to the east façade and three doors opened along the lateral wall. The church was consecrated to the Virgin Mary and during the Middle Byzantine period it was the Cathedral of the city, known as the Virgin Mary of Athens (Panagia Athiniotissa). It continued to be considered a splendid monument, as this is evident by the visit of Basil II in 1019 after his victory against the Bulgarians. During the 12th century its

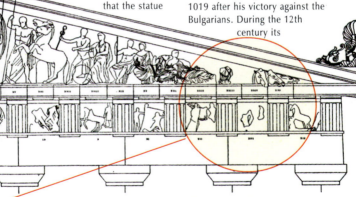

was replaced with an exact copy at the expense of Antiochus' IV, the king of Syria. Closely after the mid-2nd century AD, the traveller Pausanias visited and described the Parthenon and the statue of Athena Parthenos. In c. 362-363, the emperor Julian ordered extensive repairs in the interior of the temple, in the context of the revival of the ancient cult. However, in the end of the 5th century AD the cult of Athena seized to exist and in the beginning of the 6th century AD the Parthenon was transformed into

interior was decorated with religious paintings, traces of which have been preserved until today. When the Franks occupied Athens in 1204, the Parthenon was consecrated to Notre Dame and became the Cathedral of the Dukes of Athens; a tall campanile was built at that time at the southwest corner of the monument.

In ca. 1458 the campanile was transformed to a minaret and the Parthenon functioned as a mosque since the city was under Ottoman rule. In general

WALK 2

East Pediment

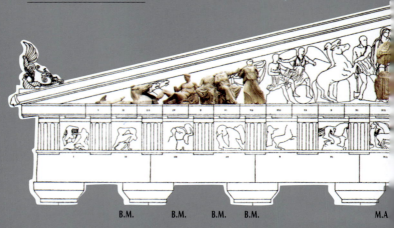

B.M.   B.M.   B.M.   B.M.   M.A.

West Pediment

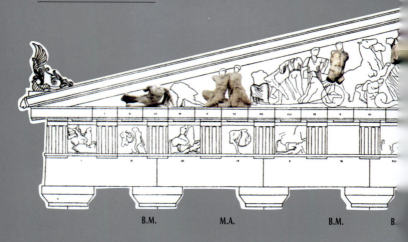

B.M.   M.A.   B.M.   B.

B.M.: BRITISH MUSEUM, M.A.: ACROPOLIS MUSEUM

ADMIRING THE PARTHENON

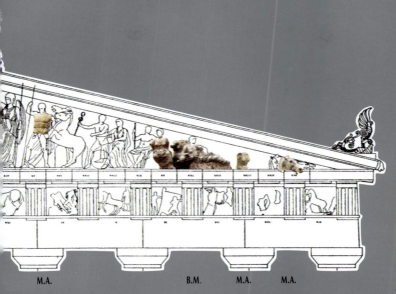

M.A.　　　　　　　　B.M.　M.A.　M.A.

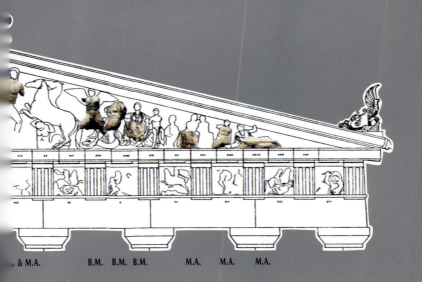

& M.A.　　B.M. B.M. B.M.　　M.A.　M.A.　M.A.

WALK 2

North Frieze

West Frieze

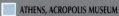 LONDON, BRITISH MUSEUM   ATHENS, ACROPOLIS MUSEUM   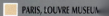 PARIS, LOUVRE MUSEUM

ADMIRING THE PARTHENON

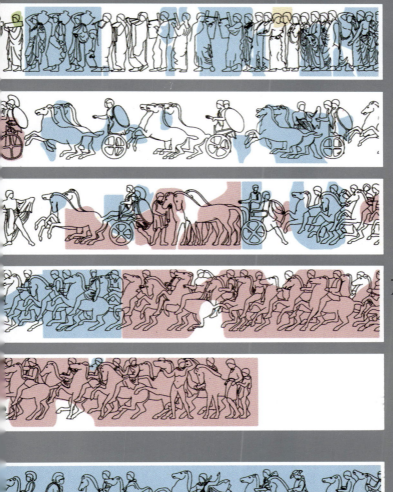

 NON-PRESERVED PARTS (SKETCHES BY CARREY)   ROME   VIENNA   PALERMO

WALK 2

South Frieze

East Frieze

	LONDON, BRITISH MUSEUM		ATHENS, ACROPOLIS MUSEUM		PARIS, LOUVRE MUSEUM

ADMIRING THE PARTHENON

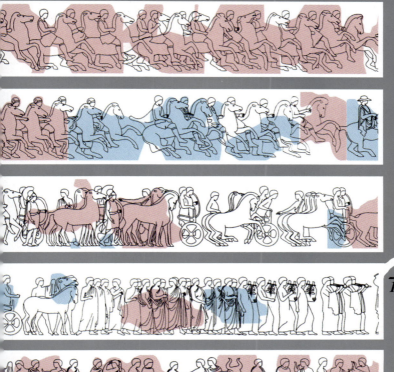

NON-PRESERVED PARTS (SKETCHES BY CARREY)

SOUTH METOPES

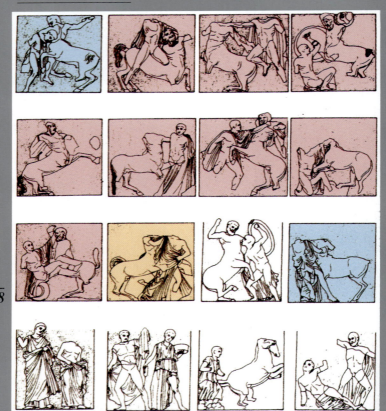

The sculptural decoration of Parthenon has been preserved in a fragmentary way. During the transformation of the ancient temple to a Christian church, the east pediment has been severely damaged, while the east, north and south metopes suffered destructions because their representations offenced the religious feeling of the early Christians. In 1674 J. Carrey made sketches of the pediments, the frieze and the south metopes, which, due to their subject (Centauromachy) and to its symbolic interpretation by the Christians as a fight between the Good and the Evil, escaped destruction. These sketches represent an invaluable guide for the parts of the monument destroyed by the explosion of 1687. In 1812 Lord Elgin detached parts of the frieze, the pediments and the south metopes from the monument and removed some more from the adjacent area. These sculptures have been transported to the British Museum. More fragments are kept in various European museums. The sculptures, which remained on the monument, suffered from the air pollution, have been removed from it and placed in the Acropolis Museum.

☐ LONDON, BRITISH MUSEUM   ☐ ATHENS, ACROPOLIS MUSEUM

p. 107: Drawing representing exaggerated the optical refinements of the Parthenon. Drawing of M. Korres in Hurwit J.M., *The Athenian Acropolis History, Mythology and Archaeology from Neolithic Era to the Present*, Cambridge University Press 1999, p. 167, fig. 131.

p. 110: Coloured drawing representation of the east pediment. Paris, *Ecole Nationale Superieure des Beaux Arts*. © Ecole Nationale Superieure des Beaux Arts, Paris.

p. 110-111: Drawing representation of the east pediment, in Hurwit J.M, as above, p. 177 fig. 143.

p. 118-119: Drawing of the metopes by J. Carrey, in Hurwit J.M, as above, p. 173 fig. 139.

p. 123: Peisistratian temple, © Dorpfeld Foundations. Alison Frantz Collection, Courtesy American School of Classical Studies, στο Hurwit J.M, as above, p. 110, fig. 82

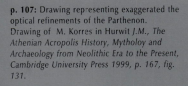

PARIS, LOUVRE MUSEUM   NON-PRESERVED PARTS (SKETCHES BY CARREY)

Representation of the "apobates" game from the north Frieze

terms however, and based on the descriptions of the Ottoman traveller of the beginning of the 17th century Evliya Tselebi, the Parthenon sustained its prestige. In 1674, Jacques Carrey, the attendant of the Marquis de Nointel, produced a series of drawings of the decorative sculptures of the building. Only a few years later, in 1687, the Venetian general –and subsequently a Doge- Francesco Morosini besieged the Ottomans in the Acropolis. A canon shell hit the Parthenon, used by the Ottomans as a powder-magazine, resulting, due to the explosion caused, in the destruction of the building and of part of its decorative sculptures.

Afterwards, Morosini attempted to remove some of the sculptures effecting in even more destruction of the Parthenon. Thus, Carrey's drawings preserved the form of the decoration which otherwise would have been unknown today. When, a little later, the Ottomans reoccupied the city, they built a small mosque in the interior of the ruined temple.

However, the greatest devastation to the building occurred in the beginning of the 19th century by the Scottish ambassador of Great Britain in Constantinople Thomas Bruce Earl of Elgin. Elgin succeeded to extract a ferman (decree) from the Sultan according to which he was allowed to get from the Acropolis as many works of art as he wished. Between the years 1801 and 1803 the greater part of the Parthenon sculptures, a Caryatid from the Erechtheion and other antiquities were removed from the monuments, transported by boat to England and later, were sold to the British Museum where they still remain. During the siege of the Acropolis in 1822, the Greek rebels, as soon as they realized that the Ottomans tore down the monuments to take and use the lead from the clamps, they preferred themselves to give their enemies the lead for the bullets.

After the liberation, restoration work began in 1841. The mosque was demolished in 1844 and for the period 1896 and 1902 more work took place. Systematic restoration was done during the years 1922 and 1933 under Nikolaos Balanos. More additions and repairs occasionally occurred until the beginning of the 1980s. At that point a study of restoration was completed and works were initiated that are still in progress.

Procession of riders from the north Frieze

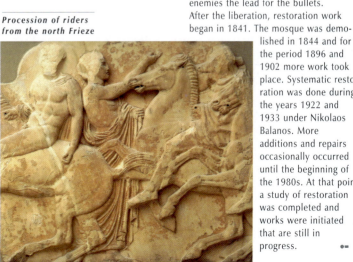

ALTAR OF ATHENA POLIAS

To the eastern side of the foundations of the Archaic temple, north-east of the Parthenon, there are a few carvings on the rock. These are probably associated with the altar of Athena Polias. This Archaic altar was destroyed during the Persian invasion of 480 BC. In Classical times, the altar was supposedly rebuilt, following its original form.

Caryatids from the SW porch of the Erechtheion

THE TEMPLE OF ROME AND AUGUSTUS

To the east of the Parthenon, traceable on the ground, is a circular foundation that has been identified as the temple of Rome and Augustus. The temple was a round monopteros, dating probably from 17–10 BC. However, archaeologists are not unanimous about the identification: some suggest that the Roman temple was in fact closer to the Erechtheion. The building was 7.35m high, with a diameter of 8.60m. It was surrounded by nine Ionic columns and did not have a cella. The inscription on the architrave still extant today mentions that the monument was dedicated by the citizens of Athens to Rome and Augustus. Pausanias, who wrote in the 2nd century, does not refer to this monument, either because he was not impressed by it, or because he intentionally avoided mentioning the Roman presence and imperial cult on such a sacred space as the Athenian Acropolis, so closely associated with the Greek religious traditions.

THE ERECHTEION AND SANCTUARY OF PANDROSOS

At the northern end of the hill of the Acropolis is the Erechtheion (the House of Erechtheus), an elaborate Ionic building built of Pentelic marble. Its original architectural design, the successful response to the ritual needs of the building and the rich sculptural decoration of its architectural elements make it one of the most important buildings of Classical times, and justify its classification as one of the most renowned buildings of Antiquity. Construction of the temple started in 421 BC, but was completed only between 409 and 405 BC. The name of the architect is not known, but the ingenious design probably points to Mnesicles. The choice of location, 40 metres to the north of the

The inscription from the temple of August and Rome

WALK 2

THE CARYATIDS

The Caryatids, perhaps the most famous women's statues of Antiquity, were named such long after their creation, possibly after the virgins of the Laconian city Caryae, who danced in honour of Artemis Caryatis. They wear a plain Doric peplos and they have their hair elaborately braided. Their hands are no longer extant, but from Roman copies we know that in one hand they held a phiale (a shallow bowl for libations). They were made by one of Pheidias' students, possibly either Alcamenes or Callimachos. Today the originals are displayed in the Museum of Acropolis, apart from one Caryatid, which is in the British Museum, along with an Ionic column from the eastern side of the Erechtheion, plundered by Lord Elgin. Exact copies take the place of these originals.

Parthenon, although problematic because of the steepness of the ground, was not accidental. The Erechteion comprised all the ancient relics of Attic cults associated with this area: the marks on the rock from the trident of Poseidon, the olive tree of Athena, the ruins of the house of Erechtheus, the tomb of Cecrops and the remains of the cult of the hero Boutes and of Pandrosos.

Architecturally, the Erechtheion is a non-symmetrical, complicated construction, with a central part, the cella, surrounded by porticos. The interior was divided by a vertical wall into two, independent parts. The eastern part had a façade consisting of six Ionic columns and was dedicated to the cult of Athena Polias. It housed the "xoanon" (wooden statue) of the goddess, which bore the sacred veil during the celebration of the Panathenaia. In front of this statue burned a golden

ADMIRING THE PARTHENON

lamp. In the western part other gods and heroes were worshipped. On the western wall, which functioned as a support, large windows opened between Ionic columns.
On the northern side an elaborate roofed entrance (prostasis) with an Ionic colonnade led through a superbly decorated door to the interior, and a smaller door led to the adjacent sanctuary of Pandrosos, daughter of Cecrops. The Pandroseion consisted of a four-sided precinct, the northern and western sides of which were enclosed by porticos. It surrounded a small temple of Pandrosos, the altar of Zeus Herkeios and the sacred olive tree of Athena.
At the south-western end of the Erechtheion one can still see today the famous porch of the Korai, the Caryatids, six female statues facing the Parthenon, who (instead of columns) elegantly support the marble roof. This porch seems

View of the Arrephorion

to have been built on the tomb of Cecrops for reasons related to the cult.
The whole building had a zone of palmettes and a frieze made of slabs of dark Eleusinian marble, with figures in relief made of white Pentelic marble. Unfortunately, this unique technique resulted in the loss of the bulk of the sculptural decoration. Part of the frieze is displayed today in the Acropolis Museum and the preserved figures suggest that the city's local myths were depicted on the frieze. In the course of time many interventions and changes of use took place at the Erectheion. It was

transformed into a church in the 6th century, into a palace in the 14th century by the Catalan conquerors of Athens and it became the Ottoman governor's harem in the 15th century. During the War of Independence it suffered serious damage (1827). Extensive restoration work has brought the monument as close to its initial form as possible. ●–

THE ANCIENT TEMPLE OF ATHENA
(THE SO-CALLED PEISISTRATIAN)

The foundations of an Archaic temple can be seen to the east of the Erechtheion. These belong to the ancient "neos" (temple), dedicated to Athena and Erechtheus. Inside, the heavenly (diipetes) xoanon of the goddess, made of olive wood and known as "hedos", was kept. This is the oldest

Old temple of Athena

temple of Athena on the Acropolis.

This was the site of the old Mycenaean palace of the Acropolis, and a temple existed here in the Geometric period. Experts cannot agree about the date of the Archaic temple, or when the various phases of construction took place. Some hold that there were two phases (beginning and end of the 6th century BC), while others affirm there was only one, a late Peisistratian phase (529–520 BC). Fragments of the sculptural decoration of the temple, such as acroteria and figures from the pedimental compositions, are on view at the Acropolis Museum.

The temple that existed here at the end of the 6th century BC was made of limestone. It was a Doric peripteral temple, with six columns along the façade and twelve at the sides, and adorned with marble pediments. After it was destroyed by the Persians in 480 BC, parts were used as building material for the construction of the north wall of the Acropolis. However, it appears that at least a section of the temple was immediately restored and probably housed the state coffers and the treasury of the Delian League until the Parthenon was built (438 BC). Although ancient writers do not offer explicit information, it seems that the old temple was burnt down again in 406/5 BC, after which it was restored anew. But all reference to it ceases after the mid-4th century BC, by which time the cults and the goddess's xoanon had been transferred to the Erechtheion.

ARRHEPHORION

Most scholars agree that the building to the north-west of the Erechtheion is the Arrhephorion or House of the Arrhephoroi. It is a south-facing,

---

ARRHEPHORIA AND ARRHEPHOROI

The Festival of the Arrephoria was celebrated in the month of Skirophorion (mid-June – mid-July), in honour of Athena. Mystic rites took place during the celebrations, which were associated with the fertility and fruitfulness of the earth. The Arrhephoroi (meaning, 'they who carry the unspoken') were virgin girls between 7 and 20 years old from distinguished Athenian families. They resided, for an unknown period of time, on the Acropolis, at the Arrhephorion, a building designed specially for them. They helped in the weaving of the peplos of Athena Polias, offered to her during the Panathenaea. Their most important responsibility, however, was to participate in the mystic rites of the Arrhephoria. One of these rites was the carrying of sacred objects (possibly little bread-like cakes in the shape of serpents and phalluses, stone pine branches and fruits), given them by the priestess. They would carry these ritual objects through a secret underground passage that led to the northern slope of the Acropolis, where a member of the priesthood received them and gave them other secret objects in return to carry up to the Acropolis.

Statuette of a Kore

The Walls of the Acropolis

square structure, built in the mid-5th century BC. Today only the foundations are visible. It originally included a pronaos and a chamber. To the west of the building was a courtyard, from which a secret passage led to the north slope of the Acropolis.

THE ACROPOLIS WALLS

As early as the Mycenaean period, the hill of the Acropolis was a naturally and artificially fortified place. The Cyclopean wall, which is discernible to the south-east of the Propylaia, dates from around 1240 BC. A little later, at the north-western corner of the Acropolis, an arched fortified wall was added, which Thucydides calls "the Pelargikon"; this wall was extended westwards during the Geometric period. It was these fortified walls that the Persians encountered when they invaded Athens in 480 BC. When the Athenians returned to the city, they feared a new attack and thus, under the orders of Themistocles, built an additional fortification around the northern slopes of the hill (479/8 BC). The Themistoclean wall incorporated parts of the monuments destroyed by the Persians. In 467 BC Cimon embanked the southern slopes of the Acropolis and erected a new isodomic fortification wall. Under Pericles the wall became even higher. During the Herulian invasion of AD 267 a new fortification was built at the western flank, part of which forms the Beulé Gate. The main stronghold of Athens remained the Acropolis or "the Castle", as it was called in Byzantine times. The wall remained the same as in Antiquity, with only a few additions. According to an inscription discovered close to Areios Pagos, in AD 1064 a tower was added to the fortifications by the metropolitan bishop of Athens, Leo. During the Frankish period, after 1204, the castle fortifications underwent important changes, mainly on the western part, and the wall was raised higher and acquired ramparts. The Beulé Gate, on the western side of the Acropolis, was sealed, and a new entrance to the castle was created under the tower, which supported the Apteros Nike Temple. The Propylaia were incorporated into the whole fortification system. Around the same time the so-called Frankish Tower was built, which was maintained until 1875, when it was demolished to enable archaeological excavations to be carried out.

THE ACROPOLIS MUSEUM

The Acropolis Museum is considered to be one of the most important museums in the world. It displays some of the masterpieces of ancient Greek art dedicated to the most significant sanctuary of Athens, that of Athena Polias and the Parthenon. The building is situated on the Sacred Rock, east of the Parthenon. It was designed by the architect Panagis Kalkos and was built between 1865 and 1874. During the 1950s it was extended eastwards. Today, construction of the new museum has begun, in the Makrigianni district, next to the Acropolis metro station, on the site of the old military hospital known as the Weiler building.

Only stone sculptures from monuments and excavations in the Acropolis area are included in the museum's collections. Pottery and bronzes are kept in the National Archaeological Museum, while inscriptions are in the Epigraphic Museum. The Acropolis Museum exhibits sculpted votive objects and pediments of the Archaic period, sculptures of the Severe style period, fragments of the Parthenon pediments, metopes and frieze, parts of the Erechtheion frieze and the parapets and frieze of the temple of Athena Nike. In addition, one can admire there the original caryatids (all but one) and the terracotta figurines and pottery from the Shrine of the Nymph excavated at the foot of the rock. Most of the pediments, metopes and the frieze of the Parthenon as well as one caryatid were stolen at the beginning of the 19th century by the Englishman, Lord Elgin. They are now exhibited at the British Museum in London. Before entering the museum one sees the owl, the sacred bird of Athena, set on a high pedestal dated to 500 BC.

In the vestibule opposite the entrance is a sculpture complex of the 5th century BC attributed to Alkamenes, Pheidias' pupil. It depicts Procne, mythical queen of Thrace, planning to murder her son Itys to avenge her husband's infidelity. In the same room, an idealized bust of Alexander the Great is also exhibited, probably the work of Leochares, who depicted the Macedonian king on the occasion of his sole visit to Athens after his victory at Chaeronea in 338 BC.

The tour of the museum's main rooms starts with a display of works of the early 6th century BC. Especially impressive is the monumental poros complex of a lioness tearing up a calf. It comes from the pediment of a large temple dated to c. 600 BC, perhaps from the ancient temple of Athena Polias. Beside it lies another, though smaller, stone pediment, belonging to a small temple or a treasury. It depicts Herakles fighting the Lernaian Hydra while his friend Iolaos waits for him in his chariot. The ancient colours (red and deep blue) have been very well preserved. Opposite, stands a marble Gorgo whose head and a small part of the body only survive. It was an acroterion of a large temple, from the beginning of the 6th century BC. It possibly belongs to the second construction phase of the ancient temple of Athena. The fragments of the marble panthers exhibited on the

The "calf-bearer", an archaic votive sculpture

left of the entrance as well as the head of the panther displayed near the second room probably belong to the frieze of the same temple. It is also likely that the fragment with the polychrome inscribed lotus flower belongs to the poros cornice of the same temple.

The sculptures in the second room are also dated to the first half of the 6th century BC. On the right, on the long wall, a poros pediment is on display, possibly from the second construction phase of the ancient temple of Athena. Herakles is shown at the one end, fighting the sea-demon Triton – half man, half fish – while at the other end stands a polychrome winged tri-bodied demon with a serpent's tail. Part of the same pediment is also possibly thought to be the scene of Herakles' apotheosis where Zeus, seated on a throne, and Hera, standing beside him, receive the hero on Olympus. The big serpents beneath the window possibly decorated the other pediment of the same temple. However, it should be noted that the above poros and marble sculptures have recently been associated with the early Archaic predecessor of the Parthenon, known from written sources as the Hekatompedon.

Statue of kore known as the "Peplophoros"

The «Rampin Rider»

One of the first freestanding votive sculptures of the sanctuary is the statue of the calf-bearer (570 BC) mounted in the middle of the room. According to the inscription on its base the statue was dedicated by someone called Rombos. Behind the calf-bearer stands the earliest of the Acropolis Korai.

Two Naxian Korai are on show in the third room. Beside them, two lions tear up a bull, a piece possibly belonging to the centre of the pediment together with Herakles, the Triton and the tri-bodied demon.

The fourth room contains marble sculptures of the 2nd half of the 6th century BC. Entering the room, the visitor faces the Horseman, part of a double votive sculpture (c. 550 BC). The original head of the figure (which has been completed by a plaster copy) is at the Louvre. The sculpture belonged to the French collector G. Rampin and has been named after him. The Horseman, his attire influenced by the East (for example his short chiton with painted palmettes and his rhomboid breeches) is called "the Persian". Around him, a group of bigger and smaller horsemen of the Late Archaic period has been collected, representing a votive group of the equestrian class. The marble dog in the middle of the room was probably the guardian of the entrance to the sanctuary of Artemis Brauronia. The marble lion-head on the dividing wall served as a waterspout of the ancient temple of Athena (c. 525 BC). Beside it is a small relief depicting Hermes leading some nymphs. Valuable exhibits in this room include statues of young girls, the Korai (maidens), the most prominent among the votive sculptures from the period 530 to 500 BC. They are lined up in chronological order along the long wall and in a semicircle at the far end of the room. The Kore beside the entrance is known as the Lyon Kore: most of her upper body and the head are plaster copies of the original in Lyon, France. Further up, stands the Peplos Kore: she wears a chiton and a richly adorned peplos. The colours on her eyes, lips and wavy hair – held by a metal wreath – are still preserved. The small-figured Kore, also richly coloured and with the sweet smile, is possibly the work of a Chian artist. At the far end of the room on both sides of the dividing wall are the heads of Korai statues. The showcases on the left contain terracotta figurines and vessels from the shrine of a nymph, excavated at the foot of the rock. A seated Athena, in the centre of the Korai semicircle, is probably the work of the great sculptor Endoios and one of the very few to have survived the Persian destruction of 480 BC. Beside her, the Kore with the almond-shaped eyes wears a chiton and a short himation fastened on the left shoulder. Her wreath and her dress were adorned with a painted meander band (500 BC).

Snake in poros

The fifth room of the museum is dominated by the bigger than life-size marble figures from the eastern pediment of the ancient temple of Athena. The subject matter of the pediment relates to the gigantomachy and the figures exhibited show Athena fighting a giant. The entire work is dated to c. 520 BC, the period when the Peisistratids gave the temple a face-lift. On the right side of the same room, stands the largest of the Korai, a work by the sculptor Antenor, dedicated by the potter Nearchos. In a small side-room, known as the alcove, the frieze of the temple of Athena Nike is exhibited. Exact cement copies have replaced the original stones on the monument. Sculptures in the Severe style (first half of the 5th century BC) have been assembled in the sixth room. The Kritios Boy stands out, the statue of a youth with long wavy hair twined around his head, the work of Kritios, teacher of Myron, and dated to 480 BC. Beside it, the head of the Blonde Youth is exhibited. Traces of golden-yellow colour are preserved in his hair. The relief of the Mourning Athena is dated

The Boy of Kritios

ADMIRING THE PARTHENON

Four horse-protome from a quadriga, from a relief of the Ekatompedon

to 460 BC. The goddess wears an Attic belted peplos and bends her head slightly towards the stele in front of her. Of particular interest is the Sulky Kore (so named because it does not have the characteristic Archaic smile), dedicated by Euthydikos.

Fragments from the west (Cecrops and his daughter, Poseidon) and the east (Selene with her chariot, horses' heads neighing) pediment of the Parthenon are exhibited in the seventh room. There is also a metope depicting a centaur grabbing a Lapith woman by the waist. A head of Iris belongs to the eastern frieze of the temple.

Fragments from the friezes of the Parthenon, the Erechtheion and the parapet of the temple of Athena Nike are shown in the eighth room. Pieces from the northern frieze of the Parthenon (440 BC) have been placed along the long wall of the room, young horsemen, chariots and apobates, hydriai-bearers, thallophoroi (olive-branch bearers) and youths leading lambs or bulls for sacrifice. The piece with the Olympian gods (Poseidon, Apollo, Artemis and Aphrodite) receiving the procession belongs to the eastern frieze. Fragments from the Erechtheion frieze (409–406 BC) are on display on the small dividing wall in the middle of the room. The figures in white marble contrast with the background of dark Eleusinian marble. The subject-matter is not certain, but probably relates to old Athenian myths. In the corner of the room pieces of the parapet from the tower of the Athena Nike temple are exhibited (410 BC) bearing scenes of Nikai leading bulls to sacrifice and a young Nike with half-open wings on her back bending to either tie or untie her sandal.

Lastly, in the ninth room, in a specially air-controlled chamber, are the original caryatids of the Erechtheion.

MONUMENTS ON THE NORTH SLOPE OF THE ACROPOLIS

Head of a kore

The north slope of the sacred rock of the Acropolis was connected to various cults in Antiquity. On the north-western side was the site of the most eminent fountain house of Classical times, a simple rectangular structure (7.80 x 6.70m) built on the natural Clepsydra spring in c. 460 BC. A paved courtyard to the north and to the east of the fountain functioned as a cistern for collecting rainwater falling from the Acropolis. The fountain house was damaged in the mid-1st century AD by landslides of natural rock, but at the beginning of the 3rd century it was restructured into a domed building.

Along the north slope of the rock are a number of sacred caves, which can only be seen if the visitor stands beneath the northern slope of the Acropolis. Unfortunately, they cannot be visited.

In front of the first cave, steps were carved in the natural rock to allow to a restricted number of the city's dignitaries to watch the Panathenaic procession. The second cave was dedicated to Apollo Hypakraios or to Pythian Apollo. According to myth, it was here that the god was united with the most beautiful daughter of Erechtheus, Kreoussa. From their divine union Ion was born, the ancestor of the Athenians. On the

The Clepsydra

inner walls of Apollo's cave are niches, still surviving today, where dedicatory reliefs and inscribed tablets were placed.

The next cave has been identified as the shrine of Olympian Zeus.

The sanctuary of Pan was situated to the east, in a smaller cave. The cult statue of the god was placed here and the carved recesses for the offerings are still discernible. The sanctuary was founded after the Athenian victory at Marathon (490 BC), when the citizens wished to express their gratitude to the god Pan, who spread panic among the Persians.

A staircase carved in natural rock was found to the east of the sanctuary. This led upstairs to the Acropolis and was used by the Arrhephoroi during mystic rites at the festival of Arrhephoria.

Surviving recesses for votive objects and offerings are carved in the rock on the northern slope of the Acropolis beneath the wall and to the east of the Erechtheion. On this site, the sanctuary of Eros and Aphrodite has been identified, dated to about the mid-5th century BC.

Until recently, it was thought that one of the caves on the north side was the site of the sanctuary of Aglauros, dedicated to one of the daughters of Cecrops, Aglauros. Today, according to the prevailing view among scholars, the sanctuary is thought to have been placed in front of the grotto of the east side of the sacred rock. Every year, the Athenian ephebes (youths) came to the sanctuary of Aglauros to swear the oath of devotion to their city.

The Aglauros Cave

3

WALK 3

1. "Acropolis" Metro Station
2. The Statue of Makrigiannis
3. The Weiler Building
4. The Ilias Lalaounis Jewelry Museum
5. The Lysikrates Monument
6. St Demetrius
7. St Catherine
8. The Hellenic Children's Museum
9. The Museum of Greek Folk Art
10. The Frissiras Museum
11. Saviour of Kottakis
12. Municipality of Athens Folk Art and Tradition Centre
13. The Jewish Museum of Greece
14. The Anglican Church
15. The Russian Church

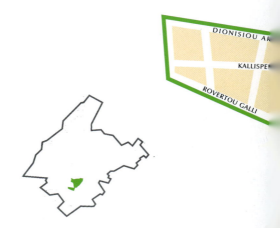

3 SMALL BUT INTERESTING MUSEUMS

Several small but interesting museums are scattered in this area. The avant-garde Children's Museum, the Jewellery Museum, where visitors can admire artifacts by the world renowned designer Lalaounis, the Museum of Folk Art, a special meeting point of rich, folk cultures, and the Jewish Museum, a reminder of Greece's important Jewish community. This Route is complete with a visit to the Anglican and Russian Churches, and presents multiple cultural aspects of Athens.

"ACROPOLIS" METRO STATION

The construction of the Athens Metro, a project dating back to the late 1970s, started in the early 1990s and has acted as impulse to the city of Athens. The first two lines started to operate in 2000, while they are expected to extend and connect with the new Suburban Railway, which is under construction as well. The Metro stations have been designed particularly tastefully, decorated with hanging works of art or replicas of archaeological findings on the walls, so that each station is a reference point of its area. Such decorations are indicative of the important excavations that preceded the construction of the underground metro tunnels, thus bringing to light exquisite findings, which were photographed, listed and removed. Several findings and photographs were displayed in prominent positions during the significant exhibition "The City under the City" at

Metro Station "Acropolis", showcases with finds

WALK 3

EXCAVATIONS IN THE MAKRIGIANNI DISTRICT

During the recent construction of the new underground system an extensive excavation programme was undertaken in the Makrigianni district, an area crucial for the study of ancient and medieval Athens. Archaeological research took place on the sites of the forthcoming new Museum of the Acropolis, the former military camp of General Makrigiannis and where the University of Athens had already been conducting excavations since the 1980s.

Metro station "Acropolis"

This area has been in continuous use from the beginning of the 3rd millennium BC. From the Geometric Period it began to be used as a cemetery, while from the end of the 8th century BC it was occupied as a settlement area, and during the Classical Period was included inside the Themistoclean fortifications. The area became prosperous during the early Byzantine era, from the 4th to the 6th centuries, as archaeological research shows: traces of luxurious, two-storey buildings with mosaic floors have been found in the district. However, the area was abandoned from the 7th century, until, gradually, during the mid- and late-Byzantine period, cemeteries and various workshops were set up here.

Metro Station "Acropolis", casts of the Parthenon Sculptures

SMALL BUT INTERESTING MUSEUMS

the Museum of Cycladic Art in 2000-2001. The Acropolis station is the most complete, thus prepossessing the passengers to what they are going to see in case they visit the sacred rock. The station is along line 2 (Sepolia - Agios Dimitrios). The archaeological decor is divided into two sections: the exact replicas of part of the sculpted decor of the Parthenon, made by the Centre for the Acropolis Studies, and the excavation findings. Casts of the sculpted decor from the east pediment as well as important display-cases with excavation findings from all historical periods (such as vessels, children's toys, gems of ancient tombs and oil lamps) are displayed on the level of the station's ticket-offices. Part of the stratigraphy, at a point from which at least six trunk roads of the ancient city passed, is shown on the passage level,

Metro Station "Acropolis" track

WALK 3

IOANNIS MAKRIGIANNIS

Ioannis Makrigiannis (1797-1864), known as General Makrigiannis, was one of the most important fighters of the Greek War of Independence of 1821. He took part in many military operations against the Ottomans and played an important role defending the Acropolis against them. He was one of the key characters of the political movement of 3rd September 1843, which forced King Otto to grant a Constitution. Apart from his revolutionary activity, Makrigiannis is particularly known for his memoirs, which were written in the popular idiom of the time and are considered as a landmark in modern Greek literature, as well as a valuable historical source.

Statue of Makrigiannis

while on the platforms there are replicas of the Parthenon's friezes.

STATUE OF MAKRIGIANNIS

On the corner of Dionissiou Areopagitou and Vironos Streets entering the area of the Plaka one can see the statue of Ioannis Makrigiannis, a leading figure of the 1821 Greek War of Independence and a property owner in the area south-east of the Acropolis that today bears his name. The statue was sculpted by Giannis Pappas and it depicts Makrigiannis clad in the traditional foustanela [skirt] holding his sword.

THE WEILER BUILDING

The Weiler Building is at the foot of the Acropolis, in the archaeological site between Makrigianni and Dionissiou Areopagitou Streets. The foundations of the building were laid in 1834; today it houses the Centre for the Acropolis Studies.
This was one of the first buildings to be constructed when Athens became the capital of Greece. It was named the Weiler building after the architect, Wilhelm von Weiler, an engineer in the Bavarian Army.
The building is an example of the Rundbogen style that developed in

The Weiler Building

Germany during the 1830s. Interestingly, the architect has allowed the building materials to be used as decorative elements: the masonry is visible without the use of plaster or paint, and the bricks around the door and window frames have a decorative function. The main characteristic of the building is the presence of arched doors and windows, similar to other urban buildings of the 1840s, such as the customs' building and warehouses in Ermoupoli on the island of Syros.
The two-storey building was designed as a military hospital for the Bavarian soldiers of King Otto. In 1930 it was used as the police headquarters. During the armed conflict of December 1944, the so called Dekemvriana, it was used by the Greek People's Liberation Army (ELAS) as their centre of operations against the British. The building was damaged and later repaired. Under the initiative of Melina Merkouri, the then Minister of Culture, it has been home to the Centre for the Acropolis Studies since 1987. At the moment the building houses the centre's store rooms, offices, research and education areas.

Golden necklace

THE ILIAS LALAOUNIS JEWELRY MUSEUM

The Ilias Lalaounis Jewelry Museum is housed in an early 20th century building on 12 Kallisperi Street, near the Acropolis. It was founded in 1993 as a private non-profit organisation dedicated to the art of jewel-making and it opened for the public in December 1994. Today its collections consist of more than 4,000 jewels and small ornaments crafted between 1940 and 2000 by Ilias Lalaounis, the museum's founder and member of the French Academy of Fine Arts. The museum's collections are separated in six categories and are on display on the two floors of the building. On the first floor the jewels from the "Golden Dawn of Art" are inspired by the Palaeolithic and Neolithic periods, as well as the finds from prehistoric caves around the Mediterranean. In the "Ilion" collection there are among others copies of the necklace and earrings, parts of the "Treasure of Priamos" that were uncovered by Heinrich

The Museum of Jewelry "Ilias Lalaounis"

Schliemann in Troy. The "Story of the Greek Jewel" consists of collections inspired by the period starting with the Bronze Age up until the Byzantine era, while the third category includes jewels inspired by European, American and Asian cultures. Two of the categories displayed on the second floor are inspired by nature and by modern technology and biology. The last category called "Special Requests" includes jewels and ornaments crafted on particular people's requests. Apart from its collections the museum has a specialist library on the history of jewel-making and the Applied Arts in general. There is a jewel-manufacturing atelier, a special events room, a shop where people can also place orders for copies of the jewels included in the collections and, finally, a coffee shop with a magnificent view of the Parthenon. The museum also boasts an active education department with various programmes and activities designed for school children, students and people with special needs.●▬

THE LYSIKRATES MONUMENT

The best-preserved choregic monument in Athens stands at the junction of Shelley and Lissikratous Streets, next to the same-named square in the Plaka, southeast of the Acropolis. An inscription, reported by the 17th century travelers, can be seen around the epistyle of the structure. According to this, Lysikrates son of Lysitheides from the deme of Kikkyna, member of the Akamantis tribe won as a choregos in the drama contest during the 334 BC Great Dionysian festival. In the same year, he raised the monument in the ancient Street of the Tripods in order to place his victory prize, the votive tripod.

The Lysikrates Monument

CHOREGIA

One of the regular liturgies in Ancient Athens, which referred to the expenses for a theater chorus undertaken as an obligatory commission by prosperous citizens. The choregos (theatre sponsor) was responsible for assembling the members of a chorus, train them, pay them a wage and costume them. The members of a tragedy chorus numbered 15, of a comedy chorus 24 and of a dithyramb chorus 50. The choregos was also responsible for a troupe of pyrrich dancers. Each time, he competed against the other choregoi for the first place. The winner could set up a choregic tripod to immortalize his name.

SMALL BUT INTERESTING MUSEUMS

The Lysikrates monument incorporated in the Monastery of the French Capuchin Monks. 18th century copper engraving.

The monument's total architectural particularities are intensified by the fact that four different building materials have been used in its construction: limestone from Piraeus, grey marble from Eleusis, marble from Hymettus and white Pentelic marble. The structure consists of a square base (ca. 3 metres long) and a tholos. The total height is over 9 metres. The base is made of a three-stepped krepidoma. Six columns stand perimetrically on it, the first examples of Corinthian order in Athens. The tholos is completed by an Ionic entablature and a conical monolithic roof. The frieze is decorated in relief with scenes from Dionysos' life. The top of the monument ends in an acanthus-shaped base where the choregic tripod was placed.
Known during the Middle Ages as "Demosthenes' Lantern" and later as "Diogenes' Lantern", the monument and its surroundings were sold in 1669 –during the Ottoman rule– to the French Capuchin monks who built a convent there. It served as a library and a guesthouse, which was visited by famous people, like Chateaubriand in 1806 and Lord Byron in 1810. During the Greek War of Independence against the Ottomans the monument was damaged. In 1845 the French state covered the expenses of the repairs, which were completed in 1892. In the beginning of the 20th century the Greek state gained the monuments' ownership by offering to France an exchange a plot in Sina Sreet where later the French Institute of Athens was built. The excavations during the period 1982-1985 as well as the earlier ones by Alexandros Filadelfeas revealed the nearby foundations of four choregic monuments. Thus, it became clear that the Street of the Tripods, a busy road in Athens leading through the Panathenaic Way to the Theatre of Dionysos, was at that section adorned with similar monuments.

THE CHURCH OF ST DEMETRIUS

The church of St Demetrius (Agios Dimitrios) is situated on Epimenidou Street,

Saint Catherine in Plaka

close to the Acropolis and near the monument of Lysikrates. It is a single-naved barrel-vaulted church, built in the 17th century. It became well known because Athanassios Diakos, a leading figure in the Greek War of Independence, was deacon here.

THE CHURCH OF ST CATHERINE

The church of St Catherine (Agia Aikaterini) is situated at the junction of Chairefontos, Lissikratous, Galanou and Goura Streets. The initial phase of the building dates back to the second quarter of the 11th century. It was originally dedicated to St Theodoros; however, in 1767 it became the metochion of the Sinaï Monastery and was re-dedicated to St Catherine.
The church was built on the site of an older, early Christian basilica and one can still see the remains of that church in the cloister: to be precise, a small part of the atrium (column and architrave) has been uncovered and preserved.
The church is of the complex tetrastyle, cross-in-square architectural type. The original façade and interior were later altered by various repairs and additions. The three semi-circular apses on the eastern side indicate the church's age. The cloisonné style used in the construction offers certain clues as to the masonry of the original building. The cross-shaped roofing of the building is significant, as is the brick pattern decoration, which can also be used to date the monument.
Once the church became the metochion of the Sinaï Monastery in the second half of the 18th century, people from Sinaï began to form a community around the church, acquiring assets and undertaking significant charitable work. Travellers who

Children's Museum

visited the church in the 19th century, and specifically in 1839, mentioned that the church was by then almost deserted and noted the existence of an icon depicting scenes from the life of Saint Catherine. In 1882 St Catherine once again became a parish church in response to public demand. Repair work and extensions also took place at this time, while the dome was last repaired in 1927. Since 1922

The Chocolate Factory in the Children's Museum

refugees from Asia Minor have kept the relics of a number of their local saints in the church.

HELLENIC CHILDREN'S MUSEUM

The Hellenic Children's Museum is housed in an early 20th-century neoclassical building at 14 Kidathineon Street, in the Plaka. The museum was founded in 1987 on the initiative of Sophia Roque-Mela, with the collaboration of a group of young experts.
The museum is a pioneering institution in that it aims to make children sensitive to and aware of the concept of the museum. The ethos of the museum is based

Exhibits from the Museum of Folk Art

on the notion that children learn most effectively through active participation and recreation.
The museum's activities are constantly evolving and cover a wide range of topics. Visiting children can act out different roles and get to learn about human activities as well as scientific concepts. They are also familiarized with the issues of recycling the protection of the environment.

The Hellenic Children's Museum organizes educational seminars for adults with regard to museum education and educational programmes for children of all ages and children with special needs.

MUSEUM OF GREEK FOLK ART

The Museum of Greek Folk Art was founded in 1918

FOLK SHADOW THEATRE (KARAGIOZIS)

Folk shadow theatre, of Asian origin, represents a particular dramatic form of expression. Greek shadow theatre is inspired by the Turkish tradition, absorbed during the period of Ottoman rule. The main character is Karagiozis, who is surrounded by caricature figures from everyday Greek life, and stars in plays inspired by Greek history and mythology, folk tales and everyday life. The figures themselves are made of leather or cardboard and are moved by the animateur behind a white screen called the "berdes". Light from behind the curtain projects the figures onto the screen.

as the Museum of Greek Handicrafts, and was originally housed in the Tzistarakis Mosque in Monastiraki Square. In 1923 it was renamed the National Museum of Decorative Arts, and in 1959 given its present name. In 1973 the collections and functions of the museum were transferred to the building at 17 Kidathinaion Street in the Plaka, where they have remained ever since.

The ground floor is dedicated to embroidery exhibits, including elaborate articles made for the matrimonial bed, using symbolic and narrative subjects. On the mezzanine is a small pottery collection from Skyros and Tsanakkale, as well as metalwork and artefacts carved in wood, such as utensils and objects of worship from all over Greece. There are also five costumes from masquerade celebrations from Nikissiani of Kavala, Kali Vrissi of Drama, Sochos of Thessaloniki, Naoussa and Skyros. Exactly opposite is a reconstruction of an entire stage, with all the popular heroes of folk shadow theatre. The first floor is largely dedicated to temporary exhibitions, while the rest of the floor houses a permanent exhibition of works by Theofilos Chatzimichail (1868–1934), an outstanding modern Greek naive painter. Among his most impressive works are murals removed from a house in Mitilini. On the second floor the visitor may admire silverwork, divided into ecclesiastical objects (crosses, chalices, cherubim, shrines and Gospel covers) and secular objects (trays, weaponry – flintlock pistols, cartridge belts, powder flasks, scimitars), as well as woman's jewellery (coronets, earrings

Traditional dresses

Agricultural equipment from the collection of the Museum of Folk Art

SMALL BUT INTERESTING MUSEUMS

and clasps).
All these objects display elaborate decorations inspired by nature as well as by Christian symbols. The third (and top) floor of the museum is dedicated to traditional costume from all over Greece. Both male and female costume is on show, festive wear – particularly for weddings – and daily costume; some is plain, some colourful and elaborately decorated.

The Museum of Greek Folk Art has also a library comprising 5,000 volumes on folk art, folklore, ethnology and museology as well as rich photographic, film and sound archives. The Conservation Laboratory for Museum Objects is staffed by specialists in the conservation of fabrics and different materials, especially wood and metal. Finally, the museum organizes educational programmes, creative workshops for children, pottery classes and shadow theatre performances. On the last Sunday of carnival, the museum mounts a festival based in Kidathinaion Street and the surrounding area: dance groups from all over Greece perform traditional carnival dances, and dances relating to fertility rites and nature worship.

The Tzistarakis Mosque (which houses the V. Kyriazopoulos Collection of Folk Pottery), the old Ottoman Baths at 8 Kirristou Street and the building at 8 Thespidos Street in the Plaka are all branches of the museum. In addition, a collection of tools relating to traditional occupations has recently been mounted at 22 Panos Street in the Plaka. This permanent exhibition has been informed by a modern approach towards the exhibition concept, and aims to familiarize visitors with the idea of work in traditional societies.

Peter Blake: "Poppy Fairy", 1981-82

THE FRISSIRAS MUSEUM

The Frissiras Museum is a modern, private museum of European and Greek painting. It was founded in 2000 in order to house the collection of its founder Vlassis Frissiras.

The museum is housed in two elegant neoclassical buildings in the Plaka in close proximity to each other that were restored to

The Frissiras Museum

their original form and were developed so that they could accommodate their new function. The building on 3 Monis Asteriou Street was constructed in 1860 and houses the permanent collection. The building on number seven of the same street was constructed in 1904; it is one of the most elegant neoclassical houses in Athens with elements of the Ionian style and houses temporary exhibitions of Greek and European painting and other cultural events.

The Frissiras collection consists of 3,000 visual art works (2,000 paintings and 1,000 drawings) by great European and Greek painters which will be shown to the public in instalments. They are works from the 20th century and their subject is human form. Among others there are works by David Hockney, Frank Auerbach, Peter Blake, Jean Rustin, Pat Andrea, Dado, Antonio Segui, Paola Rego, Vladimir Velickovic, Eduardo Arroyo, Valerio Adami, Diamantis Diamantopoulos, Giannis Moralis, Giorgos Mavroïdis, Makis Theofylaktopoulos, Chronis Botsoglou, Dikos Vizantios, John Christoforou, Nikos Baïkas, Kostas Tsoklis,

The church of Saviour of Kottakis

Nikos Kessanlis and by John Kirby, Peter Howson, Vincent Corpet, Andrea Martinelli, Clive Smith, Simon Pasieka, Giles Marrey, Matthias Schauwecker, Giorgos Lappas, Tassos Missouras, Tassos Mantzavinos, Edouardos Sakayan, Stefanos Daskalakis

and Xenofon Bistikas.
The museum also has a café and a shop. •=

THE CHURCH OF THE SAVIOUR OF KOTTAKIS

The church of the Saviour of Kottakis ("Sotira tou Kottaki") is situated between Kidathinaion and Sotiros Streets and has its festival on the day of the Transfiguration of the Saviour. The church was named after the Kottakis family, who are extensively mentioned in legal documents of the mid-18th century, but seem to have been in Athens long before then.

The original cell of the church is a domed cross-in-square that dates back to the end of

Plan of the church of Saviour of Kottakis

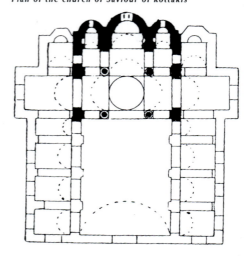

the 10th century and is, therefore, one of the earliest Byzantine churches in Athens. The large semicircular apses on the eastern side and the cross-shaped arrangement of the roof are the only remains of the original church. During the Greek War of Independence the church suffered extensive damage. Between 1827 and 1855 it functioned as the parish for the Russian community of Athens; the role was later transferred to the nearby Church of the Saviour of Lykodemos, now known as the Russian Church. During that time, as well as in 1908 and 1917, the church underwent significant repairs that altered its form.
The belfry was built in 1908.

Municipality Of Athens Folk Art And Tradition Centre

The Centre of Folk Art and Tradition of the Municipality of Athens was founded in 1980 and was housed in the residence of the great Greek folklore scholar Angeliki Hatzimichali in the Plaka, at the junction of Hatzimichali and Geronta Streets. The house, which was designed in 1924 by the architect Aristotelis Zachos, incorporates traditional and modern stylistic elements. The interior woodcut decoration was designed by Hatzimichali herself. Items from the scholar's collections are displayed thematically throughout the house, according to the function of each room.
The centre also boasts a rich folklore library, with ethnographic material and documents from Greece and the Balkans, which reflects its aim to preserve and promote the folklore cultural heritage.

The Jewish Museum

ANGELIKI HATZIMICHALI

Angeliki Hatzimichali was born in Athens in 1895. Her father, Alexios Kolivas, came from Zante. Editor of the newspaper "Proïa" and collector of Byzantine icons, he bequeathed to his daughter an interest in folklore traditions. At a time when the Athens bourgeoisie was greatly influenced by western European culture, Hatzimichali turned her attention from a very early age to the collection and study of everyday objects of folklore traditions (woodcuts, embroideries, ceramics, etc.). She was one of the most prominent members of the "Lyceum Club of Greek Women" and she founded a branch of the Lyceum in Smyrna in 1920. She travelled all over Greece and wrote numerous studies on folklore traditions, among which was her very important three-volume book on the Sarakatsanoi, a semi-nomadic people of northern Greece. She also founded numerous organisations for the promotion of folklore culture, most importantly the Association of Greek Handicraft, forerunner of the Hellenic Organisation of Small and Medium Sized Enterprises and Handicraft. She also took an active part in the revival of the Delphic Celebrations, organized by Angelos and Eva Sikelianos. She contributed to the relief and the social rehabilitation of the Greek refugees of 1922 and actively participated in the Resistance against German rule during World War II. Angeliki Hatzimichali died in 1966.

Objects from a concentration camp

JEWISH MUSEUM OF GREECE

The Jewish Museum of Greece is one of the most important of its kind across Europe. It was founded in 1977 with the initiative of the Jewish community of Athens. Its aim is to preserve, study and promote objects and documents related to the Jewish presence in Greece for the past 2,300 years.
Since 1998 the museum has been housed in its own building, a Neoclassical house of 800 square metres on 39 Nikis Street. The museum's collection consists of more than 7,000 original objects, photographs, documents and records organized in different unities, on separate levels around a central octagonal space. On the ground-floor there is the interior of the Jewish Synagogue in Patras that was transferred from there to the museum. On the first level the theme of the displays concerns the various Jewish celebrations. The collection includes various religious artifacts and traditional sugar sweets, as well as and the special tray of the Jewish Passover.
On the second level there are items of historic evidence (documents, inscriptions and books) concerning the Jewish presence in Greece from the 3rd century B.C. until the 19th century. Military uniforms, medals, photographs and publications testify to the active participation of the Jews in the Greek War of Independence and the Resistance. The following category of the displays concerns the Holocaust and the destruction of the vast majority of the Greek Jews by the Nazis. Uniforms and clothes of the prisoners in the concentration camps, photographs, documents and other objects are evidence of one of the most horrible atrocities in modern history.
In the following category there are traditional costumes and articles of clothing such as jewels, brooches, hats and shoes

Wedding dresses

covering the period from the mid-18th century until the mid-20th century, highlighting aspects of the everyday life of Jewish communities in the past. In the last level there are many religious and domestic artifacts related to important events in the course of life, clothes, embroideries, tools and household items, charms and other objects related to circumcision, religious coming-of-age, marriage and death. Apart from its permanent displays the museum organizes temporary exhibitions and various events, it has a library, a video-room, a space where educational programmes take place, and a shop.

THE ANGLICAN CHURCH

The Anglican Church is situated between Filellinon Street and Amalias Avenue and is dedicated to Saint Paul. The church was built in 1838 for the small Anglican community in Athens, who also raised the necessary funds; Henry Palmerston, the then Prime Minister of Britain, also made a donation. The inauguration of the church took place in 1843. The architect Charles Cockerell drew up the initial plans, but in 1838, before construction had begun, Christian Hansen pushed forward new designs. The resulting church is a Victorian, neo-gothic building. It is a basilica with shorter aisles on the sides that are covered by gothic apses. The walls of the church and the architrave were made of marble from Mount Hymettus, while Corinthian stone was used for the sculpted frames of the main door and windows. Only the windows and the flutes of the arches have external painted decorations. Inscriptions on the windows, walls and furniture commemorate a number of leading figures from the Anglican community, such as Richard Church, who took part in the Greek War of Independence and later became a member of the Greek Parliament. Ever since its foundation the church has been an important focus point for the English-speaking community of Athens.

THE RUSSIAN CHURCH

The church of the Saviour ("Sotira") of Lykodemos, also known as the Russian church, is situated at the junction of Filellinon Street and Amalias Avenue in the centre of Athens.

The Anglican Church

One of the most important Byzantine monuments of the 11th century, from the 19th century the church was dedicated to the Holy Trinity ("Agia Triada") and is the parish church of the Russian community in Athens. The name Sotira of Lykodemos is related to the initial dedication of the church to the Transfiguration of the Saviour and a certain donor, although there seem to have been a few variations on this name. From the variations "Sotira of Lykodemos" or "Sotira of Nikodemos" we accept the first, as it is the one that has been transmitted to our days by oral tradition. It is generally known as the Russian church because it is the focus of the Orthodox Russian community. This Byzantine church was built a little before 1031 within the perimeter of the city's defensive wall. There are two inscriptions on the church's northern wall that indicate the date when the church was built: the first one mentions the year 1031, while the second one informs us that Stephanos, the major donor, died in 1044. Archaeological research in the 19th century proved that the church was built on the site of an Early Christian basilica,

ANTONIN KAPUSTIN AND THE BYZANTINE MONUMENTS OF ATHENS

The Russian clergyman Antonin Kapustin (1817–1894) was one of the first to study Athens' Byzantine monuments. A theologian and professor of the Theological Academy in Kiev, in 1850 he became the vicar of the Russian Church in Athens. In this capacity, and with his knowledge and charisma, he supervised the excavation of the Roman baths underneath the church and the restoration of the church. Putting aside any criticism of the modification of the church's original form, one must admit that the restoration of a Byzantine church was unique at that time, when many other Byzantine monuments were left in ruin either because ancient monuments were given preference or because of extremely poor town planning. The results of Kapustin's archaeological research were published in the "Archaeological Journal" and later in a monograph in Russian. In 1874 the Russian Academy of Science published his work "Early Christian Inscriptions in Athens", the first systematic listing of Byzantine inscriptions in Athens, which is still used by experts today. Kapustin also published a list with numerous documents from the metochion of the Holy Sepulcre in Athens.

Drawing restoration of the Baptism

SMALL BUT INTERESTING MUSEUMS

LUDWIG THIERSCH AND 19TH-CENTURY GREEK PAINTING

The German painter Ludwig Thiersch (1825-1909) taught art at the School of Arts in Athens. His presence influenced art in Greece with the spread of the Nazarene style, which used subjects from the life of Christ and was influenced by the work of the famous Renaissance painter, Raphael. Thiersch's decorative work in the Russian Church in Athens (he was assisted by Spiridon Hatzigiannopoulos and Nikiforos Litras) was crucial in the development of the Greek art; it established a new style of religious painting that imitated western pictorial traditions.

which in its turn had been built over a Roman bath.
In comparison with other Byzantine monuments in Athens, the church is expansive. Even today, despite the fact that it is surrounded by much larger buildings, it still dominates the area in terms of size and quality of construction. In form a domed octagon, internally the large dome with its low drum unifies the space, and the same unified sense of grandeur is evident externally. The sense of heaviness and power created by its volumes and low roof is counteracted by the vertical motion of the tall, three-sided, narrow apses and the portals on the sides. The masonry follows a well-crafted cloisonné style. The rich brick patterns (pseudo-kufic letters and dentils) with the alternative use of bricks and stones give the exterior its sculpted look. The kufic patterns are embedded into the walls, inserted in small ceramic plates, and form a frieze across the northern and eastern walls. Some original painted decoration remains on the southern wall, where one can still see the mural paintings of Christ, St Stephen and St John the Apostle.
The katholikon of a monastery during the Byzantine period and

The Russian Church

the period of Ottoman rule, the church suffered damage from natural disasters, wars and the lack of respect on behalf of various invaders. In addition to the destruction of 1687, with the invasion of Francesco Morosini, the church was damaged by an earthquake in 1701. In 1780, when Ali Haseki was rebuilding the defensive wall, all the additional monastery buildings were demolished. It was then that the church became the metochion of the monastery of Kaissariani. The church was further damaged in 1827 with shells dropped from the Acropolis soon after the Greek War of Independence.

The half-ruined church was purchased by the Russian Government in 1847 as the parish of the Russian community of Athens. It was then that the side tribunes and the heavy belfry were added and the interior decorated. The post-Byzantine mural paintings were replaced by paintings by the German artist Ludwig Thiersch, while the low marble Byzantine screen, which was illustrated by various travéllers, was replaced by a tall Russian screen. While these alterations naturally reflect 19th-century Russian taste in art, they destroyed the church's essential Byzantine character. The work was supervised by the Greek engineer, Major Tilemachos Vlassopoulos, and the leader of the Russian community, Dean Antonin Kapustin. ●▪

THE ORTHODOX RUSSIAN COMMUNITY OF ATHENS

The interest of the Russian Tsar Nicolas I in Greek affairs had been evident during the Greek War of Independence and the early years of the Greek State (1830). The Russian Embassy in Athens regarded the Russian Church as a focal point: the church was purchased by the Russian Government and repaired with funds from the Russian community. Those in charge of the church were people of great social status and education, leading figures in the Russian community. Their many charitable activities included the funding of the Greek clergy and the restoration of numerous churches and monasteries all over Greece. Clearly those activities reflected and served the purposes of the Russian Government in regard to the religious and political affairs of the young Greek State. The Russian-born Queen Olga, in particular, contributed significantly to the development of the Russian community in Athens and the establishment of the Russian church as a cultural centre that influenced religious music, painting and craftsmanship (liturgical vestments).

The Tsar Nicolas I

4

WALK 4

1. Sintagma Square
2. The Hotel Grande Bretagne
3. The House of Parliament
4. The Ministry of Foreign Affairs
5. The Nikos Hadjikyriakos Ghikas Gallery
6. Buildings on Vassilissis Sofias Av.
7. The Sarogleion Mansion
8. The Benaki Museum
9. The Museum of Cycladic Art
10. Kolonaki Square
11. Art Deco Buildings in Kolonaki
12. St Dionysius on Skoufa Street
13. Dexameni
14. The Lycabettus Hill

4 VIEW OVER ATHENS – VIEW OVER GREECE

The visitor to Athens cannot leave the city without seeing the exhibits at the Benaki Museum. Having as its central core collections of 18th- and 19th-century objects, the museum includes exhibits from Antiquity and the Byzantine period. Not far away is another important museum, the Museum of Cycladic Art, with its unique Cycladic figurines. As a place to relax and rest, Kolonaki Square is ideal. In the evening, the view over Athens from Lycabettus Hill is magnificent.

SINTAGMA SQUARE

One could define Sintagma (Constitution) Square as the political centre of Athens and, indeed, of Greece. It is surrounded by Amalias Avenue and Vassileos Georgiou I, Stadiou and Othonos Streets. There are numerous hotels and public buildings around the square, and Parliament Square with the Monument for the Unknown Soldier and the Greek Parliament is close by. Sintagma Square is also the starting point of the city's commercial district, focused on Stadiou Street and, mainly, Ermou Street.

The square was developed during the early years of the Greek State. The Bavarian Lieutenant Hoch, who worked with the architect Leo von Klenze, was in charge of the project. The area was initially called "Palace Square" because of its proximity to King Otto's palace, which later became the Houses of Parliament. It was divided into two parts: to the east, where Parliament Square is today, and to the west, today's Sintagma Square. With the trees that were gradually planted the square became a favourite recreational spot for Athenians. From the mid-19th century the largest and most prestigious hotels were also built here, among which today the "Grande Bretagne" is the best known.

On 3 September 1843

Sintagma Square before the latest reshaping

the square was the location of a demonstration – the first among the many that have followed since then – at which crowds demanded that King Otto grant a constitution: Otto was forced to concede. This is why the western and largest part of the square was then named "Sintagma Square" (Constitution Square), while the smaller part maintained the name "Palace Square". The fact reflected symbolically the monarchy's political defeat in the constitution issue.
By the last quarter of the 19th century the square had become a high-class district with impressive private residences for the city's most prominent families. This changed during the 20th century, when the private homes were gradually replaced by public and commercial buildings, which still dominate the area to this day.
The square underwent numerous (perhaps too many) alterations, to adapt to everyday life in the capital. The latest alteration took place just before the 2004 Olympic Games. Today the square is at the centre of the capital's political and social activities. Political parties hold pre-election gatherings and demonstrations take place here; the city's major celebrations also are organised in Sintagma Square, such as that on New Year's Eve.
During the construction of the metro station excavations uncovered a plethora of archaeological finds: a road that led to the Mesogeia area, a part of the Peisistratian aquaduct (6th century BC), a large cemetery used from the late-

Showcases with archaeological finds in the Metro Station "Sintagma"

VIEW OVER ATHENS – VIEW OVER GREECE

The Hotel "Grande Bretagne"

Mycenaean until the late Roman period (1100 BC-300), pottery workshops and a complex of Roman baths.

THE HOTEL GRANDE BRETAGNE

The Hotel Grande Bretagne stands on the corner of Panepistimiou and Vassileos Georgiou I Streets and is one of Athens' oldest and most glamorous hotels.
Founded in 1866 by Savvas Kentros, the hotel was originally located in the Giannopoulos Mansion on the corner of Stadiou and Mousson Streets. When the Dimitriou Mansion, used by the French Archaeological School, was left empty in 1873, the Hotel Grande Bretagne transferred there, and has stayed there ever since. The Dimitriou Mansion was built between 1842 and 1843, to plans by Theophilus Hansen. Strongly influenced by classicism, its arched arcades on the ground and first floors and the mythological motifs in the banisters, connecting Antiquity with modern times, were typical of the building. The mansion first functioned as the residence of Ant. Dimitriou, or

SINTAGMA METRO STATION

The Sintagma Square metro station is the largest and most impressive in the entire new underground network. The main part of the station is dominated by an imaginative clock by the sculptor Theodoros. At the exit of the Ethniki Amina-Monastiraki line there is also a piece by the artist Giorgos Zongolopoulos. There are special cases for the display of the archaeological finds uncovered during the station's construction. One can see on display an important mosaic from a Roman house, as well as vases (mostly copies) found here. The large case that covers the entire western wall of the mezzanine is used to display a stratigraphic representation. The escalators lead up to a large room that is used as a space for temporary exhibitions and events.

WALK 4

THE MONUMENT TO THE UNKNOWN SOLDIER

The Monument to the Unknown Soldier is in front of the Houses of Parliament, on Amalias Avenue. Its central part, created by the sculptor Fokion Rok, depicts a dead soldier, naked, carrying only his armour, like an ancient soldier. This image was inspired by a sculpture on the pediment of the ancient temple of Aphaia in Aigina. Engraved around the soldier on the monument are writings from Pericles' Funeral Oration as it was transmitted by Thucydides. On the two sides of the monument there are copper plates listing all the military events in which Greece has taken part from the Greek War of Independence of 1821 until today. The monument was made in 1929/30, designed by the architect Emmanouil Lazaridis. It is actually a cenotaph, which, in the tradition adopted by numerous countries, commemorates all the fallen soldiers of war. The monument's style is intended to unify it with the neoclassical style and the significance of the Houses of Parliament. Furthermore, it gives the impression of a "timeless" monument, as if it were always there to remind the passer-by of Greece's glory.

The monument is guarded on a 24-hour basis by the Presidential Guard. The soldiers of the guard are called "evzonoi", who are clad in traditional 19th-century costume from southern Greece and most characteristically they wear a skirt called foustanela. There is an hourly change of guard, while on Sundays at 11 a.m. an official change of guard accompanied by military music takes place, attracting large numbers of tourists.

On Greece's national holidays of 28 October and 25 March a grandstand is placed in front of the monument for statesmen attending the parades. The monument is in general a busy tourist attraction favoured by Athenians, especially those with small children, who gather to watch the change of guard and to feed the pigeons. The space between the Monument to the Unknown Soldier and Amalias Avenue is officially called "Parliament Square", although people refer to it as the "Unknown Soldier", or simply "o agnostos" (the Unknown). Excavation during the construction of the metro station there uncovered the bed of the River Eridanos, which used to flow down from Lycabettus Hill, and also a complex of Roman baths, a bronze sculpture workshop and numerous tombs.

Limnios, a wealthy merchant living in Trieste. Between 1852 and 1856 it accommodated the guests of the royal palace and then it was leased by the French Archaeological School. In 1873 the building was bought by Stathis Lampsas and Savvas Kentros, who converted it into a luxurious hotel. It was in the Hotel Grande Bretagne that the International Olympic Committee met in 1896, the year the first modern Olympic Games were held, and it became a favourite place to stay for eminent visitors to Greece. During World War II it became the headquarters of the Greek, German and English armed forces successively. In December 1944 almost all the building was blown up during the so-called Dekemvriana, the armed conflict between the leftist Greek People's Liberating Army (ELAS) on the one hand and the Greek police and British forces on the other. In 1957 Theophilus Hansen's original building was demolished, only to be built again (according to designs by E. Vogt, realized by K. Voutsinas). The new building was taller and larger than the original, but attempts to preserve Hansen's neoclassical features failed. The last restoration was completed in 2003, when the hotel took on its current appearance.

THE HOUSE OF PARLIAMENT

The Greek Parliament building dominates the eastern side of Sintagma Square, between Amalias and Vassilissis Sofias Avenues. It was built soon after the creation of the modern Greek State as a palace for King Otto and it has housed the Greek Parliament since 1935.
The location was selected by the King Ludwig of Bavaria, Otto's father, who also lent his son money for the construction. Repayments on the loan continued even after Otto's death and were only finally paid off to Germany after the Berlin Treaty in 1878!
Building began in 1836 and work was completed in 1842; the architect in charge was Friedrich von Gaertner from Bavaria. The palace was built on the Boubounistra hill, at the site of a former church, dedicated to St Athanassios. The palace was the first monumental work in modern Athens and reintroduced the Classicist style in the city's architecture. Externally the building appears to be simple and strong with an emphasis on the horizontal lines. On the western side there is a Doric propylon made of marble from Mount Penteli. Inside, were

The Meeting Hall in the Parliament House

wall and ceiling paintings inspired by Classical, Roman and Renaissance Art. However, a great fire in 1909 destroyed the interior almost entirely. The royal family then moved to the New Palace, in what is today the Presidential Mansion. In 1924 the damaged palace was used to house the refugees from the population exchange between Greece and Turkey. Twenty years after the fire of 1909 it was decided that the Parliament and Senate should be housed in the building, so restoration work began in 1930, with Andreas Kiriazis as the architect in charge. The entire damaged central part of the building was demolished and the Parliament and Senate Assembly rooms were built. Today, apart from the meeting rooms, are the Prime Minister's and the political parties' offices and the Parliament Library. Outside the building on Amalias Avenue one can see the marble statues of Eleftherios Venizelos and Charilaos Trikoupis, two great politicians of modern Greek history. Recent excavations for the opening up of the metro and the development of parking spaces uncovered interesting archaeological finds: 145 graves dating from the Mycenaean to the Roman period, a Classical building with a black and white mosaic, a Roman workshop for the manufacture of lamps, two Hermean pillars depicting the satirical poet Eupolis and the philosopher Chrysippos, as well as a large Byzantine building complex.

THE MINISTRY OF FOREIGN AFFAIRS

The main building of the Ministry of Foreign Affairs is situated at 5 Vassilissis Sofias Avenue, at the junction with Zalokosta Street. Since 1976 it has been designated a listed building. It is also known as the Andreas Singros Mansion because for many years it was the residence of the Greek businessman of the diaspora and national benefactor, Andreas Singros. Designed by the architect Ernst Ziller, the Singros Mansion was built between 1872 and 1873. The military engineer Nikolaos Soutzos supervised the construction. According to written sources, which are available only from 1900 onwards, the mansion was a rather

The Parliament House

VIEW OVER ATHENS – VIEW OVER GREECE

The Ministry of Foreign Affairs

small, two-storey building with an attic, the only decoration being the Ionic doorposts. This original part has been preserved as the core of the present building, which has been extended east and west, making a building of five parts. Ifigeneia Mavrokordatou-Singrou, Andreas's wife, bequeathed the building to the Ministry of Foreign Affairs in 1921, on condition that it give a permanent home to the Ministry. When the Ministry was transferred here, the building was radically altered in order to achieve a classicist form: a porch with pediment was for instance added to the façade.
In 1985 the Singros Mansion was internally connected to the new building of the Ministry of Foreign Affairs at 2 Zalokosta Street.

THE NIKOS HADJIKYRIAKOS-GHIKAS GALLERY

In the Nikos Hadjikyriakos-Ghikas Gallery visitors can explore the great painter's

Andreas Singros

background. Born in Athens in 1906 to a noble family from Hydra, he became a leading figure in modern Greek art. His work was influenced by cubism, but he developed a personal, post-cubic, sensitive and lyrical style. He was a recognized and successful artist both in Greece and abroad, and from the 1930s a professor at Athens Technical University (School of Architecture), and a member of the Academy of Athens and the Royal Academy of Arts in London. His works can be admired in the most important museums and private collections all over the world.
By donating his house and collection to the Benaki Museum, Nikos Hadjikyriakos-Ghikas ensured that the public would have the opportunity to know and admire his work. The gallery opened in 1991, three years prior to his death, and was designed by the artist himself. It is situated in the heart of Athens, in a fourth-floor apartment on Kriezotou Street, where the painter spent forty years. The building, which was privately owned by the painter, was built in 1932 by the architect Konstantinos Kitsikis, and is typical of Athenian architecture between the two world wars. The top floor was added under the personal supervision of the artist, who

WALK 4

N. Hadjikyriakos-Ghikas: "Composition with rhythmic objects"

artist's photographic material and art books. Temporary exhibitions are also mounted in the gallery, highlighting different aspects of the artist's work.

BUILDINGS ON VASSILISSIS SOFIAS AVENUE

used it as an atelier and library. All the rooms have been preserved exactly as he arranged and decorated them. The permanent exhibition includes works that represent the various styles he experimented with, and, most importantly, the oil paintings he created between 1930 and 1990. Watercolour paintings, drawings and models for theatrical sets and costumes, books and manuscripts add to the collection. Ghikas also worked as a sculptor, particularly in the years 1940–70. His small copper sculptures, inspired by Greek mythology, are also on display here. Other important parts of the gallery's collection are the

Vassilissis Sofias Avenue begins at Sintagma Square and leads to the northern and eastern suburbs of Athens. Apart from its importance for the traffic, it is one of the city's most elegant and busy streets. The avenue is easily accessible via the many available means of transport; there are also two

N. Hadjikyriakos-Ghikas: "Athenian Houses"

VIEW OVER ATHENS – VIEW OVER GREECE

The French Embassy

of the Arab Bank. A bit further on towards Evangelismos Hospital, on the left, at the junction with Sekeri Street, one can see the Italian Embassy. The building was designed at the end of the 19th century by the architect Ernst Ziller and it used to be the residence of Prince Nikolaos (son of the King Constantine I and Queen Sofia). Later on it became a branch of the Grande Bretagne Hotel. The underground stations on it ("Evangelismos" and "Concert Hall"). The road was planned in 1839, however, due to various city planning problems, its opening up began in 1870. Visitors walking along Vassilissis Sofias Avenue can actually experience a "live" museum of the capital with numerous samples of the city's neoclassical and modern architecture. Starting from Sintagma on the left one can see the neoclassical building that houses the Ministry of Foreign Affairs and the building of the Egyptian Embassy. At the junction with Akadimias Street on the left is the French Embassy, a building designed by the architect Anastassios Metaxas. Further on, at the junction with Merlin Street one comes across the neoclassical building

The Rodokanakis' house. 61 Vassilisis Sofias Avenue

Vassilisis Sofias Avenue

Charokopos Mansion, which today houses the Benaki Museum, is a bit further away. The Embassy of Luxembourg is situated on 23 Vassilissis Sofias Avenue at the junction with Neofitou Vamva Street; it is housed in a modern building covered largely by glass surfaces. Further on, at the junction with Neofitou Douka Street, one can see the Kalligas building, the so-called "white apartment block", an impressive sample of a modern architectural style with selective use of classical elements, typical of the 1950s. It was designed by the architect K. Kapsambelis who was a leading figure in the urban architecture of Athens at that time. On 4 Neofitou Douka Street one can visit the Museum of Cycladic Art, a post-modern building, constructed in the 1980s, while at the junction with Irodotou Street there is another work by Ernst Ziller, the elegant and luxurious Stathatos Mansion. On the opposite side of the street there is a neoclassical building (Sarogleion) that houses the Military Officers' Club. The British Embassy is situated at the junction with Ploutarchou and Ipsilantou Streets, very close to Vassilissis Sofias Avenue, towards the Evangelismos Hospital; it was built in the 1960s, designed by Eric Bedford, Chief Architect of the British Ministry of Public Building and Works, in cooperation with the Greek architects I. Antoniadis and E. Vassiliadis. It has been built mostly of cement and glass with use of marble on the ground-floor. On 55 and 57 Vassilissis Sofias Avenue, near the "Megalis tou Genous Scholis" (Great School of the Nation) Square, opposite the glass sculpture of the "Dromeas" (Runner) and the Hilton Hotel there are two elegant apartment blocks. The two buildings incorporate Central European architectural elements with many influences from Jugendstil. They were built around 1928; however, we do not know who the architect was. After the Hilton Hotel, on the left side of Vassilissis Sofias Avenue one can see the monumental buildings of the U.S. Embassy and the Athens Concert Hall, while the other side is dominated by the neoclassical building complexes of the Aretaieio and the Ippokrateio hospitals. On 86 Vassilissis Sofias Avenue, between the two hospitals and almost opposite the U.S. Embassy there is a modern block of apartments designed after World War II by the pioneer architect Nikos Valsamakis. It is a building with emphasised horizontal lines, visible materials, forms and colours. Very close to that building, at the junction with Lampsakou Street, one can see the Antonopoulou-Kontoleontos block of apartments, one of the most characteristic examples of pre-war modernism. It was built in the early 1930s with a plain form and strong vertical lines which is apparent in the staircase openings.

SAROGLEION MANSION

At the junction of Vassilissis Sofias Avenue and Rigillis and Mourouzi Streets is Pavlou Mela (Rigillis) Square. On the south side of the square is the Saroglleion Mansion, home to the Military Officers' Club. This is a grand, two-storey, V-shaped building, designed in 1924 by the architect Alexandros Nikoloudis, the main representative of the Beaux Arts School in Athens. The building was completed in 1932 thanks to a bequest from the officer Petros Saroglou, who wanted the building to accommodate the officers of Athens' military guard.

THE BENAKI MUSEUM

The Benaki Museum was founded at the home of Emmanouil Benakis after his death in 1929. It was bequeathed to the Greek nation by his heirs to house the collection of his son, Antonis Benakis. It opened to the public in 1931.

The Saroglleion Mansion

WALK 4

THE BUILDING

The neoclassical building between Vassilissis Sofias Av. and Koumbari Street was built in 1867–68 for the merchant Ioannis Peroglou, and in 1895 was purchased by the businessman Panagis Charokopos. It was remodelled by the architect Anastassios Metaxas who designed and supervised all the alterations, which were complete by 1931. The Charokopos Mansion, as it was also known, was purchased by Emmanouil Benakis in 1910 and was redesigned so as to accommodate his social needs and those of his family. These alterations gave the building a grand entrance and a luxurious interior. In 1929-1931 the mansion was extended to the west and was redesigned again, as a museum. In 1988 construction began for the museum's new wing, which opened in 1997. Designed by Alekos and Stefanos Kalligas, this additional wing was needed to enable the wealth of the museum's collections to be displayed and its numerous activities to find a home, so that it could became a complete cultural institution. The extension also houses a library, rooms for temporary exhibitions and events and a marvellous coffee-shop. After Antonis Benakis's death, and particularly, after 1974, the initial collections, which included works of Ancient, Byzantine, Post-Byzantine, Islamic and Folk Art, were supplemented by new material. Today, the museum's collections include the Historical and Photographic Archives, the Neo-Hellenic Architecture Archives, the Department of Childhood, Toys and Games, as well as numerous works of modern and modernist Greek art. The Benaki Museum also incorporates the Museum of Islamic Art in Kerameikos, the Nikos Hadjikyriakos-Ghikas Gallery in Kolonaki and the new exhibition building near the old Gas factory (Gazi) on Piraios Street.

Gold cup

ANTIQUITIES COLLECTION

In room 1 of the museum one can see Paleolithic and Neolithic finds from various areas of Greece and Cyprus, mostly axes, figurines and

The Benaki Museum

ceramics with inscribed decorations. In room 2 are items from the Cycladic, Minoan and Mycenaean civilizations and excellent examples of pottery and metalwork from the Geometric and the Orientalising periods. Among these are two very important and rare golden cups and a silver cup from the early Helladic period, known as the Treasure of Euboea. Other noteworthy pieces are a large Attic Geometric urn and a golden crown from the Orientalising era from Kos, decorated with images of sphinxes. In the next room objects from the Archaic period are displayed, with ceramics from workshops of Attica, Boeotia and Corinth, jewels from northern Greece and Ionia (mostly ornate brooches) and sculptures from Cyprus, Naxos and Attica.
In rooms 4, 5 and 6, around the museum's main columned area, are items from the Classical period. These include red-figure pottery from the 5th century BC, white lecythi, copper helmets from Thrace and Corinth together with other weaponry items, an excellent inscribed figurine of Hercules from Boeotia, sculptures from the 5th and 4th centuries BC and Roman copies of works from the same period. There are also finds from tombs, among which one can see terracotta figurines from Attica, Boeotia and Alexandria, copper mirrors, golden jewellery and wreaths as well as marble funerary monuments.

Head of Athena

In room 7 one can see works from the Hellenistic and Roman periods. The exhibits point to the wealth and luxury of those times, with the best example being the so called Treasure of Thessalia, a group of valuable golden jewellery, much of which is decorated with semi-precious stones. There is also a uniquely crafted hair net with the bust of the goddess Athena. Among the rest of the items on display one can see Attic red-figure pottery, metal vessels from Macedonia and Asia Minor, votive and funerary reliefs, Roman copper figurines, as well as glass and ceramic vases from the same period.
The contents of room 8 form a bridge between the Ancient and the Byzantine worlds, as they include works from late Antiquity, such as a small golden statue of Venus, a marble head of Paris from Crete, jewels and small ivory ornaments, Roman portraits, and bas-reliefs from Syria and Phrygia.

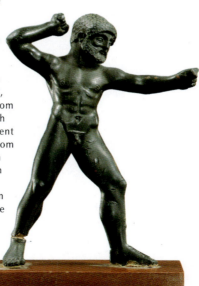

Statuette of Herakles

BYZANTINE COLLECTION

The Benaki Museum's Byzantine collection documents the development of art in the Byzantine Empire during its thousand-year history. In room 9 there are numerous items, mostly from domestic houses, which cast light on everyday life during late Antiquity (4th–7th centuries). There is a large number of particularly interesting terracotta and copper lamps, silver plates with decorations inspired by the Greco-Roman tradition, ceramic plates and ecclesiastical artefacts (incence-holders and chalices). From the same period there are also examples of the art of the first Egyptian Christians, the Copts. The Coptic collection includes silk and linen fabrics, which are influenced by the artistic preferences of the great cultural centres

Bronze lamp

THE BENAKI FAMILY

The Benaki family was one of the most prominent families in the Peloponnese before the Greek War of Independence. They held on to their wealth and status after the war and contributed greatly to the cultural and political life of Greece. Emmanouil Benakis was born in Syros in 1843 and became a cotton merchant in Alexandria. He went into politics in 1910, became a member of the Greek Parliament and later a minister, and Mayor of Athens. He was a supporter of Venizelos. Later he was imprisoned and exiled for his political beliefs; he died in 1929. He and his wife, Virginia Choremi, had five children, two of whom, Antonis and Penelopi, played a significant part in the cultural life of the country. Antonis Benakis was born in Alexandria in 1873 and came to live in Athens in 1926. From a young age he was interested in collecting. He was in friendly relationship with eminent scholars of his time whom he consulted to develop his collections. He founded the museum in 1929, naming it after his family, and ran it until his death in 1954.

His sister Penelopi was one of the greatest Greek writers, writing mostly children's books on patriotic-national themes. She was married to the businessman Stefanos Deltas. Among her best-known works are the "Story Without a Name", "The Secrets of the Swamp" and "Mad Antonis" (inspired by her brother Antonis Benakis). On the day the Germans invaded Athens in the spring of 1941, Penelopi Delta took her own life, unable to endure national humiliation.

Emmanouil Benakis

of that era, as well as items of metalwork and wooden sculptures that testify to Egypt's great economic growth, mostly during the 5th and 6th centuries.
The mid-Byzantine era (8th–12th centuries) is represented in room 10 by a limited number of significant samples of painting

Saint George

(mosaics taken from Italy and even Constantinople, manuscripts, and small bas-reliefs made of steatite and ivory) and metalwork, such as numerous cross-reliquaries and amulets and glazed pottery from Constantinople, Cyprus and Thessalonica.
In rooms 11 and 12 visitors can admire certain excellent examples of late-Byzantine painting (1204–1453) and famous post-Byzantine icons, many of which are signed by, or attributed to, great painters of the time (Angelos Akotantos, Nikolaos or Andreas Ritzos, Emmanouil Lombardos, Domenikos Theotokopoulos).
A particular mention should be made to the Byzantine jewellery from all periods in which one can see stylistic and thematic influences from the Greek-Roman jewel-making traditions, as well as the coins, which offer valuable information about the history and culture of Byzantium.

MODERN TIMES COLLECTION

The Benaki Museum's collections of religious and secular art from the 15th to the 19th centuries reveals Greek material culture during Ottoman rule.
The collections of secular art in rooms 13–24 include decorative objects and items of practical use from mainland Greece and the islands, Cyprus and Asia Minor. The rooms with the woodcut and painted internal decorations from houses of Kozani from the mid-18th century (rooms 17,19) and Hydra from the 19th century (room 24) are particularly interesting. Other important parts of the collection are the wooden painted and sculpted items, ceramics with rare decorations, metalwork, textiles and embroideries, as well as the ornate traditional costumes from various areas. There is also a very important collection of jewellery with familiar motifs, such as three-masted ships and

Abstract from the Gospels on parchment

stone sculptures from the islands. In rooms 25-28 religious artefacts of the post-Byzantine era are on display, from areas in Greece and Greek communities of the diaspora, mainly from the Black Sea, Asia Minor and Thrace. These collections have been brought by the refugees who came to Greece during the exchange of populations between Greece and Turkey. Among these items, of especial note are the woodcut screens (room 27) and epitaphs, liturgical clothes depicting the Lament and used during Good Friday services (rooms 25, 26). Rooms 29-32 show musical instruments, books, weapons, offerings and tools which portray aspects of everyday life before the Greek War of Independence of 1821. Among them there are the books of the Patriarch of Jerusalem, Chrissanthos Notaras, as well as a domestic distillation flask.
Rooms 33-36 offer relics from the Greek War of Independence of 1821 and from the foundation and expansion of the Greek State during the years of Kapodistrias, King Otto, King George I and Venizelos. Apart from weapons, emblems and depictions of the War of Independence, the collection also includes personal belongings, documents, maps and clothing of the 19th-century royal court.

Of particular historical and emotional value are the manuscripts of great Greek literary figures and the Nobel prizes of the poets Giorgos Seferis and Odysseas Elytis.
Additionally, along the corridors and the staircase the visitor can admire paintings, drawings and lithographs depicting Greece and especially Athens, those being only a few of the museum's total of almost 6,000 paintings and engravings.

Embroidered bridal pillow

OTHER ACTIVITIES

In 15 Filikis Etaireias (Kolonaki) Square, not far from the museum's main building, are the museum's Photographic Archives, founded in 1973. These include around

View of Athens from the Ilissos. Aquarelle of John Michael Wittmer, 1833

Silver fibula from a belt

300,000 negatives and 25,000 original photographs, a study area, a conservation lab and a dark room. Among the collections are the archives of Konstantinos and Petros Moraïtis, Nelly's, Voula Papaioannou, Dimitris Charissiadis and others.

The Neo-Hellenic Architecture Archives are stored on 4 Valaoritou Street; they include the archives of important Greek architects, such as Ioannis Despotopoulos, Solon Kidoniatis, Dimitris Pikionis and so on. From 1994 the Benaki Museum's Historical Archives have been housed in the Stefanos and Penelopi Delta Residence in Kifissia. They include material donated by private organizations and individuals, and are considered to be one of the best organized and most important sources for the study of modern Greek history, with collections that begin just before the 1821 Greek War of Independence up to World War II. They include the collections of Eleftherios Venizelos, Georgios Karaiskakis and Anastassis and Andreas Lontos, the archives of the Resistance during World War II, as well as those of Greek composers (Nikolaos Mantzaros, Nikolaos Skalkotas, Giannis Papaioannou), poets and writers (Dionissios Solomos, Konstantinos Kavafis (Cavafy), Grigorios Xenopoulos, Angelos Sikelianos).

MUSEUM OF CYCLADIC ART

The Museum of Cycladic Art is one of the most modern and important museums of Prehistoric and Ancient Greek art. It was founded in 1986 to host the collection of Cycladic and Ancient Greek art belonging to Nikolaos and Dolly Goulandri. The permanent collection is exhibited in the modern building on Neofitou Douka Street, designed by the architect Ioannis Vikelas. In 1991 the museum acquired a new extension, the neoclassical Stathatos Mansion, at the junction of Vasilissis Sofias Av. and Irodotou Street. The Stathatos Mansion is one of the finest specimens of neoclassical architecture in Athens. The home of the Stathatos family, it was designed by Ernst Ziller and built in 1895. It has now been restored to its original state and offers the visitor a representative picture of a 19th-century bourgeois house. As an annex to the museum it has its own magnificent entrance, but is internally connected to the new building through a specially designed corridor. In the new wing are mounted high calibre temporary exhibitions while the ground floor

Museum of Cycladic Art

is dedicated to the display of the Academy of Athens' collection of ancient Greek art.

In the main building the collections are displayed over four floors. The ground floor is occupied by the museum shop and the atrium. On the first floor one can visit the Cycladic collection, one of the most impressive and complete collections of Cycladic art in the whole world. It consists of about 350 items, displayed in modern fashion, and offers the visitor a full picture of the civilization that flourished on the Cycladic Islands in the 3rd millennium BC. Prominent among the works of art are marble figurines, some of them very rare, marble vessels and pan-shaped utensils.

On the second floor is a display of Ancient Greek art, with representative pieces dating from the Bronze Age (2nd millennium BC) to the late Roman period (4th century AD).

The third floor is dedicated to the collection of Cypriot antiquities formed by Thanos N. Zindilis. Finally, on the fourth floor the

Golden earring

Pitcher

CYCLADIC FIGURINES

The marble figurines of the early Cycladic period (3200–2000 BC) represent the main objects of artistic expression of Cycladic civilization. They reflect the anthropocentric character of this early form of art, as well as the simplicity and freedom of the islanders' lifestyle. They express both a sense of moderation and the aspiration towards monumentality. The height of the figurines varies from a few centimetres to 1.5m. Yet it is from these figurines that the genre of 'great sculpture' first emerges in the area bordering the Aegean Sea. They were made of marble with painted details. The figurines are divided in two groups: the violin-shaped group, stylized and abstract in shape, and the naturalistic group, in which the human form is more accurately traced. Some figurines reflect Cycladic society, representing pregnant women, men playing musical instruments, warriors or hunters, seated female figures as well as groups of people in family life or game scenes. Other figurines represent animals, particularly birds. A unique exhibit is the seated man with a drinking-cup (the 'toaster') and the large, almost life-size male statuette.

The impressive feature of these figurines, however, is their plastic form and the abstract tendency of the artists, who, like modern sculptors, seem to have aimed to express the essence and inner peace of the human form.

collection of Ancient Greek art formed by Karolos Politis is displayed: it was donated to the Goulandris foundation in 1989. Here also is the small collection dedicated to educational programmes, containing, among other items, the "Treasure of Keros", a hoard of broken figurines found on the island of Keros.

KOLONAKI SQUARE

The small Kolonaki Square is situated in the homonymous district in the centre of Athens and it is also known as Filikis Etaireias Square. On the square there is a bust of Emmanouil

Kolonaki square

Xanthos, one of the founders of the Filiki Etaireia (Society of Friends), the secret organisation that was formed in Odessa with the aim to prepare the Greek War of Independence in 1821. The bust was created by Thomas Thomopoulos and was placed there in 1928. In the same square one can also see the 1987 composition of the sculptor Georgios Georgiadis "Epinikio" (Triumphal).

Kolonaki Square is surrounded by luxurious, upmarket stores and cafés and is considered to be a posh area in Athens, as it is the focus point of the social life of Kolonaki, the "aristocratic" district of the centre of Athens. Many prominent Athenians still live or work in Kolonaki, the once upper class centre of Athens.

The district, however, named after a small column (kolona > kolonaki) in the square's garden, only started being built between 1858 and

Café in a street at Kolonaki

WALK 4

Block of flats, 12 Irakleitou Street

ART DECO BUILDINGS IN KOLONAKI

In the Kolonaki district are several Art Deco buildings, the most characteristic of which are the following: On 59 Skoufa Street there is an impressive apartment block, built in 1929–30, designed by the architect Kostas Kitsikis, with characteristic twin erkers that frame the main entrance like two small towers.
On 31 Skoufa Street is the building that houses the Cervantes Institute. Built in 1927, it incorporates elements from several 1930s styles, such as the arches on the ground-floor and the eccentric main entrance.
At the junction of 12 Irakleitou and Tsakalof Streets is an apartment block built in 1925 with a characteristic large pergola instead of a tiled roof.
On 7 Irakleitou Street there is an urban house built in 1928, with an overall neoclassical style combined with modern decorative elements.
At the junction of 20 Spefsippou and 27 Loukianou Streets there is an apartment block designed by Vassilis Kouremenos combining Art Deco elements with simplicity of design. The windows are characteristic of this combination, plain but surrounded by Art Deco decorative elements.

1862, towards the end of Otto's reign. At that time there was only a settlement of shepherds there from Lidoriki, who let their goats graze on Lycabettus Hill and produced milk that supplied the small – back then – city of Athens.

Block of flats, 59 Skoufa Street

Saint Dionysius on Skoufa Street

THE CHURCH OF ST DIONYSIUS ON SKOUFA STREET

The church of St Dionysius Areopagite (Agios Dionissios Areopagitis), dedicated to the first bishop and patron saint of Athens is situated on Skoufa Street between Likavitou and Dimokritou Streets. Its masonry and decoration are eclectic, combining elements from various periods and styles of church-building and indicating the seeking of a modern Greek cultural identity after the "Asia Minor Disaster" of 1922. On the same location there had been a small church since 1886 which was demolished in 1900 in order to build a larger one due to the increasing population. The church's construction began in 1923 and was completed in 1931,

☞ ANASTASSIOS ORLANDOS (1887-1979):

Orlandos was an architect and archaeologist who contributed significantly to the Classical, Byzantine and post-Byzantine studies in Greece. He was a Member of the Academy of Athens and Professor at the Technical University (1919-1940, 1943-1948) who also taught Byzantine Archaeology at the University of Athens (1939-1958). At the same time he was the Director of the Restoration Department of the Archaeological Service. He conducted numerous excavations and on-site research and was responsible for the restoration of several Classical monuments, including the Propylaea and the Parthenon, as well as numerous Christian churches throughout Greece. He made vital studies on the architecture of the Parthenon, the building materials in Ancient Greece and the architectural type of the early Christian timber-roofed basilicas. With his work of twelve volumes Archive of Byzantine Monuments in Greece (1938-1973) he made a significant contribution to further research. It was his firm belief that the archaeological sites of Greece, Ancient, Byzantine and Modern, are all part of an entity and this idea was adopted by the archaeological legislation. As an architect he designed around fifty churches, including the church of St Dionysius Areopagite on Skoufa Street and the church of St Basil (Agios Vassilios) on Metsovou Street in Athens. His research has been internationally established and his directorial skills proved crucial for the operation of numerous institutes and organizations.

WALK 4

VIEW OVER ATHENS – VIEW OVER GREECE

designed by Anastassios Orlandos. The church's decoration (1935-1939) was designed by the architect Georgios Nomikos, while the interior's pictorial decoration was made by the painter Spiros Vassiliou and his atelier between the years 1936 and 1939. The mosaics on the conches of the impressive porch were made by Sotirios Varvoglis in 1972-1973.

The church has a cross-in-square shape with an impressive interior decorated with mosaics and a well crafted marble incrustation. The pictorial decoration and the wooden screen are inspired by the religious art of Macedonia and the islands. Many icons have been offered by prominent wealthy families.

DEXAMENI

The small district of Dexameni right at the foot of Lycabettus Hill is one of the most quaint areas in Athens. It was named Dexameni (water tank) after a cistern that the Roman emperor Hadrian started to build there in 125 AD and that was completed by Antoninus Pius in 140 AD in order to provide water supply for the city. Its sources were in Tatoï at the foot of Mount Parnes. The remains of the façade of the ancient cistern are still visible on the northern side of the square in front of the modern water-tank. Also a little further to the left in a small playground there are Roman cisterns made out of white and grey marble. On the other side of the square one can see the statue of Odysseas Elytis, one of the most important 20th century Greek poets, who has won the Nobel Prize. Dexameni Square is particularly known for its café which has been a meeting point for intellectuals since the 19th century. Today apart from the café there is also an open-air cinema on the square.

LYCABETTUS HILL

The Lycabettus Hill is one of the most characteristic landmarks of Athens and is located south of the Tourkovounia Hills. It is about 300 metres high and from the top one offers a splendid view of the entire city. At its foot are the districts of Exarcheia, Neapoli,

View of Athens from the Lycabettus

Kolonaki and Ampelokipoi. The easiest way to get to the top of Lycabettus Hill is by the funicular railway. However, one can also drive up around the circular road, or even walk from Kolonaki. This route is worth the effort as it goes through the wood that covers the sides of the hill; without the Friends of the Forests Society, who systematically planted the trees between 1882 and 1915, this wood would not exist. There are two churches on Lycabettus Hill. A second road, beginning from the circular road, leads to the Church of St Isidoros, a small church (5 by 12m) built inside a cave, and which used to be called St Sidereas.

Although we do not know when exactly it was built, we do know that it existed in the mid-19th century and that it was destroyed by fire in 1930. In 1931 it was fully restored. The church of St George (Agios Georgios), which dates from 1780, is single-naved with a pendentive dome; it was built on the site of a Byzantine church which was possibly dedicated to St Elias. On the plateau around the church visitors can view the entire city, and with the telescopes supplied can look at different areas in more detail. Athenians go to Lycabettus for three reasons: to walk among the trees in the wood on the hillsides, to enjoy a drink in the bars at the top of the hill, or in the summer to watch a concert or theatrical show at the Lycabettus open-air theatre. Designed by the architect Takis Zenetos, the theatre was
built in 1964 and every summer hosts numerous events. During World War II Lycabettus Hill was used for anti-aircraft defence. Some of the guns from that period are still used today for salutes on big celebration days. Many Athenians wait up to hear the cannons fired at dawn on New Year's Day before they go to sleep after the New Year's Eve celebrations.

Saint George

5

WALK 5

1. The Athens Concert Hall
2. The Embassy of the USA
3. The Eleftherias Park
4. The Aretaieio Hospital
5. The Athens Hilton Hotel
6. The National Art Gallery
7. The Athens Conservatory
8. The War Museum
9. The Lykeion of Aristotle
10. The Byzantine and Christian Museum
11. St George Rizareios
12. The Evangelismos Hospital
13. The Marasleio Didaskaleio
14. Petrakis Monastery
15. The Gennadius Library

5. THE PANORAMA OF BYZANTINE ATHENS

In 1848, on one of the central streets of Athens, the duchess of Piacenza built her mansion, which now hosts the Byzantine Museum. It is easily accessible by the underground, and it should not be left out as it contains the largest collection of portable Byzantine icons in the world. A short away art lovers can visit the National Gallery and admire the work of Greek – mainly, but not solely – artists.

THE ATHENS CONCERT HALL

The Athens Concert Hall (Megaro Mousikis Athinon) is the fruit of the combined effort of the artistic community of Greece. As early as the 1950s, the mezzo-soprano Alexandra Triandi had spoken of the need for a multifunctional culture centre. In response to her persistent urgings, in 1956 the Government allocated a space for the construction of the Concert Hall. Among the prominent personalities who supported this effort were the great orchestra conductors Dimitris Mitropoulos and Herbert von Karajan. However, construction began only in 1976, to the designs of architect Emmanuel Vourekas and funded by the "Friends of Music Society" and Lambros Eftaxias, president of the Dekozis-Vouros Foundation. Building was interrupted in 1979 and was later resumed with the support of the Ministry of Culture (Melina Merkouri was Minister of Culture at that time). The hall was finally completed in 1991, with the support of Christos Lambrakis and other sponsors. Despite its plain exterior, the Concert Hall is luxurious inside. It has two concert halls with perfect acoustics, the "Friends of Music Hall" with a capacity seating of 2,000 and the "Dimitris Mitropoulos Hall" with seating for 450. The Athens Concert Hall houses the International Conference Centre with several conference halls: the "Alexandra Triandi

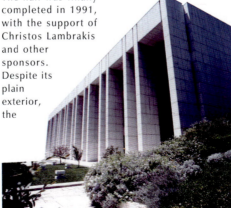

The Athens Concert Hall (Megaron Mousikis)

WALK 5

The United States Embassy

Hall" with a capacity seating of 1700 and the "Nikos Skalkotas Hall" with seating for 400, as well as other, smaller conference halls. In the Athens Concert Hall is also the Lilian Voudouri Great Music Library, a unique archive of its kind in Greece. Visual art exhibitions frequently held at the Concert Hall.

THE UNITED STATES EMBASSY

The imposing building of the United States Embassy is in Vassilissis Sofias Avenue, next to the Athens Concert Hall. It was built between 1959 and 1961 following the plans of Walter Gropius, one of the most influential architects of the 20th century and leading figure at the Bauhaus. The building is an example of modern architecture with neoclassical features. Neoclassicism appears in the austerity of the structure, the peripheral colonnade, the atrium and above all the use of white marble. The building strikes a balance between the models of Classical Antiquity and the architectural styles that prevailed in the USA when Gropius worked there. Thus, the building is a symbol of its role as the United States Embassy in Greece.

ELEFTHERIAS PARK- MUSEUM OF ELEFTHERIOS VENIZELOS

Developed in the 1960s by the architect Vokotopoulos, Eleftherias (Freedom) Park is one of the most valuable green spaces in the centre of Athens, situated on Vassilissis Sofias Avenue, next to the Athens Concert Hall. Inside the park is a statue by Giannis Pappas of the great Greek politician Eleftherios Venizelos, and behind this is a complex of buildings used by the 34th Regiment during the Balkan Wars (it is said that Venizelos used to address the soldiers there before they went off to war). During the military dictatorship (1967–74) these

Statue of Eleftherios Venizelos

buildings were used by the military police; many Greeks were questioned and tortured there.
Today, the park is a cultural centre and a place of remembrance of the events of recent Greek and Athenian history. The Athens Municipality Arts Centre is housed here in two separate buildings: one is used for temporary exhibitions and the other for seminars and other smaller scale events.
Housed separately is the Eleftherios Venizelos Museum, founded in 1986. Its collections consist of the politician's personal effects, items relating to events that took place during his lifetime (documents, photographs, postcards), as well as various pictures and portraits.
Finally, in a building behind the Arts Centre is the Museum of Antidictatorial and Democratic Resistance.

Aretaieio Hospital

The building of the neoclassical Aretaieio Hospital on 76 Vassilissis Sofias Avenue was funded by Theodoros Aretaios, Professor of Surgery at the University of Athens. The official opening of the hospital took place on 16 August 1895.
The hospital has a surgery, university gynaecology and obstetrics clinics, as well as an X-ray diagnostic department.
In 1968 busts of Theodoros and Eleni Aretaiou, sculpted by Kostas Palioglou, were put on display in the hospital.

The Athens Hilton Hotel

The Hilton hotel, one of the most distinctive buildings in Athens, stands on the corner of Vassilissis Sofias and Vassileos Alexandrou Avenues. It was built between 1958 and 1963 by a group of architects that included Emmanouil Vourekas, Prokopios Vassiliadis and Spiros Staikos. It was the first massive, tall building of post-war Athens and followed the pattern and style of the luxurious hotels of the time. The oblong building is

ELEFTHERIOS VENIZELOS (1864-1936)

Eleftherios Venizelos was born in Crete; a great politician, he became one of the most charismatic European leaders of his time. He founded the Liberal Party and served as Prime Minister of Greece in the troubled times of the Balkan Wars (1912-13), World War I, the Asia Minor campaign (1919-22) and through a part of the unsettled and creative mid-war period. Through his policies he came into conflict with the monarchy; he contributed to the expansion of the Greek State and set the basis for the modernisation of Greek society, particularly in the years 1928-32. Venizelos was adored and at the same time hated more than any other Greek politician; apart from being a landmark in Greek history, he is still a point of reference throughout Greece.

WALK 5

THE "RUNNER"

The Megali tou Genous Scholi (Great School of the Nation) Square is opposite the Hilton Hotel towards Lycabettus Hill. At the centre of the square there is a large sculpture made of horizontal glass plates that form the shape of a running man, the impressive "Runner" ("Dromeas") by Kostas Varotsos. The sculpture was initially placed in Omonoia Square but had to be transferred from there in 1994 due to the construction of the Underground. The surroundings of the sculpture are much different than Omonoia Square. However, it has been argued that the new position of the "Runner" on Vassilissis Sofias Avenue emphasizes better the dynamic character of the sculpture that is becoming a landmark of Athens.

divided into three sections, forming a curve. The edges of the curve meet the Vassilissis Sofias Avenue and Michalakopoulou Street. The important Greek artist Giannis Moralis decorated the wall overlooking Vassilissis Sofias Avenue with linear drawings that refer to Greek Antiquity. Despite the modernistic style of the building, there are obvious classical features, as with the United States Embassy.

The Athens Hilton was a step towards the tourist development of Greece in post-war years. The building, imposing in its size, distinctive lines and luxurious construction, triggered controversial opinions: some considered it a symbol of economic, technical and aesthetic progress, while others thought it spoiled the harmony of the Attic scenery. When it was built the hotel dominated the surroundings much more than today, since there were only a few sizeable buildings at the time, and the Athens Hilton soon became a touchstone for the modern city.

The Hilton Hotel

N. Gyzis: "Symphony of Spring"

NATIONAL ART GALLERY - ALEXANDROS SOUTZOS MUSEUM

The National Art Gallery - Alexandros Soutzos Museum is the most important institution in Greece devoted to the subject of the history of Greek art. The masterpieces decorating the halls of the gallery give a complete picture of the aesthetic paths and history of art of modern Greece. When the National Gallery was founded in 1900 it comprised 258 works from the collections of the University of Athens and the Technical University of Athens. The first curator was the distinguished painter Georgios Iakovidis. One year later the collection (107 paintings) of Alexandros Soutzos was donated to the National Gallery. Soutzos, a lawyer and art-lover, had spent his fortune for the creation of a large art collection and the erection of a museum of painting. The National Gallery was amalgamated with Alexandros Soutzos' bequest in 1954. The original collections were enriched by donations and bequests of artists and Greek art-lovers as well as by purchases of important works. The donation of the splendid Evripidis Koutlidis collection was of great importance and completed the presentation of the history of modern Greek painting (19th–20th centuries). The gallery's collection, which now comprises 9,500 paintings, sculptures and engravings, found its permanent home in 1976, when the present building was opened. Construction began in 1964 under architects Fatouros, Milonas and Moutsopoulos. It is a low building with two wings and follows modern architectural styles for the public buildings.

Short exhibitions of cultural interest are held in the first wing. In the halls of the second and largest wing most of the permanent collection of paintings is on display. The outstanding collection of sculptures from the 19th and 20th centuries will be accommodated in the Museum of Sculpture, in Goudi.

Priority is given to modern Greek painting and the approach of art lovers to the works of the most important Greek artists. Particular emphasis has been given to the 19th century and the first half of the 20th, century, while, due to

WALK 5

1

2

3

4

THE PANORAMA OF BYZANTINE ATHENS

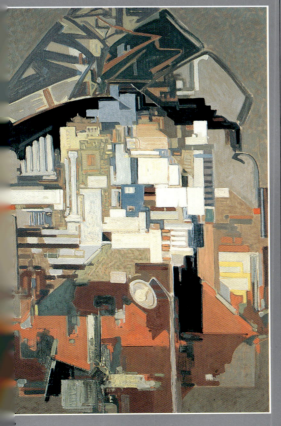

1) **I. Rizos:** "At the terrace"

2) **Th. Bryzakis:** "The Reception of Lord Byron in Mesologgi"

3) **P. Tetsis:** "Athens IV"

4) **N. Gizis:** "The Engagement of the Children"

5) **Ch. Pachis:** "The 1st of May in Corfu"

6) **A. Kontopoulos:** "Athens"

WALK 5

GIANNIS TSAROUCHIS

Giannis Tsarouchis (1919-1989), a unique artist and intellectual, was raised in Athens from a middle-class background. Very early on in his life he started to appreciate the simple working-class people for their authentic Greek character, and his ideas were mostly influenced by his teacher, Fotis Kontoglou, who also introduced him to Byzantine Art. Tsarouchis gradually developed an eclectic style in his painting. He used sharp observation and managed to depict scenes from the everyday life in a monumental manner. He loved Athens with its small streets and the authentic people who lived there. He was also a passionate photographer, capturing with his camera the faces of ordinary people and scenes and anything that would draw his attention all around Athens. He has photographed entire areas with neoclassical houses that were later demolished, thus preserving a memory of a lost world. He transferred those images into his paintings and theatrical sets. All these houses, coffee shops and scenes from the everyday life have an almost metaphysical dimension in his work. Among his most characteristic paintings are two of the "Neon" coffee-shop in Omonoia Square, where he used to spend time himself. His house in Maroussi has become a museum dedicated to his life and art.

G. Tsarouchis

G. Tsarouchis, "The Four Seasons"

lack of space, later generations of artists are presented with only a few representative works. The small though remarkable collection of 14th- to 20th-century European painting is not permanently exhibited; selected works are exhibited, depending on the space needed by temporary exhibitions.

The permanent collection of Greek painting extends to the first and the second floor of the main wing. On the first floor one can see works from the 19th century and on the second floor 20th-century works. The works are exhibited in chronological order and in thematic units. Partitions divide the space into different sub-units. In this way the visitor gains a clear view of the development of Greek painting and can admire the best examples of fine art over the course of two centuries.

The tour starts in the main hall on the first floor, on the right of the entrance. Here are the oldest works of the collection, including those of Domenikos Theotokopoulos, known in European art as El Greco. The history of modern Greek art began with the advent of painters from the Ionian islands, who are represented in here with several important paintings presented in a separate unit. Exquisite portraits, landscapes and historical scenes depict the first years of the Greek State (1832–62). The most important artist of the time is Theodoros Vrizakis, who illustrated the heroic moments of the 1821 War of Independence, while the three portraits by Nikolaos Kounelakis depicting the family of the artist are typical of the potential of the art of portraits.

Some of the most popular works were created by the academic painters who studied in Munich in the 19th century. These are presented in the unit 'The Bourgeoisie and its Artists'. Main representatives of the so-called Munich School, which dominated art in the second half of the 19th century, are Nikiforos Litras, Konstantinos Volanakis, Nikolaos Gizis and Georgios Iakovidis. The "Engagement of the Children" by Gizis, the most influential and prestigious Greek painter of his time, stands out for its maturity, while his "Art and its Spirits", "Spring Symphony" and "There Comes the Bridegroom" are splendid samples of the artist's personal style with symbolistic implications. The "Portrait of Lissandros Kaftantzoglou" by the great teacher Nikiforos Litras is admirable for its psychological analysis of the sitter. Works from the late 19th century, on display in the rest of the hall, introduce us to the different atmosphere of chromatic sensitivity inspired by Impressionism. "The Port of Copenhagen" by Ioannis

K. Maleas: "Santorini"

Altamouras stands out for its pioneering spirit and lyricism. Twentieth-century painters are presented on the second floor. Innovation, experimentation, special painting techniques and originality are characteristic of these works, which all express the Greek spirit through art. Famous artists in the unit "Towards a Greek Modernism" are Konstantinos Parthenis and Konstantinos Maleas, who are considered the "fathers of Greek painting". The "Apotheosis of Athanassios Diakos" by Konstantinos Parthenis and "Kameni Island of Santorini" by Maleas reveal the genius and uniqueness of their creators. Worth mentioning are also the works of Nikolaos Litras, who was associated with the German avant-garde.

The mid-war is represented by artists of the so-called Generation of the 30s. Important figures such as Spiros Papaloukas, Giannis Tsarouchis, Diamantis Diamantopoulos, Giannis Moralis and Nikos Hadjikyriakos-Ghikas perfectly harmonized with contemporary European styles, but also expressed Greece in art, thus widening all the opportunities offered by the past, history, tradition, folk art and modernism. The works of Nikos Hadjikyriakos-Ghikas, the main painter to adopt cubism, and the works of Giorgos Bouzianis, with the unique expressionistic language, perfectly express the modernistic tendencies of these artists. Among the works created after the Second World War and belong to the last unit of the exhibition, the most important are the "Epitaphs" by Giannis Moralis, one of the most accomplished Greek artists of the 20th century.

The small hall on the second floor has periodical exhibitions of selected modern paintings from the gallery's collection, thus completing the history of Greek painting.

ATHENS CONSERVATORY

The building of the Athens Conservatory at the junction of Vassileos Konstantinou Avenue with Rigillis Street formed part of the 1959 award-winning plan by the architect Ioannis Despotopoulos to create a cultural centre in Athens at the building

K. Parthenis: "Still art, with the Acropolis in the background"

block defined by Vassileos Konstantinou Avenue, Rigillis Street, Vassilissis Sofias Avenue and Rizari Street.

From that plan only the Conservatory was actually built between 1970 and 1977. It covers a wide space with staircases, steps and a large green space. It has two levels above the ground and two levels below the ground and it houses 35 rooms, two teaching amphitheatres, a concert room, a music library, a chapel, offices and halls for public events.

Its monumental construction with the marble coating, the excellent acoustics and the gallery on the ground-floor reflect the architect's initial aim to revive aesthetically the Ancient Agora within the space of the cultural centre that he had in mind. The building's strict geometric lines, its shiny marble façade and its provocative diagonal positioning contrasting the neighbouring city planning lines render the building's character aggressive in a certain way. Furthermore the passage through the Conservatory's galleries and the small park of the church of St Nikolaos joining Vassileos Konstantinou and Vassilissis Sofias Avenues is a pleasant experience for the visitors and an interesting place of relaxation in the centre of Athens.

The War Museum

WAR MUSEUM

The War Museum of Athens stands at the junction of Vassilissis Sofias Avenue and Rizari Street. The original plot was intended for the building of the National Gallery and was claimed by many cultural authorities to house their activities and events. In the same place there was a military campus in the mid-war, which suffered heavy damages during the movement of Nikolaos Plastiras in 1935, only to be abandoned after the war.

The museum, which was inaugurated in 1975, is today one of the most known buildings of the city due to its peculiar shape, reflecting the eclecticistic styles of the late modernism towards the end of the 1950s. Typical features of the style are the first floor, which is bigger than the ground floor, thus giving the building the shape of a cubistic atomic fungus, and the exhibition of warplanes and movable cannons in the courtyard and the balconies. It was the first museum in Athens to be equipped with a

The War Museum

modern amphitheatre for lectures and projections, conference and reception rooms as well as rooms for storage, maintenance and recording of the collections.
On the ground floor and on the mezzanine there are collections of heirlooms, weapons and objects from the operations of the Greek armed forces during the World War II, the War of Korea and the war history of Cyprus. On the first floor the visitor may wander in the Greek war and military history from prehistoric years to World War II. The museum has a rich library, whose entrance is in the courtyard with the warplanes, and a photographical archive with over 20,000 photographs from the history of the Greek armed forces.

THE LYKEION OF ARISTOTLE

Aristotle's school was named "Lykeion" (Lyceum) after the nearby temple of Lykeios Apollo. Until 1996 archaeologists believed that it was situated south of Sintagma Square, but in

ARISTOTLE AND HIS ERA

Aristotle was born in 384 BC in Stageira, Chalkidike. His father Nikomachos was physician to Amyntas II, king of Macedonia. As both his parents died when he was young, Aristotle was brought up by a family friend, Proxenos from Atarneus in Mysia. At the age of eighteen he went to Athens to study in Plato's Academy, where he remained for nineteen years, until Plato's death in 348-347 BC. When Speusippos took over as the Academy's director after this, Aristotle left Athens and travelled to Mysia and Lesvos to carry on his systematic, scientific research. In 342 BC Philip II of Macedonia invited him to Pella and hired him as the teacher of his son, Alexander; Aristotle remained in that position for two years. In the years 335-334 Aristotle returned to Athens and founded his own school, the Lykeion. The studies focused mainly on science and logic. After the death of Alexander, Aristotle suffered from the anti-Macedonian political feeling prevailing then in Athens, because of his close connection to the Macedonian royal family and he was forced to leave Athens and his school, designating Theophrastos as his successor. He retired to Chalkis, where he died in 322 BC.
Aristotle's philosophical thought focused on the scientific study of nature and society, and had widely influenced cultural life in East and West for many centuries. Numerous philosophical movements inspired by his ideas emerged in the Arab world, where many of his works were translated - and thus preserved - and in medieval Europe, where schools of thought were divided into those for and against Aristotle.

that year an archaeological find in the area between the Military Officers Club (Sarogleion) and the Athens Conservatory changed that belief: a palaestra of a gymnasium was found with evidence of two phases, one from the more recent late Hellenistic or Roman period and an earlier one from the 4th century BC. The continuous use of this space as a gymnasium led to the conclusion that it was Aristotle's Lykeion, built on the bank of the River Ilissos, in an area frequented by Socrates. The dimensions of the building's exterior walls are 50 by 48 metres. Around the 23m central yard ("ephebeion" or adolescents' space) are small, symmetrically arranged rectangular spaces. The spaces on the north-eastern and north-western side of the yard were made into "hypokausta" (heating spaces) in a later building phase, probably replacing the wash-basins of the Classical period. Along the northern side is a portico, while the southern side is underneath the Athens Conservatory. In ancient times a dense forest and plentiful water supplies surrounded the area. The nearby temple of Herakles Pankrates was discovered in 1953: its function must have been related to the Lykeion. At the moment the Lykeion cannot be visited due to ongoing excavation and restoration.

Ancient documents tell that apart from the gymnasium the Lykeion included an extensive library and a small museum with a collection that assisted students' research. The Lykeion attracted a large number of students from across the Hellenic world. When Theophrastos took over as director the school's name changed to Peripatos (Promenade), as lessons were conducted while students and teachers promenaded. The school was closed down definitively in 425.

The worship of Lykeios Apollo is one of the least known in the ancient world. The most probable etymological explanation of the word Lykeios is that it derives from the word "lykos" (wolf), signifying that the god was the protector of sheep and symbolically of young boys as they grew into adults. There is evidence of such worship in at least three locations in Athens. The most important temple was that on the bank of the River Ilissos, at a point where Athenian, archers, infantry and cavalry all met to practise, exercise and pray to Apollo. It is known that Athenians gathered there in 410 BC in order to restore democracy in the city. Lykeios Apollo was celebrated on the 12th day of the month Metageitnion (end of August), the same day that Athenians offered sacrifices to honour Zeus and Athena Polias.

The Athens School

THE BYZANTINE AND CHRISTIAN MUSEUM

The Byzantine and Christian Museum was founded in 1914. Initially it was located on the ground floor of the Academy of Athens building, but in 1930 it was permanently transferred to the Ilissia Mansion, the winter residence of the Duchess of Piacenza, in the area between Vassilissis Sofias and Vassileos Konstantinou Avenues. The mansion was completed in 1848 by the architect Stamatis Kleanthis. Its main entrance was opposite the River Ilissos, which was still visible at that time. Under Professor Georgios Sotiriou, Aristotelis Zachos turned the interior of the mansion into a museum. From 1993 work began to expand the building on three underground levels, taking advantage of the sloping ground so as to make more space available for displays. Manos Perrakis drew up the designs for this project. The present mansion is similar to its predecessor. The main entrance is still on Vassilissis Sofias Avenue, through a building with a portal, which has "ILISSIA" inscribed on the arch. The building was initially used to accommodate the servants, but today is home to the museum's offices, library and research department. Visitors going through the portal are led into a rectangular courtyard, which is defined by the mansion's lateral buildings. In the centre of the courtyard is a marble fountain and an early Christian mosaic, and on the walls around the yard are the architectural elements of various churches. The main building, one of the most important monuments in Athens, consists of two storeys and a basement. The northern side, which looks less heavy thanks to a pillared arcade, is framed by two corner tower-staircases. The narrow bas-relief panels on the building indicate the separate storeys. The external walls are revetted in marble. In general the building looks more like a Tuscan Renaissance villa with classical elements (dominant horizontal lines, low enclosed towers), as well as romantic (arched vaults, protruding roofs). When the extensions are complete all 15,000 objects of the collection will be easily displayed and the building will form part of a larger Archaeological Park, to include Aristotle's Lyceum and a small open-air amphitheatre. The Museum's large collection documents the development of art from the early Christian period to the post-Byzantine years (4th to 19th

Archangel Michael

Byzantine and Christian Museum

centuries). The collection includes sculptures, paintings and small ornaments from Greece and other parts of the Byzantine Empire, such Asia Minor, the Black Sea, Eastern Thrace, Coptic Egypt and the Danubian Principalities, which covered more or less the area of modern Romania.

The collections include around 3,000 icons, a larger number than any other museum across the world. The icons, from various parts of the Byzantine world, cover the empire's 1,000-year history as well as the post-Byzantine period, and display a variety of subjects. Among the earliest are those depicting the Virgin Mary, such as Glykofilousa (the Virgin Mary kissing Jesus affectionately) from 12th-century Northern Greece; Odegetria (Guiding Madonna) from 13th-century Cyprus; and, under various names, for example the Episkepsis (the Visitation), a mosaic from Triglia in Bithynia in Asia Minor, and the Akatamachetos (undefeated), from the 14th century. Also worthy of note is the 13th-century icon with two images of St George on either side, one painted and one sculpted, with scenes from the saint's life. Among the numerous post-Byzantine icons (15th to 19th centuries) are rare signed works of famous Cretan painters such as Angelos, Andreas Ritzos and Michael Damaskenos.

The largest part of the museum's collection consists of around 4,000 religious and secular artefacts and ornaments. Among the most noteworthy are oil lamps from Attica, Corinth, Asia Minor and North Africa, decorated with scenes from the Roman and Christian traditions, dating from the 3rd to the 6th centuries. There are also small ceramic phials of holy oil, also known as eulogies ["blessings"], which were brought back by pilgrims from the Church of St Menas, near Alexandria. The collection includes ornate crosses, reliquaries made of holy wood, post-Byzantine religious

Statuette of Orpheus

artefacts, 24 carat gold rare coins from the Byzantine Empire (the Avgeris Collection), as well as jewels from the 2nd to 7th centuries and the Treasure of Mitilini (Lesvos), accidentally discovered during excavations prior to the construction of the airport, which includes valuable artefacts, gold coins and jewels.

The sculpture collection consists of around 2,000 Byzantine and post-Byzantine pieces. They are mostly architectural elements from churches fallen into ruin in Attica, and also decorative works, such as the famous small statue of Christ-Orpheus from Aigina (4th century) and a bas-relief depicting a Nativity scene from Naxos (c. 400), a rare piece of narrative sculpture from the early Christian era.

Equally important, though less well known, is the ceramics collection, which consists of finds from excavations or shipwrecks from the area of greater Greece and from Fostat in Egypt. It includes items across the whole period of Byzantine art, for example early Christian grave offerings and Byzantine glass-coated cooking pots.

There are also numerous textiles, including Coptic material, donated to the museum by Antonis Benakis, which cover the first seven Christian centuries, and ecclesiastical textiles from the Byzantine and the post-Byzantine era (canonicals, epitaphs and antimensia), many of which are

Bronze lamp

outstanding samples of gold embroidery. The earliest among these date from the 14th to 15th centuries and imitate paintings, as their decoration is flat, while the post-Byzantine samples are influenced by western and popular art and are embossed, in imitation of metalwork. The exhibits also include manuscripts, wall paintings of the 13th and 14th centuries, mosaics, woodcuts, anthivola, copper engravings, lithographs, and copies painted by famous Greek painters, such as Fotis Kontoglou. The museum has a conservation department and since 1989 it has been organizing education programmes aimed mostly at schoolchildren, to familiarize them with the Byzantine world. •-

Th. Poulakis, "The Palm-Branch Bearer"

THE CHURCH OF ST GEORGE RIZAREIOS

Immediately next to the Evangelismos metro station, on Vassilissis Sofias Avenue, is the church

St. George of the Rizareios School

of St George (Agios Georgios) Rizareios. According to marble inscriptions on the building's façade, the church was built in 1843 in neoclassical style by the architect Armodios Vlachos. The church was funded by Georgios Rizaris, a merchant and national benefactor of Greece, who established the Rizareios Ecclesiastical School. Today the school is in Halandri, outside the Municipality of Athens proper: the old building in Vassilissis Sofias Avenue no longer exists.

The statue of the founder stands in the entrance to the church. In the rear courtyard is a large bell given by the Romanian artist Stefan Ramniceanu and putin place there in 1992.

EVANGELISMOS HOSPITAL

Evangelismos hospital is one of the largest in Athens and across Greece. It is surrounded by Gennadiou, Patera, Ipsilantou and Marasli Streets.

The construction of the hospital began on the initiative of Queen Olga in 1881, on a site donated by the Petrakis Monastery. Numerous donors supported the foundation, mostly Greeks of the diaspora, and also the then Tsar of Russia, Alexander II. The new hospital opened in 1884 with 48 beds, a significant figure at that time. There was also a nursing school, a top institution of its kind not only in Greece but also in the whole

---

EVANGELISMOS METRO STATION

During the construction of the Evangelismos metro station, excavations revealed a part of the main road that led from Athens to Mesogeia. Additionally, a 62m ceramic section of the Peisistratides' water main (end of the 6th century BC) was found. During the 4th century BC part of the area was used as a graveyard, which was later abandoned and replaced by a ceramics workshop that was in use from the 1st century BC to the 2nd century. Thirty-five burials were found, some intact, with important finds. Today the station has a special display featuring some of these finds in situ, including a marble bathtub, an urn, ceramic perfume bottles, part of the water main and the ceramic oven and water main.

Apart from these ancient finds the station is home to "Mott Station", a modern copper and neon installation by the artist Chryssa, placed in the ticketing area.

Europe. Gradually more buildings were added

The Evangelist Mark

to the hospital, always privately funded, and the complex expanded significantly. Today only the façade of the original building is visible amid the more recent buildings.

MARASLEIO DIDASKALEIO

The Marasleio Didaskaleio (School) of Primary Education is situated in Kolonaki on 4 Marasli Street. It was founded on the initiative of the Teachers Association in 1905, on a site donated by the Petrakis Monastery. The neoclassical building was designed by the architect Dimitrios Kallias and construction was funded by the Greek businessman and Russian Government official, Grigorios Maraslis.
Initially the building was used as a didaskaleio (teacher-training school). In 1924 two education specialists were placed in charge of the institution, Alexandros Delmouzos and Dimitrios Glinos. Members of the "Society for Education", they belonged to the demotic movement, which spoke up for the use of demotic (modern) Greek instead of "katharevousa", a language form closer to ancient Greek. Both were in favour of the

The Evangelist Luke

modernization of the educational system. Their new policies caused many reactions and resulted in their dismissal from the Didaskaleio, which was closed in 1926.
In 1933 the Marasleios Pedagogic Academy was founded, and, on and off, has functioned to the present day as Marasleio Didaskaleio of Primary Education, specializing in the instruction of primary school teachers.
It also houses a primary school and several experimental schools in additional buildings.

THE SAINTS ASSOMATOI - PETRAKIS MONASTERY

The Petrakis Monastery is situated in the densely populated Lykabettus district, behind Evangelismos Hospital. The main entrance to the monastery complex is on 14 Gennadiou Street, and this leads into a small garden, then to the impressive katholikon, the Church of Saints Assomatoi Taxiarches, consecrated to the Archangels; behind

> **THE SOCIETY FOR EDUCATION**
> The Society for Education ("Ekpaideftikos Omilos") was the most important of the demoticist organisations. The main aims of the society were the defence and dissemination of the demotic language and the modernisation of the educational system. It was founded in 1910 by the open-minded education specialists Manolis Triantafillidis, Dimitris Glinos and Alexandros Delmouzos, who participated in the educational reform of 1917.

the church are the administrative offices of the Church of Greece.

No written documents record the church's foundation, but architecturally the buildings can be dated to between the end of the 10th and beginning of the 11th centuries. The complex was repaired and renovated numerous times from the 15th century. The most significant renovation took place in 1673, when the monastery took on the name Petrakis, after the monk-physician Parthenios Petrakis, from Dimitsana, who financed the restoration. With a sigillion in the 18th century the monastery became patriarchal and its abbots henceforth were elected from the Petrakis family.

The monastery's katholikon is one of the oldest and most important in Athens. It is of the complex tetrastyle cross-in-square type. Of the original church only the three semi-circular apses have survived. The octagonal dome with the rounded corners and the slightly concave sides date from the later Byzantine era (1204–1453). The outer narthex was added at the beginning of the 19th century as the sanctuary was extended to the west. The church is constructed mostly of rubble masonry and only on the repaired higher parts was the cloisonné style adopted. There is a characteristic lack of brick pattern decorations. The roofs lack any strong

Petrakis Monastery, the katholikon

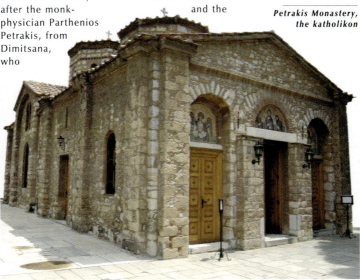

THE PETRAKIS MONASTERY IN ATHENS' MODERN HISTORY

By the mid-19th century the Petrakis Monastery acquired important landed property, thanks to the abbots' persistent drive and energy in dealing with the authorities. Many surviving legal documents, Greek and Ottoman, relate to the acquisition of land, and show that it was advantageous for the monastery to take over other monasteries nearby and used them as metochia. The monastery gradually donated the majority of its property to the public, thus becoming one of the greatest benefactors of Athens. Former monastic property was donated to found hospitals (Evangelismos, Sotiria, Singrou), religious institutions (Rizareios School), educational and cultural institutions (Athens Academy, Technical University, Gennadeios Library). The monastic community made a significant social contribution, especially during Ottoman rule, by providing people with medical care and promoting culture. Abbot Dionissios Petrakis led a delegation from Athens to Constantinople and contributed to the removal of the tyrannical Governor of Athens, Hadji Ali Haseki. The monastery financially supported the Ioannis Dekas School, founded a school of science for young Athenians and was a member of the Philomousos Society.

During the Greek War of Independence of 1821 the Ottomans plundered the monastery. After the foundation of the Greek State the monastery was used for a while as the national armoury and a military hospital. During the Balkan Wars it was used again by the Army, while after 1922 it housed Greek refugees from Turkey. During the German occupation the abbot provided Sunday meals to needy children.

Petrakis Monastery, the arch of the sacristy

graduations and this differentiates the church from other monuments of this era in Athens. As a whole, the katholikon seems to be based on the tradition of the architectural school of Constantinople. According to an elegantly written inscription over the main church's southern column, the katholikon was decorated with mural paintings in 1719, when Damaskinos was abbot of the monastery, by the painter Georgios Markou from Argos. He was the most significant religious painter in Athens and Attica during the 18th century and created a local school with numerous apprentices and a large body of work. He was influenced by Cretan painters and was also familiar with Italian art, though his own style remained conservative. On the north western side of the church is the tomb of the great Greek scholar of the Ottoman period, Konstantinos Oikonomou. ••

GENNADIUS LIBRARY

Gennadius Library is one of the richest and best organized libraries in Greece, situated between Anapiron Polemou, Aristodimou, Souidias and Gennadiou streets at the foot of Lycabettus Hill. It is housed in an impressive classicist building complex consisting of the main building of the library and several auxiliary buildings, surrounded by a large garden.
The library's story began in 1922 when the intellectual and diplomat Ioannis Gennadios donated his collection of books, consisting of 26,000 volumes, to the American School of Classical Studies at Athens. His only condition was for the collection to be kept separately and to be available to every scholar, so that Greeks could also have access to it. The Greek State offered the space for the library and the Carnegie Corporation funded its construction. The building was designed by the American architect Stuart Thomson. On the 23

The reading room of the Gennadius Library

April 1926 the official opening of the library took place with the presence of its founder and the foundation was called "Gennadeion". At the end of the 1960s the building was expanded based on a design by the Greek architect Pavlos Milonas. Since then the complex has been constantly expanded to improve the library's functionality and to add spaces of study for the promotion of the humanities. Today the library's collection consists of more than 100,000 volumes and continues to increase. The library also houses numerous important archives of great value for the study of modern Greek history, such as the archives of Gennadios, Ali Pasha of Ioannina and Heinrich Schliemann. The majority of the collections and the books concern the history of the Byzantine, the Ottoman and the modern period. The purpose of the library can be summarized in the inscription on the building's façade, a quote from Isocrates, the ancient Greek orator: "They are called Greeks who share in our culture".

Ioannis Gennadios

The Gennadius Library

WALK 6

1. The Maximos Mansion
2. The Presidential Mansion
3. The National Gardens
4. The Zappeion
5. The Hadrian's Gate
6. The Olympieion
7. The Olympieion: Other Monuments
8. The Ilissos Classical Temple
9. St Photini
10. The Basilica of Ilissos
11. The Panathenaic Stadium
12. The First Cemetery

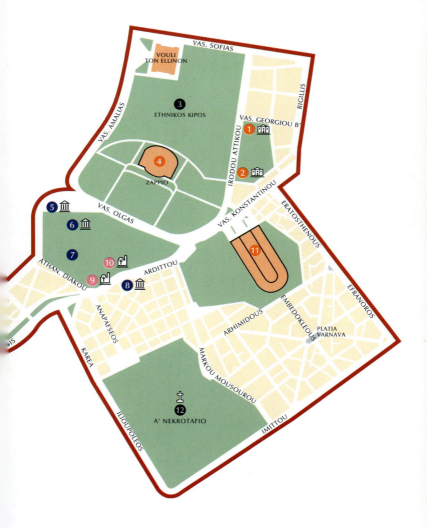

THE GARDEN OF ATHENS

On a hot day, there is no better way to chill out than to walk along the alleys of the National Garden or a take a coffee in the garden of Zappeion. These are situated in the Roman quarters of the city, built in the time of Emperor Hadrian, as attested by the inscripieion on the gate. Behind the Olympieion one can get a glimpse of the history of modern Greece through the monuments of the city's largest cemetery – in effect an open-air museum.

THE MAXIMOS MANSION

The Maximos Mansion ("Megaro Maximou") is at the crossroads of Irodou Attikou and Vassileos Georgiou II Streets. Since 1982 it has been the official residence and the office of the Greek Prime Minister. It was built in 1924 by the architect Anastassios Chelmis as the future residence of the banker Dimitrios Maximos (1873–1955), who became Foreign Minister and Prime Minister of Greece. The mansion is built over fewer storeys than other Athenian mansions, possibly for reasons of discretion, and is exactly behind the Parliament and beside the present-day Presidential Mansion, which used to be the royal residence. Originally the building consisted of a semi-basement and first floor; the second floor was built during the military dictatorship (1967–74), fortunately without spoiling the mansion's outward appearance. Chelmis was obviously influenced by Anastassios Metaxas, who built some of Athens' most important neoclassical buildings. Although the use of reinforced concrete was already widespread in 1924, and new architectural styles had taken over from neoclassicism, Chelmis built the Maximos Mansion with concrete but preserved the neoclassical features of the German bourgeois house of the early century. The façade is decorated with two elegant Ionic pillars, and the interior decoration of the Mansion (much changed because of

The Maximos Mansion

untoward interventions, mainly during the dictatorship) is very impressive.
The Maximos Mansion first functitoned as the prime minister's office when Dimitrios Maximos held that position in 1947. When he died in 1955 the building was bequeathed to the state, at first to house eminent visitors to Greece, until it was proclaimed the official residence of the Greek prime minister.

THE PRESIDENTIAL MANSION

The Presidential Mansion ("Proedriko Megaro") is situated in Irodou Attikou Street and has been the official residence of the president of the Hellenic Republic since 1974. Its story began in 1868, when the Greek Government decided to offer Crown Prince Konstantinos (later King Konstantinos I) a personal residence on the occasion of his coming of age. For this reason the royal family was allotted the land incorporating the present Presidential Mansion and the National Gardens. In 1888, when Konstantinos became engaged to Princess Sofia of Prussia, Ernst Ziller was commissioned to design the Crown Prince's palace. The plans were ready in 1890; building started in 1891 and was completed in 1897. Ziller simplified the original, unexecuted plans of the summer palace by Theophilus Hansen. The resulting building is one of the most imposing and outstanding of Ziller's works and yet looks like a private mansion. It consists of a basement, ground floor and two upper floors,

The Presidential Mansion

while the façade is divided into three parts with two side-protruding wings. The prostyle, with four Ionic pillars and a balcony on the first floor, dominates the entrance of the building.
Throughout time many changes and extensions have been made to the Presidential Mansion, such as the Hall of Credentials and the one-storeyed wing to the north (1910) as well as the extension along Vassileos Georgiou Street at the junction with Meleagrou Street

The guard of the Presidential Mansion

(1964).
When the "Old Palace" (the present Greek Parliament) was set on fire in 1909, the royal family temporarily moved here, only to settle permanently after the assassination of King Georgios I in 1913 and the accession of Konstantinos I. The building was from then on known as the "New Palace". It was not until the monarchy was abolished in 1924 that the building was for the first time retitled the Presidential Mansion. The restoration of the monarchy in 1935 brought the royal family back, until 1967, when the military dictatorship forced them to leave the country. Since 1974, when the monarchy was definitively abolished, the building has served as the Greek Presidential Mansion. ••

THE NATIONAL GARDENS

The National Gardens ("Ethnikos Kipos") are located south-east of the Greek Parliament, bordered by Amalias Avenue, Vassilissis Sofias Avenue, Irodou Attikou Street and Vassileos Konstantinou Avenue. Covering an area of about 40 acres, they constitute the largest green belt in the city centre. Athenians love to stroll here, especially in the summer, when the shade and the cool from the trees offer a respite from the baking heat. In addition to Greek flora, the gardens have trees and plants from other parts of the world, even from tropical and sub-tropical regions. Some trees are labelled, with their scientific names and the origins of the plant. In all there are about 7,000 trees and 40,000 plants in the gardens.
The original design was drawn up in 1836 by Friedrich von Gärtner, the architect of King Otto's palace (the present-day Greek Parliament). However, in 1839, on the initiative of Queen Amalia, the gardens were redesigned by the Bavarian architect Hoch, and renamed the "Royal Gardens". The Bavarian gardener Smarat was responsible for planting the trees, over an area of about 8 acres. This was the first major gardening project in Athens. Plants were imported from Italy, to give examples of sub-tropical regions in particular.
Extensions and further tree-planting as well as the garden layout were undertaken by specialist garden designers, including the Frenchman Barrot. As early as 1860 the Royal Gardens were considered a 'real wonder of gardening'. The following extract from a description of the time is a typical reaction:
"Magnificent palm trees from all parts of the East proudly tower over orange-trees and lemon-trees. The rarest flowers and the most precious

The National Gardens: the entrance with the sun dial

The "Fisherman" in the Zappeion

THEOPHILUS HANSEN (1813-1891) · CHRISTIAN HANSEN (1803-1883)

Danish architects and brothers who designed some of the most important monumental neoclassical buildings of Athens. Christian came to Greece in 1833; Theophilus, who was more involved than his brother in architectural projects in Athens, in 1838. Until 1838 they both taught at the newly established School of Arts, the forerunner of the Technical University of Athens. Theophilus later went to Vienna, where he built impressive buildings in the centre of the city, such as the Austrian Parliament (1874–83). Christian left Greece for good in 1850. He was active in Trieste and Copenhagen, where he also taught at the Academy of Architecture.

Theophilus Hansen

THE ZAPPEION OLYMPIC GAMES

The Zappeion Olympic Games were held in Athens four times: in 1859, 1870, 1875 and 1889. Apart from the 1889 event, the games were not particularly successful in terms of either organization or athletic events. However, they greatly contributed to the development of sport in Greece and paved the way for the first modern Olympic Games of 1896.

THE AIGLI CAFÉ

The Aigli café and restaurant in the Zappeion Garden close to the Zappeion Megaron, was founded in the early 20th century. The 'most enjoyable music hall of Athens', according to an old advertisement, was one of the most important social venues of the city for many years. People who frequented the hall enjoyed listening to the band playing operetta, light music and the international hits of the time. The Aigli closed down towards the end of the 1980s but opened again recently. Apart from the café-bistro, there are conference and reception rooms as well.

The open-air Aigli cinema is one of the best open-air cinemas of the city. Close beside the café-restaurant of the same name, the decorative greenery and the surrounding Zappeion Garden provide an agreeably cool shelter for

cinema-goers on summer nights in Athens.

THE GARDEN OF ATHENS

plants grow next to beautiful cisterns and shady paths, from where one can glimpse as far away as the Saronic Gulf."

Since the gardens were originally designed for royalty, the public was excluded until 1854, when the gardens opened, for Athenians only (and even then, not during the royal couple's promenade). The gardens were finally opened to the public in 1923, and renamed the National Gardens.

Today, visitors can enjoy ponds (with ducks), a small zoo, a play area, a library and a small botanical museum. There are also bronze statues of the 19th-century poet Aristotelis Valaoritis, the first Greek Governor Ioannis Kapodistrias, the Swiss philhellene Gabriel Eynard (who, together with Georgios Stavrou, co-founded the National Bank of Greece) and Jean Moreas, the Greek poet who lived in France in the late 19th century. The gardens are open to the public daily from dawn to dusk.

The Peristyle of the Zappeion Mansion

ZAPPEION

Zappeion Megaron (mansion) stands in the middle of a public garden stretching between the National Gardens, Amalias Avenue, Vassilissis Olgas Avenue and Vassileos Konstantinou Avenue. Athenians take the name Zappeion as a reference both to the Megaron and, especially, the surrounding garden. The history of the place started in the 1850s, when the wealthy merchant Evangelis Zappas (1800–65) offered to finance the athletic events modelled on the ancient Olympic Games. The then Greek government accepted the offer, but suggested

The Zappeion Mansion

that the events be accompanied by industrial, agricultural and art exhibitions, which presupposed the erection of a new building. Zappas agreed and the French architect François Boulanger began working on the plans. Although plans were drawn up, the building did not proceed because Evangelis Zappas died. In 1869 Konstantinos Zappas (1813–92), the administrator of Evangelis' will, brought forward the issue and in January 1874 it was agreed that the Zappeion Megaron should be built almost on the same place where it stands today. Initial work revealed the remains of a Roman bath and the construction was shifted to its present-day position. At the same time, in 1879, the original plans were modified by the Danish architect Theophilus Hansen, whose intervention was

THE ZAPPEION GARDEN

The greenery around Zappeion, known as Parilissia, was planted in 1886 and took its name from the Ilissos River. The former riverbed is now Vassileos Konstantinou Avenue. The 35-acre Zappeion Garden is a favourite place for Athenians to walk in, especially for those accompanying small children and, together with the nearby National Gardens, represent the two green belts in a city suffering from lack of parks. Some park benches on the side of Amalias Avenue, especially on Sunday mornings, are meeting-points for the elderly, who talk and argue vehemently about political issues. The benches of the Zappeion are considered to be more reliable than any opinion poll! The Zappeion Garden is adorned with interesting sculptures. Among them is the statue of Ioannis Varvakis, national benefactor from Epirus, by Leonidas Drossis (1870–86). Other sculptures are the "Woodcutter" (1872–75), the "Harvester" (1870) and the "Fisherman" (1874) by Dimitrios Filippotis. The composition by the French artists Henri-Michel Chapu and Alexandre Falguière, showing Greece crowning Lord Byron, stands on the corner of Amalias and Olgas Avenues. Exactly opposite the Panathinaic Stadium stand the statues of the freedom-fighter of the 1821 War for Independence, Georgios Karaiskakis, on horseback, by Michalis Tombros, and "Diskovolos" (Discus Thrower) by Konstantinos Dimitriadis.

The "Wood-cutter"

The statue of Byron and Greece

decisive. Zappeion was completed in 1888 and was inaugurated the same year, on the occasion of the fourth Zappian Olympic Games.

The Zappeion Exhibitions Hall is a masterpiece of the late Athenian classicism. The oversized Corinthian propylon (entrance) dominates the tripartite, symmetrical façade. Then comes the lofty lobby with the decorated ceiling, while one of the most beautiful cirular atriums of the 19th century follows. It is a two-storeyed peristyle with an elegant Ionic colonnade on the ground floor and columns ending in Caryatids' heads on the floor. The ensemble is characterized by successive closed and open-air spaces. The building, the vast reception square and the vast garden in front of the square present a balanced picture. On the sides of the main entrance of the Megaron stand the busts of Evangelis (1864) and Konstantinos Zappas (1893), by Ioannis Kossos and Georgios Vroutos respectively. Apart from being an exhibition hall, the Zappeion Megaron has been associated with momentous events in Greek and European history, among which are the accession of Greece to the European Economic Community on 28 May 1979 and the European Conference on 17 April 2003, just after the accession of ten new states in the European Union.

Hadrian's Gate

HADRIAN'S GATE

The monumental Hadrian's Gate is one of the landmarks of Amalias Avenue, close to the junction with Vassilissis Olgas Avenue, just outside the archaeological park of the Olympieion. The emperor Hadrian (AD 117–138) was the greatest benefactor of Athens in the Roman period, offering the city public buildings and works of art. His most important contribution to the city's welfare, however, was the expansion of the city towards the hill of Ardettus and the stadium. In order to commemorate this topographical expansion, a triumphal arch, similar to a gate, was erected close to the Olympieion, on the boundary between the old and the new parts of the city. The arch was completed in AD 131, and the emperor ceremoniously passed underneath it when he came to Athens for the inauguration of the temple of Zeus Olympios, which he had had renovated and completed.

The arch, 18 metres high and 13 metres

wide, is made of Pentelic marble and consists of two parts. The lower part forms a wall, built with regular rectangular blocks, while in the central part of the wall is an arch 6 metres wide. At the ends of this wall stand two rectangular Corinthian pillars. The second level consists of an architrave and a cornice. Corinthian columns on both sides of the wall complete the decoration of the monument. There are four small pillars with Corinthian capitals on the gate, supporting an Ionic entablature, the central part of which is crowned by a gable. The gaps between the pillars were probably filled by tympana. Statues of Theseus and Hadrian filled the central opening under the respective dedicatory inscriptions surviving on the architrave. The inscription facing the old city says, "This is Athens, formerly city of Theseus", and the one facing the new extension reads, "This is the city of Hadrian and not of Theseus". •▪

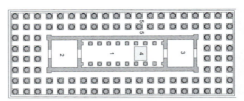

The temple of Olympian Zeus, plan

THE OLYMPEION

In the big park bordered by Vasilissis Amalias Avenue, Vasilissis Olgas Avenue, Callirrois Street and Athanassiou Diakou Street stand 15 very grandiose Corinthian columns. These are the remains of the temple of Olympian Zeus, one of the buildings with the longest history in Athens.

The period of tyrannies in the Greek cities was marked by the erection of the first monumental temples, which aimed at glorifying the city as well as its tyrant. In 515 BC the Athenian tyrant Peisistratos the Younger, following a trend already developed in Asia Minor, began the construction of a temple dedicated to the Olympian Zeus, on the western bank of the River Ilissos. According to Athenian tradition, Deucalion had built a temple on this spot just after the Deluge, in order to thank Zeus for the fact that the floodwaters had finally receded from the banks of Ilissos. The temple of Peisistratos was made of limestone in the Doric style. The drums discovered during the excavations

The temple of Olympian Zeus

attest to the huge dimensions of the initial building. The size meant, however, that construction was slow. When the Peisistratid tyranny was finally abolished, the temple remained unfinished, because of its association with the hated tyrants.
During the Hellenistic period, another monarch, Antiochus IV Epiphanes, attempted to complete the temple according to contemporary aesthetic precepts of monumental architecture. The Hellenistic temple was peripteral, built in Corinthian style. Building was carried out between 174 and 163 BC, but the temple was again not finished, due to the death of Antiochus. The temple in particular suffered from the destructive effect of Sulla's defeat of Athens in 86 BC: many of the columns were transferred to Rome to decorate the temple of Zeus Capitolinus, and others were lost in a shipwreck. At the time of Augustus some repair works did take place, but on a small scale.

Another Roman emperor, Hadrian, who adored Athens, rebuilt the temple between AD 125 and 130, and finished the construction work. The new temple was also Corinthian in style, dipteral octastyle. Its narrow sides also had a third colonnade, of eight columns, whereas the longer sides had 20 columns. The main temple was tripartite, with a closed pronaos, a cella and an adyton (holy of holies). The cella also had internal colonnades to support the roof. Here stood the colossal statue of Zeus, as well as a statue of the emperor, who apparently was worshipped in the temple as god.

The temple was surrounded by a rectangular defensive circuit 206m by 129m, supported by buttresses. A large part of this fence is still extant, either in its original form or with later repairs and reconstructions. The entrance of this defensive circuit was on the northern or north-eastern side, in the form of a propylon with four columns and two pilasters. The fenced area was ornate with several dedicatory statues and smaller buildings.

In the Byzantine period a basilical church was built in this fenced space, counteracting its pagan character. Interestingly, written accounts and engravings suggest that in the last period of the Ottoman rule, a short while before the Greek War of Independence, an ascetic, known as the Stylite, settled on one of the columns. Today, only 16 columns survive from the huge temple of the Olympian Zeus, 13 on the north-eastern side and 3 on the southern, of which the middle one has fallen on the ground, splitting its drums. The

The temple of Kronos and Rhea

The temple of Apollo Delphinios

WALK 6

The temple of Artemis Agrotera

destruction of the temple was probably due originally to natural disaster, particularly to earthquakes. However, during Ottoman rule, the drums were burned in order to produce lime, which was used as a building material. In the sacred space of the Olympieion and the banks of Ilissos River there were other smaller temples, some of which were important sanctuaries in the classical times outside the city walls.

OTHER MONUMENTS

The oldest of those sanctuaries was the temple of Apollo Delphinios, a peripteral temple in Doric style, dated in 500 B.C., situated just south of the temple of Zeus. To the right of the temple was situated an earlier building, known as the "courts at the Delphinion". It consisted of a large courtyard with many rooms along its northern side. At this court were tried those who had committed "justified" murder, protecting their life or their honour. To the south of the Olympieion was situated the temple of Apollo Pythios, known also as "The Pythion". The remains of a building discovered on this site facilitate the identification with the Pythion. The most important evidence is offered by an inscription found in situ, which was situated in the temple, according to the testimony of Thucydides. The inscription preserves an epigram according to which Peisistratos, son of Hippias, dedicated the altar built in the Pythion. In the temple there was also a statue of Apollo Pythios. Close to the Pythion, probably on the rock to the southeast of the Olympieion, there was the temple of Ge (Earth). According to Plato, in the surrounding area there were also the temples of Herakles, of Demeter and Kore, of Artemis Agrotera and of Aphrodite in the Gardens ("en kepois"). In the Roman period (124-131 A.D.) a bath complex was built to the north of the Olympieion. An important addition of the same period was the construction of the temple of Zeus Panhellenios (protector of all Greeks), further south of the archaic and classical sanctuaries of the Pythion and Delphinion. It was built under Hadrian (131-132) and was dedicated to the worship of Hadrian as Zeus and of Hera (Juno). Finally, a small Doric dipteral temple with a separate fence, on a base measuring 15.63 by 10.08 m., dedicated to Kronos and Rhea (150 A.D.) was the latest addition in this sacred space.

Artemis

The Classical Temple On The Left Bank Of Ilissos River

On Ardittou Street, on the hill just opposite Athens' open-air swimming pool, are still visible the remains of a supporting wall and the pediment of a small ancient temple. The temple had been transformed into a Christian Church and was thus maintained in this form until the 18th century, under the name "Panagia stin Petra" (Virgin Mary on the rock). Depictions of this monument exist in sketches by the English travelers Stuart and Revett (nowadays at the Benaki Museum), who visited Athens in the period between 1751 and 1754 and saw the church before its demolition.
The temple, built in the classical period, was in many ways similar to the temple of Athena Nike on the Acropolis. The architectural style chosen by the architect, possibly Kallikrates, was the ionic. In fact, this style was in this building fully developed, with a mixture of loans from the islands and with an atticizing mood of a strongly decorative character. The temple was made of white Parian marble around 448 B.C. It was amphiprostyle tetrastyle, its foundation measured 14.6 by 7.8 meters, and it had a simple architrave and frieze. Four of the slabs of this frieze have been securely identified, although their themes have not been explained in a persuasive way; nowadays they are situated in the museums of Berlin and Vienna. The temple is identified either as the "Metroon en Agrais", where the Little Mysteries were celebrated with a ritual bathing in the waters of Ilissos River, or as the temple of Artemis Agrotera.
In the 5th century the temple was transformed into a Christian church. In the beginning of the 17th century it was replaced by a smaller orthodox church, Virgin Mary on the Rock, which was later used by the Venetians as a catholic chapel. It was finally abandoned in 1674 and in 1778 it was demolished by order of the Ottoman voyvoda and the building material was incorporated in the Serpentze, around the Acropolis.

The Church Of Saint Photini

The church of St Photini (Agia Fotini) Samaritissa is situated at the beginning of Kallirois Street, near the Olympieion, on the location where the banks of the river Ilissos used to be. It is dedicated to Photini of Samareia, a prostitute who gave Christ a cup of water form the well to clench his thirst.
Today the church is particularly popular for the performing of various ceremonies as it is surrounded by a large garden in a park. It was built in 1872 on the location where during the 1830's stood the Bavarian soldiers' cemetery and

Saint Photini near the Olympieion

WALK 6

has had its present form since its renovation in 1986. It is believed that the church was built on the remains of an ancient monument dedicated to Hekate; one can still see close to the church the remains of another ancient monument dedicated to Pan.

The Basilica Of Ilissos & Martyrium Of St Leonides

The Basilica of the River Ilissos is one of the most important Early Christian monuments in Athens, situated north-east of the Olympieion, where the branches of the river form an islet. One can visit the site via Ardittou Street. The church was founded in the first half of the 5th century and is related by tradition to the manifold activities of the Empress Athinaïs-Eudokia.

The building is a three-aisled basilica with a transept vessel narthex and atrium on its western side. It originally had a timber saddle roof, and only the sanctuary was covered by a vault, or a pendentive dome, as one can deduce from the four large pillars at the ends of the semi-circular apse. The floors of the basilica and the atrium were laid with good quality mosaics depicting birds and plants. Parts of those mosaics have been preserved and are now kept in the Christian and Byzantine Museum in Athens.

The only documentary

Mosaic Floor

reference to the church can be found in a speech by Michael Choniates, Bishop of Athens, in honour of Leonides, who was martyred in Corinth alongside seven women in AD 250, during the reign of emperor Decius. It is clear from the speech that by the time of the bishop's episcopacy (end of 12th – beginning of 13th century) the Corinthian martyr's relics had been transferred to a tomb in Athens. Bishop Choniates also mentions a church dedicated to the martyr: already in a derelict state, this church can be identified as that of the Basilica of Ilissos, since underneath its north-western side there is a crypt with tombs where the remains of Leonides and his fellow-martyrs probably rest. There is also archaeological evidence connecting this basilica with another dedicated to Leonides, in Lechaio, near the spot where the martyr died.

Later documents give

LEONIDES

Leonides was Bishop of Athens in the third century; he became a martyr in Corinth together with seven women-deacons who accompanied him. His remains were brought to Athens in the mid-4th century. A martyrium was built to keep his remains and a basilica was added to it later.

no information about the monument. During the period of Latin rule, although the church was already deserted it was still referred to as the 'basilica' and it its decoration remained intact.

The church's final demise may have been caused by the flooding of the River Ilissos; but it may equally have been the work of Ali Haseki, a well-known Ottoman governor of Athens who, in order to build a new defensive wall for the city in 1778, destroyed the ancient and medieval monuments in the area, including possibly the basilica. Archaeological excavation has uncovered the church's ground plan. ••

THE PANATHENAIC STADIUM

The Panathenaic stadium is one of the most impressive monuments of Athens, lying on Vassileos Konstantinou Avenue, just opposite the garden of the Zappeion. The grandiosity and magnificence of the Stadium is accentuated by the sparkling white marble, in strong contrast with the deep green of the hills Agra

Cover page of the Olympic Anthem

THE FIRST MODERN OLYMPIC GAMES (1896)

The organization of the first modern Olympic Games in 1896 at Athens was the culmination of a series of efforts for the revival of the institution, which had already started in the first half of the 19th century. A decisive factor for the revival of one of the most successful international institutions of our times was the presence and action of Pierre de Coubertin. However, in 1896 nothing could foretell the future development of the Olympic Games in their present form. Despite the fact that the Games were a landmark of the history of modern Athens, the numbers of those times seem minimal in comparison to the contemporary numbers: only 241 athletes from 14 nations competed in 43 events.

The Games were a success and the increased needs of lodging and feeding for the athletes and the tourists were successfully met. The athletic events took place at the Panathenaic Stadium, at the shooting ground of Kallithea and in Neo Faliro. Undoubtedly one of the greatest moments of those Games, which thrilled the Greek audience, was the victory of Spiros Louis at the Marathon race, an event with which the Panathenaic Stadium is ever since related.

and Ardettus, which surround it. The Stadium is one of the few examples of successful reconstruction of an ancient monument for a modern use.

The ancient Stadium was erected in about 330 B.C. under the supervision of the orator Lykourgos, who had undertaken the financial administration of Athens. Every four years the Great Panathenaia festival was celebrated in the Stadium. The seats for the archons were wooden, whereas laymen sat on the ground. Between 139-140 and 143-144 A.D. Herodes Atticus constructed on the same spot a new stadium out of marble, with a seating capacity of about 50.000 people, as many as the Coliseum at Rome. The stadium had the shape of a horseshoe, a total length of track of 204.07 meters and a width of 33.35 meters; it was also provided with staircases among the tiers. After its completion it hosted public spectacles. With time fell into ruined and its marbles were incorporated into other buildings.

The history of the building as we see it today started in 1869-1870, when the architect Ernst Ziller excavated the area where the ancient stadium lay. In 1894, when Athens undertook the revival of the Olympic Games, it was decided that the Stadium should be reconstructed in order to host the first modern Olympics. The plans of the reconstruction were designed by the architect Anastassios Metaxas and were financed to a large extent by the businessman Georgios Averoff, president of the Greek community of Alexandria; his statue, made by G. Vroutos (1896) is erected at the entrance of the Stadium. Until March 25, 1896, day of the inauguration of the Games, only the first four rows of the Stadium were covered with marble, whereas the rest were wooden, painted white, so that no colour disharmony would exist between them and the marble ones. Simultaneously five bridges were created over the river Ilissos, which flowed just there where today is the Vassileos Konstantinou Avenue. These bridges

The "Discus-thrower"

The Panathenaic Stadium

WALK 6

facilitated the entrance to the Stadium. The construction of the arena was realized under the supervision of the British architect Charles Perry, who was at the time considered to be the top specialist in such works. The construction works were continued after the end of the 1896 Olympic Games and were completed in 1906, when the Stadium hosted the so-called "Mesolympiada" (Interim Olympics). Everything was revetted with white Pentelic marble, locker rooms were created for the athletes as well as other auxiliary rooms. A short time earlier the "Propylaia", a monumental marble construction at the entrance of the Stadium had been completed. Thus, the building took its present form and justified the attribute "Kallimarmaron" (the beautiful marble one) which the Athenians gave to it and use for denouncing it even today.

Dimitris Tofalos

The Panathenaic Stadium has 47 rows of seats, divided in two zones. The lower zone is divided in 30 tiers, whereas the upper one in 36. The seating capacity of the Stadium reaches almost 60000 spectators. Today it is used only on special occasions of public celebrations, whereas it consists the finishing point of the Marathon race, organized each year in Athens. ●●

THE FIRST CEMETERY

The First Cemetery, the main cemetery of Athens, is at the end of Anapafseos Street. According to the first document concerning the cemetery walling, it was founded in 1837, although the area, which had previously been allotted to the community of Athens by Ioannis Paparrigopoulos, was already used for this purpose. The operation regulations of the cemetery date from 1842. When Georgios Skoufos became the Mayor of Athens (1857-1861) the plan and the layout of the cemetery were worked out and the area was expanded and planted.

The cemetery is divided into sections. The oldest graves and the graves of the most eminent dead are in the area around the entrance, where stands the church of St (Agioi) Theodoroi, in the main

---

☞ THE INTERIM OLYMPICS OF 1906

The Interim Olympics of 1906 was the result of the Greek petition to the International Olympic Committee for the organization of athletic events in Athens in the interval between two consecutive Olympic Games. This petition followed the negative answer to the initial request for the permanent organization of the Games in Greece. Finally, the only Interim Olympics carried out were those of 1906. Despite the success of this event, which was the most important international athletic event organized until then, the institution did not have a future. In fact the IOC did not sanction those Games and did not include the winners among the Olympic champions.

THE GARDEN OF ATHENS

lane and in the first, fourth and fourteenth sections. The Catholics are buried in the second section of the cemetery, while the Protestants are buried in an adjoining area with a separate entrance from Markou Moussourou Street. Beside the First Cemetery on Ilioupoleos Street is the Jewish Cemetery.

The First Cemetery can provide important information about the history of Athens in the 19th and 20th centuries. Many central characters of the history of Athens and Greece have been buried there, such as the fighters of the 1821 Greek War for Independence Theodoros Kolokotronis, Ioannis Makrigiannis and Markos Botsaris, the politicians Charilaos Trikoupis and Georgios Papandreou, the national benefactor Georgios Averoff as well as figures from the spiritual world such as the modern Greek Enlightenment scholar Adamantios Koraïs, the poet Giorgos Seferis and the German archaeologist Heinrich Schliemann.

Apart from its

Averoff's funerary monument

THE 'SLEEPING MAIDEN' OF GIANNOULIS CHALEPAS

The most famous monument of the First Cemetery is the "Sleeping Maiden", the tombstone of Sofia Afentaki, a classicist work by Giannoulis Chalepas (1878). The girl seems to be sound asleep and nothing shows the rigidity of the dead body. In this way, the work fully corresponds to the model of the classicist tomb, according to which death is an eternal dreamless sleep. The sculpture owes its fame to a great degree to the artist's tragedy, as this was his last work before his schizophrenia was manifested.

Giannoulis Chalepas (1851-1938) was one of the most important representatives of modern Greek sculpture. He came from Pirgos of the island of Tinos and studied in the School of Fine Arts of the Technical University of Athens and in the Academy of Fine Arts of Munich. Other known works of Chalepas are "Satyros and Eros" (1873-1875) and the "Praying Woman" (1876-1877). Unluckily, his art, which was influenced by classicism, was shadowed by his mental illness.

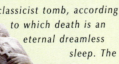

First cemetery of Athens, general view

historical value, the First Cemetery is the richest museum of 19th and 20th century Greek sculpture. In the first period of its operation the cemetery monuments followed a neoclassic line. The artists aimed to revive antiquity by adopting figures and patterns found in ancient tombstones such as tombstone oil vessels, tombstone chapels, sarcophaguses and headstones. Typical examples are the family grave of G. Koupas, the headstone of doctor Ioannis Vouros (1885) and the two sculptures by Dimitrios Filippotis: the grave of Ekaterini Antoniadou depicting the Night arriving with her children, Oneiros and Hypnos (ancient Greek deities, personifications of dream and sleep), and the aged Day departing, as well as the sarcophagus of Georgios Averoff with the exceptional marble flowers.

As years went by the idolised presentation of the dead through busts and statues gave way to more realistic depictions. One such remarkable monument is that of Michail Tossitsas (1860), made by the Fitalis brothers. Another noteworthy monument is dedicated to the 40,000 Athenians who died of famine during the Nazi occupation in the Second World War. Above all, a visit to the First Cemetery may be an opportunity for the visitor to watch closely the Greek burial customs, as burial and memorial services take place there on a daily basis.

Detail from a funerary monument

WALK 7

1. Monastiraki Square
2. St Thomas
3. St Elissaios
4. St Anna
5. The Canellopoulos Museum
6. St Nicholas
7. Transfiguration of the Saviour (Metamorfosi)
8. Museum of History of the University of Athens
9. St Symeon
10. Anafiotika
11. Rizokastron
12. St George on the Cliff
13. St Nicholas Rangabas
14. "Hellenic Society"
15. St John the Theologian
16. Monastery Dependency of the Holy Sepulchre
17. St Mary Chrissokastriotissa
18. St Spyridon and Holy Belt (Agia Zoni) of Virgin Mary
19. The Hamam of Abid Efendi
20. The Museum of Popular Instruments
21. The Medrese
22. The Tower of the Winds
23. The Fethiye Mosque
24. The Roman Agora
25. Taxiarches and Panagia Grigoroussa
26. The Plaka

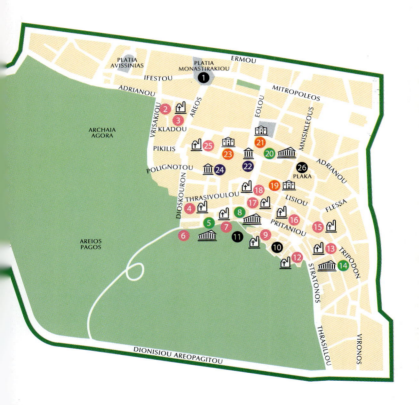

7 PLAKA: WALKING IN ATHENS' OLD CITY

The oldest district of Athens, the Plaka, is characterized by monuments of all periods, which prove that this was the heart of the city from Antiquity until modern times. Several small churches, a mosque, an Ottoman bath and the first university of Greece, together with the Roman Agora, constitute its cultural mosaic. After a walk in its narrow streets, a glass of wine in one of the little taverns under the Acropolis is a must.

MONASTIRAKI SQUARE

Monastiraki Square is situated in one of the most characteristic parts of the city centre, a meeting-point for the different faces of Athens. To the north, Athinas Street leads to Omonoia Square, the capital's central crossroads. Ermou Street, one of the city's main commercial roads, leads eastwards to Sintagma Square, the city's political centre, and westwards towards Kerameikos and the Psyrris and Thisseio districts. The Plaka at the foot of the Acropolis is south of the square. During the past few centuries the small square has been the main commercial area of Athens. Recently it has become one of the city's main tourist attractions because of its proximity to the Plaka and the Acropolis. The surrounding buildings include the Mosque of Tzistarakis, which is today a branch of the Museum of Greek Folk Art, the renovated metro station and the Church of St Mary Pantanassa, also known as the Great Monastery, which gave the square its name. The square is also surrounded by a large number of souvenir shops and restaurants that attract people on a

Square "Monastiraki"

WALK 7

Metro Station "Monastiraki"

regular basis. During the period of Ottoman rule the square was situated in the main area of the daily Lower Market. Together with the Wheat Market, which was held once a year in the Roman Agora, and the Upper Market, which was held weekly and joined with the Lower Market through Pandrossou Street, all formed the centre of the commercial and social activities of Athens. Merchants and craftsmen set up shop here, and there were also innumerable places of social contact, such as cafés, and the seats of many city authorities. Although the square's boundaries had already been established by 1860, it was not officially declared a square until 1943, following a decision by the Municipality of Athens. Over the course of time the square underwent numerous changes. During excavations in 1885 several of the monastery's adjacent buildings were demolished, and in 1907 the square was redesigned. The train station was constructed in 1895 and has the typical architectural characteristics of the time. The most recent development took place in 2003 with the unification of the archaeological sites of Athens, when the metro station was constructed and the historic square was redesigned again. These works are still in progress. Throughout its entire history the square has been a commercial centre and a place of social interaction; Monastiraki is a truly Mediterranean place, a place of contrasts, where the city's past joins its vibrant present.

THE CHURCH OF ST THOMAS

The remains of the Byzantine church of St Thomas (Agios Thomas) are situated on Vrissakiou Street, behind the Stoa of Attalos. The church's apses can be seen on the east, as well as the bases of the columns that separated the church's aisles and a plethora of marble architectural elements. The church was first built in the 6th-7th centuries and was renovated between the 9th and 10th centuries. Soon after the Ottomans had occupied the country the church was deserted and left in ruins, until the 17th century, when a new church was built on the same site. Up until the end of Ottoman rule St Thomas was the parish church of the Vrissaki district, a large parish with 54 Christian families. St Thomas was the church of the Lympones family, who were buried here and who descended from the Athenian branch of the Palaiologos family. Between 1834 and 1835 the church and the entire surrounding area were sold by the State to Prince Georgios Kantakouzinos, who demolished the church in order to build more houses. Manolis Chatzidakis excavated the major part of the church's remains.

Saint Elissaios, the Communion of the Apostles

THE CHURCH OF ST ELISSSAIOS

The remains of the church of St Elissaios (Agios Elissaios) are on Areos Street, opposite the archaeological site of Hadrian's Library on the corner of Dexippou Street.
The church was built during the period of

ALEXANDROS PAPADIAMANTIS (SKIATHOS 1851-1911)

Papadiamantis was one of the most significant Greek writers, in whose ethnographical work Athens of the 19th century is often the background. (Ethography: a genre of Greek literature aiming at describing the "authentic" mores and customs of the Greek people). Although Papadiamantis was born and died in Skiathos island, he spent the largest part of his life in Athens. He graduated from the Varvakeion High School and continued his studies at the School of Philosophy of the University of Athens. He worked as a journalist mostly in the newspaper "Acropolis" and as a translator while at the same time he wrote a large number of ethographical novels in which the protagonists were simple, poor people with whom he was truly familiar. His metaphysical quest led him to become religious and to form a close relationship with the Church. His plain and solitary way of life was the reason why he became known as the "secular monk of Greek literature". His work was appreciated mainly after his death and it has been broadly published.

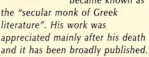

Ottoman rule, possibly during the 17th century. It belonged to Chomatianos Logothetis, a Greek who functioned as consul of England in Athens, whose house was nearby. During the German occupation, in 1943, the church was demolished against regulations by his owner, commander I. Kazakos. Historical descriptions and drawings provide information about the church's appearance: it was an aisle-less church with a wooden roof, with sculptural and architectural elements from other buildings incorporated into the external walls. This small church is connected with the city's modern history. A the end of the 19th century it was frequented by the writer Alexandros Papadiamantis and his cousin Alexandros Moraïtidis, who sung here. At that time many important scholars and writers attended mass at the church.

Lately, due to the combined efforts of the Association for Papadiamantis Studies and of the Ministry of Culture, the building has been restored; and so, a typical monument of the period of Ottoman rule, is lifted from obscurity.

THE CHURCH OF ST ANNA

Walking along Dioskouron Street towards the district of Anafiotika, one can see on the left the small church of St Anna (Agia Anna). According to the writings of several 17th-century travellers there used to be an older church on the site, also dedicated to Saint Anna. The present single-naved, barrel-vaulted building is slightly more recent. The church was built on the remains of the Pythion, an ancient temple dedicated to Artemis and Apollo-Pythios; inside the temple there used to be a sculpture of Artemis Eileithyia, goddess of child-birth. Saint Anna, to whom the church was dedicated, was also believed to protect expectant mothers. The choice of this location and these beliefs are indicative of the fusion of religions encountered so frequently in Athens.

THE CANELLOPOULOS MUSEUM

The Museum of Paul and Alexandra Canellopoulos is situated on the north slope of the Acropolis near the Ancient Agora. It is a beautiful, small museum where representative examples of Greek civilization are exhibited.

The collection belonged to Paul and Alexandra Canellopoulos.

The Museum was founded in 1976 after the collection was donated to the Greek state. It was housed in one of the most impressive neoclassical buildings in the Plaka. This mansion was constructed in the end of the 19th century and belonged to the Michaleas family. The collection contains around 6.000 objects and works of art, thus revealing the entire

Amphora signed by Nikosthenes

multiformity and extent of the Greek artistic creation from the Prehistoric period to the Modern era. The museum's exhibition has been organized in chronological and thematic units in order for the visitor to be able to follow the development and the peculiarities of Greek art.

The presentation of the exhibition objects begins in the mezzanine of museum. Here, the earliest in date among the collection objects, from the Neolithic (6800-3200 BC) and the Bronze Age (3200-1100 BC) are shown. The cult objects and those of everyday use offer notable images of the Cycladic, Minoan and Mycenaean cultures.

Golden persian jewel

Characteristic of these are the famous marble Cycladic figurines representing in an abstract way the human form, the large marble vessels ("kanteles") and the male form from Minoan Crete wearing the Minoan garment, the "zoma". Geometric pottery and figurines (900-700 BC) from Attica, the Cyclades and Cyprus represent the next period.

Among these stands out an Attic prochous of the 8th century BC bearing the characteristic Geometric decorative motifs together with herons and horses. The tour in Greek art continues on the first floor where the rich collection of Archaic (7th – 6th century BC), Classical (5th – 4th century BC) and Hellenistic (3rd – 2nd century BC) works are on display. Among the Athenian 6th century BC vases two pieces make an impression: the excellently preserved black-figure hydria with a scene of women at a fountain-house and two rare amphorae by the potter Nikosthenes with Dionysiac scenes. The funerary white-ground lekythoi, beautifully decorated, and a red-figure crater by the Dinos Painter, one of the great painters of

The Canellopoulos Museum

his time, mark the most important examples of Attic 5th century pottery. The Tanagraias, the small, pretty and especially elegant terracotta figurines of the 4th and 3rd century BC from Tanagra in Boeotia constitute a remarkable unit. Notably, the figurine of the Muse holding her lyre still carries traces of the colours that once decorated it.

The sculptures, inscriptions, coins, sealstones and vases from the Roman period complete the ancient art. The 2nd century AD marble head of Alexander the Great with the serene expression makes quite an impression as well as the Egyptian Fayum portraits that stand on the verge between ancient and Christian art.

One of the most important units of the Museum is that of the silver and gold jewelry which contains exceptional examples from all periods. Jewels that accompanied the dead, Archaic minute plates that decorated the garments, earrings, necklaces, bracelets and fingerings excite with their technical perfection and reveal the love of ancient peoples for beauty and luxury. Among the ornate Byzantine jewels, a 10th century bracelet stands out bearing demonic figures while the 18th century silver necklaces are remarkable among the works of folk art.

In the ground-floor and lower mezzanine rooms, one can view representative art works of the Byzantine and post-Byzantine periods. The collection of 270 icons is significant. A signed icon by Michael Damaskenos of the "decapitation of St Paraskevi" constitutes a valuable example of one of the most remarkable painters of the 16th century School of Crete.

THE CHURCH OF ST NICHOLAS/ST SERAPHEIM

The 17th-century remains of the Church of St Nicholas (Agios Nikolaos) can be found at the foot of the northern side of the Acropolis, after the Agraulos cave and close to Theorias Street (opposite the Museum of Paul and Alexandra Canellopoulos). According to legend, this church used to be called St Nicholas Paravas, although since 1833 it has been called St Serapheim. Judging by the church's foundations it was of the cross-in-square type which would have been unique in this area during the Ottoman period.

THE CHURCH OF THE TRANSFIGURATION OF THE SAVIOUR

Walking along Theorias Street at the northern foot of the Acropolis, after

Saint Nicholas or Saint Serapheim

THE PLAKA: WALKING IN ATHENS' OLD CITY

The Transfiguration of the Saviour

the junction with Klepsidras Street, one comes across the small Church of the Transfiguration of the Saviour (Metamorfosi tou Sotiros). Known also as Sotirakis ("small Saviour") because of its small size, the church can be dated, on stylistic grounds, to the second half of the 11th century. It is a four-columned, cross-inscribed church with a tall and elegant Athenian dome, typical of Athenian monuments of that time. Of the original church, the northern and southern sides, as well as the dome remain intact, while the eastern and western sides are more recent. The exterior walls have been built in sculpted stone surrounded by bricks, that is in the so-called cloisonné style. In some parts of the walls there are bricks cut into decorative shapes, forming rhombuses and crooked lines; these are called brickwork patterns and were frequently used for the decoration of the external walls of Byzantine monuments in southern Greece. To the south of the church is a small chapel carved in the Acropolis cliff, dedicated to St Paraskevi.

MUSEUM OF HISTORY OF THE UNIVERSITY OF ATHENS (OLD UNIVERSITY)

The Old University of Athens is situated in the Plaka, on 5 Tholou Street. Although we do not know when exactly it was built, we do know that is one of the few remaining buildings from the Ottoman period and can possibly be identified as the building depicted in the painting by Jacques Currey dating from 1674.
The building is known as the House of Kleanthis (it was purchased and developed by the architect Stamatios Kleanthis in 1831). However, according to more recent information, the house

The House of Kleanthes

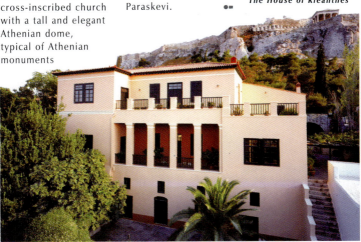

Restoration of a dentist's surgery of the begining the 20th century

belonged jointly to Kleanthis and Eduard Schaubert, the architects who in 1833 developed the first city plans for Athens. The house of the two friends was a place where artists and intellectuals gathered to discuss cultural affairs.

Chosen by the Greek Government in 1835 to house the first secondary school of Athens, only a year later the building proved to be insufficient to cover the school's expanding needs. The school was then transferred elsewhere and a few months later it was decided that the House of Kleanthis should accommodate the newly founded Greek university. The university remained here until 1841, when it was transferred to the half-finished building on Panepistimiou Street.

Later on the house was leased to the Greek Ministry of Education and after that it was used by the Army, until 1861, a year before Kleanthis's death, when it was sold to a private party. In 1963 the house was expropriated by the Archaeological Service, which declared it a listed building.

In 1967 the building was donated to the University of Athens and it was restored to its original form. Since 1987 it has been functioning as the

The Blazon of the University of Athens

STAMATIOS KLEANTHIS

Architect and city planner (1802-62). His masterpiece was the plan of the new city of Athens (1833) and the new city of Piraeus (1834) carried out in collaboration with his German colleague Eduard Schaubert. Apart from town planning, this gifted and innovative personality was also engaged in building design and a marble business. The only buildings of Kleanthis preserved in Athens today are his residence (Old University) in the Plaka and Villa Ilissia, the current Byzantine Museum.

THE PLAKA: WALKING IN ATHENS' OLD CITY

Museum of History of the University of Athens.
The museum's collections consist of rare editions of books and scientific studies, documents, decrees, newspapers, magazines, pamphlets and letters, portraits (mostly by 19th-century Greek painters), stamps and other objects related to university life (banners, flags and medals), as well as scientific instruments related to physics, chemistry, medicine and pharmacology. International conferences, scientific meetings, seminars and lectures organized by the University of Athens are held on a regular basis at the museum.

The Anafiotika

THE CHURCH OF ST SYMEON

The small Church of St Symeon (Agios Simeon) is situated in the Anafiotika district, on Theorias Street towards the Acropolis. It was initially built in the 17th century as a small single-naved barrel-vaulted basilica, but in 1847 was rebuilt by the residents of Anafi, who settled in the area and took over the church's maintenance. The icon of Virgin Mary Kalamiotissa can be seen in the church today.

ANAFIOTIKA

In Plaka there is an area called Anafiotika on the northeastern side at the foot of the Acropolis. The area was first inhabited

A small street at the Anafiotika

OTTOMAN FORTIFICATION OF ATHENS

During the first period of Ottoman rule, while the city was considerably extended beyond the fortifications, the role of the wall was downgraded. Gradually, the older Late Roman defensive wall lost its function. Walled fences and the outer sides of houses made up the city's defenses. The Acropolis fortifications were no longer relevant to the city. Only a part of the south side of the old defenses survived and was repaired, enclosing the Odeon of Herodes Atticus and the area towards the Theatre of Dionysos, known as the bastion Serpentzes. This bastion, which protected the entrance to the fort, was significantly strengthened on the eve of the disastrous siege of the Acropolis by Morosini in 1687. During the second period of Ottoman rule, the fortress was partially repaired. On the north-east side of the Acropolis the wall of Ipapanti, as it was known during the Greek War of Inependence of 1821, was built. This wall both reinforced the safety of the fortress and provided direct communication with the city through the gate near the Church of St Nicholas or Serapheim. In 1778 the voyvoda Hadji Ali Haseki supervised the defense of the city itself. He ordered the construction of a fortification wall to replace the already ruined old walls of Athens. The north section of his wall followed the ancient wall of Themistocles. To the west it surrounded the whole of the ancient Agora. Its south section included the bastion Serpentzes and extended to the ancient Olympieion. To the east, the circuit reached the modern Amalias Avenue. The new wall had a total of seven gates, which either coincided with or were close to the ancient gates. Plenty of information and descriptions, including descriptions, has been preserved on its shape because it was extant up until the War of Independence of 1821.

during the Peloponnesian War (431-404 B.C.) by people from nearby areas. During the Ottoman period workers and black slaves who had been transferred over from Ethiopia used to live there. This is why the area was called back then Kara Su or Mavroneri (Turkish / Greek for "Black Water"), or "Black People's Neighbourhood". A number of black people remained there even after the departure of the Ottomans.
In 1840 a large number of islanders, mostly from the Cyclades, and especially from the islands Anafi and Santorini, moved to Athens. They were builders in their majority, working in the numerous new constructions in the fast developing new capital.
In 1841 the entire area around the Acropolis was declared an archaeological site and it got banned to raise any new buildings there. However, several builders from Anafi decided to ignore the new regulations and started building irregularly the first houses. They worked fast, mostly during the night and helped each

other to raise roofs for the houses, since according to the new regulations no house with a roof would be demolished. Others soon followed and the entire area was named Anafiotika due to the origins (from the island of Anafi) of its new inhabitants. There were no town planning arrangements for the new houses and the streets that were opened up were small and narrow, as they are on the islands. The houses are influenced by the Cycladic architecture with the white colour being dominant.

The area's inhabitants maintained until recent years their cultural identity, avoiding marriages with people from outside their community and continuing in the same line of work, factors that contributed to their authentic character.

RIZOKASTRON

Even though many detailed aspects regarding the phases and chronology of the walls of Athens are still being researched, it is considered certain that during the medieval period the city had three defensive enclosures: the outer ancient wall, the intermediate Late Roman with the Rizokastron and the outer wall of the Acropolis.
During the medieval period, the intermediate defensive line, the Late Roman wall built after the disastrous Herulian invasion of AD 267, was of great importance. The wall started from the Acropolis Propylaia northwards, following the east side of the Panathenaic Way – where its route is

Defensive enclosure

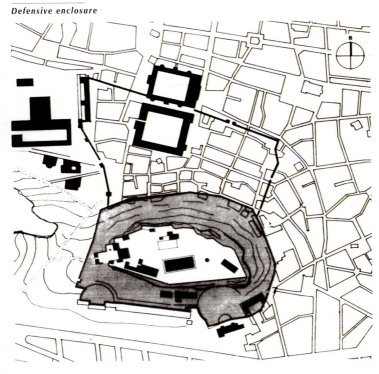

visible today – and turned eastwards at the north end of the Stoa of Attalos towards the Library of Hadrian; 350 metres further, it turned towards the Acropolis, thus enclosing a limited area of the modern-day Plaka district. The wall also extended south of the Acropolis conservation and new work, though of limited extend. Extensive additions to the defensive system took place in the Frankish period. According to the latest excavation data, in the years following 1205 an additional enclosure, the Rizokastron, was built Epicharmou, Stratonos and Thrasillou Streets and crossing the ruins of Pericles' Odeon it encircled the orchestra of the Theatre of Dionysus. The next section on the south slope ran along the course of the Late Roman wall. The Rizokastron considerably reinforced

Athens in 1820. One may see the Acropolis, the Odeon of Herodes and part of the Serpentze

surrounding the Odeon of Herodes Atticus and the Stoa of Eumenes. Architectural elements of ruined monuments were built into both faces of the wall, which was 3-3.50m thick, while roughcast bonding was used in the filling.
During the Byzantine period the city remained within the Late Roman wall. At the end of the 10th century, and between the 11th and 12th centuries, it was extended beyond the fortification wall. There is evidence of both at the foot of the Acropolis fortress. This new wall was constructed both to strengthen the defense of the fortress, where the Frankish rulers resided, and to provide greater security for the people, thus encouraging them to return to the city, which they had deserted during the siege. The Rizokastron surrounded the fortress as a perimeter. In the north part, it followed present-day Theorias and Pritaneiou Streets. Then it turned southwards along the western part of the Acropolis fortifications while its only entrance was transferred closer to the Odeon of Herodes Atticus. Around the middle of the 13th century, the Klepsydra spring was also included in the wall. The intermediate fortification wall with the Rizokastron was preserved until the end of the Middle Ages. The name "Rizokastron" continued to be used, in reference to the district north of the Acropolis.

THE PLAKA: WALKING IN ATHENS' OLD CITY

Model of a byzantine church

THE CHURCH OF ST GEORGE ON THE CLIFF

If your walk takes you to Stratonos Street, on the north-eastern side of the foot of the Acropolis, look out for the small Church of St George on the Cliff (Agios Georgios tou Vrachou).
This church was built in the 17th century and renovated during the mid-19th century, following the development of the Anafiotika area.
It is a single-naved barrel-vaulted church with blind arches on the longer sides, a popular architectural type during the Ottoman period in Athens (as in the Churches of St Symeon, Holy Power (Agia Dinami), St Athanasios Kourkouris, St Demetrius Loubardiaris).
The name of the church stems from its location at the foot of the cliff of the Acropolis. A few yards away from the garden on the eastern side one can see a memorial stone dedicated to Konstantinos Koukidis, an Acropolis guard, who, according to tradition, wrapped himself in the Greek flag and took his own life when the Germans invaded Athens on 27 April 1941.

THE CHURCH OF ST NICHOLAS RANGABAS

The Church of St Nicholas Rangabas (Agios Nikolaos Rangavas) is situated north-east of the Acropolis, between Pritaneiou and Epicharmou Streets. It dates to the first half of the 11th century and it is one of the city's most important Byzantine monuments. In more recent years it has had significant additions and alterations.
According to written sources, the name Rangabas belongs to a family well-established in Athens and Constantinople, whose best known member

Saint Nicholas Rangabas

was emperor Michael I Rangabe (811-13). There are no existing written documents regarding the foundation of the church. However, it played such an important part in medieval Athens that a whole surrounding area was named after it, as was a nearby gate on the defensive walls, the Rangabas Gate. Initially private, it eventually became, and still is, a parish church.

Experts date the building to the 11th century (1040-50) because of stylistic characteristics similar to those of numerous other churches from that period (Sotira of Lykodemos c. 1031, Kapnikarea c. 1050, St Catherine, before 1050). The church has been in its present form since the conservation work of 1979-80 that uncovered several original elements, such as the dome, the roofs and the northern side.

Examining the northeastern side one can identify the characteristic mid-Byzantine arrangement of the façades and the spaces. The large vertical tiles have been arranged in a parallel on the lower part of the wall without yet forming a cross. The masonry follows the cloisonné style, i.e. sculpted four-sided stones have been used, surrounded by bricks. There are a few decorative kufic brick patterns and there are also numerous ancient pieces of architecture in use, quite a frequent practice in this period. A particular decorative element is the double row of dentils around the whole exterior of the church. The dome is also typical of the period; small, smart, with eight sides, it belongs to the Athenian type. St Nicholas is a four-columned, domed, cross-in-square type of church, similar to that of St Asomatoi in Thisseio and the Church of the Metamorphosis on the northern side of the Acropolis. In more recent years the chapel of St Paraskevi was added on the northern side. Later on, the church, around which the area of Anafiotika had begun to develop, was extended to the west with the addition of the narthex and the belfry, while the apses on the eastern side took the form of a unified buttress.

28 Tripodon Street

THE PLAKA: WALKING IN ATHENS' OLD CITY

HELLENIC SOCIETY FOR THE PROTECTION OF THE ENVIRONMENT AND CULTURAL INHERITANCE

The headquarters of the Hellenic Society for the Protection of the Environment and Cultural Inheritance is at 28 Tripodon Street in the Plaka, in an attractive, old building. The society was established in 1971-72 with the mission to awaken interest in the protection of Greece's cultural inheritance, ecosystems and ecological balance. To this end, the society has become involved in projects that draw attention to Greece's architectural inheritance, the protection of the natural environment, endangered species and habitats as well projects that aim to improve the infrastructure for such activities and for environmental education.

The Parlour, with part of an ancient wall

The activities of the society are accompanied by cultural events, exhibitions, publications, seminars and lectures, educational programmes and tours. A member of the European Environmental Bureau since 1975, the society has been repeatedly congratulated for its activities by the pan-European federation of non-governmental heritage organizations, Europa Nostra. The society's headquarters includes a shop where books on nature and architecture, toys, ecological food and gifts are sold. The building also houses a lending library and a room designated for cultural events. A part of ancient Tripodon Street, which can be seen in the basement of the building, is of particular interest, highlighting the continuity of Athens as a city.

Ancient Wall

THE CHURCH OF ST JOHN THE THEOLOGIAN (AGIOS IOANNIS THEOLOGOS)

The church of St John the Theologian (Agios Ioannis Theologos) is situated at the junction of Erechtheos and Erotokritou Streets, under the northern side of the Acropolis. The church has been maintained in a good condition, without any significant alterations.

There are no sources referring to the church's history, however it can be dated from the late 11th or early 12th century, based on its architectural style. This dating has been verified by a copper coin from the reign of Alexios I Komnenos (1081-1118) that was found on the church's roof while it was being restored.

The church is of the two-columned, cross-in-square type with a dome and narthex, a type frequently encountered in Athenian churches during the mid-Byzantine era (10th-12th century).

The eight-sided, small, elegant dome with the marble colonettes on the edges of its sides, the so-called Athenian dome is also characteristic of the medieval monuments of Athens. With the exception of the southern side, the church's exterior masonry follows the cloisonné style, i.e. the use of sculpted stones surrounded by bricks. The contrast between the white stone and the reddish bricks creates a particular colour effect which is characteristic of the Byzantine monuments of that period.

The dome is internally supported by the walls of the sanctuary and two columns with Roman capitals. During the Byzantine era the second use of older architectural parts was quite frequent.

The church's interior painted decoration was uncovered during restoration works. The mural paintings, despite their provincial character are particularly important, as very few samples of Byzantine painting have been preserved in the churches of Athens.

On the dome there is a depiction of Christ Pantocrator ("all-sovereign") and above the sanctuary a depiction of the Ascension. On the northern compartment of the sanctuary there is a depiction of a saint on horseback, clad in armour, who could be identified as St. George. Particularly important on that painting is the realistic depiction of the horse, the detail on the saint's clothing and the overall monumental character of the scene. The mural paintings are stylistically similar to those from a number of monuments that date from the first half of the 13th century and have been crafted according to experts by a local atelier of Athens which allows their dating to the same period. ••

The Ascension (up), Riding Military Saint (down)

Monastery Dependency Of The Holy Sepulchre (Agioi Anargyroi Kolokinthi)

The Church of St Anargyroi (healing saints) Kolokinthi is

THE PLAKA: WALKING IN ATHENS' OLD CITY

> **ANARGYRIAN QUOTATIONS**
> *The Anargyrian Quotations are hand-written extracts from the unpublished work of Ioannis Benizelos (1730-1807) on the history of Athens from antiquity until 1754. They were found in the Monastery Dependency of the Holy Sepulchre in 1937 and they are now kept in the Gennadius Library.*

situated on Erechtheos Street, in the Anafiotika area, and is also known as the Monastery Dependency (Metochion) of the Holy Sepulchre, since it belongs to the Patriarchate of the Holy Sepulchre of Jerusalem. The church is typical of the style that developed exclusively in Athens during the Ottoman period. It is a part of an alley where the premises of the Exarchate in Athens are situated, together with a number of remaining cells from a former monastic building. The Church of St Anargyroi was built c. 1600. Funded by the well-established Kolokinthis family, it was built on the Palaiologos family burial site.

The priest Dimitrios Kolokinthis turned the church into a monastery in 1651 and bequeathed his whole estate to it. It was a women's monastery until 1700, then a men's monastery until the mid-18th century, when it came under the jurisdiction of the Patriarchate of Jerusalem. In 1858 it was renovated and decorated with mural paintings, while in 1972-3 the Ephorate of Byzantine Antiquities carried out conservation work on its exterior. A number of important historical documents, also known as "anargyrian quotations", have been found there.

St Anargyroi is a single-naved, barrel-vaulted church, with its vault and semi-domes ending in squinches; the church's porch and tribune were added during its renovation. The type of roofing encountered here was influenced by the Islamic public buildings of the era. The corners are made of large marble or stone blocks that were parts of older buildings, while the masonry with small, plain stones is typical of the period. There are stone arches over the windows, while at the top of the walls there is a dented cornice. One can also see traces of the brick decoration around the church's earlier entrance, alongside the contemporary one. The church's interior decoration is more recent; the wall paintings show western influences and are surrounded by classical plaster decorations. The wooden screen is neoclassical with artistic

Dependance of the Holy Sepulchre

elements from the Ottoman era, as is the marble belfry. According to the inscription underneath the entrance cornice, the church took its present form following its 1858 renovation. That was funded by the Patriarchate of Jerusalem.
In the garden one can see an old well and one of the oldest preserved street lamps in Athens.
The Church of St Anargyroi is one of the best known in Athens, particularly because of its close association with the Easter religious celebrations: this is where the Holy Light from Jerusalem first arrives on the night of Saturday before Easter Sunday, and on Good Friday the Epitaph is taken from the church in a procession around the quaint small streets of the area.

> **THE HAMAM**
>
> The Hamam was an important place of entertainment and discussion for both men and women, while balls and feasts were often held there by women visitors. According to Elisabeth Craven, who visited Athens in 1786, "the bath is the most entertaining place for women. They spend there more than five hours a day."

THE CHURCH OF VIRGIN MARY CHRISSOKASTRIOTISSA

The Church of St Mary Chrisso-kastriotissa, dedicated to the Assumption of the Virgin, is situated on the northern side of the foot of the Acropolis. It is a single-naved 17th-century church named after the fact that it was close to the city walls ("kastro" means defensive wall). According to legend, during the Ottoman rule there was always an oil-lamp burning in the church in honour of the Virgin Mary, who was believed to heal sick children. ●—

THE CHURCH OF ST SPYRIDON AND HOLY BELT OF VIRGIN MARY

In the densely populated area around Lissiou Street visitors are surprised when they come across the Church of St Spyridon and Holy Belt of Virgin Mary (Agia Zoni), as it is not easily visible among all the houses. This 16th-17th century church was initially a three-aisled basilica; it was rebuilt after the opening up of Lissiou Street and its northern aisle was removed. In ancient times there was an altar of Bacchus on the same site. ●—

THE HAMAM (TURKISH BATH) OF ABID EFENDI

The Hamam of Abid Efendi, known as the Baths of Aerides, is situated at 8 Kirristou Street in the Plaka, near the Roman Agora, and is today a branch of the Museum of Greek Folk Art, where periodic exhibitions are hosted. Its original interior spaces have been restored and may be visited.
The building, built in the 17th century, is the only surviving Ottoman public bath in Athens. Its architecture is very

Bishop's Mitra

THE PLAKA: WALKING IN ATHENS' OLD CITY

plain.
In the Ottoman period the bath was divided into three halls. First was the cloakroom, which acted as a reception, lounge, rest and recreation room. The second hall, the "cool" room, was moderately heated to prepare the body before entering the third hall, the "warm" room with running water and basins. There were small personal apartments for customers who required privacy.
In the Ottoman period both men and women used the bath, but each sex visited the bath at different hours of the day. In the 1870s this procedure was changed and new halls were built for use at the same time by both men and women.
The Hamam was open until 1965. In 1984 it was allocated to the Museum of Greek Folk Art and restoration was completed in 1998.

MUSEUM OF POPULAR INSTRUMENTS

The building which houses the Museum of Popular Instruments is situated on 1-3 Diogenous Street; it was built in 1842 as

Clay oblong folk drum

Pear-shaped lyre from Creta

the residence of Georgios Lassanis (1796–1870), who participated in the Greek War of Independence and later became a Minister of Finance.
The museum opened in 1991. The displays originated from the collection of the prominent musicologist Foivos Anogeianakis. Donated by Anogeianakis to the Greek State in 1978, the collection consists of around 1,200 18th-century musical instruments and is one of the most important of its kind throughout Greece and Europe. Visitors to the museum can admire the instruments on display and also listen to recordings of the music produced by each one of them.
The museum organizes concerts of traditional folk music from various parts of Greece and promotes the research and the study of traditional music. The main building houses the displays, the library and administration offices. The Research Centre for Ethnomusicology and the museum's warehouse, shop and archives are housed in another building nearby (the former stable-block of the Lassanis residence).

MEDRESE

The building of the medrese, the Islamic theological school, was situated between the Museum of Popular Instruments and the Fethiye Mosque on Diogenous Street. It was built by Mehmet Fahri in 1721, according to a marble inscription on its gate. The space today is property of the Greek Archaeological Service. The medrese is a basic and indispensable institution in any Muslim city. The one in Athens used to be a square building with an interior yard. Around the yard there

were eleven cells with an ambulatory, where the teaching took place. The medrese was the highest level of the Islamic education. The main subjects taught were reading, memorizing and interpretation of the Koran, religious law, theology, philosophy and Arabic, Persian and Turkish literature.
Soon after the foundation of the Greek State the medrese was turned into a prison. Later on a second store was added to the building. Its demolition started in 1914; however, due to the archaeological finds that were uncovered, several parts of the building, including the gate with the marble inscription, were maintained.

Medrese (otthoman seminary)

THE TOWER OF THE WINDS OR HOROLOGION OF ANDRONICUS OF CYRRHUS

To the east of the Roman Agora lies the Tower of the Winds, one of the better-preserved buildings of ancient Athens. In Antiquity it was called the House of Cyrrhestus, after the name of its architect, Andronicus, the Macedonian astronomer from the city of Cyrrhus in Macedonia. The ancient authors call it simply the "Horologion" (Clock). It was an important, experimental building, functioning as a wind-indicator, a hydraulic clock and a sundial. The most probable date for its construction is between 150 and 125 BC.
The monument was built on an octagonal plan: each side is 3.20 meters long and its total height is 12 meters. It was built entirely of Pentelic marble. A cylindrical annex was attached to its southern side. There were two entrances, one on the north-eastern and one on the north-western side. In front of each entrance there was a small portico with Corinthian columns. The roof was conical and tiled with marble slabs. On the tip of the cone was a marble Corinthian capital, topped with a copper Triton holding a sceptre, to gauge which direction the wind was blowing from. On the upper part of each side of the octagon stand representations in relief of the eight winds in the form of winged gods: Borreus (the north wind), Sciron (the north-west wind), Zephyr (the west

The Horologion (clock) of Cyrrhestus

THE PLAKA: WALKING IN ATHENS' OLD CITY

Lips, the SW wind, from the Tower of the Winds

wind), Lips (the south-west wind), Notos (the south-east wind), Euros (the south-east wind), Apeliotes (the east wind) and Caecias (the north-east wind). Under the reliefs, on

Danse of the Dervishes at the Tower of the Winds

each side of the octagon, as well as on the curve of the annex, there was a sundial. What remains today are the carvings on the walls showing the hours, but the metal indicators are missing. In order to estimate the time on cloudy days and at night, the interior of the House of Cyrrhestus was provided with a hydraulic water clock, which functioned with a complicated system of filling and emptying water; the cylindrical annex visible from the outside was the water tank for this machine. The exact way in which this hydraulic clock worked has not yet been revealed, although descriptions of the systems of other hydraulic clocks in Antiquity give some clue.

On the marble floor of the interior one can still see the small canals left by the clock's water pipes. The internal walls are divided into four parts, with cornices. The upper part and the interior of the roof are particularly interesting, as they form a pseudo-dome supported by eight Doric columns. The Tower of the Winds represented an innovative meteorological

Evros (the SE wind)

station, combining monumental architecture and the high technology of its time. In early Christian times it was transformed into a baptistery for an adjacent basilical church. Cyriacus of Ancona, a 15th-century traveller, mentions the building and identifies it falsely as a temple of Aiolos. In the 18th century it was transformed into a "tekke", a meeting place for Dervishes of the Mevlevi order, and called "the tekke of Braimis". Later, both the building and the surrounding neighborhood became known as Aerides (i.e. winds). The interior of the monument is closed to the public. ••

FETHIYE MOSQUE

Fethiye Cami (The Mosque of Victory) stands on the corner of

WALK 7

Fethiye Cami
(The Mosque of Victory)

Panos and Pelopida Streets near the Roman Ágora. It was built after Mehmed II Fatih (the Conqueror) came to Athens, around 1458, and just like all mosques under the same name built the same period in other Ottoman towns, it commemorates the Fall of Constantinople in 1453. Today the mosque is property of the Archaeological Society acting as a storehouse of archaeological material. The building is also known under the names "Mosque of the Wheat Market" and "Market Mosque", due to the position it held near the cereal market during the Ottoman period. Despite its historical significance, its architecture is not particularly interesting. From October 1687, after Athens was occupied by Venetian troops commanded by Francesco Morosini, until April 1688, the mosque was converted into a Catholic church dedicated to St Dionysius Areopagite. When the Venetians left the city, the mosque returned to its previous use, which finally changed after the Greek War of Independence of 1821. In 1824 the place was used as School of the Filomoussos Society (Society of the Muses' Friends), while the building was later managed by the Greek Army. As a result, the building was first used in 1843 as a guardhouse. It was either then or earlier that the minaret was pulled down according to the general trend of the times to "clean" Greece from its Ottoman past. The place was later used as a military prison, garrison headquarters and military bakery. •=

THE PLAKA: WALKING IN ATHENS' OLD CITY

ROMAN AGORA

To the east of the Ancient Agora, just on the edge of the Plaka, surrounded by M. Avriliou, Pelopida,

The Gate of Athena Archegetis

Panos, Polignotou, Epameinonda and Dioskouron Streets, lies the open space of the Roman Agora. This is a large rectangular fenced space, where one can see the remains of the market place as well as the Hellenistic Horologion of Andronicus of Cyrrhus (otherwise known as the Tower of the Winds) on the east side and the Fethiye Mosque on the west side. After the destruction of the city by Sulla in 86 BC the Ancient Agora, traditional centre of the political and economic life of the city, underwent a phase of transformation through the addition of several new buildings, many of them funded by rich Romans who were attracted to Athens. In this way, however, the operational space for merchants and artisans was dramatically reduced, and this led to the creation of a new market place to the east of the old one, on the spot where an open market already existed, used by farmers for selling produce (the "Eretria" of Strabo). In 51 BC Julius Ceasar offered to fund the construction of the new market place, which was interrupted, however, between 47 and 31 BC due to the Roman civil wars. Only in 19 BC was Octavian Augustus, victor of the wars, able to continue the construction of the market, which was finally named after him. On the western end of the new Agora a monumental gate dedicated to Athena Archegetis (Athena the Leader) was erected, placed wisely at the junction of two major streets of ancient Athens, one leading east from the ancient Agora and the other leading to the Acropolis. The gate consists of four Doric columns and a gable of Pentelic marble. According to a dedicatory inscription, it was completed in 11 BC.

What we see today is not the entire market place. Its north-western and northern

The Roman Agora, with the Fethiye Cami in the background

WALK 7

> ### 🛈 THE DEDICATORY INSCRIPTION ON THE WESTERN GATE
> *"The people of Athens from the donations given by Gaius Julius Caesar Divus and his Venerated Son Emperor God [dedicated this gate] to Athena the Leader (Archegetis) at the time when Eukles from the demos of Marathon was general of the infantry; he inherited the cure for the sake of his father Herodes who was ambassador at the time of the archon Nikias, son of Sarapion, from the demos of the Athmoneis."*

colonnades are buried underneath adjacent modern buildings. The central court, however, 111m by 98m, is still visible. It was surrounded by an Ionic peristyle on all four sides. The shops and warehouses were situated just behind this peristyle. Possibly the southern and northern sides were provided with a second peristyle, built in Doric style.
On the east side there was a second monumental gate, of gray Hymettus marble. Just beside it is situated the Horologion of Andronicus of Cyrrhus; next to this, in the middle of the 1st century BC, a rectangular building was erected, named, probably erroneously, Agoranomeion, i.e. the headquarters of the market controllers. Today one can see its façade with typical Roman arched doorways. On the architrave is discernible part of an inscription, dedicating the building to the Theoi Sebastoi (Venerated Gods) and to Athena Archegetis. Other parts of the same inscription were found in the building and on the Acropolis, yet the piece revealing the building's use and name has not been discovered. The reference to the Theoi Sebastoi leads some archaeologists to believe that it was the Sebasteion, i.e. a building dedicated to the imperial cult. Between the Agoranomeion (or Sebasteion) and the Agora are the latrinae, or public toilets, built by Emperor Vespasian. It is a rectangular building, with roof, entrance hall and a square room with benches provided with holes, under which ran the open sewage pipes.
At the time of the Emperor Hadrian the Agora was embellished; for example, with marble paving. On the inner side of the Western Gate were inscribed, on imperial demand, decrees relating to the taxation of agricultural products, especially olive oil. After the

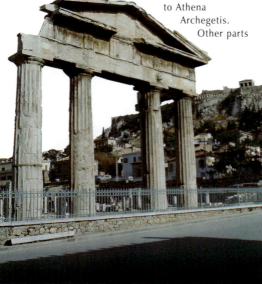

The Gate of Athena Archegetis

invasion of the Herulians (AD 267) the city's administrative and commercial centre was transferred to the Roman Agora. Finally, during the Byzantine and Ottoman periods, the area was covered with houses and workshops, at least one church and the Mosque of Mehmed II the Conqueror, known as the Fethiye Mosque. The Roman Agora was systematically excavated by the Archaeological Society in the 1930s, by Italian archaeologists between 1940 and 1942, and by Orlandos and Lazaridis in the 1960s. Since that time, the 1st Ephorate of Prehistoric and Classical Antiquities has carried out some digs. The excavations brought to light a portrait of Augustus, to be found today in the National Archaeological Museum. We also know from 18th-century engravings that at the top of the western gate there was an acroterion depicting Lucius Caesar, grandson of Augustus, on horseback. Other findings include inscriptions and architectural or sculptural decorations, most of which are exhibited in the Roman Agora. In the summer months the Roman Agora hosts occasional concerts.

Saint Elias and the Taxiarches

Church Of Taxiarches-Panagia Grigoroussa

Between the archaeological sites of Hadrian's Library and the Roman Agora, in Dexippou Street, stands the church of Taxiarches (Archangels Michael and Gabriel) and Virgin Mary (Panagia) Grigoroussa, built in the 19th century. At the same site there used to be a small church of Taxiarches in the Byzantine period. The church was of the cross-in-square two columned type with a dome. Its original form dates back to the 12th century. Later on, during the period of Frankish rule, a narthex and a belfry were added, while in the Ottoman period the Last Judgement was depicted on the facade. The church of Prophet Elias (Profitis Ilias) of the Staropazaro (wheat market) used to be a little to the north and probably was a building dating back to the Byzantine period (11th-12th cent.), converted into a church and decorated in the 15th century. Both medieval churches were pulled down around the mid-19th century during the archaeological research in the Roman Agora, which aimed to highlight classical antiquity.

The Plaka

The Plaka district stretches along the foot of the Acropolis and is enclosed by

The Taxiarches or the Church of Virgin Mary (Panagia Grigoroussa)

WALK 7

Dionissiou Areopagitou, Amalias, Nikis and Mitropoleos Streets. It is the oldest quarter of modern Athens, as its tortuous street plan, which often follows the ancient layout, suggests.

There is evidence of habitation in the Plaka from Prehistoric times, and the area has been an essential part of the city of Athens throughout its history, from Antiquity to date.

The visitor who strolls around the narrow streets of the Plaka is aware of the coexistence and sometimes the mingling of monuments or parts of them dating back to different

The Plaka

THE PLAKA: WALKING IN ATHENS' OLD CITY

Adrianou Street

periods. Columns from ancient buildings stand in front of Byzantine churches, ancient architectural features are incorporated into subsequent constructions and buildings used in different ways throughout history. What gives the Plaka its original style is that these monuments do not seem to be distant and secluded, as is the case in a museum, but are fully incorporated into the area. As a result, the different historical periods are not clearly distinguished by the layman, who finds difficulty in detecting their traces in the Plaka's complicated architecture and street plan. However, this is a charming feature of an area that has been continuously inhabited for 6,000 years.
The present-day Plaka has not changed greatly since the 19th and early 20th centuries. The buildings of the area reflect the development of popular Athenian architecture, with the internal courtyard a predominant feature, around which the architectural synthesis is laid out. Few buildings from the Ottoman period have survived. Exceptions are the building in Scholeiou Street, which takes the form of a tower-like house, known as the Church Residence, named after the philhellene and fighter in the Greek War of Independence of 1821, who lived there. Buildings from the period of King Otto, the first King of Greece, have simple ground plans and regular, symmetrically placed openings. The Lassanis Residence near the Tower of the Winds, the present-day Museum of Popular Instruments, belongs to this period. Not long after, when neoclassicism became the prevailing architectural style, a local, popular version of the style was formed, characterized by the essential presence of balconies and typical decorative features (such as ornamental edge tiles, door posts and banisters). Towards the late 19th century styles become more eclectic, with more storeys than before and numerous decorative features of different origins, which give the buildings a more luxurious look. The building at the junction of Aiolou and Pelopida Streets is typical of this style. (Today the building houses the 3rd Ephorate of Prehistoric and Classical Antiquities.) Finally, from the 1920s onwards, when the first reinforced concrete buildings emerge and architectural modernism appears, the style changes once again.
Of particular interest are the buildings and the street layout of Anafiotika in the Plaka, strongly reminiscent of the popular architecture of the Cyclades islands. The Plaka is also full of old churches, many of which date back to the Byzantine period. They are small and modest, often hidden among

the surrounding houses, thus giving the area a unique colour, especially during the Good Friday procession.

From the foundation of the Greek State to date there have been decisive moments in the development of the neighbourhood. The first was the working-out of the first city plan. According to the plan of architects Stamatios Kleanthis and Eduard Schaubert, the entire city and the Plaka itself were to be pulled down for the new city. The fact that this plan was never realized is widely considered to be the reason for the various problems of modern Athens (such as traffic). On the other hand, this was a fortunate non-event, in that the Plaka's street layout was preserved.

One century later, in the mid-war period, the Plaka had become a legend. As the capital changed radically, citizens were swept by nostalgia for "old Athens". The narrow streets and steep roads of the Plaka, the little taverns and low houses often appeared in songs of the time and became symbols of a vanishing lifestyle.

However, post-war developments affected the Plaka. The area was unable to respond to increased tourism: there was neither preparation nor a clear programme to respond to the new challenges. There was uncontrolled rebuilding, heavy

A small street at the Plaka

traffic and gradual degradation of the city centre, which led to the district's decline. At the end of the 1970s the Plaka was an area full of dilapidated buildings, with numerous tourist shops, nightclubs and bars, which had nothing to do with the area's essential character. Thanks to the coordinated efforts of the state, specialists and inhabitants of the area, a set of beneficial measures was implemented in subsequent years. Today the Plaka is worthy of its cultural wealth, with renovated buildings, tasteful cafés, restaurants, taverns and several cultural centres (such as archaeological sites, museums and theatres), which make it not an open-air museum but a lively urban area of unique beauty where past and present, the needs of tourists and of residents, as well as entertainment and culture, do not compete but complete each other.

8

WALK 8

1. Monastiraki Square
2. Pantanassa (Monastiraki)
3. The Tzistarakis Mosque
4. St Assomatoi on the Steps
5. The Hadrian's Library
6. Megali Panagia
7. Avissinias Square
8. St Philip
9. The Ancient Agora
10. The Poikile Stoa
11. The Sanctuary of Aphrodite Ourania
12. The Panathenaic Way
13. The Royal Stoa (Basileios Stoa)
14. The Stoa of Zeus Eleutherios
15. The Altar of the Twelve Gods
16. The Temple of Ares
17. The Temple of Apollo Patroos
18. The Arsenal
19. The Hephesteion (Theseion)
20. The Monument of Eponymous Heroes
21. The Old Bouleuterion and the Metroon

ARCHAEOLOGICAL SITE OF THE ANCIENT AGORA

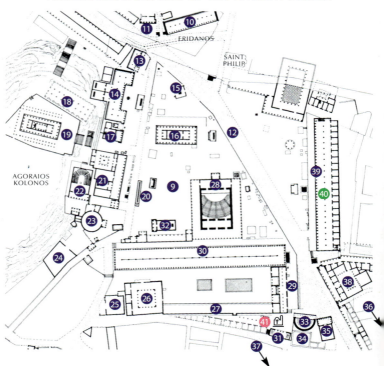

22 The New Bouleuterion (Council House)
23 The Tholos
24 The Strategeion
25 The Southwest Fountain House
26 The Heliaia
27 The South Stoa
28 The Odeon of Agrippa
29 The East Building
30 The Middle Stoa
31 The Enneakrounos
32 The Southwest Temple
33 The Nymphaeum
34 The Mint
35 The Southeast Temple
36 The Eleusinion
37 Houses in the Agora
38 The Library of Pantainos
39 The Stoa of Attalos
40 The Ancient Agora Museum
41 Holy Apostles Solaki

THE HEART OF ANCIENT ATHENS

On the way out from the underground station at Thisseio the visitor faces the temple of Hephaestus, the best preserved ancient temple in Greece. It is situated on the top of a small hill that dominates the space of the ancient Agora, the heart of the city at the time of Pericles and Socrates. A landmark in the Agora area is the building of the Stoa of Attalos, which today hosts the Agora Museum. After a tour around the ancient Agora, there is the option of an interesting walk in Athens' junk shops on Avissinias Square, just opposite the entrance to the Agora.

MONASTIRAKI SQUARE

See Route 7

THE CHURCH OF THE PANTANASSA (MONASTIRAKI)

The church of St Mary Pantanassa ("Virgin Mary queen of all") is in Monastiraki Square, between Athinas and Mitropoleos Streets, opposite the metro station. The church used to be known as the Great Monastery and later as Monastiraki ("the small monastery") and this is the origin of the name of the whole area. Excavation for the new underground station uncovered remains of floor mosaics from the 5th century, as well as remains of houses from that period. The original church was probably built on the site during the 11th century. The contemporary church dates back to the 17th century and is the best-preserved of the three-aisled barrel-vaulted basilicas that were modelled on the church of St Dionysius Areopagite. The central aisle is raised higher than the others, and is covered by a barrel vault, whereas the side aisles are covered by cross vaults. According to a patriarchal sigillion of 1678 (a document carrying the stamp of ecclesiastic authority), the Church of the Pantanassa was formerly the metochion of the Monastery of Kaissariani on Hymettus hill, it was founded by Nikolaos

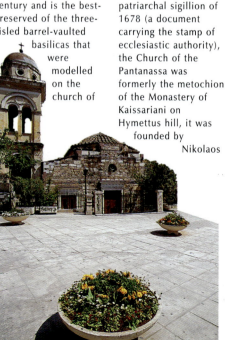

The Church of Virgin Mary (Panagia Pantanassa)

Bonefatzis (Bonefaccio) and it was a women's monastery. Later on, the church developed into the Great Monastery and the textiles produced there were sold in the nearby market. During the 18th and 19th centuries it was one of the most important parish churches in Athens. Towards the end of the 19th century, with archaeological excavation and the construction of the nearby metro station, the church lost most of its monastic buildings and was down-graded to a "monastiraki". The church underwent repairs in 1911 and its western façade was altered. The tall classicising belfry was also added at this time. At present, extensive conservation and repair work is being carried out in the interior of the church.

TZISTARAKIS MOSQUE

According to an inscription over the mosque's entrance, Mustafa Aga Tzistarakis, an Ottoman official in Athens, founded it in 1759. According to the legend, in order to build the mosque they burned a column from the Olympieion to get the necessary lime. Later on the mosque also became known by other names, such as the "Mosque of the Lower Fountain" from the fountain that used to be in the building, "Mosque of the Lower Market" and "Mosque in Monastiraki Square". After the end of the Ottoman rule the mosque's minaret was destroyed. With the foundation of the Greek State, when all the Ottoman public buildings were used by the State, the mosque was given to the army. The first piece of information that we have regarding the mosque's use as a guardhouse is from 1843. Later on the space was used as a prison, a military camp and a warehouse.
In 1915 the mosque was restored to its original form by Anastassios Orlandos. Three years later the building housed the new "Museum of Greek Handicrafts". In 1923 it was named "National Museum of Decorative Arts" and finally in 1959 it was named "Museum of Greek Folk Art". In 1973 the museum was transferred to another building and the mosque was used as an auxiliary building which housed from 1975 the display of the ceramics collection.
The destructive earthquake of 1981 caused serious damages to the mosque. In 1991, after the repairs of the damages, the mosque operated again as the museum's branch

The Tzistarakis Mosque

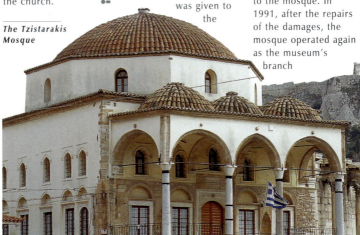

THE HEART OF ANCIENT ATHENS

and the displays of the ceramics collection was enriched with additions from the Centre for the Study of Traditional Pottery.

The displays of the collection are divided in two categories of ceramics. The first category on display in the museum's ground-floor includes works created by well known Greek potters. The second category includes ceramic objects of everyday use collected from various parts of Greece which have been put on display in the building's mezzanine.

THE CHURCH OF ST ASSOMATOI ON THE STEPS

The church known as "St Assomatoi on the Steps" (Agioi Assomatoi sta skalia) is a mid-Byzantine church dedicated to the Archangels. It used to be attached to the exterior western wall of Hadrian's Library next to its entrance and was situated a few metres south from the

The church of the Saint Assomatoi on the Steps. Copper engraving

Tzistarakis Mosque in Monastiraki Square. Today only fragments of the church's mural paintings have been preserved on the Library's wall. The church's form is known to us through its depictions by foreign travellers of the 18th and 19th century. The church was of the cross-in-square type with an octagonal dome, built in the 11th century. The inscriptions on the Library's columns indicate that the church belonged to the well-established Chalkokondylis family. It under-went repairs in 1576. At this time the mural paintings, fragments of which have been preserved, were made.

The church was demolished in around 1842 in order to carry out archaeological research to reveal finds from the classical antiquity.

HADRIAN'S LIBRARY

On the way from Monastiraki Square to Areos Street, at the junction with Adrianou Street and just next to Tzistarakis Mosque, one can see the façade of the library that Emperor Hadrian offered to the city

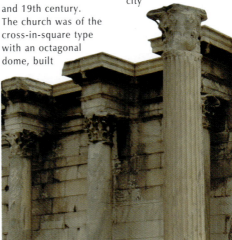

Hadrian's Library

of Athens in AD 132. The archaeological site is closed to the public during restoration and further excavation, so the visitor needs to walk farther up Adrianou Street in order to get a better view of the site: turning left to Aiolou Street one gets a panoramic view from the east. In the 2nd century AD, according to Pausanias, Hadrian's Library was the most magnificent building in Athens. It was built on a rectangular 122m by 82m, and was situated to the north of the Roman Agora. The central part of the building formed a rectangular courtyard, 82m by 60m, surrounded by a peristyle. The columns were made of Phrygian marble (pavonazzeto), dark with white and purple veins. In the central court were originally an artificial pond and a garden, where readers could relax or meditate. Today the remains of a tetraconch church are visible on the site of the pond: this is probably the earliest church in Athens, built in the first half of the 5th century.

On the northern and southern sides of the library lay the reading rooms, consisting of a rectangular and two semicircular niches, where benches were placed. The main reading room

A view of the Tetraconch

The façade of Hadrian's Library

("Bibliostasion") was situated just behind the eastern portico and consisted of a large room provided with niches and wooden shelves, where the books and manuscripts were kept. It was flanked by two smaller rooms, probably also serving as reading rooms. These small rooms opened on to two larger ones, known as lecture rooms due to the discovery of a tribune in one of them. The internal walls behind the portico were revetted with marble. People entered through the main entrance from the west, through a monumental propylon decorated with four fluted Corinthian columns made of Phrygian marble, contrasting with the Pentelic marble of the pediment and entablature. The propylon is currently being restored with new pieces of marble. Corinthian columns, of Carystian marble (cipollino), seven on each side of the gate, decorated the façade; several of them are still extant.

The library was destroyed in 267 during the Herulian invasion. Most of its internal columns were thereafter taken away to decorate other buildings. In 412 the Prefect Herculius restored the building, if in a less grandiose way. A few years later the tetraconch church referred to above was built. During the Ottoman period the mansion of the voyvoda, the supreme Ottoman administrator, was built on the site of the library. In 1835 this mansion was altered to house the soldiers of King Otto.

Excavations began under Wilhelm Doerpfeld and Stephanos Koumanoudis in 1885, following a fire, which destroyed the marketplace.

THE CHURCH OF THE TETRACONCH – MEGALI PANAGIA

In the garden of Hadrian's Library one can see the remains of what is believed to be the oldest Christian church in Athens. This is the Tetraconch, a marble central plan church founded during the 5th century. One can still see parts of the foundations and the lower walls, as well as remnants of the mosaic floor.

The church used to consist of a central square room with four conches that were accentuated by interior colonnades, an interior corridor that surrounded the room and a large narthex and atrium on the western side. The walls were covered by a marble revetment and the floors were decorated with mosaics. The fact that the church was founded in the administrative centre of the city, its differences from the basilicas constructed in Athens during the same period and the use of expensive materials indicate that the church was in fact an imperial

ATHENAIS-EUDOCIA (400-460)

The Empress Eudocia (c. 400-460) was the wife of the Byzantine Emperor Theodosius II. She was born in Athens and was the daughter of the well-known pagan philosopher Leontios. Her first name was Athenais, but she took the Christian name Eudocia when she went to Constantinople. She was known to be well educated and independently minded. During her reign she supported classical studies and she contributed to the foundation of the "Pandidakterion"(university) in Constantinople. Only fractions of her poetry have been preserved. She also was responsible for numerous construction projects in her birth-place.

building. The church's founder was probably either Herculius, Governor of Illyrikon (408-12), or the Athenian Empress Eudocia (423-460), also known as Athenais, daughter of the philosopher Leontios and wife of Theodosius II.

The Tetraconch was abandoned, possibly during the Slav invasion (582), and was replaced during the 7th century by the large three-aisled basilica that was built over the central building of Hadrian's Library's. One can still see the eastern apse and part of the colonnade of this building.

In the 11th century the basilica was replaced by an aisle-less domed cross-shaped church known as Megali Panagia ("Great Virgin Mary"). It is believed that the church's name originated from the fact that the oldest icon of Saint Mary painted by Saint Luke, was kept there. The church's architectural form and decorations are known to us mostly through the drawings of the traveller Couchaud. The monument used to have a chapel dedicated to the Holy Trinity and was demolished during the excavations following the 1885 fire that destroyed the Agora. •=

Avissinias Square

AVISSINIAS SQUARE - YOUSSOUROUM

The Avissinias Square is situated in Monastiraki, between Ifaistou and Ermou Streets. There are numerous antique shops on the square, many of which specialise in old furniture. Around the square, mostly on Ifaistou Street and in the narrow streets nearby, there is a plethora of shops selling second-hand goods, books, records and clothes. On Sunday mornings on Avissinias Square there is an open-air antique market. The district amidst Monastiraki Square, Adrianou Street, Assomaton Square and Ermou Street with the numerous antique shops is known as Youssouroum, named after a Jewish antique dealer, once vice-president of the Association of Antique Dealers, who used to run a store there. The area of Youssouroum is particularly crowded on Sunday mornings with the market. Many Athenians visit the

THE HEART OF ANCIENT ATHENS

antique shops in search of second-hand bargains, while the numerous cafés and restaurants are buzzing with young people and tourists.

The Church Of st Philip

The church of St Philip (Agios Philippos) is situated on Adrianou Street, opposite the entrance to the archaeological site of the ancient market (Agora). The church as we know it today was built in 1866 on the remains of an older one, which, according to written sources of 1821, was already in ruins. Indeed, the writings and drawings of various travellers give much information about the original church: once a three-aisled timber-roofed basilica, the earliest construction probably dated back to the 17th century. On the façade was a conch enclosing a wall painting of St Philip: it is believed that St Philip spoke here to the gathered Athenians. There are in fact indications that on this same spot, there was once another, early-Christian church underneath the existing building. The area around the church is known as "Youssourouom", a gathering spot for numerous tradesmen.

The Ancient Agora

The Agora (or market place) was an area where citizens gathered; it was the heart of public life in the ancient Greek city-state (polis). It was a venue for political meetings, trade and business, the seat of administrative and judicial affairs as well as a religious and cultural centre.
The ancient Athenian Agora extended over a large area north-west of the Acropolis, and was bordered to the south by the Areopagus, to the north by the River Eridanos and to the west by the low hill of Kolonos Agoraios. Even though it had been in use as a place of habitation and burial from the Neolithic period (3000 BC), the area only became a public place during the

Saint Philip

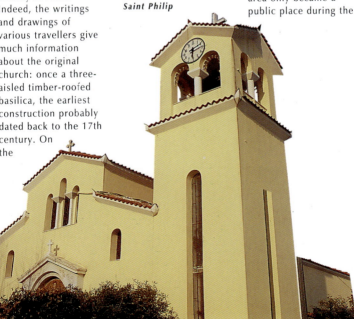

time of the legislator Solon (c. 600 BC). It was then that the basis of the Athenian constitution was firmly established. The Agora was initially an open space, and was gradually surrounded by public buildings and stoas (or porticoes), temples and altars dedicated to the gods as well as statues dedicated to distinguished citizens and foreign donors. The first public buildings of a political and religious nature were put up on the western side of the Agora in the 6th century BC. Buildings C and D are dated to Solon's time. The Altar of the Twelve Gods was founded in 522/1 BC, during Peisistratos' rule. After the political reformations of Cleisthenes (508/7 BC) the Bouleuterion, the Royal Stoa and the Heliaia served the needs of the Athenian democracy. Small sanctuaries in honour of Zeus, Apollo Patroos and the Mother of the Gods Rhea were founded at the end of

Golden banded rings

IOANNIS TRAVLOS

Ioannis Travlos was a prominent Greek architect-archaeologist of the post-war era. He was born in Rostov, Russia, in 1908 and he moved to Athens with his family when he was four. He died in Athens in 1988. He graduated from the Department of Architecture of the Athens Technical University, but from very early on he was interested in archaeological research and restoration. During the 1930's he worked in Eleusis, Megara, Olynthos and Athens, where he participated in excavation works in Pnyx, Plato's Academy and the Ancient Agora (Agora). From 1940 to 1975 he was in charge of the restoration works in the Ancient Agora, working on the Attalos' Arcade and the church of Holy Apostles Solaki. He also took part in the excavations in Olympieion, Hadrian's Library and the southern side of the Acropolis. Throughout his long career he made architectural drawings and models for numerous monuments and archaeological sites in Greece. He was also interested in the Byzantine architecture and the neoclassical architectural style in Greece. Among his most important published works are the following: "The Development of Town Planning in Athens" (1960), "Neoclassical Architecture in Greece" (1967) and "Bildlexicon zur Topographie des antiken Athen" [Pictorial Dictionary of Topography in Ancient Athens] (1971). Purely as an architect he worked on the family graves of Korizis, Andreadis and Avgerinou families in the First Cemetery of Athens.

the 6th century BC. During the same period, the first statues of distinguished citizens were set up in the Agora, such as those of the tyrant-slayers (tyrannicides) Harmodios and Aristogeiton.
During the Persian invasion of 480 BC, the buildings on the western side of the

Ivory Pyxis

Agora either suffered serious damage or were completely destroyed. Of these, the Royal Stoa, the Bouleuterion and the Altar of the Twelve Gods were restored in the 5th century BC. During the same period new important public buildings were erected for the first time to the north and south. The Stoa Poikile (the Painted Stoa), the Tholos and the Stoa of the Herms were built in the second quarter of the 5th century BC, under Cimon's initiative. The New Bouleuterion, the Stoa of Zeus Eleutherios, the South Stoa I and the Mint were built in the last quarter of the 5th century BC. The construction of the Temple of Hephaestus and Athena Ergane, the so-called "Theseion", began soon after 450 BC. Hence, the main legal, juridicial, administrative and military buildings were grouped on the western side of the Agora. Those associated with the commercial and financial life of the city were at the south.
Building activity in the Agora was renewed in about the mid-4th century BC under the patronage of the Macedonian kings Philip II (359-336 BC), Alexander III the Great (336-323 BC) and Demetrius I the Besieger (307-283 BC). But the 3rd century BC was a period of continuous civil strife and economic recession, which resulted in limited construction in the area. The support of the Hellenistic kingdoms of Egypt, Syria, Pergamon, Cappadocia and Pontus in the second half of the 2nd century BC brought a revival. This is the time when the Agora was given its characteristic rectangular shape, through the erection of multiple colonnades around its perimeter. The open central courtyard was considerably restricted when it was divided into two unequal parts by the Middle Stoa. The northern section of the Agora was bordered to the north by the Stoa Poikile, to the east by the Stoa of Attalos, to the south by the Middle Stoa and to the west by the irregular colonnade created by the Royal Stoa, the Stoa of Zeus Eleutherios, the Temple of Apollo Patroos and the Metroon, rebuilt at

Pyxis' lid

that time. The southern section of the Agora was delimited by the South Stoa II and the East Building but was completely destroyed during the Roman invasion of the city by the general Sulla in 86 BC. Henceforth, the area was used for manufacture (pottery, metalwork, marble sculpture, etc.).
In the middle of the 1st century BC the Agora acquired a new function: at the end of the century commercial activity was transferred to the new Agora built by Julius Caesar and Augustus, so that the old Agora was transformed, with the addition of buildings and pieces of art donated by Roman benefactors, into an artistic centre and recreation area. The central open courtyard of the ancient Agora was now covered by the Odeon of Agrippa and older temples, such as the temple of Ares. These were transferred from the

Detail from a red-figured vase

Attic countryside to the city-centre. The 2nd century AD marked the last great flourishing of the ancient Athenian Agora. During the reign of Trajan, the Library of Pantainos was built, and under Hadrian the Basilica and the Nympheum were constructed. In AD 267, the Agora was looted by the Herulians, a barbaric tribe from the North. The stone from the ruined buildings was used to construct a small defensive circuit wall – known as the Late Roman Wall – to the east of the Agora. After a century of abandonment, large private houses were erected south of the Agora. Shortly after AD 400, an extensive gymnasium covered the ruins of older buildings in the middle of the courtyard. Both the private houses and the gymnasium served as educational areas in a city that remained a famous cultural centre. After the destruction caused by the Slavs in the 580s, habitation in this part of the city was gradually abandoned. It was resumed, however, in the 10th century, when the Church of the Holy Apostles was built (c. 1000). In 1203 the area was devastated by invaders from Nauplion and subsequently deserted for four centuries. At the beginning of the 19th century it was inhabited anew only to suffer, between 1826 and 1827, the destruction caused by the Greek War of Independence. When the city was declared the capital of the newly established Greek state in 1834, an intensive rebuilding programme

Golden earrings of the geometric period

was initiated in the area.

Excavations in the ancient Agora were undertaken in the period from 1859 to 1912 under the guidance of the Greek Archaeological Society, while the German Archaeological Institute conducted research in the years 1896-7. A substantial number of antiquities was unearthed during the construction of the Athens-Piraeus railway in 1890-1891. From 1931 until the present day, the American School of Classical Studies has been responsible for the systematic excavation of the Agora. In order for the entire area to be unearthed, almost 400 houses had to be demolished across an area of about 120,000m².

THE POIKILE STOA (THE PAINTED STOA)

To the north of Adrianou Street one can see a large separated excavation area containing the ruins of many monuments of the ancient Agora. Among these is the west end of the Poikile Stoa, discovered only as recently as 1981. It was one of the most well-known and busy buildings in ancient Athens. Built in c. 460 BC on the north side of the Agora, the Stoa faced along the Panathenaic Way, to the Acropolis. It is a large Stoa (12.5m by 36m) with an exterior in Doric style: inside was an Ionic colonnade. Its orientation was south. It was called Poikile (meaning painted) because it was decorated with a series of wooden painted plaques by the most famous painters of the time (Polygnotos, Mikon, Panainos). These paintings, which survived until the beginning of the 5th century AD, depicted military achievements, taken from the mythology and history of Athens (the Amazonomachy, the siege and capture of Troy, the victory over the Spartans at Oinoe, the battle of Marathon). In addition to these paintings, the Athenians hung the captured arms of their defeated enemies on the Stoa's walls. In contrast to the other porticoes of the Agora, the Poikile Stoa had no designated function, but simply served as a meeting-place for citizens, being only occasionally used for official public purposes, such as the hearing of legal cases. However, it was often here that proclamations were issued, announcing those who had qualified for participation in the Eleusinian Mysteries. Furthermore, one of the most important philosophical schools of Antiquity, the Stoic, took its name from the Poikile Stoa: it was here, in about 300 BC, that the founder of Stoicism, Zenon, from Kition in Cyprus, liked to teach.

SANCTUARY OF APHRODITE OURANIA

The sanctuary of Aphrodite Ourania

The Poikile (Painted) Stoa

(Heavenly Aphrodite) was mentioned by Pausanias: it was here that he saw the cult statue of the goddess made by Pheidias. Archaeologists looking for the site of the sanctuary have hitherto searched on the northern slopes of the Kolonos Agoraios hill. However, according to a more recent view, the site must have been to the west of the Poikile Stoa. There, the ruins of an elaborate Archaic (c. 500 BC) marble altar dedicated to Aphrodite have been found. The base of the altar (5.10m by 2.40m) can be seen in the excavation area on the northern side of Adrianou Street.

THE PANATHENAIC WAY

The Panathenaic Way led from the Dipylon Gate to the Acropolis crossing the central square of the Agora diagonally. This was the route of the great processions and culmination of the Panathenaea festival, from which it received its name. Today, only a few parts of it are visible. The most characteristic section of the Panathenaic Way is that which ascends to the Acropolis, behind the church of St Apostoloi (Holy Apostles); a large part of the Way is now covered by Adrianou Street.

Although it was one of the main routes of ancient Athens, its construction appears to be quite simple. Throughout its long history the surface of the Panathenaic Way consisted largely of packed gravel that had to be renewed many times. It was in the Hellenistic period that its south-western side was bordered by a stone pipeline. The planning of the Panathenaic Way is dated to Prehistoric times, and it is known that as early as the Iron Age it led to the Kerameikos cemetery. In the 6th century BC it was incorporated into the plan of the Agora, and it served to orientate the Altar of the Twelve Gods. Along the section that skirted the Agora, ikria (special wooden tiers or grandstands) were later constructed, to allow spectators to watch the Panathenaea festivities. Excavations along the two sides of the route brought to light the sockets that held wooden posts for supporting the tiers, built in the 5th and 4th centuries BC. It appears that the Panathenaic Way hosted athletic events, at least until the construction of the large stadium in the Ilissos area in 330 BC. In 1971 the stone poles of the starting line were discovered east of the Altar of the Twelve Gods, in use in the 5th century BC. It has been also argued that during the Panathenaea an event called the "apovates dromos" took place, in which the athlete in full armour leapt on and off a swiftly moving chariot. There was also a training area for horsemen here.

The Panathenaic Way

THE HEART OF ANCIENT ATHENS

THE ROYAL STOA (BASILEIOS STOA)

The most northern structure on the west side of the Agora is a small stoa (18 by 7,5 m.), the ruins of which are not accessible to visitors. They can only be seen between Adrianou Street and the railway tracks. It is the Royal Stoa (portico), an important public building in the Agora and the seat of the archon basileus (the king archon) dated to ca. 500 BC. It is said that here Solon's laws were set up inscribed on wooden stelae, the kyrbeis. The Stoa's orientation was to the east and it was opened to the Panathenaic Way. It had eight columns in its façade and four inside, all of

The Basileios (Royal) Stoa

Doric order. The roof of the building was decorated by terracotta acroteria (corner ornaments) where mythological scenes were depicted. During the 4th century BC, small wings were added to the north and south end of the Stoa's façade.

STOA OF ZEUS ELEUTHERIOS

South of the Royal Stoa, a visitor to the ancient Agora can see part of the foundations of a large and impressive stoa (or portico), the Stoa of Zeus Eleutherios built c. 430–420 BC. Its ground plan was the shape of the Greek letter Π: the building had a Doric colonnade along its façade and an Ionic within. The traveller Pausanias saw a statue of Zeus in front of the Stoa. The internal walls were decorated with paintings on mythological and historical subjects associated with the city. The Stoa is believed to have served mostly a religious function while at the same time being the unofficial place for philosophical and political gatherings. In Roman times two chambers were annexed to the back of the Stoa, probably dedicated to imperial cult.

THE ALTAR OF THE TWELVE GODS

Descending from the north-west to the Agora's central

THE STOA OF THE HERMS

At the southwestern entrance to the Agora a number of rectangular stelae were set up, all crowned by busts of Hermes, protector of entrances and god of trade. These were known as the Herms. Numerous inscribed bases and parts of these sculptures have been found in front of the Royal Stoa. Based on the archaeological research, this is the Stoa of the Herms already known from the written sources. Nevertheless, no trace of it is preserved. It was built possibly by Cimon, shortly after 479 BC, in order to house the Herms assembled in the area.

courtyard one comes across the Altar of the Twelve Gods. This is a square peribolos (enclosure) surrounded by a low parapet. Only one of the corners is visible today: the rest of the structure has been excavated but has since been covered by railway tracks. This altar was famous in antiquity because of its use as an asylum. It was built by the archon Peisistratos the Younger in 522/1 BC and functioned as the starting point for measuring distances. Set up in almost the middle of the Agora the altar was considered to be the city centre.

TEMPLE OF ARES

The foundations of the temple and altar of Ares are situated in the middle of the Agora's open square, north of the Odeon of Agrippa. The marble Doric temple was built c. 430 BC, modelled on the architectural type of the temple of Hephaestus (Hephaisteion). It was originally founded elsewhere (possibly at Acharnai on the slopes of Mount Parnes), but was dismantled and transferred in about 15 BC to the Agora, where it was set up on new foundations. Together with the South-east and South-west temples, it belongs to the distinctive building programme during the reign of Augustus, when many fine examples of Classical architecture were transferred to the Agora, largely for the purpose of serving imperial cults.

THE ARSENAL

On the feet of the Agoraios Kolonos hill, to the northeast of the Hephaisteion, are preserved the

Temple of Apollo Patroos

foundations of a large rectangular building (measuring 17.6 by 44.4 cm.), which is dated in the beginning of the 3rd century B.C. Its interior was divided in three naves with two rows of eight supports. Pillars supported the walls and the wooden roof of the building. It was used as a space for the safekeeping of weapons and other military material. It is also possible that here was kept the oil destined for the winners of the Panathenaic contest.

TEMPLE OF APOLLO PATROOS

South of the Stoa of Zeus Eleutherios lies the temple of Apollo Patroos built after the mid-4th century BC on

Temple of Ares, view from the west

top of the remains of an Archaic apsidal temple, probably dedicated to the same god. It was an Ionic tetrastyle temple in honour of Apollo Patroos the Father of the Ionians. It contained a pronaos, a cella and an adyton (inner sanctuary) to the north. According to Pausanias, inside the temple three Apollo statues were set up: the cult statue of the god a work by the sculptor Euphranor (which is identified with the statue of Apollo Kitharodos found in the area and exhibited in the Agora Museum), the statue of Apollo Alexikakos by the sculptor Kalamis and another one by Leochares.
In front of the adyton of the temple are the remains of a small temple (dim. 5,20x3,65 m.), which has been identified as the temple of Zeus Phratrios and Athena Phratria (both protectors of the Athenian phratries) dated to the mid-4th century BC.

THE HEPHAISTEION (THESEION)

The low hill that overlooks the ancient Agora is called the hill of the Agoraios Kolonos. On the large plateau of the hill, a large Doric temple was built. Construction works began in 449 BC, were probably interrupted around 444, began again in 421 and were completed in 415 BC. The temple is a peripteral hexastyle, with 13 columns on its long sides and measuring about 31.8 by 13.8 metres. The temple's pronaos and opisthodome had a second row of columns in antis. Its similarity to the temples of Poseidon at Sounion, Ares in the Agora and Nemesis at Rhamnous have led archaeologists to the conclusion that the four temples were designed by the same architect. The Hephaisteion is the best-preserved temple in Greece. Archaeologists originally believed the temple was dedicated to the Athenian hero Theseus, who founded the city of Athens by resettlement, and whose heroic deeds are narrated in relief on the northern and southern sides of the building. It was therefore named Theseion, a name given also to the surrounding area in modern Athens

Hephaisteion (temple of Hephaestus)

(Thisseio). Systematic excavation in the Agora, however, and its relation to the written literary sources, proved that it was in fact a temple dedicated to Hephaestus and Athena, under the attribute Ergane. The two gods protected craftsmen (coppersmiths, potters, etc.), whose workshops were discovered at a short distance from the temple. In the 5th century AD the temple was transformed into a church dedicated to St George, which remained in use until 1835. Thus the building escaped damage. During the first hundred years of the Greek State it was occasionally used as a museum.

DECORATION

The temple is made almost entirely from Pentelic marble. At the end of the cella, around the interior of which ran a Π-shaped colonnade, was a podium with relief decoration on which stood the bronze statues of the two gods, made by Alcamenes probably between 421 and 415 BC. To the west of the temple a ditch was discovered, in which shards of the clay moulds used in construction were found. On the temple's façade are ten metopes depicting the labours of Herakles, while on each of the northern and southern sides are four metopes depicting the heroic deeds of Theseus. On the pronaos gate is a frieze in relief, depicting the fight between Theseus and the sons of his uncle, Pallas. The opisthodome also bears a frieze with the Centauromachy. The existence of a frieze on a Doric temple has been attributed to the influence of the Parthenon; if this archaeological assumption is true, the temple must have been completed at a date later than the Parthenon.

THE MONUMENT OF THE EPONYMOUS HEROES

On the west side of the Agora, east of the Metroon, was the site of the Monument of the Eponymous Heroes, built c. 330 BC. Today you can still see the monument's oblong pedestal (16.64m by 1.87m), on which the

The Monument of the Eponymous Heroes

bronze statues of the ten eponymous heroes of the Athenian tribes once stood. Additionally, two bronze tripods were placed at either end of the pedestal. According to Pausanias, the mythical heroes were Hippothoon, Antiochos, Aias, Leos, Erechteus, Aigeus, Oineus, Akamas, Cecrops and Pandion.

It should be noted that the Monument of the Eponymous Heroes was enclosed by a wooden fence supported by stone posts, while its façade served as a notice board for important public announcements. During the Hellenistic and Roman periods it underwent changes related to the introduction of new tribes in honour of foreign rulers who were generous to Athens. Thus, in 307/6 BC two new statues were added to the pedestal in honour of Demetrius the Besieger and his father Antigonos. This resulted in an extension of the monument to the south. In 223 BC a third statue was added, this time in honour of King Ptolemy Euergetes of Egypt. In 200 BC the statues of Demetrius the Besieger and his father were taken down and replaced by that of King Attalos I of Pergamon. In the 2nd century AD the statue of the Emperor Hadrian, as an eponymous hero, was placed on the monument.

The Metroon

THE OLD BOULEUTERION AND THE METROON

Descends from the Kolonos Agoraios Hill, to the right, a visitor to the Agora comes across a complex of ruins of various structures from different periods. This complex consists of a square building identified as the Old Bouleuterion, an Archaic temple dedicated possibly to Rhea, the mother of the gods, and the Hellenistic Metroon. The Old Bouleuterion was constructed at the beginning of the 5th century BC, to serve the Council of Five Hundred, the principal administrative body of Athens. At the end of the 5th century BC, west of the Old Bouleuterion and at the foot of Kolonos Agoraios, the city's New Bouleuterion was built, traces of which are visible today. The Old Bouleuterion did not cease to be used; rather, it was transformed into the Repository of State Archives where official public documents were stored. It was also the cult place of Rhea. In addition, it housed the cult statue of the goddess, a work of either Pheidias or Agorakritos. During the second half of the 2nd century BC the sanctuary was replaced by the new building complex of the Metroon, possibly at the expense of Attalos II. The architectural complex of the

Hellenistic Metroon (38.83m by 29.56m) consists of four rooms that face eastwards. In front of them was a colonnade of 14 Ionic columns. The northern chamber was the largest: it had an open peristyle court and an altar set up in the centre. The second room on the south was planned like a distyle temple in antis.

THE NEW BOULEUTERION (COUNCIL HOUSE)

The New Bouleuterion was a large rectangular structure (16m by 22m) to the south of the Agora. It consisted of a wide auditorium with its entrance at its south-east corner and wooden seats placed in amphitheatre style inside. Around the beginning of the 3rd century BC a porch of Ionic columns was added along the southern side of the building, and a monumental Ionic propylon was built in, the foundations of which one can trace today south-east of the Metroon.

The Old Bouleuterion

THOLOS

South of the Metroon is the site of a large round structure, the Tholos (outer diameter 18.33m), built c. 470–460 BC. It was here that the Prytaneis lived and dined, and where the temples' keys and official weights and measures were kept for safekeeping. Beneath the ruins of the Tholos private houses from the Archaic period were found, the largest of which is considered to be the House of the Peisistratids.

The entrance to the Tholos was from the east. Inside, six Ionic columns supported a conical roof while an

The foundations of the Tholos

altar stood in the middle of the floor. The building was renovated during the Roman period. An Ionic propylon was added to the entrance and the interior areas were covered with a pavement of slabs, traces of which are visible today.

THE STRATEGEION

To the south-east of the Tholos a large, trapezoid building was discovered, which comprised a central open-air courtyard (atrium), around which several rooms were arranged. This building, which is has not been maintained in good condition, dates from after the middle of the 5th century and

THE HEART OF ANCIENT ATHENS

probably formed the headquarters of the ten generals of Athens.

SOUTH-WEST FOUNTAIN HOUSE

On the south-western corner of the Agora, right next to the Heliaia, lie the ruins of a large fountain structure, which, for ignorance of its ancient name, is traditionally called the South-west Fountain House. It was built c. 350-325 BC and was perhaps the city's grandest public fountain house. A square courtyard on the north-west corner gave access, through a prostyle, to a big L-shaped basin over 100m² for the drawing of water.

HELIAIA

At the north-western end of the Agora the foundations of a square building were discovered, probably identified as the Heliaia, the most important court of justice in Athens. The original architectural plan belongs to the 6th-century BC and was a square open-air fenced courtyard measuring 26.50m by 31m. In time the building underwent several alterations, the most important of can be placed to the middle of the 2nd century BC, when an interior peristyle and a roof were added.

SOUTH STOA

The south side of the Agora is bordered by an oblong Doric portico known as the "South Stoa". Two building phases can be identified. The South Stoa I was constructed in ca. 430/420 BC and had an interior two-storeyed colonnade and 16 rooms in the back. Only a part of its foundations are visible today in the triangular area west of the Southwest Fountain House. It was a big public commercial center and the seat of the "metronomoi", those officials responsible for checking commercial life and supervising the official weights and measures.

In ca. 150 BC, the South Stoa I was torn down and was replaced by the South Stoa II. This one was built with a slightly different orientation on a much lower level than the one of the older Stoa. It was also a large Doric portico but with one colonnade and no rooms in the back. However, it retained its function as a commercial center.

ODEON OF AGRIPPA

The ruins of the Odeon of Agrippa are located behind the colossal stone giants that overlook the centre of the Agora court. It was a high building, the most impressive Roman structure in the Agora, donated by Marcus Vipsanius

The Odeon of Agrippa: Giants and Tritons

Agrippa. It was built c. 15 BC, along the north façade of the Middle Stoa,

Capital from the Odeon

for concerts and musical events. The auditorium, due to its formation as a single space 25m wide without interior abutments, had a seating capacity of about 1,000. The semicircular orchestra was paved with thin marble slabs of various colours and the low façade of the skene (stage) was decorated by marble sculptures, mostly Hermes' stelae. A two-storeyed portico surrounded the three sides (east, west, north) of the main building. The walls were decorated on the outside with high Corinthian columns and pillars. The building had one entrance to the north, which was level to the ground, and one to the south on a higher level due to the terrace of the Middle Stoa. The complete absence of interior supports, a bold architectural venture for its time, is possibly responsible for the collapse of the roof in the mid-2nd century AD. The Odeon was repaired in c. AD 170 but underwent important alterations and its function changed. On this occasion, six colossal figures of giants with serpent-tails and of Tritons with fish-tails were added to the north façade. Of these, only three are preserved. The Odeon's capacity was reduced by about one half because of the insertion of a cross-wall for stability. In its new phase, the Odeon of the Agora functioned only as an area for the philosophers' and sophists' speeches, since Athens had acquired a new Odeon in c. AD 160, that of Herodes Atticus. The Odeon of Agrippa was burnt down in 267, and a large part of its building material was incorporated into the Late Roman Wall of Athens. Four of the colossal figures were inserted into the façade of a gymnasium, which was set up in the same area some time after 400. This building was later restructured and used as the governor's quarters until the first half of the 6th century, when it was abandoned.

The East Building

EAST BUILDING

The Middle Stoa and the South Stoa II were adjacent at their eastern end to the East Building. It was built in the mid-2nd century BC and was a relatively small structure (12x40 m.) divided in length in two parts. The eastern section, which looked towards the Panathenaic Way, comprised a single room with a mosaic floor where the sockets for securing

THE HEART OF ANCIENT ATHENS

wooden tables or benches for money-changers or bankers are preserved. The west section that faced the Agora rested at a level 1,7 m. lower that the east and consisted of five square rooms. A central staircase connected the two different levels. In the first half of the 2nd century BC, the Middle Stoa, the South Stoa II and the East Building formed one big commercial center with an eastern entrance, known as the "South Square".

MIDDLE STOA

The Middle Stoa was named after its location in order to be distinguished from the other stoas of the Agora. It is a huge, possibly of commercial nature, portico (147x17,5 m.) built in ca. 180 BC, which divided the Athenian Agora in two uneven parts. It had Doric colonnades on all

Upper part of the Middle Stoa

sides. A transverse, probably Ionic, colonnade divided the interior of the Stoa into two aisles. The columns were interconnected at their lower part by parapets. The name of the financier of the Stoa is not known. Perhaps, it was the king of Pontus Pharnakes I whereas the possibility of a donation by the Attalids should not be ruled out. Nowadays, in the area one can trace the foundations of the building, parts from its krepis (steps) and many of the lower column drums.

ENNEAKROUNOS (NINE-SPOUTED FOUNTAIN HOUSE)

On the south-eastern corner of the Agora, behind the South Stoa II, are the ruins of a large fountain house dated to c. 530/520 BC. It has been identified as the Enneakrounos, a famous fountain house, which, according to the

The Middle Stoa

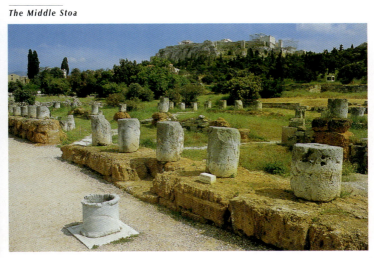

written sources, was built by either Peisistratos or his sons. However, this identification is not unchallenged: modern research tends to place the Enneakrounos on the southeast of the Agora, around the River Ilissos. For this reason scholars today prefer the use of the traditional 'South-east Fountain House'. Whatever the name, it is a large rectangular structure (6.8m by 18.2m) with a wide-spaced central room flanked by two smaller rooms on its narrow sides. The side rooms were supplied by water through spouts on the outer walls. The west room functioned as a basin from where water could be drained behind a low parapet, while in the east room one could fill up a hydria (or water jar) directly from the waterspout.

SOUTHWEST TEMPLE

In the 1st century BC a small temple was founded to the east of Tholos. With its entrance on the west side, archaeologists have named it the simply the South-western temple. Six Doric columns were incorporated in second use on its façade from a building in Thorikos, perhaps from the temple of Demeter and Kore that used to be there. The Doric architrave and the frieze were originally parts of other buildings.

THE NYMPHAEUM

Between the Church of the Holy Apostles (Agioi Apostoloi) and the Southeast Temple, a part of the fountain of the Nymphaeum is still visible. It was a large, semicircular and elaborate fountain facing north, i.e., towards the Panathenaic Way. Construction began under Hadrian and was completed around AD 140, under Antoninus Pius. It was built over the remains of the Mint, which had previously occupied this site; later on it was replaced by the Byzantine church of the Holy Apostles. In the walls of the fountain were niches decorated with statues of the Antonine imperial family, and its lower part was formed by basins, pools and springs, fed by the city's Hadrianic aqueduct.

THE MINT

Between the South-east Fountain house and the Panathenaic Way are the remains of a large, almost square area (27m by 29m), which has been identified as the Mint of Athens, dated from c. 400 BC. Today, only

Southwest Temple

the northern half of the building, used mainly as an open courtyard, is still visible. Its southern part was covered c. AD 150 by the Nymphaeum and much later (c. 1000) by the Byzantine church of Holy Apostles (Agioi Apostoloi). The main manufacturing area consisted of a big room at the south-western corner where the metallurgical furnaces and water basins were placed. Two small rooms on the south-eastern corner served as storage areas or as offices for the "supervisors", or the Mint's administrators. Here not only coins were made, but other metal objects as well.

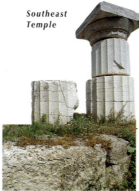

Southeast Temple

(mass of masonry) were found that comprised the base of the statue as well as fragments of a female statue of the Caryatid type but double-sized. This temple is conventionally called by the excavators "Southeast" since its suggested dedication to Athena has not been verified.

SOUTHEAST TEMPLE

In the late 1st century BC, above the ruins of the Mint a small prostyle temple was founded. Eight columns from the Classical temple of Athena at Sounion were reused in the construction of its façade. Inside the cella, piles of stones

THE ELEUSINION

To the east of the Panathenaic way, walking through the Agora towards the Acropolis, one sees the remains of the Eleusinion "en astei" (in the city), equivalent to the sanctuary of Demeter and Kore in Eleusis. The area is

ELEUSINIAN MYSTERIES

The Eleusinian Mysteries, the annual celebrations in honour of Demeter and Persephone were the first purely mystical and most important expression of religious worship in the entire ancient Greece. The Great Mysteries were held in September (Boedromion), while the Small Mysteries, or Mysteries in the Fields, were held in March (Anthesterion) in the temple of Demeter and Kore near Ilissos. Those who had been or were being initiated took a vow of silence regarding the worship practices, therefore we know very little on this matter. There is little information provided in works by Aeschylus, Sophocles, Herodotus, Aristophanes, Plutarch and Pausanias who had all been initiated. The Great Mysteries celebrations lasted nine days. On the first day there was a procession from Eleusis to Eleusinion in the Agora, while during the following days the celebrations included "things shown", "things said" and "things done". The most important ceremonies took place in the Telesterion of Eleusis. The Mysteries had a chthonic character with an eschatological content; they carried on until the early years of Christianity, while it is believed that they influenced Christian religious practices.

marked by a rectangular precinct, in the middle of which are preserved the foundations of a quite large temple (11 by 17.70 meters) with a rectangular cella. The main entrance was at the south. A small room (holy of holies) to the north served for the safekeeping of the sacred objects which were transported from the Eleusis sanctuary to the Eleusinion of Athens during the celebration of the Great Eleusinian Mysteries. This temple, dated in 490 B.C., had replaced an older one, dated at the end of the 6th century B.C. On the oblong base (2 by 15 meters) to the east of the temple were placed the so-called "attic stelae". On those stelae was inscribed a register of the sold by auction property of Alcibiades and the others who had been involved in the mutilation of the Herms and in the ridicule of the Eleusinian Mysteries in 415 B.C. In the second half of the 4th century B.C. the old entrance to the sanctuary was replaced by a

BYZANTINE HOUSES

The area around the Ancient Agora continued being inhabited until the 6th-7th century. This can be confirmed by the existence of several luxurious late Roman houses, such as the apsidal "House Γ" with a triclinium north from the Areios Pagos and by the remnants of houses in the area of Tholos and the conversion of the temple of Hephaestus (Theseion) into a Christian church (6th-7th century). Today the most probable theory is that from the late 10th century the city was limited within the late Roman walls, while during the 11th and mainly the 12th century a number of areas were developed outside the walls. Remains of Byzantine houses have been found on the east and north side of Agoraios Kolonos in the roman Market on the west side of Areios Pagos, in Kerameikos (above the Pompeion), on the southern side of the Acropolis (near the Odeon of Herodes Atticus and the Theatre of Dionysos) and in the Olympieion. The expansion of the city in those areas outside the late Roman walls is also indicated by the great number of churches that were built there. One can get a better idea regarding the type of neighborhoods in medieval Athens from the small area on the northeastern side of Agoraios Kolonos where between the 10th and 12 century a wide and densely populated neighborhood was developed. The lack of any city planning arrangements there is evident. The houses have been built on either side of a narrow street directed from the north towards the south. The houses consisted of small rooms built around a yard, which was usually whitewashed and had a small shed on one side. In most cases there have been two or three settlement stages. There used to be water wells in the yards, while food supplies were stored in large earthenware jars embedded to the floor. The constructions were cheap and only the foundations have been preserved, while the restoration of the walls has been impossible. Amidst the houses there used to be small workshops and shops. It is worth mentioning the existence of a large square building with many rooms, which might have been an indoor market, an inn, or perhaps a workshop, probably manufacturing textiles.

monumental propylon. In about the middle of the 2nd century A.D. the sanctuary was

merchants. Their ground-plan was simple. The various rooms were organized

the floor was paved with pebbles or mosaics. Many of these houses were two-storeyed. The wooden roof had terracotta tiling. Some larger and richer complexes of the 4th and 5th centuries BC have been identified as the residences of famous teachers (sophists) who, it is said, gave private lessons and offered hospitality to their favourite students.

The Eleusinion

expanded to the south, where a small portico in Doric style was built, of which only the foundations are preserved nowadays. The sanctuary was completely ruined during the Herulian invasion of 267 A.D.

HOUSES IN THE AGORA

Outside the Agora proper, on the north, west and south slope of the Areopagus, the remains of many private houses have been found. Those of the Classical and Hellenistic periods, plain in both scale and furnishings, were probably the residences of craftsmen and

around a central rectangular court, usually without a peristyle. Their number and arrangement depended on the size of the establishment. Only the lower part of the walls was of stone. The rest was made of plinths covered with lime mortar. The floors were pressed mud-earth except for the andron (the men's dining-room), where

Between the Tholos and the Middle Stoa the ruins of a house have been identified. It consisted of two rooms and a front court, where numerous metal nails and small rings, such as those used in shoe-making, have been found. In addition, the base of a cup came to light, inscribed with the identity of its owner, "of Simon". The house must have belonged to a shoe-maker, perhaps even to the Simon whose workshop, according to ancient writers, Socrates used to frequent.

THE LIBRARY OF PANTAINOS

To the south of the Stoa of Attalos was built the Library of Pantainos. Between the two buildings

Simon's house, 5th century B.C.

WALK 8

there was a paved street with colonnades, constructed around 100 A.D., which connected the Ancient and the Roman Agora. The Library of Pantainos was built around that time by the Athenian Titus Flavius Pantainos in honour of the goddess Athena, the emperor Trajan and the people of Athens. The complex comprised a rectangular courtyard with a peristyle, around which opened several rooms. The main Library hall was situated to the east. It was a large quadrate room, 10 meters long on each side, with a colonnade at the front. Its interior walls were revetted with marble. In this room were kept the books. The rooms on the western and northern side of the complex, in front of which stood an ionic colonnade were accessed from the Agora and probably served as shops or sculptors' workshops. The remains of the Library are not visible today, due to the construction of the late Roman wall, which was built with architectural parts from public buildings that were demolished during the Herulian invasion. In situ was discovered a fragmentary inscription mentioning the rules of the library, according to which loans of books were not permitted. This inscription, as well as the dedicatory inscription of the donor, are displayed in the Agora museum (Stoa of Attalos).

THE STOA OF ATTALOS

The Stoa of Attalos occupies the east side of the Athenian Agora. Built c. 150 BC with a donation from the king of Pergamon, Attalos II (159–138 BC), it is the most representative monument of the Hellenistic period in Athens. Thanks to recent restoration (1953–56), the Stoa dominates the Agora and creates for the visitor a sense of being in a living dialogue with the well-preserved temple of Hephaestus on the opposite hill. In reconstructing the Stoa, the American School of Classical Studies at Athens used much of the original architectural material. Today the Stoa houses

The inner colonnade of the Stoa of Attalos

the Ancient Agora Museum. It has served important political and cultural events, like the signing of the Accession Treaty of the European Union the 16th April 2003. The Stoa is a two-storeyed structure made of Pentelic marble, grey Hymettus marble and Attic limestone. It is about 116m long and 20m wide. A colonnade of 45 Doric columns – the lower drums are unfluted – graces the façade of the lower floor. A second colonnade of 22 unfluted Ionic columns runs along the inside. At the far end of the Stoa were 21 store-rooms, which the city lent to private merchants.

In the south-east part of the Stoa was a stairway leading to an upper floor, whose plan mirrored that of the ground floor. A colonnade of 45 Ionic columns was built along the façade. Marble parapets closed the spaces between the columns. The interior colonnade was decorated by Pergamene capitals, while at the back was a series of 21 rooms. On the epistyle of the lower floor was an inscription with the donor's name: "King Attalos son of king Attalos and the Queen Apollonis …".

The Stoa of Attalos was a large and important commercial centre, serving Athenian trade and business and offering shade in the summer and shelter from the winter rains. The building is notable for its special luxury, an unusual feature for such a frequented stoa. It is considered as the most significant monument ever donated by the kings of the Pergamene kingdom, the Attalids, to Athens. The Stoa was destroyed during the Herulian raids (267 BC) and its building material was used to construct the new defensive wall along the eastern side of the Agora, known as Rizokastro. In front of the Stoa were honorific pedestals and statues, the most remarkable of which was the pedestal with a bronze quadriga (four-horse chariot) and its rider, the donor of Stoa Attalos II. Later on, the Athenians used this monument to honour Emperor Tiberius. The foundation of the pedestal is preserved and stands in its original place in front of the middle of the Stoa façade.

The Stoa of Attalos

THE HEART OF ANCIENT ATHENS

THE ANCIENT AGORA MUSEUM (STOA OF ATTALOS)

The Ancient Agora Museum is housed in the restored Stoa of Attalos, a monument dated to c. 150 BC. The museum was restored between 1953 and 1956 to house the finds from the excavations in the Agora conducted by the American School of Classical Studies. In 1957 the Greek state took over the administration and security arrangements for both the museum and the archaeological site. The museum's special feature is that its exhibits are directly related to the

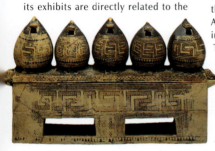

Sherds of vases used in ostracisms

functions of Athenian democracy, reflecting the Agora role at heart of the city's public life. Among the objects associated with Athenian civic life and dating from the 5th to the 2nd centuries BC are a 5th-century clepsydra (water clock) used to measure the time in the law courts, 5th-century ostraca (inscribed potsherds) used to ostracize famous politicians such as Themistocles and Aristeides, and 4th-century bronze ballots used in the law courts. Inscriptions from the 5th to 2nd centuries BC are also exhibited. Among these the horses-lists from the archives of the equestrian class hold a special position. One can also see an inscribed stele of 337/336 BC, during the period of Phrynichus' archonship, when the people of the city voted a new law against tyranny. On the relief above the decree democracy is depicted as crowning the people. Also of note is a marble kleroterion (a device for casting lots) used by the Boule (Council) during the period of the twelve tribes (3rd-2nd centuries BC). The glorious military history of the city is portrayed on an inscribed bronze shield, a piece of booty taken from the Spartans after their defeat by the Athenians at the battle of Sphacteria in 425 BC.

The Agora Museum also houses finds that reveal the commercial life of the city, such as coins spanning the period from the 6th century BC to AD 1831 as well as official weights and measures. In another room commercial amphorae are exhibited, dating from the 6th century BC to Byzantine times.

Grave goods from the area where the Agora was later established bear witness to the private life of Athenian citizens. Finds here include large amounts of household equipment, mostly pottery, found in

Pyxis in the shape of model granaries, 9th century B.C.

Plastic Vase in the shape of an athlete

WALK 8

Bronze head of Nike

hundreds of excavated ancient wells. Among the most outstanding are an ivory pyxis from a Mycenaean tomb (c. 1400 BC), with a scene of griffins attacking a deer; a pair of gold earrings (c. 850 BC); terracotta shoes (c. 900 BC) from Geometric female burials; small terracotta animal toys, found in a child's grave of the 4th century AD. Among the objects of private life are numerous finds from wells, deposits, burials, workshops and shrines. They include terracotta, bronze, ivory and glass objects from the 6th century BC to the 3rd century AD, terracotta lamps from the 7th century BC to the 11th century AD and Byzantine and Ottoman period ceramics (10th/12th to the 17th century).

Exhibits of particular importance in the museum include various ceramic vessels from the 6th century BC to the 6th century AD, in particular an aryballos in the form of a kneeling athlete who binds the victor's ribbon around his head (c. 530 BC), a red-figure kylix by Gorgos (c. 500 BC) and a black-figure krater by Exekias, showing a Hermes scene (c. 530 BC). Around the peristyle of the ground- and upper floors one can see statues and architectural elements from the 6th century BC to the 3rd century AD. Among these the following stand out: a bronze Nike head, once gilded with inlaid eyes (c. 425 BC); a marble statue of a winged Nike (possibly an acroterion of the Stoa of Zeus Eleutherios (c. 415 BC); a Nereid statue that is reminiscent of the style of the sculptor Timotheos (c. 400 BC) and was probably an acroterion of a temple roof; a fragment of a victory relief in an equestrian contest (c. 360 BC); a marble female bust, and a Herm of a sleepy Silenus, both of late 2nd century AD. Outstanding among the museum's sculptures is the statue of Apollo Patroos, a colossal cult statue by Euphranor (c. 330 BC) as well as the allegorical female figure of monumental dimensions, either Themis or Democracy, set up in front of the Royal Stoa (c. 330 BC). Lastly, on the upper floor of the Stoa, are exhibited the models of the Agora, the Acropolis and the Pnyx, where the People's Assembly met.

THE CHURCH OF HOLY APOSTLES SOLAKI

The church of Holy Apostles (Agioi Apostoloi) Solaki is situated on the south-eastern side of the Agora (the ancient market-place) at the foot of the Acropolis,

Ivory statuette of Apollo

opposite the temple of Hephaestus. It is the only monument apart from Hephaisteion that has remained intact since its foundation. Its site was not selected randomly: it was a key location during the Classical and Byzantine eras, as it was on the western side of the Panathenaic Way and the defensive wall that, after the end of the third century, was crucial to the city's defense against invasion. The church dates from the last quarter of the 10th century. It is the first significant mid-Byzantine church in Athens and the first of the so-called Athenian type. This monument is significant in the development of Byzantine architecture, being a successful combination of a central plan and a cross-in-square type building. The name Solakis probably refers to the family of donors, or sponsors of a later renovation of the church. It is said that during the 19th century the densely populated area around the church used to be called "Solaki".

The Byzantine church was built on the foundations of the 2nd-century AD Nymphaeum, while on its eastern side the foundations of an early Byzantine building have been discovered, probably a house that was demolished in order to build the church. The foundation of the church towards the end of the 10th century coincides with the beginning of a great era for Athens, which lasted until the conquest of the Franks in 1204. The church was obviously built in order to cover the ever-increasing need for parishes in a constantly developing city.

The church's ground plan consists of a four-columned cross-shaped cell covered by a dome. The four cross arms end in semi-circular niches. Between the niches there is an equal number of smaller conches. This feature indicates the architect's genius, since the smaller niches give a sense of unity to the interior of the church. The addition of the narthex to the main church is equally inventive, as the church's western niche and the two smaller ones on each side were unified with the narthex, which has the shape of the Greek letter Π. All these elements give the church a balanced and harmonious character, both externally and internally. After initial construction was completed, the northern end of the narthex was expanded in order to fit an internal arcosolium. We cannot be certain of the identity of the person who was

Holy Apostles Solaki

buried there, but it was probably the church's donor, who, according to a Byzantine tradition, had the right to be buried there together with the members of his family. The sarcophagus that exists there today was discovered by archaeologists working nearby the church, and was placed in the arcosolium by the experts who undertook the restoration. The fact that it dates from the mid-Byzantine era (together with several other elements) indicates that it used to be in the church, though we cannot be certain. Graves were also found in the main area of the church, as well as the narthex. The building shows a well crafted cloisonné style on the higher parts of the walls, while the lower parts consist of large, randomly arranged layers. The rich brickwork decorative patterns create interesting variations of colour on the church's external walls. There are characteristic taeniae with dentils and a significant variety of kufic brick patterns, as, apart from the usual shapes, there are elements that refer to Christ, such as the letters A and Ω, or an anchor-shaped cross with the initials ΙΣ ΧΣ (Greek initials for Jesus Christ). The frieze with kufic brick patterns on the upper part of the narthex was restored during renovation according to other similar examples. The dome with the light proportions is the oldest example of the Athenian type in the city. The double-light windows on the sides of the dome's drum are rare and significant. Archaeological finds and the writings of numerous travellers indicate that the church was damaged in around 1687 in the fighting between Ottomans and Venetians, which even resulted in damage to the Parthenon. In the 18th century, at the time when the church was repaired, the wall paintings were added. These are mediocre and were later much painted over. The decorations on the dome and the sanctuary are noteworthy.

Fighting between Greeks and Ottomans in 1826 must have certainly damaged the church, as was the case with all the other monuments and houses in the area. Archaeological finds and written sources inform us that the church was repaired immediately after these conflicts. Later on, in the years 1876–82 extensive work took place in repairing and extending the church, which resulted in the alteration of its form and the addition of a tasteless extension to its western side. Many parts of the marble screen (columns, architraves, panels) were built into the added extension. These parts were used to guide the experts in restoring the screen. In the mid-20th century, during excavations conducted by the American Archaeological School in the Agora, it was considered necessary to repair and restore the church. The restoration lasted two years, from February 1954 until September 1956, and restored the church to its present form, which is the closest possible to its initial state.

9

WALK 9

1. Omonoia Square
2. National Resistance Square (Kotzia Square)
3. The City Hall
4. Athinas Street
5. St Kyriaki
6. St John "around the Column"
7. St Anargyroi
8. Psirris
9. Christ of Kopidis, or Christokopidis
10. Ermou Street
11. Kapnikarea
12. St Eirene
13. Panagia Chrissospiliotissa
14. St Paraskevi
15. Panagia Romvi
16. Athens Cathedral
17. Gorgoepekoos (St Eleutherios)
18. The Monastery of St Philothei (St Andrew)
19. Hellenic Literary and Historical Archive
20. Rinaki of the Plaka
21. Cultural Foundation of the National Bank of Greece
22. Holy Power (Agia Dinami)

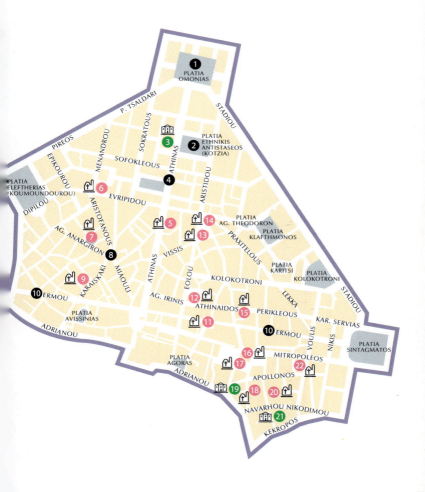

9 THE CITY HALL OF ATHENS AND THE MUNICIPAL MARKETPLACE

The City Hall is situated on a central square of Athens, surrounded by architecturally interesting buildings. Athinas Street, a popular commercial street, runs in front of the Town Hall. Visit the Varvakeios market and do not forget to see Kapnikarea Church and St Eleutherios just next to Athens Cathedral. On Ermou Street, the first commercial street of the Greek State, one can find all sorts of luxury products.

OMONOIA SQUARE

Omonoia Square has been accurately described as 'the hub of Athens and Greece'. It is a place where one can meet all kinds of people, Athenians, provincials, executives, artisans and white-collar workers, immigrants and tourists. The shape of the square highlights its function: from the square radiate outwards the most important arterial roads of the city centre – Eleftheriou Venizelou (Panepistimiou) Street, Stadiou Street, Athinas Street, Panagi Tsaldari (Piraios) Street, Agiou Konstantinou Street and 3rd Septemvriou (September) Street. Called simply Omonoia by the Athenians, this not what is normally thought of as an attractive square. But it is lively; it is a real transit centre; a place for both actual and symbolic meetings. The history of the square begins with the initial planning of the new Greek capital. According to the drawings of architects Kleanthis and Schaubert (1833), the square, which bordered the Ottoman quarter, was to become the new city centre, accommodating the palace and the most important public buildings. But the palace was finally built in present-day Sintagma Square, while the circular Otto Square was finally created on the site of the present Omonoia Square. The square was given its actual name in 1864, one year after the bloody clashes in Athens between conflicting political parties, which were formed after Otto, the first king of Greece, was exiled. The change of name into 'Omonoia (concord) Square' was a gesture to reconcile such differences. In the early 20th century Omonoia Square became the

Omonoia Square

WALK 9

Omonoia district

entertainment centre of the city. The area boasted big cafés, theatres and neoclassical buildings such as the "Megas Alexandros" (Alexander the Great) and "Bageion" Hotels at the beginning of Athinas Street. There was also a permanent platform where orchestras performed to the delight of Athenians. However, because the square was close to the lower-class Psirri and Metaxourgeio districts, it did not cater only for the aristocracy and the middle classes: it provided a meeting point for other social classes, including workers and those flocking to Athens from the provinces.

At the same time, the importance of the square as a nexus of transport gradually grew. Beside the hackney coaches stationed there, the station of the new steam-driven train came into operation in 1895, thanks to the extension of the railway line connecting Piraeus with Thisseio. In 1908 the square became the terminal of the first electrically driven tram lines. When cars multiplied in mid-war Athens, Omonoia suffered traffic congestion, a problem that has remained ever since.

It was in the mid-war period that the underground station of the electrically driven railway, which replaced the steam-driven train network, was constructed. The statues of eight of the nine Muses of Greek mythology were erected on the air-inlets of the station, which were column-shaped: one Muse was left out for the sake of symmetry. Athenians commented ironically that the square with its eight tall columns on the perimeter looked like a birthday cake. The Muses were finally considered tasteless and were taken away. After World War II the square threw in its lot in with the city of Athens. Several neoclassical buildings were pulled down and replaced by new constructions accommodating offices and, later, department stores. The expansion of Athens, mainly because of the influx of Greeks, exacerbated

THE CITY HALL OF ATHENS AND THE MUNICIPAL MARKETPLACE

> *"If you dare go to the square and learn. It is the square of every village and every city in the country. If you become familiar with this place, every place will be familiar to you. To travel from one body to another. You don't need to go anywhere else to know the Greeks; you will know them better here. They bare themselves more. 'Who knows me?' they think".*
>
> Giorgos Ioannou,
> Omonoia 1980, Odysseas, Athens 1980, p.118-120

the traffic situation in Omonoia Square. The square turned into a transit station for both people and vehicles, which has been the case ever since. Nothing remains of the entertainment centre of the early 20th century. Omonoia acquired a popular profile reflecting the wide social map of Athens and, by extension, Greece. Bakakos pharmacy on the corner of Agiou Konstantinou Street was a meeting-place for those arriving in Athens from the provinces. And today, immigrants who have come to Greece during the last few years have given Omonoia Square an air of a metropolitan centre, far from the small town of 19th-century Athens.

The hectic tempo of the square was highlighted by "the Runner", the glass sculpture by Kostas Varotsos, which today stands opposite the Athens Hilton Hotel. This piece was originally erected in the centre of Omonoia Square, triggering controversial opinions until it was removed when the square was reconstructed to enable the building of the new underground line. Travellers, commuters, immigrants and the homeless find shelter in Omonoia Square, whose traffic flow patterns have been changed countless times in recent years. Today, and after the protracted work on the new underground, the square appears finally to have acquired an impersonal look, without any particular architectural style. However, Omonoia Square continues to live its active everyday life, advancing impetuously towards the future.

Omonoia Square, the "Neon"

NATIONAL RESISTANCE SQUARE (KOTZIA SQUARE)

Ethnikis Antistaseos (National Resistance) Square, known to Athenians as Kotzia Square or City Hall Square, is opposite the Athens' City Hall and is surrounded by Athinas, Eſpolidos, Aiolou and Kratinou Streets. According to the city plan of architects Kleanthis and Schaubert (1833), the square was to be a "garden of the people" stretching in front of the King's palace to be built in Omonoia Square. The

CENTRAL BRANCH OF THE NATIONAL BANK OF GREECE

The central branch of the National Bank of Greece is in Aiolou Street near National Resistance (Kotzia) Square. It is an imposing oblong building in neoclassical style, formed from two existing buildings, the residence of Georgios Stavrou, the founder of the bank (and where the bank was originally housed), and the neighbouring "Anglia" Hotel. The latter was purchased by the bank in 1885, was joined with the original building and was completed in 1899–1900 by the architects N. and A. Balanos. The building has housed the National Bank of Greece since 1901.

plan was not carried out, however, and the area, which was a Kleanthis property, was transformed into a square connecting two of the oldest streets of modern Athens, the parallel Athinas and Aiolou Streets.

The square was originally called Loudovikou (Ludwig) Square, in honour of the King of Bavaria, who was the father of Otto, the first King of Greece. On Otto's deposition the square was renamed New Theatre Square, and a little before World War II it took on the name of Kostas Kotzias, Mayor of Athens. The square was given its present name in 1977. A great part of the present square, exactly opposite the City Hall, was occupied by the Dimotikon Theatron (Municipal Theatre) of Athens, built in 1888 on plans of Ernst Ziller. When the theatre was pulled down in 1939, Athens lost one of its cultural landmarks.

Today the square is overlooked by three important buildings, the City Hall, the Central Branch of the National Bank of Greece and the Melas Mansion, the former post office. Until 1939 the central part of the square was occupied by the building of the Municipal Theatre. Today the square is adorned by a sculpture

NEW BUILDING OF THE NATIONAL BANK OF GREECE

The new National Bank of Greece is at the junction of Aiolou and Sofokleous Streets. This building was inaugurated in 2002 and is the work of architects Eirini Sakellaridou, Morpho Papanikolaou and Maria Pollani. It is an impressive, multipurpose modern building. On the one hand, its symbolical juxtaposition with the old bank building underlines tradition, and on the other hand expresses the current energy of the modern institution. Additionally, it accommodates modern business activities and displays the archaeological findings discovered underground: in fact, the ground floor has been converted into an exhibition hall, where one can see the site of the Gate of Acharnes of ancient Athens, part of the road leading to the gate and part of Themistocles' long walls.

THE CITY HALL OF ATHENS AND THE MUNICIPAL MARKETPLACE

by Sofia Vari. Excavation work carried out during the construction of underground parking revealed, underneath the square, part of an ancient cemetery as well as pottery workshops. Among the findings on display are stone sarcophaguses and part of an ancient road.

Kotzia Square

CITY HALL

In Athinas Street, opposite the square of National Resistance (Kotzia), stands the Neoclassical building of the City Hall of Athens. It was built between 1872 and 1874 based on plans of the architect Panagiotis Kalkos. The financial difficulties had not permitted the Municipality of Athens to have its own building until then, thus the municipal

---

THE MELAS MANSION

The Melas Mansion, built by Ernst Ziller (1874), was originally the residence of Vassileios Melas, a wealthy businessman of the Greek diaspora. It is typical of the lavish yet monumental style of private architecture. The building is based on models from European cities of the time, reflecting the aesthetic and ideological views of upper class Greeks of the diaspora.
The façade of the building has three parts with two castle-like tops rising higher than the central part. The ground floor has an imposing arched form, while the parapets and the large decorative vases dominate the crest.

Vassileios Melas bequeathed the incomes from the building to Greek schools. The Athenian Club was housed here until the end of the 19th century. Between 1900 and 1972 the Melas Mansion was the central branch of the Greek Post Office. The Technical Service of the National Bank later undertook restoration, as the building had been so adapted in different periods that its original appearance had changed. The building is today leased by the National Bank of Greece and operates as its administrative and cultural centre, often hosting exhibitions and cultural events.

services had been housed in leased places. In 1872, when Mayor of Athens was Panagiotis Kyriakou, the City Council decided that a new City Hall be built on the then Loudovikou (Ludwig) Square using an amount of GrD 130,000 lent by the National Bank of Greece.

The architect Kalkos designed an unadorned, austere Neoclassical building, which extends along the horizontal rather than the vertical axis, with a Doric propylon on the façade. The offices of the Mayor and the President of the City Council, the reception room and the meeting room of the City Council, as well as the offices of the city services were originally on the first floor. On the ground floor there were shops.

The building was inaugurated on 22 April 1874 and the city services settled there on the same day. However, given that there were shops on the ground floor, there was not enough room to house the city services. Moreover,

G. Gounaropoulos, Wall painting in the hall of the City Council

during the mobilization of 1880 the building served as a military hospital and the city services were housed elsewhere until 1882.

All this, and because the building had not been preserved, led to its renovation, which started in 1901, when Spiros Merkouris was the Mayor of Athens. There were extensive restoration works and the space was rearranged. A luxurious reception room was created on the first floor, while the ground floor housed the offices of the city services. The second renovation of the building started

The City Hall of Athens

THE CITY HALL OF ATHENS AND THE MUNICIPAL MARKETPLACE

in 1935, when Konstantinos Kotzias was the Mayor of Athens. During the works the first floor was built, the entrances of the ground floor were transformed into windows and the lowest part of the building was faced with white marble. However, those changes, and particularly the addition of the new floor, corrupted the architectural style of the building and the proportions were upset. The last change was made in 1994-1995 aiming to restore –as far as possible– the original look of the City Hall by using former decorations such as cornices and a parapet, which had been removed during the previous renovation. Today the building of the City Hall is functionally and aesthetically incorporated into both the environment of the square that opens before it and Athinas Street. The position of the building, between the modern hub of Omonoia Square and the Acropolis, highlights the historical genuineness and the energy of modern Athens.

ATHINAS STREET

Athinas Street, one of the most commercial streets of Athens, connects Omonoia Square with Monastiraki Square. Unlike Ermou Street and Kolonaki, where one can find plenty of clothing and cosmetics stores, Athinas Street offers everyday, goods. Two of the city's biggest street markets are held here, Varvakeios Market and Lachanagora (vegetable market), and in addition there are may shops selling tools, paints and ironware. Due to its commercial nature, Athinas Street is a multicultural place thronging with colourful crowds. Behind the Theatre Square the city's immigrants, Poles, Russians, Pakistanis, Indians and Chinese, have their stores and restaurants. The role of Athinas Street as

---

THE PAINTINGS OF THE CITY HALL

In 1937 the painters Fotis Kontoglou and Giorgos Gounaropoulos were assigned the task of decorating the building with paintings. Kontoglou painted in his own unique style, reminiscent of the Byzantine icons, four compositions inspired by the mythology and the history of Athens, which can be seen in the transaction room of the ground floor. On the first floor and in the old reading room the painter created an impressive array of forty people covering the entire Greek history from mythology until the Greek War of Independence of 1821, while there is a parallel zone depicting respective scenes from Greek mythology and history. The painter Giorgos Gounaropoulos decorated the room of the City Council with a sizeable wall-painting 113 m^2 depicting mythological and historical scenes related to Athens.

F. Kontoglou, "Fighters of the Revolution of 1821"

VARVAKEIOS MARKET

The Varvakeios, or Municipal, Market of Athens is the busiest market of the city. The building was built between 1877-1886, reminiscent of the respective European markets of the same period. The central food market of Athens was transferred there

from its previous position, at the end of Aiolou Street. The market gave Athinas Street its "popular" character and made it one of the principal commercial centres of the city, the one most frequented by the lower social groups of Athens. Today the clients of Varvakeios Market are Athenians of all social classes, attracted by both prices and product variety. The building houses the fish market, while lots of groceries exist on the sides of the building on Athinas,

Evripidou and Sofokleous streets. Behind the building is the arcade of the meat market where, among the shops, there are some small taverns that remain open overnight.

marketplace is highlighted by the fact that the street was the centre of prostitution in Athens. The visitor may therefore be surprised to see the City Hall in this street, opposite National Resistance Square (or Kotzia Square, as it is known), which is famous for its monumental buildings. But let us start form the beginning. Athinas Street is one of the oldest streets in Athens. It opened in 1835 and faced innumerable difficulties because the street crossed the centre of the former Ottoman town. According to Kleanthis' and Schaubert's plan, the part of the street nearest to present-day Omonoia Square would be a large square, the so-called 'garden of the people', with lots of greenery, imposing buildings and shops. The plan was finally abandoned in 1851. However, hotels, houses and shops had already been built in Athinas Street. Theatre Square, Varvakeios Square (the present-day vegetable market, where the Varvakeio Lyceum, which no longer exists, was erected in 1859), and Commercial Market Square (present-day Varvakeios Market) were formed later. The City Hall, Varvakeios Central Market and the City Theatre – demolished as

THE CITY HALL OF ATHENS AND THE MUNICIPAL MARKETPLACE

early as 1939 – were erected in the 1870s, while the luxurious Bageion and Megas Alexandros (Alexander the Great) hotels were built at the junction of Omonoia Square with Athinas Street in the early 20th century. Athinas Street gradually became divided in character: the upper end near Omonoia Square was luxurious in character, while the opposite end near Monastiraki was significantly lower in the social scale, due to the Central Market and its proximity to the old quarters of Athens. This dichotomy was intensified after Asia Minor refugees were accommodated here in shacks in the 1920s. In the mid-war period many houses were converted into cheap hotels, which after the Second World War accommodated Greeks from the provinces.
Towards the end of the 20th century the architecture of Athinas Street changed to a certain extent. Several dilapidated buildings were pulled down and office buildings and department stores of questionable aesthetic value were built instead. However, a considerable part of the architectural wealth of the street, ranging from neoclassicism to modernism, has been preserved and is being restored.
Athinas Street, the road that symbolically connects the present with the past of the city of Athens, Omonoia Square and the Acropolis, has acted as witness to the city's social history. Today the street reflects the energy and metropolitan character of the multicultural city of Athens.

Athinas Street, 1906

THE CHURCH OF ST KYRIAKI

The church of St Kyriaki (Agia Kiriaki) is situated on Athinas Street a few yards away from the junction with Evripidou Street, towards Monastiraki. Founded by the Sklepas family, it is a small aisle-less barrel-vaulted church

dating back to the post-Byzantine period. The sculpted doorframe of the entrance, the plain stone masonry and the blind arches in the middle of each of the longer sides are the church's main characteristics.

THE CHURCH OF ST JOHN "AROUND THE COLUMN"

The church of St John "around the Column" ("Agios Ioannis stin kolona") is situated in a small garden on Evripidou Street, which is located in the market. Its unique form and the religious beliefs with which it is associated make it one of the most interesting Byzantine buildings in Athens. The church is a single-naved basilica built around a Corinthian pillar (column) that rises right through its roof. The pillar was part of an earlier monument that used to stand on the site; and this is why the church carries the soubriquet 'around the Column'.
The church is associated with a number of interesting religious beliefs: it is dedicated to Saint John, who is known as thermastis (meaning "warming") and who was believed to relieve people from high fever and heal them. This belief is related to the function of the site in ancient times: there was once here an ancient sanctuary of Asclepios with a monument dedicated to the Athenian physician Taxaris, who was said to cure people suffering from a high temperature. It is worth adding that a high temperature was the main symptom of malaria, a common

Saint John at the Column

ailment in Athens until the beginning of the 20th century. The belief was so widely accepted that until recent years one could see the many coloured threads that people used to tie around the pillar in praying for recovery.

THE CHURCH AND SQUARE OF ST ANARGYROI

The church of St. Anargyroi (Agioi Anargyroi) is situated in the middle of the homonymous square in the Psirri district, surrounded by Agion Anargiron, Taki, Aristofanous and Katsikogianni Streets. The church was built over an older Byzantine one, which was destroyed in 1827 by the Ottoman army that besieged the Acropolis. The church has been at its present state after the re-building of 1832 and the repairs of 1908. The building has strong Byzantine influences, is of the cross-in-square type and has two belfries on its western side. Apart from the architectural style, the Byzantine influences are evident in the exterior decorations with the

THE CITY HALL OF ATHENS AND THE MUNICIPAL MARKETPLACE

> *Towards the end of his life [Saint John] erected a pillar on the ground and tied up lots of coloured silk threads representing every single ailment and put them around the base of the pillar. He then said, 'When I die, people who are sick can come here and tie a silk thread around the pillar and the thread will have to be the colour of their ailment and they will have to repeat three times: "Saint John, I tie up my ailment and I ask you to untie it" and so, they will be healed'.*
>
> Unknown author, cited in: Liza Micheli,
> Athens in Minor Tones, Dromena, Athens 1987

characteristic dentils. In Agioiß Anargyroi Square there are numerous open-air coffee shops and restaurants.

PSIRRIS

The neighbourhood of Psirris, one of the oldest in Athens, lies between Monastiraki, the historical city centre, the neighbourhood of Metaxourgeio and Kerameikos. Until few years ago Psirris was no more than a popular Athenian suburb, full of light industrial and artisanal workshops and small handicraft businesses closely packed into an area of tiny, low, neoclassical houses and numerous small chapels. Many of these houses were empty, as their owners had moved to better quarters, while several buildings were almost in ruins. Present-day Psirris is completely different, especially at night: it is now full of restaurants, bars, clubs, art halls and theatres and has become a mainstream entertainment area for many Athenian youngsters.

Psirris was originally on the outskirts of Ottoman Athens: in 1860 the chapel of Saint John "around the Column" ("Agios Ioannis stin kolona") in Evripidou Street was described as a "rural chapel". The neighbourhood inhabitants belonged mainly to the lower social strata. Despite the changes of the 19th century, the popular character of Psirris remained. The capital's expansion from east to west along the axis of Ermou Street was accompanied by the extension of the city's light industry. Thus, Psirris expanded and became filled with small stores, handicraft businesses and workshops.

At the same time, Psirris, and especially Assomaton Square, became the focal point for vehicles arriving from Piraeus. Indeed, one of the two terminal stations of the then steam-driven railway connecting Athens with Piraeus was constructed in 1869 on the site of

Saint Anargyroi, Psirri

present-day Thisseio Station. As a result, light industrial units serving the transport industry were established in the area: fodder-sellers, saddlers, coachbuilders, carpenters and metal workshops. In late 19th-century Psirris there were many cafés, popular restaurants and meeting-places not only for locals but for students and intellectuals as well.

The social history of Psirris after the establishment of the modern Greek state is of particular interest. Immediately after the 1821 Revolution former fighters, the jobless and refugees, frequented the numerous cafés of the neighbourhood; and leaders of political parties used to choose their bodyguards and henchmen from such people. The area had a peculiar social character with workers and middle-class people coexisting with the city's dropouts. Typical figures were "tramboukos" (thug), "koutsavakis" (bully) and "mangas" (smart guy), who trod a path between the proletariat and the underworld, often also involved with the police as informers. Their lifestyle and private codes of honour worked on the prejudices and imagination of the Athenian middle class, while intellectuals and artists depicted them romantically in literature and theatre. The decisive blow to the microcosm of Psirris was given by the Head of the Military Police of Athens-Piraeus, Dimitrios Bairaktaris, in the late 19th

Psirri district

THE ROMANCE OF LORD BYRON

The English poet and ardent philhellene Lord Byron lived in the house (no longer extant) of Mr Makris's widow in Psirris in 1809. The short romance between Lord Byron and his landlady's daughter, Teresa Makris, known as the "Beauty of Athens", is thought to have taken place there. It is not quite clear whether the poet was hopelessly in love with the twelve-year-old Teresa or if the story is just another romantic exaggeration. At all events, it was a story that survived for a long time and has now faded. Psirris, with the hectic lifestyle of the present city, is far from the romantic world of Lord Byron.

THE CITY HALL OF ATHENS AND THE MUNICIPAL MARKETPLACE

> **THE CRIMINAL COURT**
>
> Such was the lack of public buildings in the city that, a few years after Athens was proclaimed capital of the newly born Greek state, the Danish architect Christian Hansen undertook the task of converting the church of Agia Eleoussa (Virgin Mary the Merciful), in the street of the same name, into the Criminal Court. The building that accommodated the Criminal Court for several years from 1837 is today abandoned: only a few people are aware of its strange history.

century. Usual punishment methods were beating, hair-cutting and cutting of one coat-sleeve. The "koutsavakides" used to leave one coat-sleeve hanging from the shoulder without the arm inside, to indicate their social identity and their readiness to take part in fights.

In the second half of the 20th century Psirris was downgraded, together with the neighbouring suburb of Metaxourgeio. Although it continued to house industry organized in small- and medium-sized businesses, its importance as a place to live was greatly reduced. Popular hotels and brothels were housed in the small and badly preserved buildings. Today the neighbourhood reflects the multicultural character of the city of Athens: on an imaginary line connecting Theatre Square with Eleftherias (Freedom) Square (Koumoundourou) there are stores and restaurants established by economic immigrants. At the same time, the expansion of the entertainment and cultural activities of the city to the west, from the Plaka to Pireos Street, has left its mark at Psirris. On Saturday nights the neighbourhood squares are full of people until early morning, while traffic on Ermou and Assomaton Streets is heavier than during working days.

THE CHURCH OF CHRIST OF KOPIDIS OR CHRISTOKOPIDIS

The church of Christ of Kopidis, or Christokopidis is situated between Christokopidou and Aisopou Streets in the densely populated Psyrris area. It was initially built in the 17th century and was named after its donor, Kopidis. The present form of the church (domed cross-in-square) and the two belfries on its western side date from the 19th century.

Psirri Square

The Christ of Kopidis is one of the oldest and most important parochial churches in Athens. According to some sources, during the Ottoman period the parish of Kopidis was highly populated. This can furthermore be proven by the fact that it is located right in the centre of an area that gradually expanded around the church. Because of the shortage of public buildings when Athens became the capital of Greece in 1834, the church was used for a while to house the Areios Pagos, the Greek Supreme Court. The Danish architect Christian Hansen was responsible for the alterations necessary for the new use of the church. ●■

ERMOU STREET

Ermou Street, the main shopping street in Athens, begins at the ancient cemetery of Kerameikos and leads to Sintagma Square. It was opened up early on, when Stamatis Kleanthis and Eduard Schaubert were preparing the first city plans for Athens in 1833. From the beginning it was meant to be a commercial street; hence it was named after Hermes, the ancient god of commerce.

When, in 1856, the Government decided to build a railway connecting Athens with Piraeus, it was agreed that the terminal station would be in Thisseio, next to Ermou Street, which thus became the main road entering the city from the port. From the following year work began to widen up the road, including some necessary demolition. With this development Ermou Street gradually became one of the most crowded in the city with numerous textile and jewellery shops, cafés and hotels, mainly in the section between Monastiraki and Sintagma.

In the Monastiraki to Thisseio section a different kind of activity developed, with ironmongers, antique and building material outlets. These shops were actually a part of the greater open-air market of the area.

In the recent years the Ermou Street to Sintagma Square and Aiolou Street sections have been turned into a pedestrian zone, thus becoming the main shopping street and a favourite place for walks. The old traditional textile shops have been replaced by modern clothing, shoe and cosmetics shops. The strong commercial

Ermou Street, a busy commercial street

THE CITY HALL OF ATHENS AND THE MUNICIPAL MARKETPLACE

The paved way in Ermou Street

activity on Ermou Street, also supported by the restoration of numerous buildings, revived this historic street of Athens. Apart from numerous shops and cafés one can find musicians, street sellers, "laterna"- (a kind of barrel-organ) players, sellers of roasted chestnuts and various street artists. The part of the street between Aiolou Street and Assomaton Square maintains its working-class commercial character. The last part between Assomaton Square and Piraios Street has also been turned into a pedestrian zone within the framework of the project of unification of archaeological sites of Athens.

THE CHURCH OF KAPNIKAREA

One of the most important Byzantine monuments in Athens is situated in the middle of Ermou Street. The church is dedicated to St. Mary, but is better known as Kapnikarea. It is a complex tetrastyle cross-in-square church that dates back to 1050. The higher parts of the masonry follow the cloisonné style, while the lower parts consist of large courses arranged so that they form crosses. The elements that lead experts to date the church to 1050 are the few kufic brick patterns, the limited use of dentils and the particular arrangement of the windows. The dome is typically Athenian with its light proportions. The graduated roofs and the alternative use of straight and curved lines contribute aesthetically to a sense of grace and harmony. The element of the colour variations with the abundant use of kufic brick patterns is less visible here than in earlier monuments, instead the emphasis is placed on the stones' sculptural values. Soon after the church's foundation, a chapel dedicated to St Barbara was added on its northern side. The outer narthex as we know it today was added on the western side of the church and chapel during that time as well, and initially it was an open portico. The small columned porch on the narthex's southern entrance was built in the 12th century. In 1834, during the opening up of Ermou Street, the

CAFÉS AND CLUBS ON ERMOU STREET

The popular cafés and clubs on Ermou Street were part of Athenian social life of during the 19th century. One of those was the "Beautiful Greece" ("Oraia Hellas") at the junction with Aiolou Street, frequented by many Athenians who went there to discuss current political affairs. Near the junction of Ermou and Piraios Streets was the "Green Tree" ("Prassino Dendro") Club, frequented by Bavarians who came to Greece with King Otto; concerts, balls and gambling took place there.

THE NAME KAPNIKAREA

There are various theories regarding the origins of the name Kapnikarea. Most probably the name relates to the "kapnikon", a certain tax imposed during the Byzantine era. According to this explanation, the church was sponsored by an executive who might have been in charge of collecting this tax, or simply carried the family name Kapnikares.

In older documents we encounter variations of the name, most frequently the name "Kamoucharea", originating from the word "kamouchas" (luxurious textile). These other theories however regarding the church's name are no longer accepted.

The church also used to be called "the Princess's church" based on a tradition that connected the most important churches in

Athens with Athenian empresses of Byzantium. During the 19th century the church was also known as "Panagia of Prentzas" ("St. Mary of Prentzas") probably because of its association with a sponsor, or donor of an important icon that might have been kept in the chapel, though none of this has been proven.

It is worth mentioning that even today Athenians might say that an old, ugly woman "looks like Kapnikarea", probably in reference to the poor state that the church was in at the beginning of the 19th century.

church that had by then been damaged and deserted during the Greek War of Independence came close to being demolished. This would have been a hasty solution, applied already to other Byzantine monuments to serve the needs of the new capital and to satisfy the zeal of certain experts who wanted to focus exclusively on the study of ancient monuments. Then with the intervention of Ludwig of Bavaria, King Otto's father, the church was rescued. The church also escaped demolition in 1863 with the intervention of the Bishop of Athens. The church's interior marble screen was crafted later and it is a copy of the screen in the Monastery of Kaissariani. The church's pictorial decorations date from the mid-20th century (1942) and were created by the famous icon-painter Fotis Kontoglou and his group. The mosaic over the entrance was crafted by Elli Voïla in 1936.

The church of Kapnikarea now belongs to the University of Athens.

Saint Eirene

The Church Of St Eirene

The church of St Eirene (Agia Irini) is situated between Aiolou and Athinaidos Streets on the location of an earlier church dedicated to the same saint, which had been repaired soon after the creation of the Greek State to be used as the Cathedral. When in 1842 it was decided to build a new Cathedral, the local community asked that it were built on the same location. Although their efforts were unsuccessful, a part of the funds that had already been collected for the Cathedral were used to fund the building of the new church of St Eirene.
The new church was designed by Lissandros Kaftantzoglou and construction began in August 1846. The local community, the Municipality of Athens and the Public Revenue Office funded the project.
The church is a three-aisled domed basilica. On the plainly decorated façade there are three vaults and on the upper part there are lobed windows with a pediment. At the ends of the façade stand two belfries. It is evident that the church's form is a combination of religious architecture with the neoclassical style.
There are three semi-circular conches in the interior, one in the sanctuary and two on the sides, whereas arcades with columns separate the aisles. The church was opened in 1850 in a half-finished state and was completed in 1892, when its decoration works were finished.

The Church Of Virgin Mary Chrissospiliotissa

The church of Panagia (Virgin Mary) Chrissospiliotissa is situated between Aiolou and Chrissospiliotissis Streets. This ornate church is a sample of the eclectic style that was dominant in Greece during the 19th century. It is an impressive two-storey building with two belfries on each side of the narthex.
The older Byzantine church that occupied this site was ruined during the Greek War of Independence, but was repaired in 1835

Saint Eirene, interior

and used again. Preparations for the construction of a larger church began in 1846; however, due to various difficulties and bureaucratic matters, the work began only in 1863.

Dimitrios Zezos drew up plans for the new church, successfully combining the Byzantine style with ancient Greek elements. But before even the foundations had been lain, Zezos passed away and Panagis Kalkos took over the supervision of the project, on existing designs. When Kalkos himself died, Ernst Ziller took over and changed the design of the dome, a fact that upset the local community. This resulted in the intervention of the Mayor of Athens, Dimitrios Soutsos, who, as an engineer himself, redesigned the dome as it is today. The religious paintings and decorations were completed in 1892. The costs for rebuilding and decorating were funded by a large number of Athenians. •−

THE CHURCH OF ST PARASKEVI

The tiny church of St Paraskevi is situated to the north of the church of Chrissospiliotissa on Aiolou Street. This single-naved barrel-vaulted church was built during the period of Ottoman rule and is a metochion of the Monastery of Phaneromeni. The internal wall paintings were created during the Modern period. •−

THE CHURCH OF VIRGIN ROMVI OR ROUMBI

The church of Panagia (Virgin Mary) Romvi or Roumbi is situated between Evangelistrias and Ermou Streets. There are no written sources giving details on this monument. The name Romvis, or Roumbis, obviously refers to the church's founder, and there are numerous legal documents from the Ottoman period in which an Athenian family of that name is mentioned. The church is a three-

The Chrissospiliotissa

THE CITY HALL OF ATHENS AND THE MUNICIPAL MARKETPLACE

aisled basilica that was probably built at the beginning of the Ottoman era; its external walls were altered as a result of repairs in more recent years. The aisles are covered by vaults, the central one ending in conches. There is an additional building on the northern side of the church divided by a colonnade in two long compartments, of which the northern one is used as a chapel.

The church of Virgin Mary of Romvi

ATHENS CATHEDRAL

Athens Cathedral is situated in Mitropoleos [Cathedral] Square, on the street of the same name, which connects Sintagma Square with Monastiraki. Building began in 1842 and was completed by 1862. Dedicated to the Annunciation of the Virgin ("Evangelismos tis Theotokou"), the Cathedral is a three-aisled, domed basilica. Many consider that the building's mixture of architectural models spoils its stylistic unity.

The cost of construction exceeded the predicted amount of 700,000 drachmas, a particularly high sum for that time; the difference was covered partly by the sale of ecclesiastical property and partly by donations, mostly from King Otto and the wealthy Sinas family, who lived in Vienna.

The church was built in four stages. The architect Theophilus Hansen prepared the first drawings, which resulted in that part of the building up to the first series of windows. Then, in 1843, construction work was interrupted due to financial problems. Three years later Dimitrios Zezos took over and introduced a Greco-Byzantine style. On his death in 1857 the Municipality of Athens asked the French architect François Boulanger to continue the project. Boulanger collaborated with Panagiotis Kalkos, who was responsible for the actual execution of the project. Material from ruined Byzantine churches was used in the construction process. The internal wall

The Cathedral of Athens

paintings by Spiridon Giallinas and Alexander Seitz follow Byzantine tradition, while the ornaments were made by the painter Konstantinos Fanellis from Smyrna. The sculptural architectural elements, the capitals and the pulpit, were designed by the sculptor Georgios Fitalis. The numerous stylistic alterations effected during construction led to an ill-defined architectural character, especially by comparison with the church of Gorgoepekoos right next to the Cathedral. Characteristically, the lower part of the church, designed by Hansen, looks smaller in relation to the rest of the building.

THE CHURCH OF GORGOEPEKOOS (ST ELEUTHERIOS)

The church of Virgin Mary Gorgoepekoos is situated in Mitropoleos Square, next to the contemporary Cathedral of the Annunciation, and is also known as the Small Cathedral. One of the very few churches to have maintained its original form, it also boasts unique external sculptural decoration. Gorgoepekoos is a Byzantine church from the end of the 12th century, the period when Michael Choniates was Bishop of Athens (1180–1204). According to legend, Empress Eirene of Athens founded the church in 787. During the Ottoman period

The Cathedral of Athens

THE CITY HALL OF ATHENS AND THE MUNICIPAL MARKETPLACE

> **RELIGIOUS SYNCRETISM**
> *Gorgoepekoos constitutes another example of the fusion (syncretism) between ancient and Christian religious traditions: it was built on the remains of an ancient temple dedicated to Eileithyia, the goddess of childbirth. The same beliefs were later applied by the Christians to St Mary Gorgoepekoos, the adjective "gorgoepekoos" meaning he/she who grants requests quickly: the church was dedicated to Gorgoepekoos and Christian women went there to pray for a quick and painless labour*

the church formed part of the episcopal mansion, and was called "katholikon". In 1841, after the foundation of the Greek State, the church was used as the National Library, housing the first collection of books donated to the Orphanage of Aigina. The church underwent repairs in 1863 and was later also dedicated to St Eleutherios.
The church is built as a cross-in-square with a three-part narthex whose middle part is vaulted and taller than the other two.
The dome is the most characteristic and best preserved example of the Athenian type and is, therefore, particularly important. Built largely of marble – bricks or stones have hardly been used apart from the dome – the lower part consists of undecorated marble blocks, whereas in the higher part there are ninety ancient Greek, Roman, early Christian and Byzantine walled-in reliefs. A number of these were used in a way similar to their original function, while

The Church of Gorgoepekoos, walled-in reliefs

plaques with engraved scenes formed a frieze around all sides of the church.
The variety of walled-in reliefs is particularly interesting. Among them there are plaques from the 9th and 10th centuries using designs of oriental origin (animals, plants, representations of the tree of life, etc.), or stemming from folk traditions. There are also sculptures with trophies of the Panathenaic Games representing athletic games, and roman triumphs, as well as others of Byzantine origin with oriental sphinxes, geometric shapes, animals and plants. A 4th-century BC cornice has also survived, representing celebrations from the Attic calendar, including a scene showing of

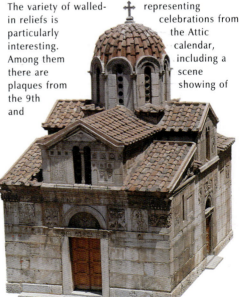

MICHAEL CHONIATES (c. 1138-1222)

Michael Choniates was a writer and Bishop of Athens (1182–1204); he was later canonised. Well educated and with a great respect for the classical legacy of Athens, he frequently complained in his writings about the city's cultural decline. As Bishop of Athens he relieved the population of its heavy taxes and also led the resistance against the siege raised by Leo Sgouros (1203). Following the occupation of Athens by the Franks in 1204, Choniates refused to accept the new situation and sought refuge first on the island of Kea and then in Euboea. From 1233–4 there appeared many depictions of Choniates in churches throughout Athens, which suggests that he was canonised soon after his death.

Herakles with Hebe. It is interesting to note that the artisans attempted to Christianize these ancient sculptures by adding the symbol of the cross between different scenes

THE MONASTERY OF ST PHILOTHEI (CHURCH OF ST ANDREW)

The small church of St Andrew (Agios Andreas) is situated on St Filotheis Street, near the Cathedral and the Archbishop of Athens' offices, an area

The Church of Gorgoepekoos, parapet decorated with an eagle

crowded with shops selling religious artefacts. In around 1550, during the Ottoman rule, the Athenian nun Philothei, whose family name was Regoula, or Rigoula Benizelou, founded a women's monastery in this area: there was once an early-Christian basilica here. The monastery housed a hostel and a hospital where the nuns looked after people regardless of their religious background, as well as a girls' school. The monastery's "katholikon", a three-aisled basilica

EIRENE OF ATHENS (752-803)

Eirene was Empress of Byzantium, wife of Leo IV and mother of Constantine VI, born in Athens. After the death of Leo she came into power as the guardian of her young son; later she removed him from the throne and became the first Empress (797-802). She lost her throne to Nikephoros I in 802 and was exiled to Lesvos, where she died. Eirene restored the icon worship, which had been banned in the Byzantine Empire by the so-called "eikonomachoi" (iconoclasts). She was active in charitable work and her international policy was quite successful, however her financial policies in the long term proved damaging for the public.

dedicated to St Andrew, was demolished in 1890, together with the rest of the monastery, in order to build the Archbishop's offices. A crypt was built from the remains of the early-Christian basilica.

HELLENIC LITERARY AND HISTORICAL ARCHIVE

The Hellenic Literary and Historical Archive (ELIA) is a centre for the collection, preserve and research of a unique material, which is of great value for the study of Greek history and which might have been lost otherwise. ELIA was founded in 1980 and since then it has expanded its manifold activity based in its two buildings on Agiou Andreou Street. The first building is a five-storey neoclassical house from the mid-war period that belongs to ELIA; it houses the library, the collection of family and personal archives, museum items and everyday objects, as well as the administration offices. The second building is opposite the first one and belongs to the Rizareios Ecclesiastical School; it houses the Photographic Archive, the Egyptian Hellenism Department and the Map Collection. The library of ELIA includes more than 100,000 printed volumes from the 19th and the 20th century. Particular reference should be made to the series of Greek calendars, magazines and newspapers, as well as the Greek printed material that has been published in Egypt. The library also includes a rare collection of popular literature, as well as printed material produced by Greeks of the diaspora.

OBJECTS

Through ELIA's exhibitions and publications, one can realise the wealth of its collections of objects: professional tools, pieces of machinery, toys, product packaging, decorative objects, household items and clothes. There are also everyday objects that usually get neglected, such as the tickets issued by the conductors of horse-led trams and the sheet with the

---

ST PHILOTHEI OF ATHENS

Regoula or Rigoula Benizelou was born in Athens in 1522. She came from an aristocratic family: her father, Angelos Benizelos, belonged to a well-known Athenian family and her mother was born to the Palaiologos family. When Rigoula was still in her teens she married Andreas Cheilas and became a nurse. Soon after, however, she was widowed and became a nun, taking on the name Philothei. Her charitable work, her support for the Christian women in the Acropolis' harem and her preaching angered the Ottoman authorities, so that she was arrested and tortured. She was martyred on 19 February 1589 – now the date of her commemoration in the religious calendar. Her relics are kept in Athens Cathedral, and she is the patron saint of the wealthy suburb in Athens named after her (Filothei).

wishes of the distributor of the newspaper "Asty" from 1898. Many items from the beginning of the 20th century are on display in the permanent exhibition "Travelogue of Athens" in the Cultural Centre of the Municipality of Athens "Melina Merkouri".

ARCHIVES

The best-known collection of ELIA consists of the private archives of individuals who played an important part in the country's politics, culture and finance. This is why the collection reflects the history of organisations, political parties, commercial ventures, businesses, banks, as well as of simple individuals and social groups, such as the 1922 refugees.
The Photographic Archive includes more than 300,000 photographs and negatives from the 19th and the 20th century. Part of the archive includes albums and photographic archives of individuals and families from the 19th and the 20th century. There are photographs by well known photographers, such as Moraïtis, Konstantinou and Boeringer, as well as the archive of Dimitris Papadimou (1918-1994). There are also albums from the period 1855-1860 and negatives on glass plates and film, as well as thousands of postcards from Greece and abroad. The Map Collection consists of more than 2,000 maps from the period 1830-1950 most of which concern Greece and the Balkans. Among them there are specific thematic and statistical maps illustrating the development of the Greek State.
From March 2000 ELIA's collection also includes shadow theatre figures, playbills and theatre sets, paper cut-outs with motifs from the shadow theatre, leaflets about

C.P. Cavafy

The Central building of the Hellenic Literary and Historical Archive

ROMAN BATHS

Excavations carried out in Thoukididou Street have brought to light the ruins of Roman baths. Such buildings are typical of the Roman era, when Athens was enriched with many buildings, including baths. Today the visitor can clearly see both the various rooms of the baths and the column bases.

Karagiozis, the leading figure of shadow theatre, LPs with shadow theatre plays, printed material concerning the Greek shadow theatre (advertising sheets, programmes, cards, posters) and handwritten notebooks with shadow theatre plays. The collection also includes a record of press cuttings and photographs concerning the history of shadow theatre in Greece. There is a separate collection with photographic and printed material archives from the most important Greek communities of Egypt, those in Alexandria, Mansura, Cairo, Port Said, Suez, Ismaelia, as well as the archive of the Patriarchate of Alexandria. This detailed collection sheds valuable light onto the life of a lost by now part of Greek diaspora. •▪

RINAKI OF THE PLAKA

The small, recently restored post-Byzantine Church of St Eirene (Agia Irini), known as Rinaki of the Plaka, stands in Navarchou Nikodimou Street, near Agias Filotheis Street. It is a plain, single-room church, built in about the 17th century. The diminutive "Rinaki" reveals the locals' familiarity with the church. •▪

CULTURAL FOUNDATION OF THE NATIONAL BANK OF GREECE

The Cultural Foundation of the National Bank of Greece is housed in a building on 13 Thoukydidou Street. It is a particularly interesting building as it one of the few remaining from the Ottoman period. It has been built around a spacious internal closed courtyard, and was formerly used as a residential complex and a hostel. It is a plain two-storey building with many openings on its façade. In addition to producing its various publications, the foundation mounts temporary exhibitions here. •▪

The Cultural Foundation of the National Bank of Greece

The Church Of Holy Power (Agia Dinami)

The small church of Agia Dinami (dedicated to the Birth of Virgin Mary) is situated on Mitropoleos Street, near the entrance to the Greek Ministry of Education and Religion. According to legend, Agia Dinami was believed to protect women in labour; women would go to church to pray for a safe and painless delivery.

This small barrel-vaulted church was built during the first years of the Ottoman rule and since the 16th century has been a metochion of the Monastery of Penteli. During the Greek War of Independence it was used as a bullet-manufacturing factory. Its present form dates from its renovation in 1912. The sculpted lintel above the entrance is particularly impressive.
An inscription found on the site suggests that the church was built on the site of an ancient temple dedicated to Herakles. The inscription reads, ΗΡΑΚΛΕΙΔΙ [ΟΜΕΙΩ ΚΑΙ] ΑΝΗΘΗΚΕΝ (dedicated to Herakles).

The Church of Holy Power (Agia Dinami)

10

WALK 10a

1. The Eynard Mansion
2. The National Theatre of Greece
3. St Constantine
4. Karaïskakis Square
5. The Peloponnissou Station
6. The Larissis Station
7. Metaxourgeio
8. The Former Athens Conservatory
9. The Municipal Gallery
10. The Museum of Islamic Arts
11. St George on Piraios Street
12. The Athinaïs
13. Votanikos
14. The Plato's Academy

WALK *10b*

1. The Kerameikos
2. Technopolis
3. The Cultural Centre "Melina Merkouri"
4. Industrial Buildings of Piraios Street
5. Refugee Settlements In Piraios Street
6. The "Hellenic Cosmos"
7. The Athens School of Fine Arts

10 AN UNUSUAL WALK

Piraios Street is the street that from Antiquity onwards connects the city of Athens with its port. At its start is the Municipal Gallery, in the building of the old city nursery. Further down one sees industrial buildings that have been transformed into kernels of cultural activity: the Technopolis in a former gas factory, the Melina Merkouri Cultural Centre in the Poulopoulos hat-making factory, Hellenic Cosmos in the former Viosol metal processing factory.

ROUTE 10a

THE EYNARD MANSION

At 20 Agiou Konstantinou Street, next to the National Theatre, stands the Eynard Mansion, the main exhibition centre of the Cultural Foundation of the National Bank of Greece (MIET). It is a neoclassical building named after the Swiss philhellene Jean-Gabriel Eynard, who contributed to the establishment of the bank in 1841 and was a friend and supporter of Ioannis Kapodistrias.
The important "Victor and Niovi Melas Cartographic Archive" is housed here including rare maps by European map makers of the

Archive of Cartography

16th-18th centuries, old atlases, portolans and gazetteers, such as that of Chrissanthos Notaras, as well as one of the few original copies of the "Charta" (map) of the late 18th century Greek revolutionary Rigas Velestinlis (Feraios) in perfect condition. The archive, part of which is permanently on display, and the book collection are open to the students of charts.
At the Eynard Mansion there is a room dedicated to the important Greek actors Katina Paxinou (1900-1973) and Alexis Minotis (1900-

Eynard's Mansion

1990) with photographs, books, theatrical programmes, mock-ups and sketches as well as costumes. The other rooms of the Mansion accommodate periodical art exhibitions.

National Theatre Of Greece

The National Theatre, on Agiou Konstantinou Street (opposite the church dedicated to St Constantine) is one of the city's most imposing buildings. It was designed by the architect Ernst Ziller, who was influenced by European theatres of the time such as the People's Theatre (Volkstheater) of Vienna, but finally decided for a style reminiscent of the Italian Renaissance. The protruding Corinthian columns of the façade, which stand on oblong bases at ground-floor level, are typical of the building. The façade was modelled on Hadrian's Library. Funding came partly in the form of a donation to George I, the then King of Greece, from the Greek merchant of the diaspora Stefanos Rallis. Construction began in 1895, but work was interrupted in 1897 because of the Greek-Ottoman war and because Rallis' money was running out. Two more donations from Greeks of the diaspora, together with contributions from the revenue office, saved the day. The building was finally completed in autumn 1901 and was opened on 24 November of the same year. The mechanical and electrical installations were among the best of its time. The theatre was restored and modified in 1960, when it was also extended towards Menandrou Street, thus taking its present form.

The building housed the Royal Theatre between 1901 and 1908, when its function was suspended, although it hosted occasional performances of foreign theatre companies. In 1930 the former Royal Theatre was re-established as the National Theatre, the monarchy having been

The National Theatre

abolished in Greece, and in 1932 performances resumed. The National Theatre was soon to become the most important theatrical establishment in Greece, recruiting almost all the great actors of the time. "Arma Thespidos" (Chariot of Thespis), a mobile theatre company touring Greece and abroad, was established in 1939 within the framework of the National Theatre and has been performing ever since.

The repertoire of the National Theatre ranges from classical to modern drama. However, particular emphasis has always been given to ancient drama. The performance of Sophocles' Elektra in 1938 at Epidaurus theatre was a pivotal moment for the theatrical world, as it initiated the use of the ancient theatres for classical drama performances. The next performance at Epidaurus was given in 1954 with Euripides' Hippolytos directed by Dimitris Rontiris. One year later the National Theatre inaugurated the Epidaurus Festival. Among the most famous actors that either starred or studied in the National Theatre were Katina Paxinou, Alexis Minotis and Melina Merkouri. Today the National Theatre has five stages, three of which are in Ziller's building. The Central Stage seats 658, the New Stage 114 and the Experimental Stage seats 100 people. The other two stages are in the Rex building on Eleftheriou Venizelou (Panepistimiou) Street.

The entrance of the National Theatre

THE CHURCH OF ST CONSTANTINE

The large and impressive church of St Constantine (Agios Konstantinos) is situated on the eponymous street, Agiou Konstantinou, which begins at Omonoia Square and

LISSANDROS KAFTANTZOGLOU

Kaftantzoglou (1811-1885) was an important architect and engineer whose work is related to several of the most important buildings in Athens in the 19th century, such as the Technical University, the Arsakeion and the church of St. Constantine. He was  *one of the strongest supporters of the classicistic style in architecture. In his role as the director of the "School of the Arts" (later Technical University) between 1844 and 1862 he contributed to the upgrading of the study of architecture in Greece.*

ends in Karaïskakis Square. The city council decided to build a church dedicated to St Constantine in 1869, to celebrate the birth of the Prince Royal and future King Constantine I. Funds were raised by collection; Lissandros Kaftantzoglou designed the building. Construction began in 1871 and was completed in 1893, when the church was inaugurated. Queen Olga, Prince Constantine's mother, paid for the decoration and other miscellaneous works necessary to complete the church.

The architect defined the style of the church as Greek. As at St Eirene on Aiolou Street, every effort was made to apply neoclassical design to religious architecture: Kaftantzoglou despised the Byzantine style and believed that modern Greek architecture should be modelled upon ancient Greek style.
The result, according to many architects, is a failure. Despite its imposing, lavish character – due largely to its size and the extensive use of marble – the building is not well proportioned, but seems heavy and overbearing.

KARAÏSKAKIS SQUARE

Karaïskakis Square is crucial for the traffic connecting the center of Athens with the western suburbs and the rail station. Since 1999 the Underground station of Metaxourgeio has been on the square.
The largest part of the square is occupied by the "Monument of the Fallen Aviators", created by the sculptor Evangelos Moustakas and representing the fall of mythical Icarus on a prismatic pedestal. The sculpture has also a metal sphere at the end of the space occupied by the

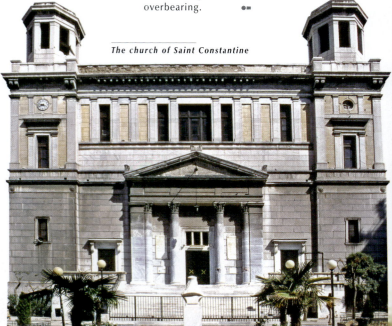

The church of Saint Constantine

AN UNUSUAL WALK

Karaiskakis Square and the "Monument of the Fallen Aviators"

monument designed by the architect Ioannis Moustakas in 2000. The square's sculptured decorations also include a work by Gabriella Simosi called "Birds" created in 1989.

PELOPONNISSOU STATION

Peloponnissou Station is one of the two great railway stations of Athens. It is an oblong building (63 x 20m), divided into three parts. The central part protrudes and has a big arched door with a clock above. The two side parts are similar to the central one, only smaller. All three parts lead to trapezoid wooden constructions covered with curved metal sheets, while the ground-floor wings connecting the three parts are covered with a double wooden roof. The artistic, hammered metal constructions located at different points of the station, and particularly at the entrance and the platform, are typical of the building.

The station was probably built in 1889, but it took its present form between 1912 and 1913, modelled on the "Chemins de fer Orientaux" station at Constantinople. However, the Peloponnissou Station is not so exotic as its model because it is a mixture of neoclassical, central European and art nouveau elements. Thus, the perfect symmetry along the axis of the main entrance and the successive rooms communicating with the corridors as well

Peloponnisou Railway Station

as the scotias and the door posts, which are the main decorative elements of the station, may be considered neoclassical. On the other hand, the main entrance, the shelters and the metal constructions are typical examples of the art nouveau style, while the domes on the roof remind us of central European railway stations. The station has generally preserved its original appearance and has been designated one of the city's historical monuments. ●▪

LARISSIS STATION

Larissis Station of Athens is the greatest station of the railway line leading to Northern Greece. It was designed and built in the early 20th century. Although the exact year is not known, it is believed that it was built in 1904, the year that the railway line was put into operation by the French manufacturing company.
As regards its architectural style, it is a typical example of Greek neoclassicism. It consisted of 15 arched openings, symmetrical to the entrance and the clock, where similar openings existed to the side of the platform. It was decorated with horizontal lines, scotias and door posts. The central two-storeyed part was connected on both sides with ground floor wings.
Today the station has nothing to do with the station of the early 20th century. In the 1970s there were systematic interventions that completely changed its look. As a result, a false ceiling covered the ground floor shelter of the platform, the details of the lime-cast disappeared and the shelter of the front entrance covered the arches. ●▪

METAXOURGEIO

Metaxourgeio is the quintessential working-class district of Athens, situated between Psirris, from which it is separated by Piraios Street, and Akadimia Platonos (Plato's Academy). The district was developed during the third quarter of the 19th century, when population increase resulted in the expansion of the city to the west. Its name originated from the silk factory that was situated here. Metaxourgeio's inhabitants came mostly from the Peloponnese and the islands; they worked

Larissis Railway Station

AN UNUSUAL WALK

"Metaxourgeio" Square

in the numerous little shops, industries and workshops crammed in between the residential buildings. Between the two world wars Metaxourgeio remained a working-class and lower middle-class district, buzzing with social and cultural activity and favoured by many actors and artists. After World War II, living conditions in the area deteriorated and many homeowners moved to better neighbourhoods. Today, Metaxourgeio maintains its working class character as an ever-increasing number of immigrants from abroad settle here. On the other hand, that part of the district closer to Piraios Street is gradually developing into a culture and entertainment area, similar to Psirris and Gazi.

THE SILK FACTORY

In 1833 the Danish architect Christian Hansen began the construction of a plain, elongated building to be used as a market. The property owner, Georgios Kantakouzinos, was hoping that the construction of the new city centre in the Kerameikos area, according to the city plans of the Bavarian architect Leo von Klenze, would contribute to the further development of the neighbouring area. However, the market was never completed, and the new city centre was transferred to what is today Sintagma Square. The half-finished building, which dominated the barren area, was redesigned in 1853 to house a silk factory, which was active until 1875. It was Greece's first steam-powered factory. During the 1880s the building was turned into a two-storey housing complex with strong neoclassical architectural elements. The Municipality of Athens acquired the building in 1993. Today it is undergoing restoration and repair. The best-preserved part of the complex is on Millerou Street, at the point where it meets Megalou Alexandrou, Germanikou, and Leonidou Streets.

Drawn restoration of the factory

THE FORMER ATHENS CONSERVATORY

The building at 35 Piraios Street is today the National Theatre's School of Drama. This, and another two-storey building on the opposite side of the street, used to belong to the family of G. Vlachoutzis, a nobleman from Wallachia. Both buildings were the first modern constructions on Piraios Street in the 19th century, and until 1836 they housed the Viceroyalty's offices. In that year the Bavarian lieutenant and army engineer Friedrich von Zentner installed his equipment in one of the buildings, and the following year the newly founded Royal School of Arts (which would later form Athens' Technical University) was housed there, at his suggestion.

The Technical University was transferred to its new premises on Patission Street in 1873 and the building on Piraios Street was given to the Music and Drama Society to accommodate the Athens Conservatory. In the 1970s the Conservatory was again transferred, and the National Theatre's Drama School has been housed in the Vlachoutzis building ever since.

The exterior of the building has been gradually altered and an extra storey was added in 1845. The architect who designed it remains unknown; however, it is believed that it may have been Stamatis Kleanthis.

THE MUNICIPAL GALLERY

The Municipal Gallery of Athens is situated on 51 Piraios Street in Eleftherias (Koumoundourou) Square. Built between 1872 and 1875, this elegant neoclassical building was designed by the architect Panagiotis Kalkos. It has a clear, symmetrical form and

E. Michelis: "The Clock of Cyrrhestus".

consists of a central aisle and two transverse wings. At the front of the building is an arched vault, and the wings are covered by pediments. The building housed the city nursery until 1977, and in 1982 was renovated in order to be used as the municipal gallery. Prior to this renovation, the city nursery was also a foundling hospital, an

The Municipal Gallery

AN UNUSUAL WALK

G. Gounaropoulos: "Still Life"

Michalis Tompros and Thanassis Apartis. Furthermore, there are architectural drawings of important neoclassical buildings by Ernst Ziller and Theophilus Hansen. Due to the gallery's limited space, only a part of these collections is on permanent display, but there are also many temporary exhibitions.

institution indicative of historical social attitudes towards unwanted children. The municipal collection, which is housed on the Gallery, goes back to 1923. The main part of this collection was acquired by the Municipality of Athens in the years 1930–40, through purchases from national and private galleries, as well as donations. Today the collection consists of around 2,500 works, mostly by 20th-century Greek artists, such as Georgios Iakovidis, Konstantinos Parthenis, Georgios Bouzianis, Georgios Gounaropoulos, Nikos Engonopoulos, Giannis Moralis and Spiros Papaloukas, among others. It includes numerous important engravings by Ioannis Kefallinos, Vasso Katraki and Tassos. There are also sculptures by Dimitrios Philippotis, Georgios Fitalis, Georgios Bonanos,

MUSEUM OF ISLAMIC ARTS

The Museum of Islamic Arts is a part of the Benaki

N. Engonopoulos: "Orestes and Pylades"

Museum, situated on 22 Assomaton and 12 Dipilou Streets. It used to be the residence of Lampros Eftaxias, honorary president of the Benaki Museum's governing body. The residence actually consisted of two houses, one three-storey, the other two-storey. In 1989 they were declared as listed buildings and their restoration began in

A clay globe

1996; the new museum opened in June 2004. During restoration parts of an ancient wall and tombs were discovered at foundation level and a number of spaces in the buildings were adjusted in order to display these finds. This is the only museum of Islamic Art in the Balkans; it has a rich collection of artefacts covering a period of thirteen centuries. The collection was initially acquired by the museum's founder, Antonis Benakis, and later by donation and purchase. It includes ceramics, metal objects, textiles, wood engravings, glassworks, as well as seals, weapons and golden ornaments. There are four display areas: objects from the 7th to 12th centuries are displayed in the first, and artefacts from the 12th to the 16th centuries in the second. In the third area is a marble inlaid interior of a 17th-century mansion in Cairo, as well as treasures from Iran and Turkey. Finally, in the fourth room there is a collection of weapons and jewels from Iran dating from the Qajar period (1796–1925).

Golden jewelry

Bronze candelabrum

THE CHURCH OF ST GEORGE ON PIRAIOS STREET

The church of St George (Agios Georgios) on Piraios Street is one of the most elegant examples of modern religious architecture in Athens. Built in 1900, it was designed by Ernst Ziller and formed part of the wider building complex of the Georgios and Aikaterini Chatzikostas Orphanage, designed by the same architect. The church was surrounded by the boundary wall of this institution, which meant that it was not visible or easily accessible to the public. With the demolition of the orphanage in 1963, however, this early work of the German architect could be admired. Ziller attempted to develop a particular type of small, Christian church, an impressive, dominating

AN UNUSUAL WALK

Saint George in Piraios Street

dome that covers most of the building, decorative arched endings on the upper walls, multilobed windows and pediments at the ends of the cruciform plan. The imaginativeness and elegance of St George's church are unfortunately missing from the later church of Holy Trinity (Agia Triada) of 1925, which is situated on the other side of Piraios Street. Its bulk has blocked to a great extent the view towards the Kerameikos. •■

ATHINAÏS

The Athinaïs multi-complex is situated on 34-36 Kastorias Street in the district of Votanikos, near Kerameikos and Iera Odos.
The complex is housed in a building that before World War II was used as a silk factory, designed by the architect Thomas Gazetas. During World War II the building was used as a shelter, but after the end of the war the factory was back in operation, until the 1950s when it closed permanently and the space was used as a warehouse. The Mamidakis Business Group began renovating the 6,500 square metre-building in 2000. Special attention was given to the project by Marilena Mamidakis and her husband Nassos Kokkineas.
The building, which reflects the city's characteristic industrial architectural style of the first half of the 20th century, with the masonry left visible and the use of iron on the windows and façades, has been transformed into a unique space of culture and entertainment for Athens.
The complex includes a conference area,

Exhibition Center "Athinaïs"

PIERIDES MUSEUM

The Pierides Museum of Ancient Cypriot Art, in the Athinaïs complex, was opened on 12 February 2001. The museum displays a part of the archaeological collection of the Pierides Museum–Laïki Group Cultural Centre in Larnaca, Cyprus. The exhibits cover a period of 9,000 years, representing examples of Cypriot archaeology from the Neolithic period to the end of the Middle Ages.
The collection focuses on the island's Prehistoric period, especially the Bronze Age, when Cyprus was a major production and export centre of bronze and linked into the commercial network of eastern Mediterranean. Items include ceramics and statuettes of both men and women, and especially the red polished pottery vases (painted with red varnish) and the Cypriot white slip bowls, which are found only in Cyprus. The plank-shaped human figurines are of particular interest.
Developments in the Geometrical period and Phoenician colonization of Kition in Cyprus are clearly evident in Geometrical pottery – in the typical Phoenician vessels with black patterns on red background, which are either imported or made on the island. The dishes, the vessels and the pots exhibited in the museum are typical of this and the Archaic period. The bichrome vases with depictions of birds of the 'free pictorial style' are unique examples of pottery painting.
Objects from the Classical, Hellenistic and Roman periods are comparatively fewer than Prehistoric artefacts; they are mainly vessels and items of everyday use as well as statuettes in pottery and stone. Among them are the sealed pottery vessels from the Roman period, the terracotta lamps and iridescent glass vessels of different colours and shapes. Greek art in the Classical period obviously influenced Cyprus, as did Egyptian art in the Hellenistic period, when Cyprus was within the Ptolemaic sphere of influence. Finally, the turbulent Middle Ages, when Cyprus was successively occupied by Venetians, Franks and the Knights Templar during the crusades, is represented by the glazed pottery vases of 13th to 15th centuries, depicting birds, animals and mythological creatures.

The Emerging Aphrodite

exhibition spaces, cinema, music stage, theatre, restaurants, bars and a children's music stage; it also houses the Pierides Museum of Ancient Cypriot Art.

Votanikos

VOTANIKOS

The Votanikos Garden is situated at the beginning of Iera Odos. This is the country's first botanic garden and was first developed in 1838 by Fraas, professor of botany. During the period of Ottoman rule, the farm of the city's voyvoda, Hadji Ali Haseki, was situated here. A number of buildings have survived from this period, including the remains of Haseki's residence, a water fountain, a defensive enclosure and a 19th-century greenhouse and well.
After the foundation of the Greek State, Haseki's entire estate became public property and was gradually developed into a botanic garden. The garden contains, among others, large palm-trees and tall cypress trees, which have been preserved from the original garden. The Votanikos Garden has given its name to the surrounding, densely populated area, which includes the Agricultural University of Athens.

PLATO'S ACADEMY

The Akademeia (or Ekademeia) area was situated in the south of the ancient city, close to the banks of the River Kephissos, within the limits of Kolonos. Its name derived from the hero Academos (or Ecademos). It was here that Plato, a student of Socrates and one of the most brilliant philosophers of Antiquity, founded his philosophical school in 387 BC. Today the Academeia archaeological site is situated in the middle of a large park, very pleasant for walks but not particularly well known to Athenians. The area has been inhabited continuously since the Late Helladic period (1550–1100) BC. In the 6th century BC. one of Athens' three gymnasiums was built here and later a grove was created at the instigation of Cimon. The area was connected to the city centre via a street starting at the Dipylon Gate and flanked by public tombs.

Plato

AN UNUSUAL WALK

The oldest trace of habitation is a vaulted building dated to the Early Helladic period (3rd millennium BC), which has been named the House of the Hero Akademos. Excavations have also revealed a sacred house of the Geometric period, tombs, remains of temples and sports grounds. The gymnasium as we see it today dates from the 1st century and consists of a large rectangular building with an interior peristyle. Next to it lies another building with a peristyle, which could have been the ring of the 4th-century gymnasium. Both these buildings are related to Plato's school of philosophy.

The Academy of Plato

PLATO AND HIS SCHOOL

Plato was born in 428/7 BC. Both his parents were members of the Athenian aristocracy, and his teachers were Kratylos and, consequently, Socrates. He elaborated his philosophical ideas in a series of dialogues, where he recognized the superior and absolute Idea as the regulator of nature and society. He founded his own school when he returned to Athens after a long absence, during which he travelled extensively in order to overcome his distress at the death of his teacher and the general political ambience in the city. Students at his school were primarily concerned with philosophy, and particularly the contemplation of the world of ideas. The syllabus was unusually broad, comprising everything from mathematics to aesthetics, ethics and political theory. Plato taught here for almost forty years, until 347 BC, when he died. When he appointed Speusippos as his successor, Aristotle, who had been a student of Plato for twenty years, abandoned the school and founded his own, which he called Lykeion (Lyceum). Plato's Academy remained operative until AD 529, when all philosophical schools were shut down in compliance with an edict of Justinian. In the Renaissance the concept of the academy was revived and further developed internationally; so that in modern western civilization it constitutes the supreme cultural, scientific and artistic authority in each country.

The Academy of Plato: mosaic from Naples

WALK 10

ROUTE 10b

KERAMEIKOS

See Walk 1

TECHNOPOLIS - GAS FACTORY (GAZI)

Exhibit in the "Technopolis" of the City of Athens

The Technopolis (City of the Arts) of Athens is situated on Piraios Street, at the junction with Ermou Street; it is housed in the old gas factory, hence it is also known as Gazi (gas). Through the reconstruction of the area by the City of Athens, the old factory, a true architectural jewel, has been transformed into a centre of cultural activity.

Technopolis is a showcase for art and technology and houses exhibitions, happenings and festivals of art, state-of-the-art science and digital technology. The city's radio station is also installed here. The Piraios Street district used to be one of the most important industrial zones in Athens. The gas factory, which opened in 1862, was crucial to the district's industrial development, producing gas that was used for lighting throughout the city. The buildings constructed during the early stages of the project followed the French early industrial Romanticism style. The factory's second phase began in 1896, when, to meet the increased demand for lighting brought on by the Olympic Games, it was extended and took more or less the form it still has today.
These new demands for gas necessitated further changes during its third phase of operations (1920–50), which was marked by German technology and industrial architecture (Constructivism).

Gas Factory

AN UNUSUAL WALK

An Athenian district

The factory ceased to be operational in 1983, after 120 years of production. The building complex was declared a monument of industrial civilization and is unique throughout Europe. It is also an important monument in the history of industrial architecture.

CULTURAL CENTRE "MELINA MERKOURI"

The Cultural Centre of the City of Athens "Melina Merkouri" is on 66 Irakleidon and Thessalonikis Streets in the district of Thisseio, very close to the Poulopoulou Bridge. It is housed in an impressive industrial building where the Poulopoulos hat factory used to be. It has been a listed building since 1985 and it belongs to the City of Athens.
It is a stone building with a simple architectural design and tiled roof. The use of iron one the windows and facades is interesting, as is its trapezoid shape.
The Centre organises temporary exhibitions, events and concerts.

THE NEIGHBOURHOOD OF GAZI (GAS FACTORY – "GAZOCHORI")

The Gazi district, known to Athenians also as Gazochori, extends between Peiraios and Konstantinoupoleos Streets near the former gas factory, the present-day Technopolis of the City of Athens. The neighbourhood is built on part of the ancient Demos of Kerameikos and is widely considered to be a part of the wider area of Kerameikos. The area was settled in the second half of the 19th century and developed quickly into the main working-class district of Athens because of its proximity to Peiraios Street, the industrial hub of the city. In the early 20th century the Gazochori, full of makeshift shanties and huts, was a place of poverty, misery and a nest of contagious diseases.
Today the neighbourhood is far from this. The expansion of the cultural and entertainment zone of the city, together with the transformation of the gas factory into a cultural centre, has led to the opening of bars and restaurants and the restoration of buildings and public areas. Gazi has gradually been transformed into a multicultural centre, where immigrants coexist with those who come for entertainment and cultural events. The area also attracts Athenian volunteer organizations, which aim to improve the status of immigrants and avoid social and cultural exclusion

WALK 10

MELINA MERKOURI

The actress and politician Melina Merkouri was born in Athens in 1922. She played her first leading part in the theatre in 1949 and made her film debut in 1955 with Michalis Kakogiannis' Stella. She became known internationally through her collaboration with the director (and from 1966 husband) Jules Dassin, in films such as Never on a Sunday (1960), Phaedra (1962) and Top Capi (1964). During Greece's military dictatorship military dictatorship in Greece (1967–74) Melina Merkouri voluntarily moved abroad, where she tried to raise international awareness of the dictatorship. After her return to Greece she became a politician; for many years was Minister of Culture. Until her death in 1994 she campaigned for the return of the Elgin marbles Marbles of Parthenon, removed from the Parthenon by Lord Elgin at the beginning of the 19th century, and now on display at the British Museum.

A charismatic actress with a strong personality, Melina Merkouri was loved by Greeks everywhere and a symbol of Greece abroad.

On the first floor there is a permanent exhibition called "Travelogue of Athens" which was organised with the participation of the Hellenic Literary and Historical Archive; it presents the neighbourhoods of Athens at the beginning of the 20th century. In the exhibition one can see mural paintings, the interior of a neoclassical house, authentic clothing articles of that time, shop windows with the merchandise that was available in those years, as well as a small open-air coffee-shop.

INDUSTRIAL BUILDINGS OF PIRAIOS STREET

Piraios / Panagi Tsaldari Street runs along the ancient route that connected Athens (the city) with Piraeus (the port). The present road largely follows the north part of the long walls,

The Cultural Center "Melina Merkouri"

which stood here from the 5th century until 86 BC, when the Romans pulled them down. The construction of a long straight avenue was included in the city plan worked out by Stamatis Kleanthis and Eduard Schaubert. The economical solution of a road that would follow the existing path from Kerameikos to the port was finally preferred. The part from Omonoia Square to Gazi was adorned with neoclassical public buildings and bourgeois residences, hotels and shops. The construction of the road was completed in 1836 and until 1869 it was the main thoroughfare to the port, by means of a horse-drawn bus, the so-called omnibus, which started from Ermou Street. However, the Athens-Piraeus railway, constructed in 1869, superseded the road, despite improvements carried out in the early 20th century and during the mid-war period.
The opening of the silk factory (1853) and especially the new coal gas factory at Gazi, on the boundaries of the capital (1862), signalled the transformation of Piraios Street into a road of industry and manufacture. The first factories were built at both ends of Piraios Street; the exact location can thus indicate the period in which the various industries were built. Towards Piraeus is the Pavlidis chocolate factory, built between 1876 and 1884, within a short distance from the Poulopoulos hat factory (1886). The slaughter houses, built by the engineer K. Zannos (1914–17), and possibly the late neoclassical buildings of Sikiaridis textile industry (the present Athens School of Fine Arts) belong to the same first period of industrialization of Piraios Street.
Heavy industries were built near the refugee settlements (Tavros, Kallithea and Agios Ioannis Rentis) during a second period, from the mid-war period until the 1970s. Metal processing was the main activity of industries such as Halkor (1937), Viosol (1940–7, the present Foundation of the Hellenic World) and Chalivourgiki (steel industry). Other industries were APCO Plastics (1959, designed by architect Takis Zenetos), which produced chemical products, and the rear buildings of the Greek textile mills.
Thanks to the coordinated activities of private and public authorities, today Piraios Street is being transformed from an area of industrial monuments into a road bristling with cultural and recreation centres.

REFUGEE SETTLEMENTS IN PIRAIOS STREET

The present-day refugee blocks of flats in Piraios Street in the Municipality of Tavros were built largely during the military dictatorship of 1967–74, as replacements for the refugee shacks of the time.
Refugee shacks had been erected in the 1920s on both sides of Piraios Street. The so-called German shacks ("Germanika"), built with German indemnities after World War I, were on the right-hand side, in the direction of Piraeus, between Piraios Street and Konstantinoupoleos Street. This quarter was mainly inhabited by refugees from Constantinople and Smyrna. On the whole this settlement was of better quality than that on the opposite side of Piraios Street because building

there had been financially aided by post-war indemnities. There were 126 constructions, each housing an average of six to eight families. The buildings were replaced during the dictatorship of 1967-1974 by the blocks of flats that the visitor can see today.

On the opposite side of Piraios Street were more poorly built refugee settlements. Inhabited by refugees from Antalya in south-western Asia Minor, this settlement was called "Attaleiotika" (from Antalya). These huts were partly replaced by blocks of flats during the dictatorship of Ioannis Metaxas (1936–40); many more were replaced between 1967 and 1974. Most of the blocks built during the dictatorship of Metaxas were restored in the 1990s. ••

"Sikiarideio", named after the industry's owner. The complex consists of fourteen single-storeyed and two-storeyed buildings covering a space of 28,451 square metres and a large ground behind the buildings. It seems the complex was built in two phases, the first one being a late Neoclassical one for the three buildings on Piraios Street and a second one with the modern buildings of the 20th century. The neoclassical buildings are not completely preserved but one can still see their monumental entrances; they are arranged in a Π-shaped complex forming a yard towards Piraios Street. From the central building only the façade has been preserved.

The Athens School of Fine Arts purchased this area in 1992 and was housed there after the restoration and remodelling of the buildings by the architect Michalis Souvatzidis and his team in 1995-1997. The School's history is related with the Technical University, which was founded in 1836-1837 as a Sunday "School of the Arts" in the Vlachoutzis house on Piraios Street. From 1840 one branch of the by then full-time "School of the Arts" was the "School of Fine Art", which from 1843 became a higher educational institution for teaching the fine arts.

In 1873 the School was transferred to the new buildings on Patission Street and from 1887 it operated as the independent "School of Fine Art" within the Technical University. In 1910 it was separated from it and in 1929-1930 it was renamed "Athens

ATHENS SCHOOL OF FINE ARTS

The Athens School of Fine Arts on 256 Piraios Street occupies a large area with industrial buildings which used to belong to the "Hellenic Textiles SA."; the complex was also known as

N. Litras, "Nude"

AN UNUSUAL WALK

Guided Tour of pupils in FHW exhibition area

School of Fine Arts" and established as an independent educational institution equal to the Technical University.

Today the area of the former "Sikirideio" houses the workshops, the teaching rooms, the administration and the School's library. There are vast rooms for the display of the works created by the students. The Athens School of Fine Arts has also one of the largest areas in Athens that can be used for the organization of cultural events and international exhibitions.

Many important Greek artists have studied and taught at the Athens School of Fine Arts. Among the School's professors were Nikiforos Litras and his son Nikolaos, Konstantinos Parthenis, Georgios Iakovidis, Giannis Moralis and Filippos Margaritis, the pioneer of Greek photography. ••

HELLENIC COSMOS

Hellenic Cosmos, the innovative and multifunctional cultural centre of the Foundation of the Hellenic World (FHW), occupies the former VIOSOL factory at 254 Piraios Street. The building was designed by the architect Solon Kidoniatis and completed on 28 October 1940 in an industrial area that was then 'outside the city'. During World War II the building was requisitioned by the army and it was not until 1947 that it returned to civilian use, when a pipe manufacturing company took it over. In 1996 it was acquired by FHW, redesigned and opened as its cultural centre in March 1998. Today Hellenic Cosmos is not

The Cultural Center "Hellenic Cosmos"

Model of the new buildings of the "Hellenic Cosmos"

confined to this building, but extends into the area behind the former factory, which in previous decades was occupied by small, artisan workshops. The area is gradually being transformed from a light-industrial suburb into an area of cultural development.
Hellenic Cosmos houses unique virtual reality systems designed for the research and promotion of cultural heritage, where representations of ancient Greek monuments and cities are on display. At the same time, exhibitions on Greek history and culture, as well as special educational programmes are organized here. The Cyber Hall, an innovative Internet café dedicated to Greek history, also functions here, while the museum shop offers, among other articles, all the Foundation's productions.
In Thisseio, at 38 Poulopoulou Street, a former, mid-war industrial unit (a hat factory) that was once used as a technical school, a restaurant and a bar, is today home to FHW's creative and research sectors, with offices, a library and special digital laboratories for 3D graphics and representations, virtual reality systems, multimedia and digital cartography. ●●

11

WALK 11

1. St Nicholas (Thon Estate)
2. All Saints (Agioi Pantes)
3. The Refugees' Housing Block
4. Pedion tou Areos
5. Victoria Square
6. The National Archaeological Museum
7. The Technical University
8. Exarcheia
9. The Strefis Hill

11 THE NATIONAL ARCHAEOLOGICAL MUSEUM

Taking the underground down to Victoria station and turning right in Patission Street, one comes to the country's largest archaeological museum. Here are displayed some of the most important works of art from Antiquity, such as the golden jewellery and mask of Agamemnon, kouroi and korai with their enigmatic smiles, vases, utensils and other objects.

THE CHURCH OF ST NICHOLAS (THON ESTATE)

Nikolaos Thon was a financial expert and advisor to King George I; in 1880 he built his mansion on the corner of Alexandras and Kifissias Avenues, in an area of around two acres to a design by the architect Ernst Ziller. The same architect designed the small church there, named St Nicholas (Agios Nikolaos), after its donor. During the fighting that followed the liberation of Athens in December 1944 the mansion was looted and destroyed.

Saint Nicholas (Thon Estate)

THE CHURCH OF ALL SAINTS

The small Byzantine Church of Agioi Pantes (All Saints) is situated on Kiriakou Street near "Apostolos Nikolaïdis" Stadium (football ground of Panathinaïkos FC) in Ambelokipoi. The church has been in its present form since the renovation and restoration of 1956 under the supervision of the member of the Athens Academy Anastassios Orlandos and with the collaboration of Manolis Chatzidakis, Ephor of Byzantine Antiquities.
There is no information regarding the church's foundation or history. It can, however, be dated to the 11th century on the basis of its architectural form. The fact that the church is situated in a remote suburb of the medieval city of Athens, as well as certain archaeological finds (during excavation in the area several buildings were found related to the church), indicate that the

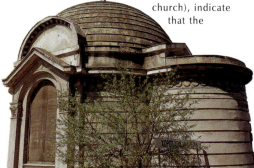

WALK 11

The Church of All Saints

church used to be the katholikon of a Byzantine monastery. The church is of the four-columned cross-in-square type with an eight-sided dome. The façades are modelled according to the Athenian churches of this era. The masonry follows the cloisonné style, and there is plain decoration only on the frames of the windows and openings. The numerous ancient architectural elements incorporated into the walls, many which have inscriptions, are particularly interesting.
Today the church is the metochion of the Petraki Monastery.

MANOLIS CHATZIDAKIS (1909-1998)

Manolis Chatzidakis, born in Crete, was an expert in Byzantine studies, contributing greatly to the methodical study of Byzantine art and its appreciation as part of European art. He was the director of the Benaki Museum (1941-1973) and Director of the 1st Ephorate of Byzantine Antiquities (1943-1960), conducting a number of important archaeological excavations in Athens and in Delphi. His directorial skills while he was in charge of the Byzantine Museum (1960-1967) and as a member of the Academy of Athens (1980-1998) led to the founding and organization of the Centre for the Study of Byzantine and post-Byzantine Art of the Academy of Athens and the organization of the Laboratory of Restoration of Paintings and Mosaics in the Byzantine Museum. He was in charge of the restoration of numerous churches in Greece and abroad, such as the Sinai Monastery, the church of St. George in Venice and the church of the Holy Sepulcre in Jerusalem.

His work focuses in the research of the religious painting of the Byzantine and post-Byzantine period. He made a great contribution to the study of the Cretan School after the fall of Constantinople (1464) and more specifically of the painter Theophanes, and he researched thoroughly the inter-relations between Byzantine and Western art. This internationally acknowledged scholar, who was for many years the Secretary General of the International Association of Byzantine Studies, published also numerous articles in the Press in order to raise the public awareness regarding matters related to the Byzantine, folk, and contemporary Greek art.

Manolis Chatzidakis, oil painting by I. Pappas

REFUGEES' HOUSING BLOCKS

The last remaining parts of a large refugees' housing complex are situated on Alexandras Avenue, opposite "Apostolos Nikola_dis" Stadium; they were constructed between 1922 and 1936 in the midst of military camps and public buildings. The housing complex used to occupy the area between Pedion tou Areos (Field of Mars) and Lycabettus Hill. It was built in order to house the large numbers of refugees who came to Greece from Asia Minor in the years 1922-1924. Only two parts are preserved today from the last stage of the refugees' housing project (1932-1936), on Alexandras Avenue and further down from the Lycabettus ring. The blocks were designed by the architects Dimitrios Kiriakos, Kimon Laskaris and Vassilis Tsagris. The project was completed through the collaboration of the Municipality of Athens with the Ministry for Public Healthcare. Construction work was completed in 1936 with eight apartment blocks and a total of 228 flats. Each block is separated in four or five sections with their own entrance and staircase. The flats have one or two bedrooms each, plus a kitchen and bathroom, and for every three flats there is one laundry space on the roof of each section. The buildings have a plain and clear form with small balconies and well-lit staircases with glass windows. They combine elements of the central European modernist architecture of that era with the sociability of the refugee neighbourhood. They form a unique example of social housing in Greece, a project which successfully combined effective social policies with the architectural and town planning avant-garde of the time. Unfortunately, the refugee housing blocks are not in a good state of preservation. The initial plan for the arrangement of this area, which consisted in the preservation and restoration of two of them and the creation of a park on the place of the remaining has not yet been realized.

PEDION TOU AREOS

The Field of Mars ("Pedion tou Areos") is one of

Refugee's housing blocks in Alexandras Avenue

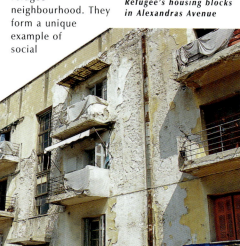

Athens' few parks and a favourite spot for local residents, who come here to walk and talk. Situated between Alexandras Avenue and Mavromataion, Evelpidon, Moustoxidi and Bousgou Streets, it covers an area of 277,000 square metres. Its name originated from the fact that it used to be (polygon), because of the polygonal wooden bandstand where military music was played.

During the 19th century and until the 1920s, when the map of Athens was altered with the arrival of Greek refugees, this area was considered to be a part of the countryside, outside the city's boundaries.

continued to enjoy the park.

The site took its present form in 1934, when it was decided to develop it as a park for the Athenian public, as well as developing the so called "Heroes Avenue", for which the Athens Municipality commissioned from the Association of

THE SCULPTURES AT THE PEDION TOU AREOS (FIELD OF MARS)

At the Pedion tou Areos there is a collection of important sculptures typical of the modern Greek history. The statue of Athena by the sculptor V. Falireas and the architects F. and E. Kidoniatis that dominates the entrance from Alexandras Avenue is a monument for the fallen British, Australian and New Zealander soldiers during World War II. The Cenotaph of the Sacred Band ("Ieros Lochos") referring to the army corps that was formed by Greek students who perished in the Greek War of Independence is the earliest monument of modern Athens. Privately funded and constructed in 1843, it was based on the plan of the famous architect Stamatis Kleanthis. Another unique monument is that of Alexandros Ipsilantis created by Leonidas Drossis. The hero is "sleeping" on a sarcophagus. The sixteen busts of freedom fighters of the Greek Revolution of 1821, placed in "Heroes Avenue" and created by sixteen sculptors between 1934-1937 are also worth mentioning.

The statue of Athena

the exercise yard of the Athens' Guard. Since 1900 the area has been particularly associated with military education, especially when the Evelpidon (Military) School was built on the park's eastern side and the Equestrian School was built on Mavromataion Street. The park was also called Poligono

During the first years of King Otto's reign the royal couple promenaded here every Sunday; but they ceased to visit the park after 1859, when the "Skiadika" uprising took place: a group of people led by students began a three-year opposition campaign which resulted in Otto's departure in 1862. However, the public

Greek Sculptors marble busts of all the leading figures of the 1821 Greek War of Independence. This initiative resulted in the creation in 1937 of a unique Greek war memorial with sculptures of great fighters, such as Athanassios Diakos, Konstantinos Kanaris, Georgios Karaïskakis, Manto Mavrogenous,

THE NATIONAL ARCHAEOLOGICAL MUSEUM

The Field of Mars (Pedion tou Areos)

Nikitaras and Bouboulina. The busts were made by established artists of the time, such as Athanassios Apartis, Michail Tombros and Fokion Rok.
In the middle of the square at the junction of Alexandras Avenue and Mavromataion Street is a copper statue of King Constantine I of Greece on horseback, by the Italian architect Constantino Vetriani and the Italian sculptor Francesco Parisi.
Today the Field of Mars is one of the largest green spaces in Athens. Open-air exhibitions take place there, such as the annual Flower Show. Apart from these special events, visitors come to the park daily for recreational purposes and it is a favourite spot for local children to play. ●■

VICTORIA SQUARE

The construction of Victoria Square ("Platia Viktorias") started in 1872. It was initially called Kiriakou Square, named after Panagis Kiriakos, the then Mayor of Athens (1870-1879), whose house was nearby. It was soon renamed Victoria Square in honour of the Queen of England.
In the centre of the square there is a copper sculpture by the German sculptor Johannes Pfuhl (1846-1914) depicting Theseus saving Hippodameia. The work was made in 1881 and was given as present to the Municipality of Athens in 1927. It was originally erected in Sintagma Square but was transferred to its present position in 1938.
Number 3 of the square houses the Athenian offices of the Peloponnesian Folklore Foundation, while a beautiful building of the late neoclassicism at number 7_ of the nearby Guilford Street houses the church of St Francis and St Clara of the Italian Catholic community.
The square used to be a traditional hangout of both the original Athenians and the sports fans of the FC Panathinaikos, especially the café named after Mimis Domazos, the famous former captain of the football team. Today the presence of a considerable number of economic immigrants gives the area a multicultural character. ●■

Sculpture at Victoria square

The National Archaeological Museum

> **HISTORY**

The National Archaeological Museum, the largest and most representative archaeological museum in Greece, is situated in the center of the city, in a block between Tossitsa Street, Ipirou Street, Bouboulinas Street and 28 October (Patission) Street, where the mueum's entrance is). It was built in three stages at the second half of the 19th century, and despite numerous alterations and additions that were made in order to serve new requirements, the building basically retains its neoclassical style. The need to create an archaeological museum was felt already since the foundation of the modern Greek State. The first such museum was founded by Ioannis Kapodistrias in Aigina in 1829, and as soon as Athens became the state capital the archaeological collections were housed in different premises, for example at Hephaisteion, the University and the Technical University. In 1858 an international architectural competition to select the location and design of the museum took place, but with no result. Finally, in 1865, Eleni Tossitsa donated a large plot near the Technical University for the construction of the building. There was already since 1858 a sum of 200,000 drachmas available for the building, donated by Dimitrios Vernardakis from St Petersburg, a Greek of the diaspora and a national benefactor. The construction began in 1866 and was completed in 1880.

The initial designs were made by the German architect of Romanticism Ludwig Lange and were realized, with certain alterations, by Panagis Chalkos, the architect in charge. In 1874 the western wing of the so-called "Central Museum" was

Red-figured pelike

The National Archaeological Museum

completed. In 1881, at the initiative of Charilaos Trikoupis, the museum was renamed "National Archaeological Museum". The southern wing was completed in 1885 and the western wing in 1889. In 1888 the famous architect Ernst Ziller took over the final stages of the project; he redesigned the building's façade and made several alterations to the original design. In 1891 the Archaeological Society donated to the museum the archaeological finds collected from various excavation projects in Greece. With the plethora of archaeological finds in the 20th century the museum had to be expanded: work began in 1931. The small houses on the eastern side, where the guards lived, and the apse of the initial building had to be demolished, and in their place the eastern two-storey wing was built, designed by G. Nomikos. The construction was completed in 1939 and all the offices were transferred there.

During World War II all the antiquities were removed, placed in boxes and buried. They were gradually put back on display between 1945 and 1964, under the supervision of the museum's director Christos Karouzos. At the same time, storehouses were built at the north wing of the old building. At the 1999 earthquakes the building suffered heavy damages. Subsequently, the museum closed for the public in order for renovation works to be carried on and for the museum's collections to be rearranged in view of the 2004 Olympics. Since June 2004 part of the permanent collections are on display for the public. There is also a large exhibition for the Olympic Games, with objects both from Greece itself and on loan from numerous European and American museums.

Golden cup from Vapheio

COLLECTIONS

The National Archaeological Museum houses representative collections from the Prehistoric years to the late Roman period.

PREHISTORIC COLLECTION

The Prehistoric collection is displayed on the ground floor, in rooms 3-6. In room 5 there are Neolithic objects (6800-3300 BC) and objects from the early and mid-Bronze period (third millennium and 2000-1700 BC respectively). There are noteworthy ceramic finds from the important Neolithic sites at Dimini and Sesklo in Thessaly, as well as early and middle Helladic ceramics from various locations in Boeotia, Attica and Phthiotis. Some objects from Schliemann's excavations in Troy are also on display. Room 6 houses the Cycladic collection

"Kroisos"

A neolithic vase from Dimini

with the famous marble figurines from cemeteries of the third millennium BC together with numerous bronze tools and vessels. Items representative of Mycenaean civilisation are displayed in room 4 and the adjacent small room 3. Among them stand out the excellent 16th-century BC finds that Schliemann excavated from Mycenaean Circle A Graves, as well as finds from the earlier Circle B Graves. Most notable are the gold funerary masks covering the faces of deceased leaders, stone relief stelae, vessels of gold, silver, electrum (an alloy of gold and silver), crystal and alabaster, golden and amber jewels, and small bronze knives decorated with gold, silver and niellum inlays, depicting battles and hunting scenes.

There are also finds from the vaulted tombs in Mycenae and other locations in the Peloponnese (Tiryns and Dendra in Argolis, Pylos in Messenia and Vafeio in Lakonia) including stone, bronze and ceramic pots, figurines, ivory objects, golden seals and rings with precious and semi-precious stones, glass and faience. Most notably there are two golden cups in relief decoration from Vafeio depicting scenes of the capture of a bull. There are also finds from the citadel of Mycenae, such as an group in ivory depicting two goddesses with a child, a painted limestone head of a goddess and the famous warriors' vase dating from the 12th century BC.

SCULPTURE COLLECTION

The major part of the rooms of the ground floor are devoted to the exhibition of sculpture from the 7th century BC to the Roman period. The rooms have been arranged in chronological order. In room 7 the visitor can see sculpture of the daedalic style, dating from the 7th century, including the poros metopes from Athena's temple in Mycenae and the kore (statue of a girl) dedicated by Nikandre, from Naxos, to the goddess Artemis at Delos; this is the earliest known life-size stone statue in ancient Greek

Amphora from the Dipylon cemetery

The "harp-player"

sculpture. The room is dominated by the colossal Geometric amphora attributed to the Dipylon Painter, one of the first Greek works of art to show the human figure (750 BC), representing the exposition of the body of the dead and the mourning in his honour. In rooms 8–13 are Archaic sculptures from the end of the 7th until the beginning of the 5th centuries. Prominent are kouroi (statues of boys) from Sounion, Anavyssos and Volomandra in Attica, Melos and the sanctuary of Ptoon in Boeotia, including the important grave statue of Aristodikos from 500 BC, which marks the liberation of the human figure from archaic stillness and preconises the Classical art. Equally remarkable is the statue of Phrasikleia (kore) discovered in Merenta in Attica.

Votive relief

In rooms 14 and 15 are works belonging to the severe style (480–450 BC), including the votive stela of an athlete from Sounion placing a wreath on his head, and a relief from Eleusis depicting Demeter, Persephone and Triptolemos. Room 15 is dominated by the famous bronze statue of Zeus, or Poseidon, from Artemision in Euboea, dating from 460 BC and attributed to the sculptor Kalamis. In room 16 there are gravestones from cemeteries in Attica, including that of a young man from Salamis from 430 BC. In room 17 there are parts of metopes, sculptures from the decoration of the temple of Hera in Argos with scenes of Greeks fighting the Amazons and a marble head from the statue of the goddess. Room 18 displays gravestones, including that of Hegeso (end of the 5th century BC) from the cemetery of Kerameikos; the dead woman is shown seated opposite a slave who is holding a jewel case (pyxis). Rooms 19–20 include works from the Roman period, copies of famous bronze sculptures of the Classical period. The importance of the statue of Varvakeios Athena (3rd century BC) lays more in its being a copy of the gold and ivory statue of Athena from the Parthenon made by Pheidias, than in its aesthetic value. Two well-known pieces are displayed in room 21 on the way from the ground-floor to the first floor: the statue of Diadoumenos, a marble Roman copy of a work by the sculptor Polykleitos from Argos (mid-fifth century BC) and the copper statue of a jockey from Artemision dating from the mid-2nd century BC. In room 34 on the other side of the staircase that leads up to the first floor there are several stelae and a marble altar on display. In room 22 one finds architectural sculptures from the temple of

"Aristodikos"

Asklepios in Epidaurus that date from the 4th century BC, while in rooms 23 and 24 are displayed gravestones of the 4th-century BC, including the excellent gravestone of Ilissos (c. 340 BC), produced by the workshop of the famous sculptor Skopas. Rooms 25–27 include votive reliefs from various areas of Greece, as well as documentary and honorary reliefs from Attica. In room 28 there are works from the late Classical period (4th century BC), such as the bronze statue of a young man from Marathon, possibly made by Praxiteles, and the bronze statue of a boy in his teens from Antikythera, sculpted by Euphranor, both dating from around 340-330 BC, as well as the gravestone of Aristonautes. In rooms 29–33 bronze and marble statues from the Hellenistic and Roman periods are displayed, including the famous statue of Poseidon from Melos, the colossal statues of Damophon from the temple of Despoina in Lykosoura (Arcadia), the "wounded Galatian" and the group of Aphrodite and Pan from Delos, the bronze statue of Octavian and the bust of Antinous, Emperor Hadrian's protégé.

"Poseidon or Zeus from Artemision"

BRONZE COLLECTION

The antiquities exhibited in room 36 once belonged to Konstantinos Karapanos, a politician and amateur archaeologist from Ipiros, and come from the excavations he conducted himself at Dodone and Corfu, but from purchases as well. The collection includes excellent bronze objects, mostly statuettes, such as the young man on a horse from Dodone (550-540 BC), a woman wearing the peplos from Pindos (460 BC) and a dancing satyr, created by a Corinthian workshop (second half of the 6th century BC). There are also inscribed metal sheets, tools, mirrors, fibulae, implements, weapons and fragments of large bronze vessels from Dodone, terracota figurines and small tablets from the lesser sanctuary of Artemis in Corfu as well as and the heads from Roman statues and Attic gravestones.

In room 37 there are also bronze

objects on display from various areas of Greece (statuettes, vessels, implements, fibulae, weapons) from the Geometric and early Archaic periods, as well as

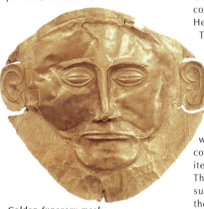

Golden funerary mask

jewellery made of precious metals mostly found in sanctuaries. In the future, rooms 37a, 38 and 39 will display bronze objects (mostly statuettes of athletes and animals as well as fragments of vessles) from the sanctuaries of the Acropolis and Olympia.

EGYPTIAN COLLECTION

The Egyptian collection is housed in rooms 40 and 41. It consists mainly of donations from two Greeks who lived in Egypt, Ioannis Dimitriou from Alexandria and Alexandros Rostovisz from Cairo. This collection was only recently displayed next to the masterpieces of Greek art. It is one of the richest collections worldwide including works of art from the Neolithic period to the end of the Roman era. It also includes a large number of sarcophagi and mummies.

THE STATHATOS COLLECTION

The Stathatos collection is housed in room 42; it includes 970 objects ranging from the Middle Bronze Age to the post-Byzantine years, mainly jewellery, metal objects and vessels, as well as stone and ceramic vases. Of particular artistic value are considered the golden jewels of the Hellenistic period from Demetrias in Thessaly and from Karpenissi.

THE THERA COLLECTION

The collection from Thera (Santorini) is displayed in room 48 on the first floor. The impressive frescoes from Akrotiri with their vivid colours and wonderful compositions are justly considered to be among the finest items of the museum's collections. The fact that they have survived in such excellent condition is due to the island's volcanic explosion, which covered the houses of the prehistoric town in volcanic ash. The paintings include the scene of the naval expedition with the earliest known depiction of a town in ancient Greek art, the images of fisherman, monkeys, boxing children, one of the earliest depictions of a sport event in Greece and the fresco of the spring. Apart from the paintings visitors can admire here

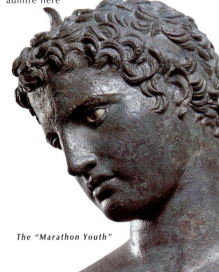

The "Marathon Youth"

WALK 11

The Spring, detail from a Theran fresco

excellent ceramics, bronze and stone artefacts from Thera.

COLLECTION OF VASE AND SMALL ORNAMENTS

The collection of vases is displayed in rooms 49–56 on the first floor. Representative finds from the Protogeometric to the later Classical period (11th–4th centuries BC) are arranged in chronological order. Protogeometric and Geometric vases, mainly from Attic workshops, found in the cemeteries of Nea Ionia, Areios Pagos, Kerameikos and Dipylon, are displayed in room 49. Here one can admire an amphora by the Dipylon Painter, which depicts a funeral procession (similar to that in the collection of sculptures in room 7). There are also two terracotta heads of figurines from the Amyklaion in Lakonia. In room 50 are presented Geometric vases and figurines of various workshops (from Attica, Boeotia, Corinth, Thessaly). Among these the Dipylon crater with its great volume and the quality of the representation of the funeral procession stands apart. In room 51 are displayed vases of the Orientalising period (7th century BC) in the so called Protoattic style, found in Attic cemeteries, as well as early cycladic amphoras (the so called Melian amphoras), jugs in the wild goat style and various small scale artefacts. In room 52 are exhibited Corinthian, Attic and Boeotian black-figured vases as well as a series of important votives from the sanctuaries of Hera in Perachora and Argos, Artemis Orthia in Sparta and Apollo

Geometric krater

THE NATIONAL ARCHAEOLOGICAL MUSEUM

in Thermon in Aetolia. Among the most significant displays here are the ceramic model of a temple from Heraion in Perachora, the painted metopes from Thermon dating from the 7th century, and the wooden panels from Pitsas in Korinthia. In room 53 are black-figured vases of the 6th century BC, terracotta sarcophagi found in the 1920-21 excavations in Clazomenae, small finds from various sanctuaries in Athens and a selection of finds from Lemnos, among which is the stela of a warrior with an inscription in an Etruscan dialect. In room 54 there are black- and red-figured vases from the late Archaic (500–480 BC) and the early Classical (480–460 BC) periods. In room 55 there is an extensive collection of Attic white lekythoi mostly of Attic and Euboean provenance, as well as red-figured vases. Room 56 displays vases and figurines from the late 5th and the 4th centuries.

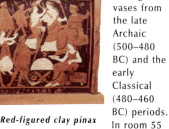
Red-figured clay pinax

Group of three figures in ivory

THE EPIGRAPHIC MUSEUM

The southern section of the Archaeological Museum, with its entrance on Tossitsa Street, houses the Epigraphic Museum, which possesses the largest collection of Greek inscriptions in the world (a total of over 15,000). The earlier inscriptions are in room 11, while the most historically significant inscriptions from various periods can be seen in room 9. The inscriptions in room 1 are the tribute lists of the First Athenian Confederacy; these are invaluable documents for the study of the history of Classical Greece. The earliest inscription from this collection (454–453 BC) is an impressive block of stone 3.5m high.

The "Youth from Antikythera"

TECHNICAL UNIVERSITY

The Athens Technical University ("Ethniko Metsovio Politechneio") is situated on 28 October (Patission) Street, next to the Archaeological Museum. The building was designed by the architect Lissandros Kaftantzoglou and is one of the most important neoclassical buildings of the 19th century.

From the early years of the Greek State the need for the creation of a school for technical education was evident, so the Royal School of the Arts was founded in 1836-7, and initially housed in the Vlachoutzis building on Peiraios Street, where the National Theatre Drama School is today. At first it was a basic training school for builders with the Bavarian Army. The architect Friedrich von Zentner was the first director. Gradually the programme of studies was upgraded and more specialized technical subjects were introduced. In 1887 the school became a higher education institution and developed as the main training university for architects and engineers.

The original building on Peiraios Street proved to be too small for the school's increasing needs. In 1852 Nikolaos Stournaris, business partner of the wealthy merchant Michail Tossitsas from Metsovo in Ipiros, donated the sum of 500,000 drachmas for a new building on 28 October Street. Tossitsas himself added to the donation with his bequest, and so did his wife Eleni, who actually donated

THE UPRISING OF THE POLYTECHNEIO

The student population was the only element of the Greek society to organize a massive movement against the military regime of 1967-74. Their most significant action was the uprising of the Technical University in November 1973, the highpoint of the student movements that had begun in March that year with the takeover of the Law School. In November students took over the Technical University, urging people to resist the dictators. After a few days, on the evening of 17 November, a tank broke into the university through the main entrance and military and police forces put an end to the uprising using violence, leaving several casualties. The uprising contributed to the international isolation of the dictators and their final fall from power. Since then the Technical University has been not only an educational institution, but also a place of memory and a symbol of civic duty.

A sculpture by Memos Makris called "Head in Honour of the Dead" in the university's courtyard shows a large-scale man's head fallen to the ground in memory of the dead students of 1973.

National Technical University of Athens

EXARCHEIA

The quarter of Exarcheia was formed between 1870 and 1880 on the then boundaries of the city and took its name around 1900 from the grocery of Exarchos, at the junction of Themistokleous and Solomou Streets. The area has achieved a high social importance, since it is near the Technical University of Athens; moreover, many intellectuals and artists live there. Exarcheia is also famous as a meeting point for friends as well as for social and political groups. Places of particular importance in Exarcheia Square are the "Vox" cinema (at the junction of Themistokleous and Arachovis Streets) and, exactly opposite, the Antonopoulos block of flats (on the corner of 61 Arachovis and 80 Themistokleous Streets). Among the oldest open-air cinemas of Athens, "Vox" was designated as a listed building in 1997 together with 47 more open-air cinemas all over Greece. The

the land. Construction began in 1862 but was interrupted in 1870 due to lack of funding; it resumed in 1873, thanks to Georgios Averoff, also from Metsovo, who funded the project until it was completed in 1876. In 1873 the Technical University was transferred from Peiraios Street to the half-finished building of Patission Street. The Technical University complex consists of three buildings symmetrically arranged. The central Averoff building dominates, with its two storeys and marble staircase that leads into a propylon with four Ionic columns. The building has a semi-circular part at the back where the main events room is situated. In front of this building are two T-shaped single-storey buildings (with Doric vaults on the façades), which were initially used as the Prytaneum and the School of Fine Arts. Since the transfer of the Technical University to the new complex in the Zografou district, the building on Patission Street houses the Department of Architecture and various administration offices.

Monument in honour of the dead at the uprising of the Polytechneio

building served other purposes as well. After the war it served as training place for boxing and wrestling, while today it houses a modern café-bookshop.
The Antonopoulos block of flats, known as the "Blue apartment house", thanks to its original external colour, is a typical example of the mid-war modernist Greek architecture. It was designed by Kiriakoulis Panagiotakos (1903-1982) and decorated in collaboration with the painter Spiros Papaloukas, thus combining the modernistic views with the colours of Byzantine icons.
The building consists of the basement, the ground floor and six floors with 38 flats in total and four ground floor stores on the side of the square. In the rooftop, apart from the usual offices, there is a lounge for the dwellers in order to meet and socialise.
The original dark blue colour has been replaced by a lighter blue.
Higher up at 69 Themistokleous Street, the "Theatre of Exarcheia" is a typical example of recent alteration (1987-1989) of a neoclassical house into a small modern theatre.

The block of flats of Antonopoulos

The Exarcheia Theater

STREFIS HILL

The small, green Strefis Hill is in the district of Exarcheia. Until the beginning of the 20th century this was the limit of the city of Athens. Together with the other smaller or higher hills, such as Lycabettus, Ardettus, Philopappos Hill and the Acropolis, Strefis Hill dominates the city's space and morphology. The hill is very close to the centre of the Exarcheia district and a focal point for the local community. With its trees and the small theatre there it offers people a valuable recreation space.

12

WALK 12

1. Omonoia Square
2. The National Bank
3. The National Printing House
4. The 25th March (Klafthmonos) Square
5. St Theodoroi
6. The Museum of the City of Athens
7. St George Karitsis
8. Building at the junction of Stadiou and Chr. Lada Streets
9. The Old Parliament
10. The Army Share Fund Mansion
11. The Numismatic Museum
12. The Bank of Greece
13. The Catholic Church (St Dionysius)
14. The Ophthalmic Clinic
15. The Agricultural Bank of Greece
16. The Academy of Athens
17. The University of Athens
18. The National Library
19. The Rallis House
20. The Alpha Bank
21. The Arsakeion
22. The Rex Theatre
23. Kaniggos Square
24. The Old Building of the Hellenic Conservatory
25. The German Archaeological Institute
26. Zoodochos Pege
27. The Greek National Opera
28. The Cultural Centre of the Municipality of Athens
29. The Kostis Palamas Building
30. The Faculty of Law
31. The University's Chemistry Laboratory

12

THE CENTER OF THE CENTER AND ITS CHARMS

With the multicultural Omonoia as a starting point, and walking up Stadiou Street, one reaches the Museum of the City of Athens and the Old Parliament, (Historical Museum). On El. Venizelou Street three neoclassical buildings predominate, the Academy, the University and the Library. Not far from them, on the same street, is the Numismatic Museum. For a short break the best place is the cafeteria of the Cultural Centre of the Municipality of Athens on Akadimias Street.

OMONOIA SQUARE

See Walk 9

NATIONAL BANK

The branch of the National Bank on Stadiou Street occupies two conjoining buildings that used to house the bank's main branch and head office. These were purpose-built in 1845, four years after the bank's foundation. The neoclassical building took its present form in 1899 under architect Vassilios Hatzis.

NATIONAL PRINTING HOUSE

The building between Stadiou, Santaroza and Arsaki Streets was built in 1835 on a state-owned plot of land opposite the artillery camp as the Royal Printing and Lithography House, designed by architect Joseph Hoffer. It was one of the first public buildings constructed during King Otto's reign, at a cost of 40,339.25 drachmas. The building was illustrated in a 1837 etching, as seen from the corner of Stadiou and Santaroza Streets. It consisted of a ground floor and a semi-basement on Santaroza Street, as well as a spacious room above the ground floor, which was the manager's residence. Half the building – the entire second floor – was destroyed by fire in 1854. In 1905 the National Printing House was transferred to a new building on Kapodistriou Street; by 1931, according to historical sources, the old building on

National Bank of Greece

The National Printing House

> **MONUMENT OF THE NATIONAL RECONCILIATION**
> The large bronze sculpture on Klafthmonos Square made by Vassilis Domopoulos consists of three women who join their raised arms forming a pyramid. It was placed on the square in 1988 as a symbol of the end of the era of political divisions and discriminations in the public affairs of Greece.

Stadiou Street had been deserted and ruined. At about this time (1931-1932) repairs were carried out and a second floor was added, the façades were developed and the sides on Santaroza, Panepistimiou and Arsaki Streets were added. Until recently the building housed the Athens Court of the First Instance.

25th MARCH (KLAFTHMONOS) SQUARE

Most Athenians know the square in the historic centre of Athens in the midst of Stadiou, Dragatsaniou, Paleon Patron Germanou and Paparrigopoulou Streets as Klafthmonos Square, however it is officially called 25th March Square.
The name Klafthmonos (lamentation) originated from a former practice followed by the civil servants every time that the government changed: prior to 1911 civil servants did not have a permanent status, therefore every time that the government changed most of them would lose their jobs, being replaced by those who supported the new government; the civil servants who had lost their jobs would usually gather in this square, where the Ministry of Finance used to be situated until 1939, in order to protest and lament their misery. Underneath the square there is a parking facility; while it was

The Saint Theodoroi

being constructed excavations uncovered parts of the Themistoclean Wall.

THE CHURCH OF ST THEODOROI

On the south-western side of Klafthmonos Square, at the junction of Dragatsaniou and Agion Theodoron Streets one can see the church of St Theodoroi (Agioi Threodoroi).
On the church's western side there are two marble plates with inscriptions mounted on the wall. The first one officially announces that the church was renovated by an administrative official of the Byzantine Empire called Nikolaos Kalomalos. On the second, smaller plate there is an inscription with a date that probably corresponds with the year 1065. Although experts seem to be divided regarding the identification of the date with the year, in

which the church was renovated, one can assume that the church dates back to the mid-11th century, based on its architectural and morphological characteristics. The church is a variation of the distyle cross-in-square type. Its exterior is particularly interesting: the few small openings on the walls are conservative, if one considers the period when the church was built, while the belfry is obviously a more recent addition. The dome is eight-sided with double-light windows. The cloisonné style of the masonry is a testimony to the technicians' skill and care, while the large stones that support the masonry on the lower parts of the walls are mounted decoratively so that they form crosses. The church has interesting ceramic decorations: pseudo-kufic patterns, a frieze with small ceramic plates with kufic-like reliefs and other decorative elements, dentils and brick arches around the windows.

The church of St Theodoroi is almost contemporary to the nearby church of Kapnikarea, but of heavier proportions, more severe structure and more conservative choices. In a stylistic overview one could say that the church stands out rather through its strength than through the grace and the rhythm of its characteristic small roofs. The church was damaged during the Greek War of Independence and was repaired in 1840.

Room in the Museum Vouros-Eutaxias

MUSEUM OF THE CITY OF ATHENS

The Museum of the City of Athens is situated in Klafthmonos Square, at 5 and 7 Paparrigopoulou Street. Founded in 1973, it began to function in 1980 and in 1990 received the award of the Academy of Athens. The museum houses the art and historical collection of its founder, Lambros Eftaxias, including paintings, engravings, furniture, everyday objects, and important relics from medieval and more recent Greek history – from the period of Frankish rule to the 19th century. The museum is housed in two of the oldest buildings in Athens, which are now connected by a

The Museum of the City of Athens

covered bridge. The building at 7 Paparrigopoulou Street was for a time the residence of King Otto and Queen Amalia; the building is therefore also known as the "Old Palace". This is why on the first floor of the museum are reconstructed with the original furniture Amalia's reception room, Otto's reception room, the hall of the throne, as well as Otto's study and library.
There are interesting collections of paintings, watercolours and engravings by travellers who visited Athens, and the large, 1674 oil painting by Jacques Carrey (3x5m) is one of the most important sources of information on Athens in the 17th century. There is also an interesting plaster model of Athens as it was in 1842, to a scale of 1:1,000 by Ioannis Travlos and Nikos Gerasimov. The model was based on a drawing of the city by Fr. Stauffert made between 1836 and 1843, and on numerous photographs, written sources and drawings. The model offers a picture of Athens when it had only 25,000 inhabitants and was gradually being transformed into the capital of the newly founded Greek State. The museum contributes to the city's cultural life with lectures, concerts and exhibitions.

Athens in a copper engraving of 1805

THE CHURCH OF ST GEORGE KARITSIS

The church of St George (Agios Georgios) Karitsis is situated at the junction of Parnassou and Christou Lada Streets, very close to the Museum of the City of Athens.
The church as we know it today is a three-aisled, domed basilica and was built on the location of an older Byzantine church that belonged to the Karykes family (hence the name "Karitsis"). In 1845 Efrosini Negri, Ioannis Filimon, the Leonardou family and local parishioners decided to fund the

J. Carrey (1674): "The Parthenon before the bombardment by Morosini"

Saint George Karitsis

demolition of the older church and the construction of a new one. Useful and important architectural materials from the old building were incorporated into the new one, for example the columns and several decorative elements. Lissandros Kaftantzoglou, the church's architect, maintained the Byzantine style, as requested by the donors, and the new church was completed in 1849.

BUILDING AT THE JUNCTION OF STADIOU AND CHRISTOU LADA STREETS

The building at the junction of Stadiou and Christou Lada Streets, where the cinemas "Apollo" and "Attikon" are housed, as well as numerous shops, was designed by the architect Ernst Ziller in the second half of the 19th century. It is a building with neoclassical elements at the ridge and with tower-like constructions on the corners of the façade. The two cinemas were built later in the building's atrium. The "Attikon" hall was built in 1914 as a theatre; in 1918 it was developed as a cinema designed by the architect Alexandros Nikoloudis. "Apollo" was also built as a theatre in 1915 in the location where the older theatre "Panorama" used to be and in 1918 it was also turned into a cinema. Both cinemas today are among the city's most popular venues.

NATIONAL HISTORICAL MUSEUM – OLD PARLIAMENT

The National Historical Museum is located in Stadiou Street, a short distance from Sintagma Square. It was built on the site of the former residence of Al.

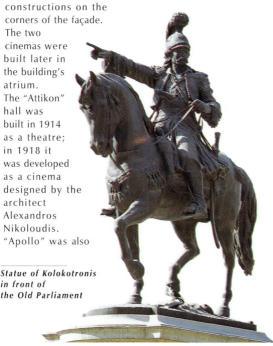

Statue of Kolokotronis in front of the Old Parliament

WALK 12

> ### 👉 THE HISTORICAL AND ETHNOLOGICAL SOCIETY OF GREECE
>
> *The Society was established in 1882 by prominent scholars and artists. Among them were Timoleon Filimon (first president of the Society), Nikolaos Politis, Spyridon Lambros, Dimitrios Kambouroglou, Antonios Miliarakis and Georgios Drosinis. The society's aim is to preserve and promote the material and spiritual monuments of modern Greek history. It established the Historical Ethnological Museum in 1896, the forerunner of the National Historical Museum, which was housed in a room of the Technical University of Athens. Today, apart from the National Historical Museum, the society disposes of a Historical Archive and a Library and has been active in the fields of research and publishing.*

Kontostavlos, one of the richest merchants of Athens, and, even earlier, in 1834, it was the residence of King Otto of Greece. After the constitutional movement of 3 September 1843 and the grant of a constitution by Otto in 1844, the building became the seat of Greece's Parliament and was used for meetings of the Parliament and the Senate.

In October 1854 the building was completely destroyed by fire. A new, neoclassical building was built in 1858, designed by the architect François Boulanger. Designed primarily as a parliament building, it included two amphitheatres, one for parliamentary meetings and another for meetings of the Senate. Construction stopped soon after commencement due to financial difficulties; by the time they resumed in 1863, the institution of the Senate had been abolished, which necessitated a change of plan, and the necessary modifications were undertaken by the Greek architect Panagiotis Kalkos. The building was completed in 1871 and housed the Parliament from 1875 to 1935 (when the institution was transferred to the Old Palace in Syntagma Square). The building then served as the Ministry of Justice, and from 1962 it has housed the National Historical Museum, created by the Historical and Ethnological Society of Greece.

The museum's collection covers modern Greek history and folklore from the 15th to the 20th

The Army Share Fund Mansion

centuries. Exhibits from the periods of Frankish and Ottoman rule (15th to 19th centuries) are displayed, and the preparation, outbreak and development of the War of Independence of 1821. There are also exhibits connected with prominent Greek scholars and clergymen, the philhellenes, Ioannis Kapodistrias (the first Governor of Greece, between 1828 and 1831), the reign of Otto, first King of Greece (1833–62), the reign of King George I (1864-1913), the Balkan Wars (1912-1913), the Asia Minor Campaign (1919–22) and the Greek-Italian War of 1940–41. The historical units consist of collections of historical and folklore material including weaponry, flags, works of art, memorabilia, medals, personal items of historical figures, furniture, folk costume, items from everyday life and folk art.
In the area around the Old Parliament one can find three statues: on the square leading from Stadiou Street is the statue of Theodoros Kolokotronis on horseback, one of the great figures of the

Traditional dress

Greek War of Independence of 1821. Created by Lazaros Sochos in 1900, the statue was erected in the square in 1904. The base is decorated by two reliefs depicting scenes from Greek

Greek soldier of 1821

War of Independence, the battle of Dervenakia and the Assembly of the Peloponnesian Senate. On the sides of the museum there are statues of two outstanding Greek politicians of the 19th century, Charilaos Trikoupis (by Thomas Thomopoulos, 1920) and Theodoros Diligiannis, the Prime Minister who was assassinated by the entrance to the Parliament in 1905 (by Georgios Dimitriadis, 1924).

THE ARMY SHARE FUND MANSION

The Army Share Fund Mansion, a landmark project of Athenian mid-war architecture, is one of the few buildings in Athens that covers an entire street. The building is surrounded by Stadiou, Amerikis, Eleftheriou Venizelou (Panepistimiou) and Voukourestiou Streets.
The mansion, standing on the site of the former royal stables, was built according to French public building models of the time. It rises to six floors and its imposing appearance combines features of modern

The "Iliou Melathron", nowadays the Numismatic Museum

classicism and Art Deco. The plans were drawn up by architects Leonidas Bonis and Vassileios Kassandras.
It was built in three stages between 1928 to 1938. Shops and offices were originally built on the side of Stadiou Street, when the arcade connecting Voukourestiou and Amerikis Streets, the "Palace" Theatre with a seating capacity of about 2,000 as well as the "Aliki" Theatre in Amerikis Street, which originally acted as an entertainment hall and later as a cinema, were constructed. The Panepistimiou Street side was formed at the last stage of building. The famous "Zonars" café-patisserie, once a meeting point for intellectuals and artists, was a feature here until a few years ago.

THE NUMISMATIC MUSEUM-ILIOU MELATHRON

The Numismatic Museum is situated on Eleftheriou Venizelou (Panepistimiou) Street, very close to Sintagma Square and Parliament House. It is housed in the so-called Iliou Melathron, the historic house of the famous German archaeologist Heinrich Schliemann (1822–90), who excavated Troy (ancient Ilion) and Mycenae. The museum was founded in 1834 and boasts an important collection of coins, molybdobulls, stathmia, medals and precious stones from ancient Greece, Rome, Byzantium, the Orient, medieval and modern Europe, America and modern Greece. It is unique in Greece and one of the most important museums of its kind in the world. Before the collections were permanently housed in Schliemann's house, they were kept at Athens University, the Athens Academy and the National Archaeological Museum, while during the German rule they were safely kept in the vaults of the Bank of Greece.

The Iliou Melathron was built in the years 1878–80 by the German architect Ernst Ziller (1837–1923). It shows the influence of the buildings of the Italian Renaissance,

THE CENTER OF THE CENTER AND ITS CHARMS

HEINRICH SCHLIEMANN

The German Heinrich Schliemann (1822-1890) throughout his adventurous life gained as a businessman great wealth. When he was forty years old, he turned to archaeology and set out to fulfill his life dream, the discovery of Homer's world. He was the pioneer of prehistoric archaeology, he who proved the existence of the world of Mycenae. His excavations at Troy, Mycenae, Orchomenos, Tiryns and Ithaca caused great sensation, admiration but also controversy. His love for Greece and its culture as well as his marriage to Sophia Engastromenou (Kastrioti) connected him closely to Greece, which became his second homeland.

adapted however to late 19th-century neoclassicism. It is considered to be one of the city's most characteristic neoclassical buildings and one of Ziller's most important works. The building has a garden on three of its sides, and its ground plan is an almost perfect square. Its celebrated façade with arched verandas and Ionic colonnades, marks this as one of the most impressive houses in Athens.

Inside the walls and ceilings have been decorated with paintings by the Slovenian artist Yuri Subic and are mostly copies of the mural paintings in Pompeii. The mosaic floors by Italian craftsmen depict various geometric patterns, as well as objects uncovered by Schliemann in the excavations at Troy and Mycenae. The house was officially opened on 30 January 1881; it cost a total of 439,650 drachmas, a truly impressive amount for those days.

The Iliou Melathron was purchased by the state in 1927 and for a while was used as the premises of the Supreme Court (Areios Pagos). In 1984 it was renovated and this is when the Numismatic Museum was transferred there. In 1998 the museum's permanent exhibition was mounted on the first floor, where the Schliemann family

ERNST ZILLER (1837-1923)

Ziller was one of the most important architects of the 19th century. Born in Dresden, he came to Greece in 1862 as an assistant to Theophilus Hansen for the construction of the Academy, and remained in Greece for the rest of his life.

He designed churches, public buildings, monuments, graves, mansions and houses in Athens and other cities. He frequently combined elements from Roman and Renaissance architecture with various Greek styles. His great reputation meant that buildings designed by other architects were often attributed to him. Among his most significant works are the National Theatre (1882–1900), the Presidential Mansion (1891–97), the Military Academy or Evelpidon School (1889–94) and the church of St Lucas (Agios Loukas) on Patission Street; however his most typical work is the house of Heinrich Schliemann, also known as Iliou Melathron.

used to socialize. The transfer of the museum's entire collection and functions was completed at the beginning of 2003. The main parts of the museum's collections have been donated by a number of wealthy Greeks. The most significant collections in quantity and variety of types are those donated by the Zosimades Brothers (1857), Giannis Dimitriou (1892) and Grigorios Empedoklis (1953). The first of these collections included over 18,000 coins and medals, the other two around 10,000 and 7,800 coins respectively. The exhibition begins in the old reception rooms, with information on the building and its architect, while there are also important highlights of Schliemann's work and his coin collection. In the reception hall, the Esperides hall, one can find out about the use of various metals for transactions, the invention and wide use of coins, metals and methods for the cutting of ancient coins, as well as treasures, i.e., collections of ancient coins. In the study room, or Literary Salon, there are several series of "strong" ancient coins, for example from Athens and from the kingdom of Alexander the Great. In the adjacent room the coins on display highlight the various images that they carry. In the space where the dining-room used to be, parts of the donated collections are on display. Finally there is a room with photographic and archival material. On the second floor restoration work on the wall paintings and mosaics is still being carried out; once that is completed there will be an exhibition of Roman, Byzantine, medieval and more recent coins, as well as molybdobulls, stathmia and medals.

BANK OF GREECE

The Bank of Greece stretches over a large block in central Athens, the midst of Panepistimiou (Eleftheriou Venizelou), Stadiou, Omirou and Edward Law Streets. The Bank was founded in 1927 and began operating in 1928, although construction did not begin until 1933. Designed by Nikolaos Zoumboulidis and Konstantinos Papadakis, the building was officially opened on 4 April 1938; it is typical of

The Bank of Greece

The Catholic Church of Saint Dionysius

Athenian public building of the mid-war period, especially of the style that followed the neoclassical pattern. The building was gradually added to. The first extension took place after World War II, when the building was extended towards Omirou and Edward Law Streets. The second took place during the 1970s, towards Stadiou Street, when the building took over the entire block. In 1982 another storey was added. The building was listed as a historical monument in 1989. ••

THE CATHOLIC CHURCH OF ST DIONYSIUS

The Catholic church of Athens, dedicated to St Dionysius Areopagite (Agios Dionissios Areopagitis), is situated on the corner of Eleftheriou Venizelou (Panepistimiou) and Omirou Streets. It was designed by Leo von Klenze in 1844, however, due to lack of funding the design was altered and simplified by Lissandros Kaftantzoglou. The construction of the church, which is a three-aisled basilica, began in 1853 and was completed in 1865. Impressive marble steps lead up to the church, while the Renaissance-style porch designed by Kaftantzoglou is also interesting. The porch has three entrances to the three aisles of the basilica. The four-storey belfry is a little higher than the church's roof. All work on the building was completed in 1887 with a collection among the Catholic community of the island of Syros. The church of St Dionysius ever since it was built has been the main point of focus for the Catholic community of Athens from both, Greece and abroad. ••

THE OPHTHALMIC CLINIC

The quite unique building of the Ophthalmic Clinic is between Eleftheriou Venizelou (Panepistimiou) and Sina Streets, next to the Catholic church of St Dionysius Areopagite. The building is in strong contrast with the so-called "Neoclassical Trilogy" formed by the buildings of the National Library,

The Ophthalmic Clinic

the University of Athens and the Academy, therefore it is particularly interesting.

The clinic's history began in 1843, when by royal decree it was decided that a separate ophthalmic clinic should be built in order to avoid transmission of ophthalmic diseases to other patients. The Danish architect Christian Hansen first designed a neoclassical building. The foundations were laid in April 1847, however the progress of the construction was slow, due to lack of funding. In 1850 Hansen left Greece and two years later the architect Lissandros Kaftantzoglou took over the project and re-designed the building following a Byzantine-like style by demand of King Otto. The building was completed in 1854.

In 1868 the Opthalmic Clinic was donated to the Faculty of Medicine of the University of Athens. The limited space led to the decision to add another storey to the building. The project was supervised by the army architect Gerassimos Metaxas and was completed in 1869. The building took its present form in 1881 with the addition of other smaller sections.

The Agricultural Bank

AGRICULTURAL BANK OF GREECE

The building of the Agricultural Bank (Agrotiki Trapeza) of Greece is situated at the junction of Eleftheriou Venizelou (Panepistimiou) and Edward Law Streets. Initially it was the mansion of the Italian mineralogist and businessman Gian Baptista Serpieri. The characteristic neoclassical building was designed by the architect and military engineer Anastassios

The Academy of Athens

THE CENTER OF THE CENTER AND ITS CHARMS

The Academy of Athens, a detail of the roof

THE ACADEMY

The Athens Academy is an imposing building at the junction of Eleftheriou Venizelou (Panepistimiou) and Sina Streets, between the university and the Ophthalmic Clinic. It is typical of 19th-century neoclassical architecture, and, together with the neighbouring university buildings and the National Library, forms part of Athens' so-called "neoclassical trilogy", one of the most important architectural units of the city.

With the establishment of the modern Greek State came the demand for an academy of arts and sciences. In 1856 Simon Sinas, a rich merchant and banker based in Austria and Ambassador of Greece in Vienna, offered considerable funds for the construction of the academy. When Sinas died, his wife Ifigeneia supervised the project. Construction began in 1859, under the Danish architect Theophilus Hansen. But Hansen's professional obligations did not allow him to reside in Greece, so in 1861 he engaged the young architect Ernst Ziller to supervise the project. The academy trilogy is perhaps the most monumental creation of Athenian classicism and certainly one of the most typical examples of its kind in Theophilos and the construction was completed in 1881. Later on the artist and decorator G. Bilancioni took over the building's painted decoration which was completed in 1884. The Agricultural Bank that was founded in 1929 was first housed in this building in that same year and since then its main branch remains there.●■

SCULPTURE

There are many sculptures in the Athens Academy. The seated statues of Socrates and Plato in front of the building, the central pediment depicting the birth of Athena and the building's emblem, the statues of Athena and Apollo on two high Ionic columns, are works of the sculptor Leonidas Drossis. The eight small pediments on the sides of the building, by Franz Melnitzki, depict Athena offering art and science to the Athenians. The bust of donor Simon Sinas stands in front of the building, among the gods of wisdom and light and the most eminent philosophers of Greek Antiquity, thus chosen to adorn the principal spiritual institution of Greece.

Statue of Athena

WALK 12

The Academy of Athens, pediment

Europe. The ground plan is symmetrical and consists of three wings, connected by two shorter transverse wings. The central building, which houses the Academy's conference hall, is an amphiprostyle Ionic temple with elements from the eastern part of the Erechtheion of the Acropolis. The right-hand side of the building houses the library and the left side the administrative offices. Built almost exclusively in Pentelic marble, the mansion is lit by six marble lamp-posts. The main conference hall is adorned with wall-paintings by Christian Griepenkerl, depicting the legend of Prometheus. The paintings express monumental and idealistic qualities, and are clearly influenced by Michelangelo. The building was completed in 1885, almost thirty years after it was founded. Between 1890 and 1940 the academy's eastern wing accommodated the Numismatic Museum, especially designed by Ernest Ziller. At various times the building has housed objects and services more or less relevant to its mission, including the General State Archives and the collections of the Byzantine Museum. It became the seat of the Athens Academy in 1926, when that institution was established. The academy, as most homonymous institutions in other countries, comprises the most important members of the communities of science and art in Greece. Its most significant events include the awarding of prizes to notable scientists and artists.

THE NATIONAL AND KAPODISTRIAN UNIVERSITY OF ATHENS

The National and Kapodistrian University of Athens is in Eleftheriou Venizelou (Panepistimiou) Street, between the two other buildings of the so-called "neoclassical trilogy" of Athens, the National Library and the Academy. Founded in 1839, the university was designed by the Danish architect

> ### STATUES
> Four emblematic figures of modern Greek history adorn the university's propylaia. The statues of the revolutionary Rigas Feraios by Ioannis Kossos and the Patriarch of Constantinople Gregorios V by Georgios Fitalis stand in front of the building, while beside the stairways of the propylaia are seated statues of the scholar Adamantios Koraïs and the first governor of Greece, Ioannis Kapodistrias. In front of the building, inside the garden, is a statue of the British politician William Gladstone.
>
>
> *I. Kapodistrias*

THE CENTER OF THE CENTER AND ITS CHARMS

"PANEPISTIMIO" METRO STATION

> The "Panepistimio" metro station is decorated on the level of the ticket-offices. In terms of modern art, there is a relief by Giannis Moralis decorating the space above the staircases, while in terms of archaeology, there are display-cases with pottery such as various objects, small sarcophaguses, small spherical vessels for oil (aryballoi), other vessels, loom equipment and oil lamps. Many of these vessels are exact replicas, made with the same methods of baking as the original ones

Christian Hansen, who followed contemporary neoclassical models. When he left Greece in 1843 the project was completed by different architects, such as Anastassios Theofilas and Lissandros Kaftantzoglou. The University of Athens has occupied this building since 1864, when it was transferred from the so-called "Old University" of the architects Stamatis Kleanthis and Eduard Schaubert in the Plaka.

The plain yet elegant façade has the form of an arcade with rectangular pillars. The middle of the arcade is set off by an Ionic entrance (propylon) and the edges form two solid parts. Both pillars and capitals are modelled on the propylaia of the Acropolis. On the interior of the arcade there is a wall painting designed by the Bavarian artist Karl Rahl and painted by the Polish painter Edward Lebiedzky, depicting the renaissance of the arts and sciences in the Greece of King Otto. The painter Vicenzo Lanza painted the interior of the building. On the ground floor there were four classrooms, amphitheatres and administrative rooms, while the first floor housed the assembly hall (where official ceremonies took place), the public library and the museum of natural history. Today the building houses the administrative services, the deanery and the assembly hall of the university.
The building was funded by donations from King Otto, the

The University of Athens

The core of the building is a synthesis of three two-storeyed wings forming a double T-shape, and it forms, together with the two symmetrical courtyards, a rectangle. Prince of Serbia, Milos Obrenovic, and other wealthy families. Restoration was completed in 1864 after financial difficulties had been overcome.

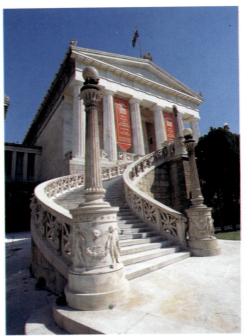

National Library

THE NATIONAL LIBRARY

Vallianeios National Library stands on the corner of Eleftheriou Venizelou (Panepistimiou) and Ippokratous Streets and forms part of the "neoclassical trilogy" of Athens (together with the University and the Academy).
This cluster of buildings was founded in 1887, designed by Theophilus Hansen and supervised by Ernst Ziller, in order to house the National Gallery, which until then had been accommodated in the neighbouring university building. The then Prime Minister, Charilaos Trikoupis, had the initiative to construct the Library. The project was funded by the Vallianos brothers, Russian Greeks, while the Greek State contributed financially to the completion of works. The building is a monumental neoclassical mixture of pentelic marble and consists of three solid parts: the middle part houses the reading room and the two side parts accommodate the books themselves. The entrance is a Doric prostyle, modelled on the temple of Hephaestus in the Agora. Access is by means of two monumental curved marble stairways, based on Renaissance models. The central pediment and the window panels were to be decorated with sculptures and the reading room with wall-paintings. However, due to financial constraints the commissions from the Viennese sculptor Schwerzek were not executed. A statue of the donor Panagis Vallianos stands in front of the building and statues of his brothers, Marinos and Andreas, made by the sculptor Georgios Bonanos, stand in the front alley.
The National Library moved into the finished building in 1903, where it has remained to date. It has a rich collection of books exceeding 3,000,000 titles, among which there are many rare editions. Collections of newspapers and magazines from the 19th and 20th centuries as

THE READING ROOM

The arrangement of the reading room in the National Library is of particular interest as it has an Ionic peristyle and is roofed by a glass ceiling. The original construction of cast-iron bookstands is very interesting.

The Orpheus' Arcade

well as engravings, maps and both Greek and foreign manuscripts, dating from the 9th to the 19th centuries, are also kept in the National Library.

THE RALLIS HOUSE

Immediately opposite the University, at the corner of 10 Koraï Street and Panepistimiou Street, there is one of the oldest middle class houses of Athens, built before 1844, which gives us a good idea of the size of buildings before the appearance of the majestic private mansions. The building housed some of the most important families and figures, such as the families of Dimitrios Soutzos and Andreas Singros as well as the family of Dimitrios Rallis, the former Prime Minister of Greece. The house was renovated in 1998 as during the previous years it had served commercial purposes.

ALPHA BANK

The head office and main branch of Alpha Bank is at the junction of Eleftheriou Venizelou (Panepistimiou) and Pesmazoglou Streets. It consists of two buildings where the Ionian Bank and the Laiki Bank were formerly housed. The old building of the Ionian Bank on Pesmazoglou Street was built in 1911 and was expanded in 1917. Its exterior is influenced by the neoclassical style that was developed by the Scottish architect Robert Adam. The old building of the Laiki Bank on Eleftheriou Venizelou Street is also a neoclassical one and it was built in 1925. Both buildings were remodelled by the architect Anastassios Metaxas. In 2000 Alpha Bank acquired both buildings and joined their interior spaces in order to house its main branch.

EDUCATIONAL SOCIETY
The Educational Society was founded in 1836. Its aim was to promote education. The founders placed particular importance on the girls' education, which until then was neglected. The society is the oldest active educational organization in Greece and has been very active in education and cultural matters to this day.

ARSAKEIO

The grand, classical two-storey building on Pesmazoglou and Eleftheriou Venizelou (Panepistimiou) Street is the Arsakeio Mansion. It was built on the initiative of the Educational Society as

ART THEATRE "KAROLOS KUHN"

Karolos Kuhn

Model of I. Tsarouchis, for a performance of the "Birds"

The entrance to the older stage of the Art Theatre, also known as "Basement", is on 5 Pesmazoglou Street (the second stage of the theatre is on 14 Frinichou Street in the Plaka). The theatre and the homonymous drama school were founded in 1942 by the great Greek director Karolos Kuhn (1908–87), and from 1954 both were housed in the basement of the old Orpheus Cinema in the Arsakeio building complex. Kuhn used this stage to present pioneering productions from the international repertory, with emphasis on great 20th-century playwrights (Brecht, Lorca, Williams, Pirandello, Beckett, etc.), modern Greek writers (Kampanellis, Anagnostaki, Skourtis, Kechaïdis, etc.) and ancient drama. The most significant productions of ancient drama were the Persians by Aeschylus and the Birds by Aristophanes.

Most of the important Greek actors of the second half of the 20th century graduated from the Art Theatre's drama school. In 1949 Melina Merkouri played her first leading role there in "A Streetcar Named Desire" by Tennessee Williams.

Sophocles, "Oedipus at Colonus", 2002

two schools, a girls' school and a nursery. Today the Arsakeio building complex houses the State Council, the administrative offices of the Educational Society (whose schools are located in several Athenian suburbs), the Book Gallery and the Art Theatre ("Theatro Technis").

The foundations of the Arsakeio were laid in 1846 in a plot of land purchased by the Educational Society from the Zoodochos Pege Monastery of Andros. Initially Stamatis Kleanthis was in charge of designing the building; however, later on the architect Lissandros Kaftantzoglou took over, which created tension between the two architects. The building encloses an interior courtyard. The narrower wings on Eleftheriou Venizelou Street have pediments, while the main entrance stands out with its pediment and Doric columns. At the top of the pediment is Leonidas Drossis's sculpted head of Athena, the goddess of wisdom. Building materials from the Acropolis were used in the construction of Arsakeio, but towards the end of the 20th century, as repairs were made to the Arsakeio, many of those stones were removed and returned to the Acropolis.

The Educational Society funded the initial construction of the building, but by 1850, when the shortage of funds became apparent, Apostolos Arsakis, a wealthy Greek of the diaspora, stepped in to support the project, and so the building was completed in 1852: as a token of their appreciation, the society named the school Arsakeio.

With additional donations from Arsakis and others the society purchased the rest of the street, towards Stadiou Street, including the buildings of the Tossitseio Girls' School and the nursery of Simon Sinas. Both these new buildings were also designed by Lissandros Kaftantzoglou, thus maintaining the stylistic unity and the plain, austere look of the whole complex. At the beginning of the 20th century these buildings were replaced by a new structure, with shops on the ground floor. The architect Konstantinos Maroudis designed the new project and created an impressive arcade with a light glass roof to harmonize the new building with the Arsakeio. The arcade is known as Arsakeio Arcade, or Orpheus' Arcade,

named after the Orpheus Cinema that was built in the centre of the mansion in 1937. This is the part of the complex where the State Council is housed today.
In 1996 the Educational Society founded the Book Gallery, a permanent exhibition of books from the main publishing houses in Athens and at the same time an important cultural space in the city centre. Its entrance is in the Arsakeio Arcade.

Rex theatre, performance of the "Students" by the National Theatre

THE REX THEATRE

The Rex building is in 48 Eleftheriou Venizelou (Panepistimiou) Street. It dates back to 1937 and has been one of Athens' most important centres of entertainment from its inception. Designed by architects Leonidas Bonis and Vassileios Kassandras, who had studied in Paris and were obviously influenced by contemporary international styles, the Rex building was a pioneering construction. Its external features, which emphasize vertical lines, remind one the skyscrapers of the time, while inside its series of rooms reflect French architectural models. The basement

MARIKA KOTOPOULI

The great Greek actress Marika Kotopouli was born in Athens in 1887. Born into a family of actors, she made her stage debut when still a child. At a young age she took on leading roles at the Royal Theatre, and in 1908 put together her own theatre ensemble with which she worked on numerous great productions of contemporary and ancient drama. She performed in plays such as Euripides' "Hecuba", directed by Fotos Politis in the Panathenaic Stadium (1927) and Schiller's "Mary Stewart" (1932) in which she worked with the other great actress of her time, Kiveli. In 1937 she acquired a new theatre in the Rex building. Her career was interrupted during the German occupation, but she returned to the stage in 1944 when she played Klytaimnestra with great success in the National Theatre's production of Aeschylos' "Oresteia". In 1950, four years before her death, she founded the Kotopouli Award for young actresses.

Marika Kotopouli was an actress of great talent and technical ability, who worked with all the important directors of her time and was successful in all types of drama, from musical varieties to ancient tragedy.

accommodated the Cineac movie theatre, which had seating for 582. The Rex movie theatre was on the ground floor: the stalls had seating capacity for 803, the circle for 321 and the gallery for 448. Above the Rex itself was the Kotopouli Theatre: here, the stalls could seat 626, the circle had 222 and the 15 boxes and gallery a further 276. With its excellent acoustic, the building was for a long time one of the finest of its kind in Athens.

In 1982 the Kotopouli Theatre was destroyed by fire. Since then the mansion has been designated a listed building belonging to the Ministry of Culture, and has been restored. The halls of the Cineac movie theatre and the Kotopouli Theatre are used as stages for the National Theatre, while the Rex movie theatre has been transformed into an entertainment hall.

KANIGGOS SQUARE

Kaniggos Square is at the end of Akadimias Street. It was named after the English politician George Canning, the Foreign Secretary whose attitude influenced the English policy in favour of the Greek War of Independence. His bust stands on the square and was made by the British Francis Chantrey, one of the most important sculptors of the first half of the 19th century. The sculpture was created in 1834 but it was erected on the square in 1931. Kaniggos Square is a major hub with lots of bus stations; at the square is also situated the Ministry of Commerce.

George Canning

THE OLD BUILDING OF THE HELLENIC CONSERVATORY

The old building of the Hellenic Conservatory on Phidiou Street attracts hardly any attention because of its poor state of preservation and its proximity to the imposing German Archaeological Institute. But it is one of the oldest and most historic buildings of Athens. A two-storey structure with a plain, neoclassical façade and French windows, it was designed in

The Orchestra director Dimitris Mitropoulos

1840 as the home of General Anton Prokesch-Osten, the Ambassador of the Hapsburg Empire in Greece from 1833 to 1840. Stamatis Kleanthis and Eduard Schaubert, the first city planners of modern Athens, were the architects. At the end of the 19th century the house was acquired by the Bavarian pianist Lina von Lottner and from 1899 to 1919 the Lottner Conservatoire was housed here. In 1903 this conservatoire merged with the Apollo Music Society, which published the magazine of this name.

The Hellenic Conservatory operated here from 1919 until 1966; its founder and director until 1926 was Manolis Kalomiris, the most important figure of the Greek national music school, and one of the leading composers of symphonic music in Greece. Great Greek musicians also taught here, including Dimitris Mitropoulos, for many years director of the New York Philharmonic. Today, the building belongs to the Association of the National Bank Employees.

GERMAN ARCHAEOLOGICAL INSTITUTE

The building at the corner of Phidiou and Charilaou Trikoupi Streets is related to the history of the German Archaeological Institute of Athens which has been housed there since 1888. It was built in 1887-1888 designed by the architect Ernst

The German Archaeological Institute

Ziller and initially it belonged to Heinrich Schliemann who donated to the German State in 1899.

The building is a three-storey neoclassical mansion with a grand interior entrance and staircase and rich painted decorations. Initially it was surrounded by a garden that reached Panepistimiou Street. In 1900 a two-storey building was added on the side towards Charilaou Trikoupi Street to house the Institute's library, designed by the archaeologist and architect Wilhelm Dörpfeld and funded by the proceeds of the sale of the garden. The building was renovated in 1983-1985 by the team of Professor Pavlos Milonas.

The building houses the library, the rich photographic collection, the offices and the institute's guest-house. The German Archaeological Institute of Athens has been active since the 9 December 1874 and it conducts excavation projects in numerous archaeological sites in Greece, such as Olympia, Kerameikos, Boeotia, Aegina and Tiryns.

CHURCH OF ZOODOCHOS PEGE

The church of Zoodochos Pege

The National Opera. Performance of the "La Finta Giardineria" by Mozart

(Holy Fountain of Life) is situated on Akadimias Street. The building's construction began in 1846 and was completed in 1852, with the exception of the belfry, which was built in around 1900. The church's construction was funded by a collection among the parishioners and by the Municipality of Athens. The architect Dimitrios Zezos from Ipiros designed the building, which is actually his most important work. The church is a basilica with two side entrances, a belfry and single-light windows with dentils. The exterior is plastered and has limited decorative elements; hence the church's simple, unpretentious look, which stood in contrast with the classicistic style that was dominant in that time.

The interior's pictorial decoration was completed in 1880, while new mural paintings were added in 1930.

Greek National Opera

The building of the Greek National Opera is on 59-61 Akadimias Street. The Greek National Opera is the first and only opera house in Greece. It was founded in 1939 as part of the Royal Theatre and since 1944 it has been an autonomous organisation.

Forerunner of the Greek National Opera was the Greek Melo-drama which had been founded in 1888 and, despite all its financial problems, remained active until 1939 with international success; it was succeeded by the

WALK 12

THE CENTER OF THE CENTER AND ITS CHARMS

Greek National Opera. At present the Greek National Opera organises productions of operas for adults and children, of ballet, musicals, concerts, as well as lectures. The Greek National Opera has an archive, a music library and a museum with costumes, stage designs, sheet music and memorabilia from important productions.

The Cultural Centre of the City of Athens

CULTURAL CENTRE OF THE CITY OF ATHENS

The contemporary Cultural Centre of the Municipality of Athens with its garden takes over an entire block in the heart of Athens surrounded by Akadimias, Massalias, Solonos and Asklipiou Streets. It was built in 1836-1838 but its architect remains unknown. The construction was funded by Ludwig, King of Bavaria, father of Greece's first monarch, King Otto, as well as by wealthy diaspora Greeks. Since 1842 the building functioned as a Public Hospital- as opposed to the Military Hospital (Weiler

THE THEATRE MUSEUM

The Museum and Study Centre of the Greek Theatre was founded in 1938 by the Greek Theatre Writers Society and, since 1977 it has been housed in the basement of the Cultural Centre. Apart from the exhibits the museum has an extensive library and a collection of records related to the Greek Theatre, which has been computerised since 1992. The items on display include photographs, playbills from the 19th and 20th century, theatrical sets and costumes, as well as models and significant memorabilia from shows, or personal items of great actors. The displays are separated in the following categories: Modern Greek Theatre, Opera, Musical Theatre and Variety, Ancient Greek Drama and Puppet Theatre. There are also a number of impressively replicated dressing rooms of many leading Greek actors.

KOSTIS PALAMAS

Kostis Palamas is one of the most important poets of modern Greece. He was born in 1859 in Patras, grew up in Messolongi and in 1875 came to Athens to study. However, he gave up his studies to pursue a career in literature. He worked as secretary at the University of Athens from 1897 and later became secretary general of the university, while in 1926 he became one of the founding members of the Academy of Athens. He was the most important poet of the 1880 Generation, a group that reformed Greek literature after the Romantic period. Palamas also participated in the demotic movement, which urged the use of the demotic (modern Greek language) in Greek literature instead of the so-called "katharévousa", a language form closer to ancient Greek. Palamas believed in poetry's potential as a factor of promoting national and social development. During the unsettled period between the Greek-Ottoman war of 1897 and the uprising in Goudi in 1909, Palamas expressed through his work ("The Dodecalogue of a Gypsy" and "The King's Flute") his strong support for a total cultural transformation of the Greek society. His poetry is symbolic, rich in form and content, expressive and original. He was greatly respected and admired by his peers and the public generally. His funeral in 1943 turned out to be a massive public protest against the German occupation.

PALAMAS AND ATHENS

Palamas spent most of his life in Athens. The following citation from "The King's Flute" is a proof of his deep affection for the Greek capital:

The day is early and the sun is bright,
And Athens is a sapphire in Earth's ring
Light everywhere; and light makes everything
stand out in bold outline; nothing is left
in semi-darkness to seem like a dream,
A misty cloud, or a reality
The mighty and the humble, are all seen.

(Translation by T.P. Stefanides / G.C. Katsimbalis)

Building) in the area of Makrigianni - where the poor citizens of Athens were looked after. In 1858 two new wings were added due to an ever-increasing popular demand and the building housed the city's university hospital for over a century. In 1972 the building was renovated with the architect Kimon Laskaris in charge and since then it has been used as the Cultural Centre of the Municipality of Athens with numerous offices and events rooms. There is a café on the ground floor and the Theatre Museum is in the basement.
In the garden in front of the building one can see the statues of the poet Kostis Palamas (sculpted by V. Falireas in 1975), the actress Kiveli, the theatre writer Pantelis Horn and the busts of the first city planners of modern Athens Stamatis Kleanthis and Eduard Schaubert. The small church of St Anargyroi, which used to be the hospital's church, is behind the building on the side of Solonos Street. The pedestrian Massalias Street and the wide pavement on Solonos Street is a popular gathering point for large numbers of young people, mostly students of the Faculty of Law, which occupies the next block.

THE KOSTIS PALAMAS BUILDING

The neoclassical Kostis Palamas building belongs to the University of Athens and stands next to the Cultural Centre of the Municipality of Athens. It was built in 1856–1857 as the Lykeion (secondary school) Papadopoulou by the architect Stamatis Kleanthis or by Kostas Deinokratis. A little later it housed the laboratories of the School of Sciences and of the Faculties of Medicine and Pharmacy of the University, as well as the city's mortuary. Later still, the Natural History Museum and the Pedagogical Museum occupied the building. Today it houses the Cultural Centre of the University of Athens and the Theatre Museum's library.
At the junction of Sina and Akadimias Streets is the Monument to the Resistance by Giorgos Nikolaidis, erected in 1991 in honour of the university students, teachers and employees of the Athens University who were killed in the Resistance against the Germans between 1941 and 1944.

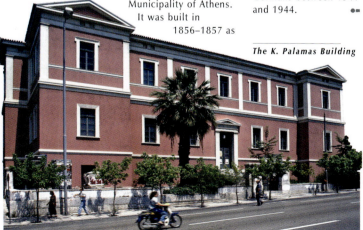

The K. Palamas Building

THE FACULTY OF LAW

The Faculty of Law buildings were built in the mid-war period to house the Athens University's Faculties of Law, Philosophy and Theology.
The complex consists of the neoclassical building at 3 Sina Street, built around 1880 as an extension to the university, and including the Oikonomidis Hall, and the Mansion of Theoretical Sciences in Solonos Street, erected in Bauhaus style in 1933–36 by Emmanouil Kriezis. The two buildings were connected by means of a subsequent extension behind the mansion, which was demolished after the 1999 earthquake. A new extension to the mansion was built in the same area between 2003 and 2004. The Oikonomidis Building was designated a listed building in 1975 and its neoclassical form restored, with a new entrance from Massalias Street.
In the 1980s the Faculties of Theology and Philosophy were transferred to the university campus at Zografou.
Most of Greece's prime ministers and important political figures have graduated from the Faculty of Law, and the first massive demonstration of students against the military dictatorship of 1967–74 took place here in February 1973.

THE UNIVERSITY'S CHEMISTRY LABORATORY

The university's Chemistry Laboratory is situated at the junction of Solonos and Mavromichali Streets and is the first building where science was taught in Greece. Although the decision to build was taken by the University Senate in 1868, work at a specially designated site did not begin until 1887, because of financial difficulties. Until then the Chemistry Laboratory had been housed in several buildings, among which was the ground floor of the university. The plans of the new building were drawn up by the architect Ernst Ziller. However, Anastassios Christomanos, Professor of Chemistry, made the final alterations to the design.
The building was completed in 1890, when it began to operate normally as a chemistry laboratory. It was much destroyed by fire in 1911: restoration commenced in 1914 and was complete by 1918. The second floor was built later and the third in 1926, while at the same time a vast amphitheatre was constructed and additional buildings erected in Navarinou Street.
During the Asia Minor campaign of 1919–1922, the radio equipment that provided contact with the Greek expeditionary force was set up in the building; the illegal radio station during the Nazi occupation of Greece was also housed here.
The laboratory has been designated a listed building by the Ministry of Culture. Today it is home to the Museum of Natural Sciences and Technology, which belongs to Athens University's School of Sciences and Faculty of Pharmacy. The museum's collection comprises 7,000 unique scientific instruments, including optical, printing and sound equipment, radiation and electricity sources as well as instruments for analysis and measurement.
In addition, the building also houses part of the university's Department of Pedagogy.
The Chemical Laboratory is associated with the struggles of the students and the youth against the junta and for democratic liberties in general.

IN THE PERIPHERY OF ATHENS

The entire Attica is very rich in monuments and natural beauties. By the Sacred Way one arrives to the Sanctuary of Demeter and Kore in Eleusis. Brief stop at the Dafni Monastery for the mosaics of incomparable beauty. Enchanting sunsets from Poseidon's temple on cape Sounion. Sacred and historical memories of Brauron and Marathon. And closer to the city, the revitalizing breath of the green lung at the Kaissariani Monastery.

THE MONASTERY OF KAISSARIANI

The Monastery of Kaissariani, dedicated to the Presentation of Virgin Mary, is an archaeological site about 7 kilometres away from the centre of Athens, in a green valley at the foot of Hymettus Hill. It was built in the 1st century near the remains of the ancient temple of Demeter (Telesterion) and possibly Aphrodite. The discovery of the foundations of a three-aisled, 5th-6th-century basilica indicates that the area developed during the early Byzantine era. In the 10th century, on high ground south-west of the monastery, a church was built, in the transitional style, the forerunner of the cross-in-square type. Not far away, south of the church, the Catholic Church of St Mark was built during the period of Frankish rule; hence the area was called the Frank Monastery. The oldest existing documents relating to the Monastery of Kaissariani are from the early 13th century; they include a letter from Michael Choniates and a document from Pope Innocentius III, in which the monastery is referred to as "Santa Syriani". However, we still do not know how the monastery came to be built, or the origin of its name. On the other hand, there is plenty of evidence relating to the monastery's history and function during the period of Ottoman rule: the monastery maintained its autonomy at this time, and developed into a significant cultural centre, with links to a number of prominent families in Athens, such as the Benizeloi. From the monastery's Byzantine phase only the main church of the katholikon and the bathhouse – a rare find of its kind – have survived. The main church (second half of the 11th century) is simple and gracious. It is of the semi-complex cross-inscribed type, built with cloisonné

View of the monastery of Kaissariani

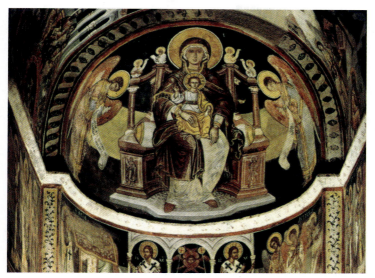

Monastery of Kaissariani, view of the niche of the Holy of Holies

masonry. The eight-sided dome without colonnettes and a straight cornice forms an exception to the typical Athenian dome, which has a billowy cornice. During the 16th century the barrel-vaulted Chapel of St Anthony (Agios Antonios) was added to the southern side. The narthex with the low dome was added in the 17th century, while the belfry was added in the 19th century. During the Ottoman period the adjacent structures were also added, such as the dining-room, the kitchen, the "tower of Benizelos", the cells and so on.

The original iconography has not survived: the wall paintings one sees today are from the post-Byzantine period. The narthex was painted in 1682 by Ioannis Ipatos from the Peloponnese, as the inscription over the entrance indicates. The Holy Trinity (Agia Triada) is depicted on the dome, while other areas depict scenes from the life of Virgin Mary and the parables, such as the Poor Lazarus and the Imprudent Wealthy Man. The successive scenes, depicting a mass of people, are narrative in character and are indirectly related to everyday life in the countryside. The wall paintings in the main part of the church are from the early 18th century. Here the painting generally follows the style developed in Mount Athos during the 16th century and exhibits the characteristically conservative character of the ecclesiastical painting of the time.

The monastery has been in its present state since the 1950s, when it was attempted to restore the complex to its 11th-century form.

Mass is celebrated in the monastery only on 21 November (the Presentation of the Virgin Mary) and on Good Friday.

THE MONASTERY OF DAFNI

The Monastery of Dafni is situated in Dafni, about 10 kilometres away from the centre of Athens, possibly on the location of the ancient temple of Daphneios Apollo; it is the largest monastery in Athens and one of the most significant Byzantine monuments. Written sources offer very little information about the monastery. Dedicated to the Assumption of the Virgin, it was founded in the early Byzantine period (5th–6th centuries), as is indicated by parts of the surrounding fence, remains of monastic cells, and an oblong building, possibly the monastery's hospital or dining hall that can be dated to that period.

It appears that, over time, the monastery was abandoned and gradually fell into ruin. In around 1080 the church we know today was built and decorated with excellent mosaics. The donors remain unknown, but to judge from the excellent quality, the skilled craftsmanship and the avant-garde style of the building and its mosaics, they must have had close links with Constantinople.

In about 1207–11, during the period of Frankish rule, the monastery came under Cistercian order and was used as a burial ground for the dukes of Athens; it remained under the control of the Franks until the occupation of Athens by the Ottomans in 1456. The catholicon is a domed octagon, similar to that of the Church of Sotira of Lykodemos (pre 1031) in the centre of Athens, with which it has a lot in common. The katholikon is particularly renowned for its mosaics. Its walls are decorated with seventeen scenes from the life of Christ and the Virgin Mary, as well as

The katholikon of the monastery of Dafni

Representation of the Crucifixion

numerous saints. The pictorial decoration is arranged so that scenes from the life of Christ are counter-balanced by scenes from the life of the Virgin, which occupy an equally large space since the church is dedicated to the Virgin Mary.

Aesthetically the mosaics have been greatly influenced by classical traditions. The figures are tall and thin with beautifully modelled features and graceful movement on an abstract gold background. The harmoniously balanced compositions, the soft colour contrasts and the grace of the beautiful faces make this monumental work one of the masterpieces of Byzantine art. The monastery has had an adventurous history in the more recent years: after the period of Ottoman rule it was used as a military camp, a mental hospital and a sheep-fold. The great damages it suffered from earthquakes at the end of the 19th century alerted the experts, who, led by Georgios Lampakis, began to repair it. The monastery was the first Byzantine building the State chose to restore, despite the controversial campaign that began in 1889, which brought an awareness of the need to maintain and study the remnants of an entire era (Byzantine) that until then had been ignored in favour of classical antiquities.

Systematic restoration began in 1955, but, after the 1981 and 1999 earthquakes, UNESCO declared the monastery a listed building, initiating further restoration.

OMORPHOKLISSIA ("BEAUTIFUL CHURCH" OR THE CHURCH OF ST GEORGE)

The Omorphoklissia is situated in Galatsi, in an uninhabited area at the foot of the Tourkovounia Hill. The church has always been dedicated to St George; the first reference to the name Omorphoklissia is an inscription of 1769 on the sanctuary screen. The church is a distyle, cross-inscribed building with a small dome, dating from the third quarter of the 12th century. It has a narthex on the western side and a chapel to the south that must have been built at the same time as the main church, despite the stylistic differences. The masonry is high quality, in the cloisonné style, with the exception of the narthex, which is made of bricks, small stones and a good deal of mortar. The strict succession of the roofs and the elegant, eight-sided dome are typical of mid-Byzantine Athenian churches. There are a few sculptured decorations internally and externally, including a Gothic rosette on the chapel's westernmost cross vault. The interior is characterized by balanced forms, a hierarchical arrangement of space and the famous mural paintings dating from the last two decades of the 13th century. Originally the whole of the interior was covered with mural paintings, many of which have been destroyed with time and human interference. The harmonious arrangement of the compositions adds to the monument's unique grandeur. The paintings were created by a group of experienced and skilled artists who followed the artistic styles of their time. One can identify individual stylistic traits in the use of line and colour, as well as in

Galatsi, Omorphoklissia ("The Beautiful Church")

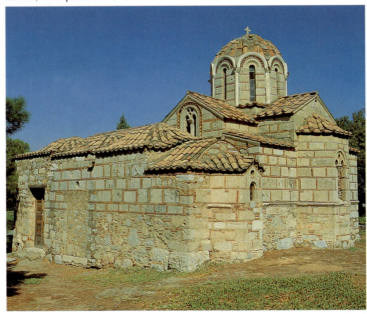

Galatsi, Omorphoklissia, Prophet Daniel

the use of space and the third dimension, and occasionally one can detect western influences in their work. The iconographic programme, especially in the south chapel, indicates complicated theological symbolism. According to an inscription on the main gate the sanctuary screen was decorated in 1743. Today people can celebrate Mass here on St George's day. On this occasion the visitor may admire the interior decoration of the church.

Galatsi, Omorphoklissia ("The Beautiful Church"), wall panel depicting the "Last Supper"

BRAURONA

Two kilometres along the country road from Markopoulo to Porto Rafti a junction to the left leads to Braurona, 8 kilometres away. After another 3 kilometres north-east from Markopoulo, on the left-hand side of the road is a medieval tower (Vraona Tower), where traces of an early Greek settlement have been found. On a hill above Vravrona Bay, an important prehistoric settlement has been discovered. Founded in the Neolithic Period, the settlement prospered as a fortified acropolis in the mid-Greek and early Mycenaean Period (2000–1600 BC). During the early Archaic and Classical Periods, the town of the Philaïdes grew up, with the agricultural temple of Brauronia Artemis, on the northern side of the bay.

SANCTUARY OF BRAURONIA ARTEMIS

On the north-eastern side of the Prehistoric acropolis, the Archaeological Society have been conducting systematic excavations since 1948. They have discovered much of the sanctuary of Brauronia Artemis, one of the oldest and most important sanctuaries in Attica. The Classical temple of Artemis (first half of the 5th century BC) is a Doric temple with a three-aisled nave and a deep adyton, situated to the north of the small post-Byzantine Church of St George, which is on the site of an older, archaic temple. Eight metres away from the south-eastern corner of the temple of Artemis the Sacred Cave was found, which was related to the worship of Iphigeneia. Earlier remains of worship around the cave date from the 8th century BC.

In around 425–415 BC the sanctuary was expanded with the construction of a Π-shaped Doric stoa built around a large, closed interior courtyard, which had an opening towards the temple of Artemis. On the northern part of the stoa behind the façade colonnade, where many offerings were placed, was a series of six rooms (called houses in inscriptions) with tiled floors. Each room contained eleven wooden beds arranged in a circle with seven marble tables in front of them. One can still see the holes in the ground where the beds were attached with lead. There were similar rooms in the shorter western side of the stoa. Among them was the courtyard's central entrance. The houses were the residences of the young virgin girls who offered their

Votive relief from the sanctuary of Artemis at Braurona

services to the sanctuary.
From the middle of the northern wing a narrow passage led behind the stoa to where, at a later construction phase, a narrow stoa was built with an opening to the south and 37 stone steps, which were used to support wooden posts where the women used to hang the dresses that they dedicated to the goddess. In the open-air corridor in front of the stoa many statue bases and bas-reliefs have been found. This entire area was probably used for the permanent display of offerings to the temple. At its eastern and western ends were two identical propyla with a column between the door-posts on the exterior and two doors on the interior. Further west from the western propylon is an ancient stone bridge over the River Erasinos.

MUSEUM OF BRAURONA

The Museum of Braurona houses numerous finds from the temple excavations. Among them is a series of marble statues of the "bears" (young girls and, occasionally, boys) entrusted by their parents to the goddess. There are bas-relief offerings with scenes of local worship, ceramic figurines of Artemis, a series of pots with scenes of girls' dances, jewels, mirrors and many inscriptions – lists of offerings from worshippers – all providing valuable information about the history of the temple and the worship of Artemis-Iphigeneia. The museum displays finds from the Prehistoric settlement and the tombs of Braurona, the Mycenaean tombs of Perati and from a number of cemeteries in Attica (Anavyssos, Merenta, etc.).

THE CULT OF THE BRAURONIA ARTEMIS

Artemis of Braurona was worshipped as the goddess of vegetation, protectress of seeds and animals, the goddess of hunting and country life and protectress of women in their domestic chores and, crucially, at childbirth. In the sanctuary of Artemis in Braurona the clothes of women, who either had died at childbirth or had an easy childbirth, were dedicated to the goddess. According to legend, some Athenians had once killed a bear in the sanctuary, and so, by way of redemption, the goddess had demanded that unmarried girls should dedicate their lives to the sanctuary. This is why young girls between five and ten years old offered their services to the sanctuary and were called "bears". In official celebrations they wore yellow robes and imitated bear dances; bears were the goddess's sacred animals.

Official celebrations, called Braetbronia, were held every four years and included a procession from the sanctuary to the Acropolis in Athens, dances of young virgins around the goddess's altar, athletic games and musical competitions. In addition to Artemis, other deities were worshipped here, including Iphigeneia, protectress of women in labour. Also, the virgin priestess, daughter of Agamemnon (as Euripides tells us in the eponymous tragedy), came to Braurona when she left Tauris bringing with her the ancient xoanon (wooden statue) of Artemis and founded the worship of Artemis in Attica. Later she died and was buried here. From the end of the 5th century BC, Apollo, the brother of Artemis was also worshipped here.

ELEUSIS

Eleusis (Elefsina) is 17 kilometres away from the centre of Athens and it is one of the best-known archaeological sites in Greece. In ancient times it was a part of Athens, but always maintained its particularity as the most important religious centre dedicated to Demeter and Persephone, with the celebrations of the Eleusinian Mysteries. Eleusis was connected with Athens through the Hiera Odos [the Sacred Road], along which worshippers would walk during the celebrations. The temple was surrounded by walls built at various periods; the earliest, from the time of Peisistratos in the 6th century BC, were entirely destroyed by Alaric the Goth in 395.

The last part of the Hiera Odos has survived and is included in the archaeological site of the sanctuary of Eleusis. It leads to a large courtyard of the Roman period, where worshippers would gather to prepare and watch the parade of the Eleusinian celebrations. The courtyard is surrounded by colonnades, a water fountain, a podium for the officials and two triumphal Roman apses. In the middle are the remains of the temple of Propylaia Artemis and Father Poseidon, a 3rd-century four-columned temple, and altars dedicated to the two deities.

The sanctuary's northern entrance is dominated by the Large Propylaia, an exact copy of the central part of the Propylaia of the Acropolis in Athens. The Small Propylaia, forming the entrance to the main room of the sanctuary, were built in 54: only two caryatids have survived, one kept at the museum of Eleusis, the other in Cambridge, England. In the interior of the Propylaia part of the processional road leads to the Telesterion (see below), through the Ploutoneion. It is believed that there used to be a small temple in antis here in the 4th century BC, where according to legend the gates of Hades used to be. Further south from the sanctuary is an exedra and the temple of Hekate, while on the other side of the processional road is a rock, identified as the Sullen Stone, where Demeter came to rest when

Eleusis. The archaeological site

she arrived in Eleusis.

The Telesterion is the place where the processional road terminates. It is the most important building of the shrine, the focus of the goddess's worship. Archaeologists have found remains from several constructional stages: an early Telesterion from the era of Solon (beginning of the 6th century BC) followed by a square room with columns and a colonnade on one side from the era of Peisistratos (third quarter of the 6th century BC). This building was destroyed by the Persians in 479 BC. The third Telesterion remained incomplete and dates from the era of Cimon, after the Persian wars. The room was rectangular. In the Periclean era the architect Iktinos designed a large square building that was not completed until the 4th century BC, when a Doric colonnade was added to the south with fourteen columns attributed to the Eleusinian architect Philon (317–307 BC). The building was destroyed during the invasion of the Kostoboks in 170 and was rebuilt in classical style during the era of the Emperor Marcus Aurelius.

The rectangular building measured 56 by 54.5 metres. Each of the internal sides had eight steps carved out of rock, or made of brick. It had six doors, two on each of the northern, eastern and southern side. In the centre was a palace, a rectangular building where the sacred symbols of Demeter were placed and only the high priest was allowed to enter. To the south and east of the Telesterion were two squares with administrative and auxiliary buildings.

In the museum south-west of the Telesterion are sculptures and architectural parts elements from the temple, from the Classical to the Roman period, as well as ceramic pots and small ornaments from the tombs of the western cemetery of Eleusis. The most important finds, such as the bas-relief of Triptolemos, the pediment from a treasure of the Parthenon period and the ceramic painted plate of Ninnio dedicated to Demeter and Kore have all been transferred to the National Archaeological Museum.

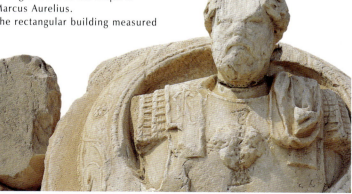

PIRAEUS

Piraeus is the port of Athens, the largest port in Greece and one of the largest in the eastern Mediterranean, about 8 kilometres away from the city centre.
There are many archaeological remains in Piraeus from its heyday, between the 5th and 1st centuries BC. The history of Piraeus begins in the early 5th century BC, when Themistocles decided to fortify the city's three ports and to build and base the Athenian fleet there, with the creation of a navy yard. Construction began during the 470s BC, after the Persian Wars, following a city planning system devised by the architect Hippodamos from Miletos; in around 460 BC Piraeus was connected with Athens via the Long Walls. From the 5th century BC Piraeus was a commercial and military naval port and a meeting point for merchants from Greece and abroad, as well as a stronghold of democracy. During the Hellenistic period it was frequently occupied by the Macedonians, while it was almost entirely destroyed by the Roman general Sulla in 88 BC.
The remains of the fortification are impressive; in many parts of Piraeus they remain today as they were at the time of General Konon in 394 BC, but especially along the coast of Piraeus (along a 2.5 kilometre stretch). One can see two gates, the gate of the city (tou Asteos, 394 BC), through which passed the carriage way that led to Athens, and the gate of Hetioneia (411 BC) on the northern side of Kantharos Bay (today's port) on the Kastraki Hill in Drapetsona.
Of the ancient navy yard, parts of three docks survive today, and can be seen in the basement of an apartment block on the Moutsopoulou coast, as can parts of four others recently discovered in the port of Mounychia (Mikrolimano). The port's best-known building was the "skeuotheke", designed by Philon after the mid-4th century BC: this was excavated in 1988 on the north-western corner of the port of Zea (Passalimani). Over a century earlier an inscription was found

The Walls of Piraeus, along the coast

listing in detail all the instructions left by Philon. It was an oblong building, 130 by18m, where various parts and fittings of ships, such as sails, ropes, cables and tents were kept. The skeuotheke was completely destroyed by Sulla in 88 BC, so that only the entrance can be seen today, in the internal courtyard of an apartment block on Ipsilantou Street. Very few remains of the commercial port (Kantharos Bay) have been preserved. One of the town's most important monuments is the small 2nd century BC theatre, a copy of the theatre of Dionysos in Athens, which has been well preserved in the courtyard of the Archaeological Museum of Piraeus. Many temples have been identified at various locations, such as the important temple of Artemis in Mounychia; however, little has survived. In the courtyard of the University of Piraeus one can see the foundations of a part of the ancient, Classical settlement.

Bronze statue of Athena

PIRAEUS MUSEUM

Piraeus Museum is one of the most important archaeological museums in Greece, restored in 1988. Its collections include finds from Piraeus, such as an inscription listing the boundaries of the city's famous market, a ship's copper ram and most importantly three magnificent 4th-century BC statues (two statues of Artemis and one of Athena), as well as an Archaic statue of Apollo. The statues had been hidden for safekeeping in a warehouse on the port just before the destruction of 88 BC. The museum's collection also includes important sculptures from the temple of Cybele in Moschato, gravestones and monumental sculptures such as the famous temple-like monument from Kallithea (4th century BC) and finds from tombs in Peiraiki, Mesogeia and Salamis, dated between the Mycenaean and the Roman periods.

SOUNION

Sounion was once one of the most important and densely populated demes in ancient Attica. It has been inhabited since Prehistoric times, as is evident from tombs discovered in the area. During the Archaic period Sounion's two temples were founded, the temple of Poseidon and the temple of Athena Sounias, both of which, during the Classical period, were incorporated into Pericles' building plans and further developed. Sounion was occupied by the Macedonians between the second half of the 4th century and 229 BC, when it returned to Athenian rule. During the Roman period both the town and its temples went into decline. This is perhaps the reason why the traveller Pausanias, visiting Athens in the 2nd century, mistakenly identified the temple on the peninsula as that of Athena. In later years the remains of the temple of Poseidon dominated the peninsula, which was named Cavo-Colones (Column Cape). The temple attracted many European travellers during the 18th and 19th centuries, several of whom actually carved their names on the building – Lord Byron's name is carved on the second pillar beside the entrance to the temple. The earliest archaeological research at the temple of Poseidon began as early as the end of the 18th century, while the Sounion temples were systematically excavated by the Archaeological Society from the end of the 19th century.

SANCTUARY OF POSEIDON

At the top of the Sounio peninsula, on the southernmost tip of Attica, past and present visitors have admired the remains of the temple of Poseidon, one of the most beautiful monuments of Greece and a foretaste of the magnificent monuments of Athens from the time of Pericles.

Visitors enter the archaeological site through an opening in the fortifications constructed by Athens in around 412 BC, during the Peloponnesian War. The top of the peninsula is dominated by the temple of Poseidon, which was built on flat ground and surrounded by a separate courtyard. The entrance was to the north through an impressive Doric propylon built during the Classical period, while to the west of the propylon were porticos that protected pilgrims from the sun, rain and, especially, strong winds.

The surviving temple was built in about 444–440 BC on the site of an older, limestone Doric temple,

Sounion, temple of Poseidon

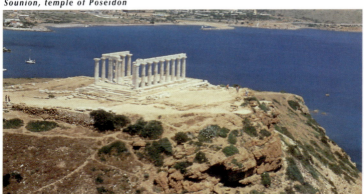

which was destroyed by the Persians in 480 BC, but whose remains were incorporated into the foundations of the new one. The new Doric temple was made of marble, with an ambulatory measuring 13.47 by 31.12 metres, with 6 rows of 13 columns. Particular notable is the thinness of the columns, which, although Doric, resemble elegant and graceful Ionic columns. The outer temple's entablature is interesting, with an Ionic frieze depicting the battles of the Centaurs and the Giants. Unfortunately, only very few pieces of pedimental sculpture have been survived. It is believed that on the eastern pediment was a sculpture depicting the fight between Poseidon and Athena over who would rule Athens. The temple of Poseidon in Sounion has been attributed to the architect who designed the temple of Hephaestus and Athena (Theseion), the temple of Mars in the Athenian Agora and the temple of Nemesis in Rhamnous.

It is probable that there were also houses for the guards and temple staff on the fortified peninsula, as well as for the town's residents. On the north-eastern point two 3rd-century docks have been found, which were used for the safe anchorage and repair of military vessels.

THE SANCTUARY OF ATHENA SOUNIAS

The sanctuary of Athena Sounias, smaller and less impressive than that of Poseidon, is on a low hill approximately 500 metres away from the sanctuary of Poseidon. Dating from the second half of the 5th century BC, the complex consisted of a polygonal courtyard and an Ionic temple with a colonnade on the eastern and southern sides. The marble temple measured 19 by 14.5 m., and had four internal columns. During the reign of Augustus (31–14 BC) the temple was demolished and the building materials used in the construction of the south-eastern temple in the Athenian Agora North-east of the temple of Athena was a smaller (5 by 6.8 metres) Doric temple, perhaps dedicated to Artemis and probably from the Classical period. On the northern part of the hill it is believed there was a shrine to Phrontis, helmsman to Menelaos, who, according to Homer's Odyssey, died and was buried in the sanctuary of Sounion.

The "kouros from Sounion"

Rhamnous

The remains of ancient Rhamnous are situated close to village Souli in northeastern Attica, just on the Euboean gulf. Rhamnous was a deme of the tribe of Aiantis. It is the best preserved deme of ancient Attica, as the area has not been built over since antiquity and the buildings were covered with earth until the excavations, which started in 1813 by the Dilettanti Society and were continued at the end of the 19th and throughout the 20th century.
Along the settlement ran a broad street, which ended at the fort by the sea and was divided in two parts, the southern and the northern street. The entrance to the archaeological site lies to the south. The first monuments that the visitor meets are two funerary precincts and the burial monuments of important families, such as the monuments of Menestides, Euphranor and Diophantides (4th century B.C.). Just after them is situated the so-called Western House, a typical rural estate with room for the animals or the rural tasks.
Just north of the Western House, in a residential building complex, was situated the temple of the goddess Nemesis, the most important sanctuary of Rhamnous and one of the most prominent temples in Attica. Its earliest phase dates in the beginning of the 6th century B.C. Around the end of the century it was replaced by a Doric temple of poros limestone, which was destroyed, probably by the Persians during the 480-479 B.C. invasions. In the course of the 5th century it was replaced by a small temple, which functioned more like a treasury; in its cella were discovered important sculptures, such as the statue of Themis by Chairestratos. In the middle of the century however was built the large temple of Nemesis, which has been attributed to the architect who designed the Hephesteion (the so-called Theseion) in the Agora of Athens. The temple was peripteral hexastyle, double in antis. Some parts remained unfinished. The sculpted decoration was limited to the akroteria of the top and the corners.
The real gem of the temple was the statue of Nemesis, a work by Agorakritos, which is found broken in

Rhamnous, the archaeological site

THE CULT OF NEMESIS

Nemesis was the goddess who symbolized the fare distribution of wealth, the solving of dissent and the punishment in case of hybris. The cult of the goddess at Rhamnous has been related to the period of the Persian Wars, although it was older. It was considered a chthonic deity, whereas sometimes she was worshipped in combination with the goddess of Justice per se, i.e. Themis, mentioned on inscriptions of Rhamnous.

hundreds of pieces. In 45 –46 A.D. the temple was related to the post-mortem imperial worship of Livia and Augustus. The temple bears also repairs and dedications by the rich sophist Herodes Atticus from nearby Marathon. It was however destroyed at the end of the 4th century by Christians, who also smashed the statue of the goddess. Architectural parts of the temple and pieces of the statues have been gathered in a covered area, which functions like a temporary museum. The sanctuary comprised also an altar to the east, a stoa to the north and a monumental fountain just in front of it. The northern street continued flanked by funerary stelae and monuments, many of which constitute fine examples of classical sculpture. It ended at the fort, a hill fortified with an 800 meters long wall. The fort was founded by the Athenians at the end of the 5th century B.C., in order to secure free navigation in the Euboic Gulf and the steady income of provisions in crops to Athens. The Athenian Ephebes served their duty there. In Hellenistic times, particularly in the first half of the 3rd century B.C., it was used by the Macedonians and the Ptolemies. The upper part of the fort had a second row of fortifications and comprised the military installations. At the lowest part there were some private houses and public buildings, such as the gymnasium, the theatre and the temples of Dionysos and Hero Archegetes. Another sanctuary, of Amphiaraos, was situated to the northwest of the fortress gate.

Funerary stela from Rhamnous

THE AMPHIAREION IN OROPOS

The remains of the Amphiareion, the sanctuary of the chthonic deity and hero Amphiaraos, were found about six kilometres southwest of the Skala Oropou, on the road connecting Markopoulo Oropou with Kalamos. The sanctuary is situated in an idyllic location, in a ravine with pine-trees. The Amphiareion was founded at the end of the 5th century BC as a therapeutic shrine. Its administration was always dependent upon the political situation in Oropos, which at times was an independent city and at other times under the rule of Athens or Boeotia. The official celebrations in honour of Amphiaraos were called Amphiareia. The Great Amphiareia was held every four years and included music and poetry competitions and athletic games, while the Small Amphiareia was an annual celebration.

Visitors entering the archaeological site can see on the left a series of some thirty inscribed statue bases from the Hellenistic and Roman periods. The remains of a portico were found behind them, which was probably the area of the encoemeterion, where sick people slept in wait for the god to reveal their cure to them in their dreams. To the west of the space, where offerings were made, the remains of a small temple (5.5 by 4 metres) were found dating from the early 4th century BC, probably the older temple of Amphiaraos. On the right of the present entrance to the site one can see the remains of the larger temple of Amphiaraos, where there was a marble statue of the god. The Doric temple measured 28.16 by 14 metres and was built soon before the mid-4th century BC. It consisted of a pronaos, cella and a smaller room at the end which was probably the adyton or treasury. At the front of the temple, on the north side, was a healing water spring mentioned by Pausanias and the large altar (8.9 by 4.6 metres) built in the 4th century BC, dedicated to numerous gods and heroes. North of the altar was the so-called "theatre by the altar", consisting of semicircular stone steps where pilgrims would sit and watch the presentation of offerings and various other events. South-east of the altar the remains of a paved hall have been found,

The Amphiareion

which has been identified as part of a complex of baths (for men).
Further to the east there are remains of the Long Stoa, a large portico (110.15 by 10.78 metres) built in c. 350 BC, which was probably again the area of the encoemeterion. From here pilgrims might watch the games that took place in the stadium, located in the area between the portico and the ravine.

The dedication of Archinus to Amphiaraos

What remains of the building today are parts of the walls and of the Doric columns from the façade and the Ionian columns from the interior. The sanctuary's theatre was situated behind the Long Stoa, built in the 2nd century BC, with a capacity of about 3,000–4,000. The theatre's cavea was wooden, the orchestra was horseshoe-shaped and around it there was an arrangement of five ornate marble thrones, mainly used by the priests. From the two-storey scene one can admire today the restored proskenion.

Next to the Long Stoa is a square building of the 4th century BC, identified as a complex of baths (for women). In the late Roman period the building reverted back to use as thermae.

A small settlement developed on the south-western side of the sanctuary, especially during the Hellenistic years, with numerous buildings providing accommodation and services for the pilgrims and sick people visiting the temple. Among these buildings is a large four-sided columned building identified as an agora, a clepsydra (hydraulic clock), houses, hostels, shops and many other auxiliary buildings.

The Amphiareion was excavated by the Greek Archaeological Society between 1884 and 1929. It is one of the most magical archaeological sites in Greece.

 AMPHIARAOS

Amphiaraos, the son of Oikleus, was legendary for his wisdom and ability in divination. He reigned in Argos together with Adrastos and took part in the operation against Thebes. He was believed to have escaped the pursuit of his enemies through the intervention of Zeus, who used his thunderbolt to strike an opening in the ground, allowing Amphiaraos and his horses to vanish.

MARATHON

The village of Marathon is around 30 kilometres away from the centre of Athens. It is one of the most important archaeological sites of Attica, with monuments from the Prehistoric to the Roman periods. The most significant monument is the Tomb of the Marathon fighters, the 192 Athenians who were killed in the battle of Marathon against the Persian invaders in 490 BC. The tumulus is 9m high, has a 185m perimeter and 50m diameter. Certain parts of the trophy built by the Athenians after the battle have been preserved; they were embedded in the medieval tower of the Church of Panagia (Virgin Mary) Mesosporitissa and today are on display in the Marathon Museum. In the Brexiza area, north of the former US military base in Nea Makri, are two more significant monuments. The first is the temple of the Egyptian Gods, where archaeological research is still being carried out today. Interesting life-size and larger statues have been found here. The second monument is the Herodes Atticus baths east of the Egyptian temple and dating from the second century. The busts of Roman emperors found there are on display in the Louvre and the Ashmolean Museum in Oxford.

The Tumulus (Burial Mound) of Marathon

A settlement has been discovered in the Plassi area, with traces of houses from the Neolithic, the early-Helladic, the mid-Helladic and the Mycenaean periods. Two significant Prehistoric cemeteries are situated in Tsepi (early-Helladic) and in Vrana (mid-Helladic). The recently renovated Marathon Museum is very close to the latter. Its collection consists of finds from these Prehistoric settlements, ceramics and other finds from graves of the Geometric, Archaic and Classical periods. Other artefacts include pots from a nearby tomb, probably of the citizens of Plataea who were killed in the battle of 490 BC, and several offerings from the tomb of the Athenians, as well as other finds from the area. There is a significant number of tombstones dating from the Classical to the Roman periods, found in the area of greater Marathon, statues of Herodes Atticus and members of the emperor's family from the area around the tomb, as well as Roman statues from the temple of the Egyptian Gods.

Funerary stela from Marathon

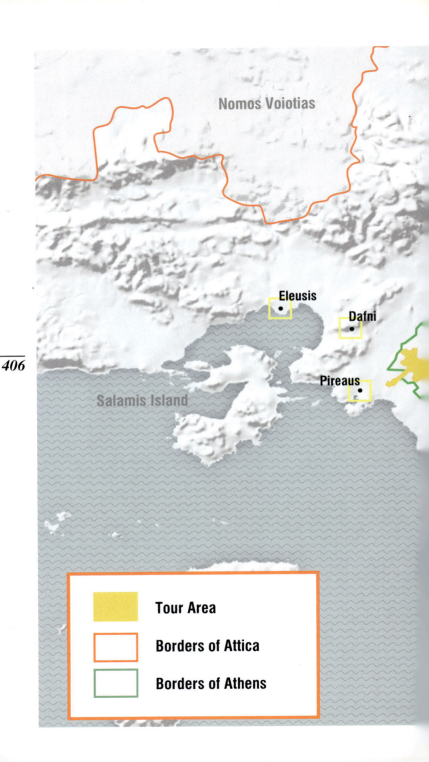

Glossary

Adyton: the most sacred part of a church/temple usually separated from the nave by a wall. Only priests were allowed access to it.

Anthivolio: drawing of a picture used to produce copies of it.

Antimensium: holy ceremonial textile placed on the altar (mensa) during Mass, or replacing the altar.

Apoptygma: a folding on the upper part of the robe on depictions of women. Usually it reached down to the woman's waist, or went lower with a belt around the waist.

Apse: curved or semi-circular construction connecting two vertical architectural parts, columns or pillars. Sometimes synonymous with "conch".

Arch: bow-shaped architectural part used to support a roof. Blind arches are the ones found on side walls and have a supportive or decorative function.

Arcosolium: vaulted grave carved in a rock during the early Christian period, or built into the walls of churches during the mid- and late Byzantine period.

Art Deco: an artistic movement expressed in the architecture and decorative arts during the 1920s and 1930s. It is characterized by a modern sense of elegance away from classical models. It used simple geometric forms, stylised patterns and a mixture of dissimilar, artificial and natural materials.

Atrium: the central yard of a building, surrounded by colonnades.

Bath: public or private ancient bath including an underground heating system and cisterns with hot water.

Amazonomachy (battle of the Amazons): the battle of the Athenians with the Amazons, the fighter-women who lived around the Black Sea. According to the myth the Amazons marched out against Athens to take revenge for the Amazon Antiope, taken by Theseus. Despite their bravery the Amazons lost. In the art of ancient Athens there is a clear political symbolism in the depictions of the battle of the Amazons: the Amazons symbolise the Persians and the battle reflects the Persian Wars.

Bauhaus: an artistic and architectural movement that blossomed in Germany through the homonymous school of architecture and applied arts. The movement aimed to promote a modern art and architecture based on industrial technology, the wide use of materials such as cement, glass and metal, the preference for cubic forms and the principles of logic and functionality. The work of artists and architects should obey a "socially responsible" planning programme.

Beaux-Arts: the architectural style of Beaux-Arts was named after the "Ecole des Beaux Arts" in Paris; it blossomed in the late 19th and early 20th century. It is an eclectic version of neoclassicism incorporating elements from classical Greek, Roman and Renaissance architecture. It places an emphasis on symmetry, the wide use of decorative elements and monumental dimensions.

Brickwork patterns: the decoration of the exterior walls of Byzantine churches with bricks, or other enclosed ceramics in various shapes and combinations.

Buttress: wooden or stone abutment for an apse or wall.

Byzantine style (neo-Byzantine style): this style incorporates elements from the Byzantine

GLOSSARY

architecture in classicistic compositions. Those efforts reflect a neo-Byzantine "movement" evident mostly in religious architecture and less frequently in public buildings, such as the Opthalmic Clinic.

Centauromachy (battle of the Centaurs): the battle of the Centaurs (mythical creatures of the Greek Mythology with the body of a horse and a human head and torso) against the Lapiths (a brave people from Thessaly). The Battle of the Centaurs was a favourite subject in ancient Greek art.

Chiton: ancient Greek men and women's item of clothing. It was a linen or woollen rectangular garment, wrapped around the body and fixed with fibulas.

Cistercian order: Monastic order of the Catholic Church, founded in eastern France in 1098 by the abbot Robert of Molesme.

Coffer: a hollow alcove formed on a ceiling with engraved or painted decorations.

Conch: rectangular or semi-circular recess on a wall with decorative or functional purpose. Sometimes synonymous with "apse".

Coptic art: the art that flourished in Christian Egypt mainly from the 4th century until the mid-7th century (640), when the country was occupied by the Arabs.

Course: horizontal layer of stones or bricks.

Cross vault: a kind of vaulted roofing for square or rectangular buildings, mainly for Byzantine churches. It occurs by the section of two semi-cylindrical vaults.

Eclecticism: the combination of elements from various artistic styles for the creation of an original work.

Encoemeterion: a space in the shrine of Asclepius and other religious healing places in ancient Greece where the sick people were hypnotised, possibly with the use of hallucinogenic drugs. In their sleep the sick people would have a dream sent by the gods revealing the method with which they would be cured.

Erker: strong architectural protrusion from the level of the façades. In Greece there are classicistic buildings with autonomous erkers and modernist apartment blocks with combinations of erker-balconies. Regarding the shaping of the buildings' façades the erkers are characterised by sharp edges and the use of plain, geometric decorative shapes. The erker, a typical feature of mid-war architecture, was banned by law in Greece in 1937 because it was supposed to violate the clarity of the building lines.

Exarchate: ecclesiastical district under an Exarch, a representative of the Patriarchate with administrative and ecclesiastic responsibilities.

Gigantomachy (battle of the Giants): the battle of the gods of Olympus against the mythical Giants, children of the Earth (Gaia) and Uranus, hugely built and with frightening strength. The battle of the Giants was a favourite subject in ancient Greek art, mainly in architectural sculpture.

Gorgoneion: the head of the Medusa/Gorgo, the mythical monster who had snakes on her head instead of hair and was killed by Perseus with the support of Athena. In ancient Greek art it decorates the aegis (a kind of breastplate made of goat's skin) and the shield of Athena.

Glazing: glass-coating of the external surfaces of ceramic pots.

Hypokauston: the main system for the heating of ancient baths. The word means literally a "furnace that burns underneath". With this system the room's floor was supported by small poles and the space underneath the floor was heated by the circulation of hot air, while the heat was transferred through the walls by conductors.

Indictio: a fortnight, a circle of fifteen days, used as a time unit during the Medieval period, according to the Roman tradition.

Italian Renaissance: the architecture of the Italian Renaissance is characterised by the wide use and adaptation of elements from the Roman architecture, such as the vaulted roofs, the arched constructions, the generally circular or spherical forms, the colonnades and the various decorative elements. This style was used in numerous religious and public buildings in Italian cities, mainly in Florence and Rome.

Jugendstil: this was an expression of the Art Nouveau artistic movement in Central Europe. The Art Nouveau movement began at the end of the 19th century as a reaction to neoclassicism and was expressed in painting, architecture, sculpture and the applied arts; among its characteristics were lack of symmetry, decorative mood and use of exotic, dream-like forms. In Central Europe Jugendstil was represented mostly by the Sezession artists, a movement that appeared mainly in Munich, Vienna and Berlin with the aim to break free from academic art.

Katholikon: the main church of a monastery.

Light (of a window): the arched opening or window in Byzantine churches. Depending on the number of lights, there are single-light, double-light and three-light windows.

Metochion: small monastery estate, usually belonging to a larger independent monastery. The church in that estate is also called metochion.

Molybdobull: an inscribed lead seal, used frequently to seal official documents during the mid-Byzantine era.

Monopteros temple: an ancient temple with only one row of columns around the nave.

Niche: see "apse" and "conch".

Opus caementicium: an enduring sort of Roman masonry. It is made with a mixture of mortar and smashed stones, which is then thrown into wooden moulds for the construction of arches and vaults.

Orthostates: rectangular stone placed vertically at the lower part of a wall.

Ostracism: condemning verdict for the exile of politicians, reached by voting during which the voters wrote the name of the person to be exiled on a ceramic sherd (ostrakon).

Palmette: decorative element in the form of a flower or bud.

Panel: low wooden or stone closure, often with bas-relief decorations, e.g. marble panel in Byzantine churches closing the openings at the lower part of screens and between the columns of the side aisles.

Patriarchal monastery: a monastery under the jurisdiction of the Patriarchate, autonomous from the administration of the local Bishop. According to tradition the Patriarch has the right to found a monastery in an area of his jurisdiction and he sends a cross, which is placed in the monastery's foundations symbolising the monastery's dependence on the Patriarchate.

GLOSSARY

Peplos: ancient Greek woman's cloth, long and sleeveless, fixed by pins on the shoulders and a belt around the waist.

Peristyle: a row of columns around a building or an interior yard, cloister.

Pillar: a square pole.

Popular neoclassicism: the term refers to the use and adaptation of neoclassical elements for the construction of houses for the middle and lower social strata. The houses, therefore, had a limited decoration and lacked a monumental character. There are characteristic examples of such houses in Athens (Thisseio, Psirris) and in provincial towns of Greece.

Porch: the covered space at the front of a gate on a building's entrance.

Poros stone: soft stone with porous composition, used widely in ancient Greek architecture and sculpture.

Portal: large, exterior gate, the main entrance to a mansion, a temple etc.

Portico: see "Stoa"

Portolan: a nautical map with information on the coasts and ports.

Propylon: monumental building at the entrance of ancient temples or public building complexes.

Rubble masonry: masonry with the use of rough stones.

Rundbogenstil (style of circular arches): a movement of revival of the early medieval Romanic architecture that began in Munich during the 1830s. The Romanic architecture uses plain forms, balance between horizontal and vertical lines and circular arches at the openings.

Semi-dome: architectural part shaped like a quarter of a sphere, found over apses and conches, particularly popular in Byzantine churches.

Shipyard (Neosoikos): a covered space in a port where ships were built or repaired.

Sigillion: imperial or patriarchal document. A patriarchal sigillion usually confirmed the status of the patriarchal monasteries.

Squinch: a conch bridging the corners of a square compartment transforming it into an octagon. It was used to support the domes of Byzantine churches.

Stathmion: a metallic (usually copper) weight used to measure the weight of solid goods on the scales.

Stoa: a long building with a roof supported by one or two colonnades parallel to its back wall.

Triclinium: a dining room or reception hall in luxurious houses of the Roman and late Roman period.

Tholos: circular construction with a conical or hemispherical roof.

Victorian Gothic style: British version of the neo-Gothic style in the second half of the 19th century. This style incorporates elements from the medieval Gothic style (emphasised height, strong, pointed architectural parts with sharp endings, sculptured decorations, narrow arches with acute angles) for the construction of churches and public buildings.

Xoanon: wooden statue of a deity, used from the late Archaic until the early Classical period.

Bibliography

Bastea, E., *The Creation of Modern Athens: Planning the Myth*, Cambridge 2000

Bleicken, J., *Die Athenische Demokratie*, Paderborn 1988

Brouskari, M., *The Acropolis Museum : a descriptive catalogue*, Athens 1974

Brouskari, M., *Musée de l'Acropole: Catalogue descriptif*, Athènes 1974

Brouskari, M., *The Monuments of the Acropolis*, Athens 1997

Brouskari, M., *The Paul and Alexandra Canellopoulos Museum, A Guide*, Athens 1985

Burgel, G., *Le miracle athénien au XXe siècle*, Paris 2002

Burn A.R., *The living past of Greece: a time traveler's tour of historic and prehistoric places*, London 1993

Camp, J., *The Athenian Agora: Excavations in the Heart of Classical Athens*, New York 1992

Camp, J., *The Athenian Agora: A Guide to the Excavation and Museum*, Athens 1990.

Camp, J., *The Archaeology of Athens*, New Haven 2001

Cheetham N., *Medieval Greece*, New Haven 1981

Frantz Alison, *The Athenian Agora XXIV, Late Antiquity, A.D. 267-700*, Princeton 1988

Goette, Rupprecht, H., *Athens, Attica and the Megarid: An Archaeological Guide*, Routledge 2001

Gregorovius, F., *Geschichte der Stadt Athen im Mittelalter. Von der Zeit Justinians bis zur türkischen Eroberung*, München 1983

Habicht, C., *Athen : die Geschichte der Stadt in hellenistischer Zeit*, München 1995

Habicht, C., *Athens from Alexander to Antony*, Cambridge 1997

Habicht, C., *Pausanias' Guide to ancient Greece*, Berkeley 1985

Habicht, C., *Pausanias und seine "Beschreibung Griechenlands"*, München 1985

Hurwit, J.M., *The Athenian Acropolis : history, mythology, and archaeology from the Neolithic era to the present*, Cambridge 1999

Jenkins, I., *The Parthenon Frieze*, London 1994

Karouzou, S., *Nationalmuseum, Illustrierter Führer durch das Museum;* Athen 1980

Karouzou, S., *National Museum, Illustrated Guide to the Museum*, Athens 1985

Kazanaki-Lappa M., "Medieval Athens", in Laiou A.E. (ed.), *The Economic History of Byzantium: From the Seventh through the Fifteenth Century*, Washington 2002

Kitroeff, A., *War-Time Jews: the Case of Athens*, Athens: Hellenic Foundation for European and Foreign Policy, 1995

Knigge, U., *The Athenian Kerameikos : history, monuments, excavations*, Athens 1991

Knigge, U., *Der Kerameikos von Athen: Führung durch Ausgrabungen und Geschichte*, Athen 1988

Korres M., Bouras Ch. et.al. (eds), *Athens: From the Classical Period to the Present Day (5th Century B.C.-A.D. 2000)*, New Castle 2003

Llewellyn Smith M., *Athens: A Cultural and Literary History (Cities of the Imagination)*, Northampton 2004

Llewellyn Smith, M., *Olympics in Athens: 1896-2004*, London 2004

MacKenzie, M., *Turkish Athens: The Forgotten Centuries, 1456-1832*, London 1992

Mee, C., Spawforth, A., *Greece : an Oxford archaeological guide*, Oxford 2001

Meier, C., *Athen. Ein Neubeginn der Weltgeschichte*, München 1995

Mossé, Cl., *Histoire d' une democratie: Athènes, des origines a la conquete mecedonienne*, Paris 1971

Osborne, R., *Demos: the Discovery of Classical Attika*, Cambridge 1985

Papageorgiou-Venetas, A., *Athens: The Ancient Heritage and the Historic Cityscape in a Modern Metropolis*, Athens 1994

Papageorgiou-Venetas, A., *Eduard Schaubert 1804-1860. Der städtebauliche Nachlaß zur Planung der Städte Athen und Piräus*, Mannheim 2001

Papageorgiou-Venetas, A., *Haupstadt Athen. Ein Stadtgedanke des Klassizismus*, München 1994

Prevelakis, G., *Athènes: Urbanisme, culture et politique*, Paris 2000

Protestou, E., *Athen. Ein Führer zur zeitgenössischen Architektur*, Köln 1998

Protestou, E., *Athens: A Guide to Recent Architecture*, London 1998

Robertson, M., Franz A., *The Parthenon Frieze*, London 1975

Rupp, D. W., Peripatoi: *Athenian Walks, Road*, Athens, 2002

Sanders G.D.R., *The archeology of Medieval Greece*, Oxford 1996

Schuller, W., *Griechische Geschichte*, München 1991

Schuller, W., *Die Herrschaft der Athener im ersten attischen Seebund*, Berlin 1974

Setton K., *Athens in the Middle Ages*, London 1975

Setton K., *Catalan domination of Athens, 1311-1388*, London 1975

Starr, Ch. G., *The Birth of Athenian Democracy. The Assembly in the Fifth Century B.C.*, New York/Oxford 1990

Tobin, J., *Herodes Atticus and the City of Athens. Patronage and Conflict under the Antonines*, Amsterdam 1997

Travlos, J., *Pictorial Dictionary of Ancient Athens*, London 1971

Travlos, J., *Bildlexicon zur Topographie des antiken Athen*, Tübingen 1971

Travlos, J., *Bildlexikon zur Topographie des antiken Attica*, Tübingen 1988

Waterfield R., *Athens: A History – from ancient ideal to modern city*, New York 2004

Wycherley, R.E., *The Stones of Athens*, New Jersey 1978

Publication
City of Athens

Design and Creation
Foundation of Hellenic World (FHW)

General Project Coordinator
Dimitris Efraimoglou, FHW's Managing Director

Production Consultant
Athina Rikaki

Publishing Consultant, Art Director
Kostas- Iraklis Georgiou*

Photography
Giannis Giannelos*

The following members of FHW's staff collaborated for this publication:

Publishing Editor
Kleopatra Ferla

Texts
Guentcho Banev, Maria-Dimitra Dawson, Daphne Dimitriadou, Georgia Kalogeropoulou, Afroditi Kamara, Gianna Katsiamboura, Euridiki Leka, Dimitris Paleothodoros, Vassilis Papadopoulos, Emilia Salvanou, S. Mohammad Shariat-Panahi, Vassilis Siametis, Athanasios Sideris, Vassiliki Spyropoulou, Yorgos Tzedopoulos, Michalis Warlas

Scientific Editors
Gianna Katsiamboura, Athanasios Sideris, Yorgos Tzedopoulos

Translation
Giorgos Velentzas*, Daphne Dimitriadou, Afroditi Kamara, Christina Kotsaki*, Sevi Spyridogiannaki*
Editor: Elizabeth Stone*, Yorgos Tzedopoulos

Selection and Administration of Illustrated Material
Zografia Bidikoudi, Despina Moschou, Vassilis Papadopoulos, Vassiliki Spyropoulou

Map Design
Dimos Giannakakos, Fotini Kladia, Giorgos Sidiropoulos

Architectural Drawings
Maria Lafazani

Creative Team
Gina Grapsia, Panagiotis Panopoulos

Desktop Publishing
Vana Panopoulou*

*Collaborators of the Foundation of the Hellenic World

The City of Athens would like to thank Loretta Gaitis for her permission to use a photograph of a Giannis Gaitis' painting. The City of Athens would also like to thank the following organizations for their permission to use their photographic material:
- Municipal Gallery, Athens
- "Technopolis"
- Cultural Centre of the City of Athens
- City of Athens Press Office

And the following institutions and individuals:
- Archaeological Receipts Fund, Athens
- 1st Ephorate of Prehistoric and Classical Antiquities, Athens
- 2nd Ephorate of Prehistoric and Classical Antiquities, Athens
- 3rd Ephorate of Prehistoric and Classical Antiquities, Athens
- 1st Ephorate of Byzantine Antiquities, Athens
- National Archaeological Museum, Athens
- Acropolis Museum, Athens
- Agora Museum, Athens
- Numismatic Museum, Athens
- National Art Gallery and Alexandros Soutzos Museum, Athens
- Byzantine and Christian Museum, Athens
- Benaki Museum, Athens
- Kerameikos Museum, Athens
- War Museum of Athens
- Museum of the City of Athens, Vouros-Eutaxias Foundation, Athens
- The Jewish Museum of Greece, Athens
- N.P. Goulandris Foundation-Museum of Cycladic Art, Athens
- Photo Archive of the G. Psaropoulos Family Foundation - Centre for the Study of Traditional Pottery, Athens
- Ilias Lalaounis Jewelry Museum, Athens
- The Hellenic Children's Museum, Athens
- Museum of Greek Folk Art, Athens
- Frissiras Museum of Contemporary European and Greek Art, Athens
- National Historical Museum - Historical and Ethnological Society of Greece, Athens
- Paul and Alexandra Canellopoulos Museum, Athens
- Pierides Museum of Ancient Cypriot Art, Athens
- Museum of Popular Instruments - Research Center for Ethnomusicology, Athens
- Museum of the History of the University of Athens
- Museum and Study Center of the Greek Theatre, Athens
- Archaeological Museum, Piraeus
- Arhaeological Museum of Brauron
- Archaeological Museum of Rhodes
- Gennadius Library, Athens
- German Archaeological Institute, Athens
- Hellenic Literary and Historical Archive, Athens
- Hellenic Olympic Committee, Athens
- Unification of Athens Archaeological Sites S.A.
- Filekpaideftiki Etaireia, Athens
- The Archaeological Society in Athens
- The Greek National Opera, Athens
- Art Theatre "Karolos Kuhn"
- Atelier Spiros Vassileiou, Athens
- Hellenic Society for the Protection of the Environment and Cultural Inheritance, Athens
- National Theatre, Athens
- Cultural Foundation of the National Bank of Greece, Athens
- Athens Concert Hall (phot. Stefanos Karamanian)
- Hellenic Festival S.A., Athens (phot. Charis Bilios)
- "Multi-purpose venue" Athinais, Athens
- "I. SIDERIS" Publications, Athens
- "MELISSA" Publications, Athens
- "KOTINOS" Publications and Photographic Archive, Athens
- K. Ioannidis Collection, Athens
- I. Bastias Collection, Athens
- I. Pappas Collection, Athens
- Eustathios I. Finopoulos Collection, Athens
- Thanassis Papaioannou Private Collection
- Christos Zioulas Archive

PHOTOGRAPHIC ARCHIVES - PHOTOGRAPHERS
- G. Giannelos Photographic Archive, Athens
- Studio KONTOS/PHOTOSTOCK, Athens
- Alkis Xanthakis, Athens
- Vassilis Makris, Athens
- Paterakis BROS, Athens

INDEX

A

Academy of Athens 369
Academy, Sculpture 369
Acropolis 99
  Acropolis Walls 125
  Acropolis Museum 126
  Acropolis, North Slope Monuments 129
  Acropolis, South Slope Monuments 89
  Agrippa Monument 102
  Altar of Athena Polias 121
  Arrhephorion 124
  Athena, Figures 101
  Caryatids 122
  Chalkotheke 105
  Chryselephantine Statue of Athena 109
  Propylaia 102
  Temples - Shrines
    Ancient Temple of Athena 123
    Artemis Brauronia 104
    Athena Nike 103
    Erechteion 121
    Pandion 105
    Pandrossos 121
    Parthenon 106
    Rome and Augustus 121
    Zeus Polieus 105
Agora Ancient 259
  Altar of Twelve Gods 265
  Arsenal 266
  Byzantine Houses 276
  East Building 272
  Eleusinion 275
  Enneakrounos 273
  Heliaia 271
  Hephaisteion (Theseion) 267
  Houses in the Agora 277
  Library of Pantainos 277
  Metroon 269
  Mint 274
  Monument of the Eponymous Heroes 268
  Museum of Ancient Agora 281
  New Bouleuterion 270
  Nymphaeum 274
  Odeon of Agrippa 271
  Old Bouleuterion 269
  Panathenaic Way 264
  Sanctuary of Aphrodite Ourania 263
  Southeast Temple 275
  Southwest Fountain House 271
  South-west Temple 274
  Stoas
    Attalos 279
    Herms 265
    Middle 273
    Poikile 263
    Royal 265
    South 271
    Zeus Eleutherios 265
  Strategeion 270
  Temple of Apollo Patroos 266
  Temple of Ares 266
  Tholos 270
Aigli Café 206
Amphiaraos 403
Amphiareio in Oropos 402
Anafiotika 231
Antiquities of the St Marina Area 78
Areios Pagos 81
Aretaieio Hospital 181
Aristotle 190
Aristotle, Lykeion of 190
Army Share Fund Mansion 363
Arrhephoria-Arrhephoroi 124
Arsakeio 373
Art Theatre 'Karolos Kuhn' 374
Asclepieion 94
Athena Nike, Temple 103
Athenais – Eudocia 257
Athenais Multi-complex 325
Athens
  Cathedral 305
  City Hall 291
  Concert Hall 179
  Conservatory 188
  Conservatory, Former 322
  History 18
  Mythology 15
  Natural Environment 12
Attalos Stoa 279

INDEX

B

Banks
  Agricultural Bank of Greece 368
  Alpha Bank 373
  Bank of Greece 366
  National Bank of Greece, Central Branch 290
  National Bank of Greece, New Building 290
  National Bank of Greece, Stadiou Str. 357
Benaki Family 166
Braurona 392
Brauronia Artemis, Sanctuary 392
Brauronia Artemis, Cult 393

C

Caryatids 122
Cemetery, First 218
Cemetery, First, "Sleeping Maiden" 219
Chatzidakis, Manolis 340
Choniates, Michael 308
Choregia 138
Churches
  All Saints 339
  Anglikan 147
  Cathedral 305
  Catholic Church, St Dionysius 367
  Christ of Kopidis 299
  Dependency of the Holy Sepulchre 238
  Gorgoepekoos / St Eleutherios 306
  Holy Apostles Solaki 282
  Holy Power 312
  Kapnikarea 301
  Megali Panagia 257
  Omorphoklissia 390
  Panagia Grigorousa / Taxiarches 247
  Pantanassa 253
  Rinaki of Plaka 311
  Russian Church 147
  Sotera of Kottakis 144
  St Anargyroi 296
  St Anna 226
  St Assomatoi 63
  St Assomatoi on the Steps 255
  St Athanassios Kourkouris 77
  St Catherine 140
  St Constantine 317
  St Demetrius 139
  St Demetrius Loubardiaris 83
  St Dionysius, Skoufa Street 173
  St George Karitsis 360
  St George on the Cliff 235
  St George, Piraios Street 324
  St George Rizareios 195
  St Eirene 303
  St Elissaios 225
  St John "Around the Column" 296
  St John the Theologian 237
  St Kyriaki 296
  St Leonides Martyrium 215
  St Marina, Thisseio 79
  St Nicholas / St Serapheim 228
  St Nicholas Rangabas 235
  St Nicholas, Thon Estate 339
  St Paraskevi 304
  St Philip 259
  St Photini 213
  St Spyridon and Holy Belt 240
  St Symeon 231
  St Theodoroi 358
  St Thomas 224
  Tetraconch 257
  Transfiguration of the Saviour 228
  Virgin Mary Chrissokastriotissa 240
  Virgin Mary Chrissospiliotissa 303
  Virgin Mary Romvi 304
  Zoodochos Pege 378
City Hall 291
City Hall, the Paintings 293
Criminal Court 299
Cultural Centre of the City of Athens 381
Cultural Centre "Hellenic Cosmos" 335
Cultural Centre "Melina Merkouri" 331
Cultural Foundation of the National Bank 311

D

Dexameni 175
Dionysos, Sanctuary 90
Dionysius Areopagite, St 82

E

Educational Society 373
Eirene of Athens 308
Eleftherias Park 180
Eleusinian Mysteries 275

INDEX

Eleusis 394
Erechtheion 121
Eumenes, Stoa 95
Evangelismos Hospital 195
Exarcheia 353
Eynard Mansion 315

F

Faculty of Law 384
Fethiye Mosque 243
Folk Shadow Theatre 141

G

Gazi Neighbourhood 331
Gennadius Library 199
German Archaeological Institute 378
Grand Bretagne Hotel 155
Greek National Opera 379

H

Hadrian's Library 255
Hadrian's Gate 209
Hamam of Abid Efendi 240
Hansen, Christian 206
Hansen, Theophilus 206
Hatzimichali, Angeliki 145
Hellenic Conservatory, Old Building 377
Hellenic Literary and Historical Archive 309
Hellenic Society for the Protection of the Environment and Cultural Inheritance 237
Hephaisteion (Theseion) 267
Herodeion 97
Herodes Atticus 97
Hill of the Muses 83
Hill of Strefis 354
Hilton Hotel 181
Historical and Ethnological Society 362
History of Athens 18
Horologion of Andronicus of Cyrrhus 242
House of Proklos 89

I

Iliou Melathron 364
Ilissos, Classical Temple 213
Ilissos, Basilica 215

Interim Olympics 218

J

Jewish Synagogue 64

K

Kaftantzoglou, Lissandros 317
Kapustin, Antonin 148
Kerameikos 65
　Burial customs, Classical Athens 66
　Dipylon and Fountain-House 69
　Funery Periboloi and Monuments 71
　Kerameikos Cemetery 71
　Kerameikos Museum 75
　Pompeion 70
　Sacred Gate 68
　Themistoclean Wall 67
　Tumuli (Tombs) 74
Kleanthis, Stamatios 230
Kolonaki, Art Deco Buildings 172
Kotopouli, Marika 376

L

Leonides 215
Lord Byron 298
Lycabettus Hill 175
Lykeion of Aristotle 190
Lysikrates Monument 138

M

Makrigianni District, Excavations 134
Makrigiannis, Ioannis 136
Makrigiannis, Statue 136
Marasleio Didaskaleio 196
Marathon 404
Maximos Mansion 203
Medrese 241
Melas Mansion 291
Merkouri, Melina 332
Metaxourgeio 320
Metaxourgeio, Silk Factory 321
Ministry of Foreign Affairs 158
Mythology of Athens 15
Monasteries
　Dafni 388

Kaissariani 386
Petrakis Monastery 196
St Philothei 308
Monument of the National Reconciliation 358
Monument to the Unknown Soldier 156
Monuments of the North Slope of Acropolis 129
Monuments of the South Slope of Acropolis 89
Museums
Acropolis 126
Ancient Agora 279
Atelier of Spiros Vassileiou 85
Athens Municipal Gallery 322
Benaki 163
Braurona 393
Byzantine and Christian 192
Canellopoulos 226
Centre for the Study of Traditional Pottery 64
City of Athens 359
Cycladic Art 169
Eleftherios Venizelos 180
Frissiras 143
Greek Folk Art 141
Hadjikyriakos-Ghikas Gallery 159
Hellenic Children's 141
Hellenic Cosmos 335
Islamic Arts 324
Jewish 146
Kerameikos 75
Lalaounis, Museum of Jewellery, 137
Municipality of Athens Folk Art and Tradition Centre 145
National Archaeological 344
National Art Gallery 183
National Historical-Old Parliament 362
Numismatic-Iliou Melathron 364
Pierides, Ancient Cypriot Art 326
Piraeus 397
Popular Instruments 241
Theatre 381
University of Athens 229
War 189

N

National and Kapodistrian University of Athens 370
National and Kapodistrian University of Athens, Statues 370
National Gardens 205
National Library 372
National Printing House 357
National Theatre of Greece 316
Natural Environment of Athens 12
Nemesis, Cult 401
Nikias Choregic Monument 95

O

Observatory 80
Odeon of Herodes Atticus 97
Odeon of Pericles 93
Old Parliament 362
Olympieion 210
Olympic Games, Modern, First 216
Ophthalmic Clinic 367
Orlandos, Anastassios 173
Oropos, Amphiareio 402
Ottoman Fortification of Athens 232

P

Palamas, Kostis 382
Palamas Kostis Building 383
Panathenaic Stadium 216
Panathenaic Way 264
Parliament House 157
Parthenon 106
Parthenon, Optical Refinements 107
Papadiamantis, Alexandros 225
Pedion tou Areos 341
Pedion tou Areos, Sculptures 342
Pheidias 110
Philoppapos Monument 83
Philothei of Athens 309
Pikionis, Dimitrios 85
Piraeus 396
Plaka 247
Plato 329
Plato's Academy 327
Pnyx 80
Presidential Mansion 204
Propylaia 102
Psirris 297

R

Rallis House 373
Refugee Settlements in Piraios Street 333
Refugees' Housing Blocks in Alexandras Av. 341
Rex Theatre 376
Rhamnous 400
Rizokastron 233
Roman Agora 245
Roman Baths 311
Russian Orthodox Community 150

S

Sarogleion Mansion 163
Schliemann, Heinrich 365
School of Fine Arts 334
Squares
   Avissinias (Youssourouom) 258
   Kaniggos 377
   Karaiskakis 318
   Klafthmonos 358
   Kolonaki 171
   Kotzia 289
   Monastiraki 223
   National Resistance (Kotzia) 289
   Omonoia 287
   Sintagma 153
   Agioi Anargyroi 296
   Thisseio 78
   Victoria 343
Society for Education 197
Sounion 398
Stations
   Metro Acropolis 133
   Metro Evangelismos 195
   Metro Panepistimio 371
   Metro Sintagma 155
   Railway Larissis 320
   Railway Peloponnisou 319
Streets and Avenues
   Alexandras, Refugee Housing Blocks 341
   Apostolou Pavlou 77
   Athinas 293
   Dionissiou Areopagitou 89
   Ermou 300
   Ermou, Cafés and Clubs 301
   Piraios, Industrial Buildings 332
   Piraios, Refugee Settlements 333
   Stadiou-C. Lada, Building 361
   Vassilissis Sofias, Buildings 160
   Vassilissis Sofias, the "Runner" Sculpture 182

T

Technical University 352
Technical University, Uprising of 352
Technopolis-Gazi 330
Theatre of Dionysos 91
Theseion 267
Thiersch, Ludwig 149
Thrasyllus Choregic Monument 93
Tower of the Winds 242
Travlos, Ioannis 260
Tsarouchis, Giannis 186
Tzistarakis Mosque 254

U

United States Embassy 180
University's Chemistry Laboratory 384
University of Athens 370

V

Varvakeios Market 294
Venizelos Eleftherios 181
Votanikos 327

W

Weiler Building 136

Z

Zappeioi Olympic Games 206
Zappeion 207
Zappeion Garden 208
Ziller, Ernst 365

1. Giannis Gaitis, Patineur, 1980.
Oil on canvas

Athens, Collection Kostas Ioannidis

2. Runner in stadion race from a panathenaic amphora 460 BC.
Bologna, Museo Civico Archeologico
© Ministero Per I Beni E Le Attivita Culturali